SOCIOLOGY TODAY

VOLUME II

hARPER ✦ ᴛoRchBooᴋs

A reference-list of Harper Torchbooks, classified by subjects, is printed at the end of this volume.

RESEARCHES IN THE SOCIAL, CULTURAL AND BEHAVIORAL SCIENCES

edited by BENJAMIN NELSON

SOCIOLOGY TODAY

VOLUME II

Problems and Prospects

EDITED BY

ROBERT K. MERTON
LEONARD BROOM
LEONARD S. COTTRELL, JR.

HARPER TORCHBOOKS
The Academy Library
HARPER & ROW, PUBLISHERS
NEW YORK AND EVANSTON

SOCIOLOGY TODAY

Copyright © 1959 by Basic Books Inc.

Printed in the United States of America

This book was first published in 1959 in one volume by
Basic Books, Inc., and is here reprinted by arrangement.

First HARPER TORCHBOOK edition published 1965 by
Harper & Row, Publishers, Incorporated
49 East 33rd Street
New York, New York 10016

Library of Congress Catalog Card No. 58-14277

Contents

VOLUME II

III
The Group
and
the Person

11
Personality and Social Structure

ALEX INKELES

Harvard University

It is perhaps a reflection of the intellectual insecurity of social scientists that they spend an inordinate amount of time and energy defining the "boundaries" of their respective fields as if these were holy lands which had to be defended against expansive, barbaric, and heathen invaders. This need for a clear professional identity leads to a striving for ideological purity, and often from their earliest student days those entering the field are carefully watched for signs of dangerous pantheistic belief. The discipline's name designates not so much a focus of study or a mode of analysis as a banner around which the faithful rally. In sociology this tendency expresses itself in the attempt to analyze social phenomena with a method which strictly excludes psychological theory and data. Those who take this position do so, of course, with the most authoritative of sanctions, since it was Durkheim's explicit purpose, in the first great modern work in sociology, to demonstrate that suicide rates could not be explained by individual psychology. As he defined the task of that great work, it was "to determine the productive causes of suicide directly. . . . Disregarding the individual as such, his motives and his ideas, we shall seek directly the states of the various social environments (religious confessions, family, political society, occupational groups, etc.) in terms of which the variations of suicide occur." And, again, after reviewing the psychological and other

theories on suicide, he declared: "Wholly different are the results obtained when we forgot the individual and sought the causes of the sui-
cidal aptitude of each society in the nature of the societies themselves.
. . . The social suicide rate can be explained only sociologically." [1]

Durkheim was fighting to press back the waters of a veritable sea
of psychologism in order to expose beneath the surface the solid ledge
of societal factors and to create an awareness of the explicit and distinctively social attributes of situations which generated suicide. Considering the difficulty he faced, it may be that the only course open to
him was simultaneously to insist on the *exclusive* relevance of social
factors. Be that as it may, we are no longer living in Durkheim's time.
Our criterion should be not disciplinary purity but, rather, the adequacy of our analysis. The central thesis of this paper is that adequate
sociological analysis of many problems is either impossible or severely
limited unless we make explicit use of psychological theory and data in
conjunction with sociological theory and data. Indeed, I would assert
that very little sociological analysis is ever done without using at least
an implicit psychological theory. It seems evident that in making this
theory explicit and bringing psychological data to bear systematically on
sociological problems we cannot fail but improve the scope and adequacy of sociological analysis.

Obviously, we cannot proceed further without clarifying the meaning of "sociological" and "psychological" as the terms are used here.
I do not believe it very helpful to define the fields in terms of what the
individuals bearing the respective professional labels generally "do."
For one thing, people who wear quite different professional labels often
"do" the same thing. This difficulty is avoided if each discipline is defined in terms of a discrete, central analytic focus or problem. For purposes of this discussion, I will treat sociology as the study of the
structure and functioning of social systems—that is, relatively enduring
systems of action shared by groups of people, large or small. Psychology
I take to be the study of the structure and functioning of the personal
system, the system of action which characterizes a particular biological
organism, notably a human being. According to these definitions, many
professional psychologists who are mainly concerned with the efficiency
of small groups (a social-system problem) are actually doing sociologi-

[1] Emile Durkheim, *Suicide* (trans. J. A. Spaulding and George Simpson), Free Press, 1951, pp. 151, 299.

cal analysis, and those sociologists whose main effort is to discover the individual qualities which predispose one to suicide or crime (a personal-system problem) are dealing with psychology. (This may raise some difficulties about the criteria of membership in professional societies, but our concern here is fortunately not with that problem but with conceptual clarification.)

To establish this conceptual distinction is not, however, to indicate that in practice those interested in social structures can proceed with their analysis without reference to the conceptually distinct problems of psychology. On the contrary, my main purpose is to stress that use of the theory and data of personality systems is essential to an understanding of the stable functioning or the change of social systems. In particular, I wish to stress the importance for sociological analysis of: (1) a general theory of personality—for example, the Freudian theory—and (2) knowledge about the particular personality components in the population or group acting in any social system or subsystem. In thus attempting a modest theoretically oriented assessment of the field, I hope to point to some of the outstanding work that has been done and to suggest the main lines of future work.

The Role of a General Theory of Personality

The student of a social structure seeks to explain the action consequences of a particular set of institutional arrangements. In order to do this, he must correctly estimate the meaning of those arrangements or their effect on the human personality. All institutional arrangements are ultimately mediated through individual human action. The consequences of any institutional arrangement, therefore, depend, at least in part, upon its effect on the human personality, broadly conceived. The human personality system thus becomes one of the main intervening variables in any estimate of the effects of one aspect of social structure on another. The need for a theory of personality is perhaps most evident in the study of those "rates" which represent the summary or end product of thousands or millions of individual decisions and acts, yet which are of distinctive size for different societies or cultures. To illustrate the role which personality theory can and should play in such analysis, I must limit myself to the briefest consideration of two—suicide and delinquency rates. The same type of analysis is, however, equally relevant to other "rate" problems, such as that presented by the frequency and pattern of residential and occupational mobility.

In his strictly sociological analysis, Durkheim found that the rate of suicide, particularly egoistic suicide, was determined by the degree of integration of particular social structures—whether church, family, political party, or national state. Even those who are most skeptical of Durkheim's analysis cannot deny the fact that he has exposed the main pattern of correlation. But one is left in serious doubt as to the causal nexus which converts a state of integration of social structure into a rate of suicide. Indeed, despite his intention to go "directly" to the causes of suicide, "disregarding the individual as such, his motives and his ideas," Durkheim was in the end forced to introduce a general theory of personality as the intervening variable between, on the one hand, the state of integration of social structures and, on the other hand, the varying rates of suicide he sought to explain. To the question of how the origin of suicide could lie in the degree of integration of a social structure, he replied by referring to man's "psychological constitution," which, he said, "needs an object transcending it." This object is lacking in the weakly integrated society, and consequently "the individual, having too keen a feeling for himself and his own value . . . wishes to be his own only goal, and as such an objective cannot satisfy him, drags out languidly and indifferently an existence which henceforth seems meaningless to him." [2]

This is not the place for an evaluation of the adequacy of the psychological theory that Durkheim finally used or the consequences of his failure to introduce this theory explicitly and systematically into the analysis. I wish, rather, to stress the uneven development in the study of suicide. Durkheim's brilliant analysis provided so definitive an argument and so strong a model that for nearly sixty years there was virtually no advance in our understanding of the phenomenon. Generations of students, taught to take *Le Suicide* as the model of sociological analysis, went through their training and out into the world to do battle for "pure"—*i.e.*, nonpsychological—sociological analysis, whatever the cost.

It has been only recently, in the work of Henry and Short on *Suicide and Homicide*,[3] that a major advance has been made in re-

[2] *Ibid.*, pp. 151, 208-16, 356.

[3] A. F. Henry and J. F. Short, *Suicide and Homicide*, Free Press, 1954.

search on this important area. It behooves us, therefore, to ask what made this advance possible. Not the discovery of mountains of new data, although some new data are introduced. Nor does the advance stem from the application of new methods, statistical or otherwise, that were not available in Durkheim's time. The achievement of Henry and Short has, rather, been made possible largely by their systematic use of an explicit psychodynamic theory in conjunction with Durkheim's theory of the role of social integration and social restraint. Henry and Short treat suicide as an act of aggression following from restraint and consequent frustration. They assume that both suicide and homicide have this characteristic,[4] although the two responses differ in the direction in which the aggression is expressed—in the former case inward, in the latter outward. By combining in their analysis the situational factor stressed by Durkheim—namely, the degree of external restraint—and the personality factor of propensity to express aggression inwardly or outwardly, Henry and Short are able to suggest important connections between suicide and homicide rates, to resolve certain contradictions in Durkheim's analysis, to explain some new data in a manner consistent with the rest of the analysis, and to suggest important lines of further research. All this is accomplished without any "reduction" in the importance of the sociological factors, and certainly without reduction of the social reality to personality. This small work is a landmark which surely points the road along which we will or should be travelling in the next decades.

Durkheim and the study of suicide provide the model case, but the importance of my point depends on the existence of other cases. Time permits only the briefest allusion to a parallel development at a much later date, this time in the study of juvenile delinquency. In his classic study of *Delinquency Areas,* Shaw [5] developed an explanation strikingly parallel to Durkheim's theory of suicide. Differential rates of delinquency, he found, are determined by the degree of community disorganization and the consequent weakening of social control. (Shaw

[4] It is not sufficiently realized, even by Henry and Short, how clearly Durkheim saw this connection. He said: "Anomy, in fact, begets a state of exasperation and irritated weariness which may turn against the person himself or another according to the circumstances; in the first case, we have suicide, in the second, homicide." *Op. cit.,* p. 357.

[5] C. R. Shaw, *Delinquency Areas,* University of Chicago Press, 1931.

also added a new element, the conception of the delinquency area as having a special subculture and of delinquency as learned cultural behavior. Although significant, this conception is not of great importance for our present purposes.) Like Durkheim, however, Shaw failed to specify the mechanism by means of which a quality of the community could be translated into the individual actions which ultimately produce the delinquency rate.

In this area, too, progress has been slow, for it was not until twenty years later, in the Gluecks' *Unravelling Juvenile Delinquency*,[6] that community disorganization was meaningfully linked to delinquency rates through the intervening variable of the personality types typically generated under such conditions of disorganization. In their monumental study, the Gluecks have enabled us to see why the previously noticed social conditions in delinquency areas produce the delinquent act, by revealing the creation of response propensities toward delinquent acts in the personalities subjected to those special conditions. They also have enabled us thereby to understand what Shaw could not explain—why only a minority of those exposed to the delinquent subculture actually learn the culture.

This analysis does not, however, minimize the importance of the delinquent subculture or of the objective characteristics of the delinquency area—physical decay in a district in transition to industry, heavy representation of racial or ethnic minorities, high rates of alcoholism and crime, and seriously disrupted family life. But it does vastly increase both our understanding of the phenomenon and our ability to predict and control it through the juxtaposition and integration—but not reduction—of the social and the psychodynamic elements of the situation.

The cases of the suicide and delinquency rates clearly illustrate the kind of model with which we have been operating and enable us to compare it with the model of analysis I am proposing. Sociologists generally begin with some rate, such as the rate of delinquency in a given district or of social mobility out of a given class, perhaps because it is brought to their attention as a "social problem." Their task then is to discover the prior state of the social system which caused or produced the observed rate. The conclusion is generally formulated as a

---

[6] S. Glueck and E. Glueck, *Unravelling Juvenile Delinquency*, Commonwealth Fund, 1950.

sociological *S-R* proposition, in which *S* is the state of society and *R* the resultant rate. Durkheim, for example, began with variations in the rate of suicide (R_s) and sought to explain them through variations in the degree of integration of society (S_i).

It is not unintentional that to describe the standard model of sociological analysis I have used a set of symbols and a formula identical with those of stimulus-response theory. In my opinion, the psychological *S-R* (stimulus-response) theory has its analogue in the sociological *S-R* (or state-rate) theory. Both suffer seriously from failure to utilize an explicit theory of the human personality, and its general and specific propensities, as an intervening variable between their respective *S*'s and *R*'s. Introducing this personality factor (*P*) permits several important reformulations of the model of analysis, involving rearrangements of the same basic elements according to the focus of the study.

The simplest formula, $(S) (P) = R$, although probably far from adequate, would nevertheless be greatly superior to the *S-R* formula, since it provides for the simultaneous effect of two elements influencing action. Without some general theory of the nature of human personality, it is impossible to explain why the absence of social integration should in some cases produce, not Durkheim's egoistic suicide, but mental illness or homicide—or nothing. It is also impossible, without such a theory, to explain why the suicide rate is not generated by high states of integration, or by any other social condition, instead of Durkheim's low state of social integration.

Furthermore, recognition that social conditions and personality are distinct and to some degree independently operating determinants of social action provides the basis for additional differentiation which is crucial to an analysis of certain patterns of action. For example, the external restraint of the individual's situation, in the terms of Henry and Short, varies from high (S_{hr}) to low (S_{lr}). Even assuming that personality is a constant, the formulae $(S_{hr}) (P) = R_h$ and $(S_{lr}) (P) = R_s$ describe two situations of frustration which may produce either homicide or suicide, depending on the degree of external restraint to which the individual is subjected. In addition, it is clear that personality will not be a constant but will itself vary—in this case, most importantly along the dimension from intropunitiveness, which would dispose the individual to suicide, to extrapunitiveness, which would dispose him, rather, to homicide. Obviously, a rich matrix of

factors can emerge which would make quite refined analysis and prediction possible.

This is not the place in which to elaborate these considerations.
I wish to stress, however, that in the examples given above there is
no "reduction" of either the psychological or the sociological variable.
The result is a product of the interaction of the sociological and psychological variables of situation and personality.

Personality and Social Movements.   In addition to its role in explaining the levels of social action which can be expressed as population
rates, a general theory of personality is of great importance in the analysis of major social movements or processes.

Max Weber, perhaps the greatest sociological student of large-
scale social processes, was not lacking in psychological acuity. Indeed,
in many ways his analysis of the influence of Protestantism on capitalism [7] is a specification of the personality types which predispose toward
and are a necessary condition for the development of capitalism. Nevertheless, the basic formulation of his problem—what elements in the
economic ethic of Protestantism account for its encouragement of capitalism—does not particularly require the intervention of a general
theory of human personality. The personality type is given, at least implicitly, in the religious ethic, and the problem is largely to show the
translation of the ethic into action in the economic realm.

Among more recent studies of the social consequences of capitalism, the work of Erich Fromm is an outstanding example of the application of a general theory of personality to explain social movements
which follow from a particular form of social organization. In *Escape
from Freedom,*[8] Fromm asks no less a question than what is the effect
of capitalism as a socioeconomic system on man conceived in terms of
a general theory of the human personality.

The framework of Fromm's analysis is the very general problem of
"the role which psychological factors play as active forces in the social
process." He explores the problem mainly with reference to the effect
of two general needs—the need for relatedness to others, and the need
for freedom or autonomy. These needs are rooted "not in the bodily

[7] M. Weber, *The Protestant Ethic and the Spirit of Capitalism* (trans.
T. Parsons), Scribner's, 1930.

[8] E. Fromm, *Escape From Freedom*, Farrar and Rinehart, 1941, p. 19.

processes but in the very essence of the human mode and practice of life." Of the first, "the need to avoid aloneness," he says: "[The] lack of relatedness to values, symbols, patterns, we may call moral aloneness and state that moral aloneness is as intolerable as physical aloneness, or rather that physical aloneness becomes unbearable only if it implies also moral aloneness." It is the state "which man most dreads." The quality of freedom is less precisely defined, but it seems to mean freedom from instinctual and other restraints which prevent individuation, the fulfillment of innate growth potential, or the "growth of self-strength."

Having postulated these two general human needs, Fromm asserts that all human history has been characterized by "conflict and strife" because:

> Each step in the direction of growing individuation threatened people with new insecurities. Primary bonds once severed, cannot be mended. . . . However, if the economic, social, and political conditions on which the whole process of human individuation depends do not offer a basis for the realization of individuality . . . while at the same time people have lost those ties which gave them security, this lag makes freedom an unbearable burden. . . . Powerful tendencies arise to escape from this kind of freedom into submission or some kind of relationship to man and the world which promises relief from uncertainty, even if it deprives the individual of his freedom.[9]

Within this framework, Fromm traces the history of modern man, from the Middle Ages through the Reformation to the establishment of modern democracies and their counterpart in modern totalitarianism of the fascist variety. His work is extremely ambitious. Since he is attempting to fit a given theory to the sweep of several centuries of man's history, he has the historian's advantage of being sure in advance that his theory will be consonant with the facts he selects. Nevertheless, Fromm has added something to social history and to our understanding of modern man. Indeed, *Escape from Freedom* is probably one of the most distinguished works of social science of the twentieth century. But my purpose in introducing it here is not to argue in support of its thesis. The importance of Fromm's work for this analysis lies in his explicit use of a general theory of human personality as an independent element in the analysis of a continuing process of social change.

Fromm's general formula, as we have said, specifies that man must

[9] *Ibid.*, pp. 36-37.

have both a high degree of relatedness to others and freedom from restraints which prevent individuation. In social contexts which increase individuation but undercut relatedness, there will be a drive to regain such relatedness by a surrender of freedom to group purposes. Presumably any period could be assessed in terms of its potential for change according to its ability to satisfy these needs.

It is greatly to Fromm's credit that he does not try to derive the character of the economic and political structure from these general human needs. He holds, quite properly, that "psychological forces have a dynamism of their own" and asserts that while "the expression of human needs . . . can be molded, [the needs themselves] cannot be uprooted." Nevertheless, he recognizes that "economic forces must be understood not as psychological motivations but as objective conditions . . . dependent on objective factors, such as the natural productive forces, technique, geographical factors. . . ." [10] In this respect his work is superior to Freud's and to Kardiner's.[11] The latter, although he exempts economic relations, attempts to derive the main outlines of myth, religion, and other projective systems almost exclusively from the specific child-rearing disciplines of the culture.

Certain links between Fromm's work and Erikson's may be established. According to Erikson, the entry of America, Germany, and Russia into the industrial era created "a need in the youth of all these countries for a new, a fraternal conscience."

> Industrial revolution, world-wide communication, standardization, centralization, and mechanization threaten the identities which man has inherited from primitive, agrarian, feudal and patrician cultures. What inner equilibrium these cultures had to offer is now endangered on a gigantic scale. As the fear of loss of identity dominates much of our irrational motivation, it calls upon the whole arsenal of fear which is left in each individual from the mere fact of his childhood. In this emergency masses of people become ready to seek salvation in some reactionary pseudo-identity.[12]

Erikson does not develop this position systematically. The same deficiency afflicts Cantril's *Psychology of Social Movements*,[13] but it

[10] *Ibid.*, p. 298.

[11] A. Kardiner, *The Psychological Frontiers of Society*, Columbia University Press, 1945.

[12] E. Erikson, *Childhood and Society*, Norton, 1950, pp. 243, 368.

[13] H. Cantril, *The Psychology of Social Movements*, Wiley, 1941.

nevertheless deserves brief comment. Cantril seeks to show the relevance for social analysis of a variety of psychological concepts, qualities, or processes, such as attitudes, frames of reference, and the functional autonomy of motives. He also emphasizes the importance of certain ego needs in the functioning of any personality, particularly the need for status, or self-integrity. Of this need, he says, "an individual is constantly trying to maintain or enhance his own feeling of self-regard." In addition, he posits a need for meaning, for a frame which permits man to see events as organized or structured and subject to explanation. He then seeks to explain lynching mobs, the Father Divine cult, the Oxford Movement, the Townsend Plan, and the Nazi Party as social movements which arose or were successful in part because they offered to meet these and other needs under conditions in which they were substantially unfulfilled or threatened.

For those who demand proof by means of successful prediction under controlled laboratory conditions, analyses such as those of Fromm, Erikson, and Cantril are not likely to be too convincing. Given any reasonable list of human needs, no author should have great difficulty in showing that in any historical situation he might select one or more of these needs was not adequately met. To demonstrate any *necessary* connection between the deprivation of the need and the emergence of a social movement, he would have to show that in all other situations in which the movement did not arise the need had been fulfilled. Failing that improbable demonstration, he would at least have to predict the emergence of specific movements under conditions in which the deprivation is known to be developing. This too is a difficult task, partly because of the lack of adequate measures of psychosocial deprivation. Those that we do have are expensive and difficult to use on so large a scale as a whole society. In addition, prediction is difficult because we cannot easily find a sufficient number of cases involving the same deprivation, in order to test its general role in stimulating social movements. All this is quite apart from the problems which stem from the role of independent political, economic, or psychological forces, which may suppress the development of a social movement despite marked deprivations. Further difficulties inhere in the fact that deprivation of the same need may lead, in different times and cultures, to quite diverse responses, not all of them easily recognizable as "social movements."

Despite these massive difficulties, increased understanding of the response propensities of peoples subjected to unusual, extreme, persistent, or critical deprivation will continue to be needed and sought. The great social movements of the past will continue to demand explanation, and new movements will constantly arise to challenge the imagination. With a few notable exceptions, such as *When Prophecy Fails*,[14] little has been done by sociologists and psychologists to meet this challenge, even though substantial and indeed rich data are available. For example, the "cargo cult" or its analogue—with its startling abandonment of native sources of sustenance and its pathetic anticipation of an unlimited flow of white man's goods—has been reported in a sufficiently large number of cases in widely dispersed culture areas to suggest that there is some general mechanism in human nature which produces this specific type of manifestation. Closer study of such problems not only would promise increased understanding of the dynamics of social movements but would contribute to our understanding of the dynamics of human personality.

Since the "psychologizing" of social organization is in bad repute with many social scientists, and perhaps deservedly so, it is important to stress certain crucial differences between the approach developed here and some which have been important in the past. Psychological theories of society and social movements have mainly been of two types. The first derives social behavior and institutions directly from the psychological properties of the human psyche, including, in the case of Freud, the psychological history of the race. A typical if extreme example is the assertion that man has an aggressive instinct and that therefore we have war.[15] The second, which Sorokin has labelled the "psychologistic" school of sociology, simply reduces or translates all social phenomena into psychological terms; in its modern version, it asserts that the only "real" social phenomena or variables are the personalities, the individual psychologies, of those who make up any given group.

Fromm, Erikson and Cantril cannot be made to fit in either of these patterns. As the quotation on page 258 demonstrates, Fromm recognizes social institutions, particularly systems of economic organiza-

[14] L. Festinger, H. W. Riecken, and S. Schachter, *When Prophecy Fails*, University of Minnesota Press, 1956.

[15] See T. H. Pear (ed.), *Psychological Factors of Peace and War*, Philosophical Library, 1950.

tion, as relatively independent variables, with their own history and laws of development. He does not treat them as mere projections of personality or need systems. These authors also recognize that many processes in political or economic systems, such as the accumulation of capital, cannot be reduced to or fully described in psychological terms. The essence of this mode of analysis, rather, lies in its insistence that all forms of social organization have personal meaning or psychological implications for the participants, and that different social systems have different psychic meanings. The pattern these authors have followed in their analyses is to state, on the basis of general personality theory, certain general human needs or drives; then to examine a given social setting to assess its effect cn those needs. Where the needs are not satisfied or are met in a peculiar way, they again draw on personality theory to suggest the typical modes of human response to such frustration. They then assess the effects of the personal reaction on the social system, with especial attention to the prospects for equilibrium or further frustrations which may set in motion a different social movement. In this model, the action propensities in the individual are derived, not from society, but from a general theory of the human personality. In turn, culture and social structure are perceived historically, not as derived from or reduced to personality factors. But they act on personality and, according to their mode of influence, produce reactions from personality which may generate movements of social change in the original sociocultural system.

The Role of Modal Personality Patterns

Not only does the student of social structure need an adequate general theory of personality; it may also be important for him to measure the particular qualities of personality which characterize the "population" of any given social structure. Such information is of great importance in the study of at least two major sociological problems: (1) the recruitment of persons into, and the adequacy of their performance in, the major social roles; and (2) the integration and change of the diverse institutions that make up a society.

Sociologists have traditionally explained regular role performance as a logical consequence of the system of sanctions imposed on those who fail to meet, and rewards granted to those who do meet, the expectations of society. Performance is thus seen as largely dependent on factors "outside" the person. The only thing that need be posited as "inside," in this view, is the general desire to avoid punishment and to gain rewards. Important as such "drives" may be, they do not seem sufficient to explain the complex phenomenon of differential role performance. Without in any way challenging the crucial importance of the objective factors which determine role behavior, I wish to stress that recruitment into roles and the quality of role performance may to an important degree be influenced by personal qualities in individuals which predispose them to move toward one or another role, and which have a marked effect on the quality of their role performance once they have been placed. It must be assumed, further, that this happens on a sufficiently large scale to be a crucial factor in determining the functioning of any social system. To the degree that this is true, to predict the functioning of a particular institution, of a small- or large-scale social system, we need to know not only the system of statuses but also the distribution of personality characteristics in the population at large and among the incumbents of particular roles.

Although there is considerable surface plausibility in this assumption, few studies deal with the problem. Two studies do give us the opportunity to observe at least the effects of differing personality patterns in the participants, although in a structurally constant environment. In the study by Haythorn and his associates [16] a number of four-man discussion groups were formed. Each group was shown a silent film on human relations in industry and given the task of composing and recording a dialogue to fit the film. The subjects had been previously rated on authoritarianism (F scale). One type of group was composed of men all of whom were very high in authoritarianism. Members of the other type were all low scorers. Although the two types of group were alike in structure in that no leader had been appointed and no rules for reaching an agreement specified, their behavioral patterns varied significantly. In groups composed of those low on the authoritarianism scale, more positive affect was shown, there was greater concern for the feeling of others, and fewer efforts were made to direct others. In each of the two types of group there developed what the researchers describe as a distinctive "group culture." Although it derived from the modal personality patterns of the

---

[16] W. Haythorn *et al.*, "The Behavior of Authoritarian and Equalitarian Personalities in Groups," *Hum. Relat.*, 9 (1956), 57-74.

members, this "culture" was similar to what would have been expected had the norms of the group been formally structured as democratic or authoritarian.

A comparable but more complex pattern is represented in the work of Schutz.[17] He also composed groups by selecting members on the basis of a personality test, but the groups were arranged to be "compatible" or "incompatible." The personality test discriminated among individuals described as "personal" or "counter-personal" in their orientation toward interpersonal relations. The "personal" individuals were more concerned than the "counter-personal" with the smoothness of interpersonal relations; those rated as "counter-personal" were less considerate of the individual, less concerned with good relations, and more concerned with getting the job done. The compatible groups were homogeneous; that is, all the members were the same type, either personal or counter-personal. In the incompatible groups, both types of interpersonal orientation were represented. On a variety of tasks involving problem-solving by the groups, the compatible sets had a significantly higher productivity or effectiveness score. Follow-up revealed that members of the compatible groups experienced greater satisfaction with their group and with their own participation in it.

In neither of these studies was the formal social structure of the group varied significantly, although in the Haythorn study the shift from emergent to appointed leaders represents a structural change not yet systematically reported on as of this writing. Until the social structure of such groups is also brought under experimental control, sociologists will wonder how important these personality factors are as compared to variable aspects of structure such as the pattern of leadership, the rules determining the rights of members, the methods of assigning individuals to tasks and of handling grievances, the forms for internal communication, and the size of the groups. Until the variables of both personality and structure are simultaneously controlled and the relative impact of each on group effectiveness is tested, we can explain only a limited part of the observed variance. Indeed, we may be explaining only a very small part of the variance, since the combined impact of personality and structural variables may produce effects far

[17] W. C. Schutz, "What Makes Groups Productive," *Hum. Relat.,* 8 (1955), 429-65.

more massive than might be suggested by a simple additive approach to the two "independent" variables. Clearly this field is one for major exploitation in the future.

Since such studies seem to presume small-group research under laboratory conditions, a word is perhaps in order on two commonly raised objections to such laboratory studies, both bearing on their relevance to "real" social situations. The first holds that the rigorous selection of personality types in these carefully composed groups limits their relevance, because in "natural" groups structural factors generally produce a more or less random assortment of personality types. The validity of this assertion is, of course, open to test. Studies of the personality composition of occupational groups, such as those by Roe or Swanson,[18] and other studies on social-class groupings suggest that within major subgroups of the population personality types may in fact be much less random than is commonly supposed. But, of course, even a random distribution of personality types is, after all, a distribution, and its relation to performance and group process can be studied.

The other, and perhaps weightier, objection to laboratory studies charges that such composed groups are "artificial" and that the applicability of the findings of these studies to "real" situations which produce "genuine" personal commitment is, therefore, limited. Those who make this assertion often have no idea how real and complete is the commitment of participants in experiments based on group discussion or competitive games. Be that as it may, the answer would seem to be that if laboratory groups do not elicit effective personal commitment then the effect of personality on role performance should be studied in "real" situations—in school, in the family, on the job, in politics. Sociologists have not been distinguished by either the alacrity or the thoroughness with which they have approached this task. Yet solid evidence is gradually being accumulated which reveals that even in the "real" world particular statuses often attract or recruit preponderantly for one or another personality characteristic. This fact has a substantial effect on individual adjustment to roles and the general quality of institutional functioning.

Whether they are based on recruitment or on development on the

[18] A. Roe, *The Psychology of Occupations*, Wiley, 1956; G. E. Swanson, "Agitation Through the Press: A Study of the Personalities of Publicists," *Pub. Opin. Quart.*, 20 (1956), 441-56.

job, such modal personality differences are relevant to the sociologist only if they can be shown to affect individual role performance and consequently institutional functioning. Studies in which data on personality and on role performance are simultaneously reported are rare, and little has been done systematically to exploit the promising lead which Merton [19] gave us years ago. The few available studies do indicate marked effects of personality on role performance. In a study of the performance of nurses' aides in a mental hospital as judged by their supervisors, Gilbert and Levinson [20] rated them as "custodial" or "humanistic" in their treatment of patients. Aides rated as "custodial" made more threats to patients and placed prime emphasis on keeping the wards quiet. The "humanistic" aides were more friendly and respectful to the patients and assumed the role of "social" therapist for their wards. For the female aides in three Boston hospitals, the rank-order correlation between custodialism in the treatment of patients and score on authoritarianism in personality as measured by the F scale was .75.

Several outstanding studies relate personality to school performance. Rosen [21] drew a sample of students stratified by social class from public high schools in New Haven and obtained measures of achievement motivation and school performance. Those who scored high on need achievement tended to make good grades, 69 percent having "B" or better as against 35 percent of those with low need achievement. A test of value orientations, incidentally, failed to discriminate significantly the low- and high-grade performers. Need achievement was also very highly associated with social class, but a separate control run on class showed that it had virtually no independent effect on grade performance when achievement motivation was controlled.

Stern, Stein, and Bloom [22] obtained a series of performance measures for two groups of 61 students who were rated, respectively, high

---

[19] R. Merton, "Bureaucratic Structure and Personality," *Soc. Forces,* *18* (1940), 560-68.

[20] D. Gilbert and D. J. Levinson, "Role Performance, Ideology and Personality in Mental Hospital Aides," in M. Greenblatt and others (eds.), *The Patient and the Mental Hospital,* Free Press, 1957.

[21] B. C. Rosen, "The Achievement Syndrome: A Psycho-cultural Dimension of Social Stratification," *Amer. sociol. Rev., 21* (1956), 203-11.

[22] G. G. Stern, M. I. Stein, and B. S. Bloom, *Methods in Personality Assessment,* Free Press, 1956.

and low on stereopathy, a trait broadly similar to authoritarianism (F scale). Intelligence accounted for only a modest part of the variance in the stereopathy score, but any possible effect of differences in intelligence between the two groups was controlled by matching on this dimension. On entrance and placement examinations, there were marked differences in the performance of the two groups in tests on the humanities, social sciences, and English. By contrast, there was only random variation in their performance in biological sciences, physical sciences, and mathematics. The emphasis at the college concerned (presumably the University of Chicago) was on "capacity for detachment, for delaying resolution or closure, and for tolerating ambiguous relatives rather than demanding structural absolutes." This placed a premium on qualities which were characteristic of nonstereopaths and relatively lacking in those high in stereopathy. Such qualities were, however, obviously less important in the natural-sciences and mathematics examinations, for which fields the requirements and tests are also more standardized.

Striking differences also emerged in the later school performance of the two groups. At the end of the first year, 20 percent of the stereopathic students had withdrawn from the college whereas none of the nonstereopaths had done so—a difference significant at the .001 level. Intelligence made virtually no difference in this performance. The complaints of the withdrawing stereopathic students strongly suggested that their action resulted from a lack of congruence between their personality and their consequent ambitions and hopes, on the one hand, and on the other the special requirements of the particular college they had entered. They complained most about the seeming lack of discipline, the refusal of instructors to give the "right" answers, and the separation between course content and their immediate and practical vocational interests This outcome was largely as had been predicted from an examination of the distinctive qualities of education at the particular college and the distinctive personality attributes of the stereopathic students.

It is clear from these studies that role recruitment and particularly role performance cannot safely be predicted solely on the basis of the extrinsic features of the status and its place in the larger social structure. The personalities of those occupying the statuses will strongly influence the quality of their role performance. And since it seems likely that personalities are not randomly recruited to statuses, the effects of the modal personality patterns in any given group of status incumbents may be a massive influence on the quality of role performance in the group. The impact on other parts of the social structure may therefore be substantial. We see again, as in our earlier observations on social rates, that both social structure and personality must be treated as important independent but interacting variables influencing the flow of the social process.

As this task is pursued, furthermore, sociologists will increasingly discover how impoverished and inadequate is their conceptual scheme in the very area in which they feel so secure. Although sociologists give a central place in their conceptual scheme to the role concept, it is surprising to discover how undeveloped this area of study is. There is, for example, no standard set of concepts or categories which could be used to describe *any* typical role or set of roles in a way that is sociologically meaningful, does some justice to its complexity, and permits systematic comparison with other roles. The devising of such a set of categories, particularly one which will have meaning with reference to personality variables, is a necessary precondition for launching the program of fruitful research which invites our attention here.

Personality and the Social System. If the study of personality as it influences role recruitment and performance seems to pose major methodological problems, they are as naught compared to the problems posed for him who seeks to discover the role that personality patterns play in the integration and change of social systems. The concept of "national character" not only is old but has long been under attack for its presumed kinship with discredited theories about racial psychology. However eager we may be to avoid seeming prejudiced, or worse still "racist," as scientists we cannot avoid dealing systematically with the question: Is there a significant difference among various national or subnational populations in the distribution of discrete traits or personality types, and, if so, how does this affect the functioning of the social system? Can we assume that a given social structure will operate in much the same way regardless of the set of personalities placed in that context? What stimulus to social change follows from the lack of congruence between personality needs and system requirements, and what limitations on such change follow from the lack of certain motivations in the participants?

No one has ever tested a national population or even a major subpopulation using either an adequate sample or adequate psychological instruments.[23] All assertions or denials of national, subnational, regional, or class differences of major magnitudes, therefore, remain mere statements of faith. And until we have accumulated the basic facts, the other questions, of course, must also be held in abeyance. To answer questions such as those above, we must be able to measure in an adequate sample of a national population the distribution of personality traits and personality syndromes or types, much as we now chart the distribution of attitudes and voting intentions. Before we attempt this difficult task of measurement, we need to know what elements of personality should be measured for purposes of sociological analysis. Having measured important personality dimensions in such populations, we need to learn how to interpret the results, and then to integrate our findings with data on the structural aspects of the system, to develop predictive propositions, and to test the adequacy of our theory in new populations and situations.

Although this may sound exceedingly ambitious, we are much closer to the attainment of this objective than many realize. Recent theoretical efforts have moved us far toward the delineation of some of the components of personality which we assume to be of greatest relevance for social-system analysis. In the last two decades, substantial progress has been made in devising apparently valid and reliable personality tests which can be easily and simply administered to large samples—notably, modifications of the sentence-completion test, the TAT, and other paper-and-pencil tests. Indeed, very limited and simple personality tests on a single dimension have already been included in national opinion surveys. Many dilemmas, particularly those involving the cross-cultural validity of psychological tests, still are unresolved, but the path ahead seems fairly clear and the prognosis good. And, in fact, we can point to several pilot studies based on extremely small populations which represent in capsule form what we must learn to

[23] In a study undertaken for the Joint Commission on Mental Illness and Health, the Survey Research Center of the University of Michigan in March 1957 recorded the responses of one of its national samples to a set of TAT cards. The study, directed by Drs. Gerald Gurin and Joseph Veroff, used a special set of cards developed in collaboration with Dr. John Atkinson. Scored for need achievement, power, and affiliation, they will give us the first partial assessment of personality modes in a major national population.

do for larger populations—*e.g.*, the study by Kaplan and Plaut of the Hutterites [24] and Spindler's exceptional study of personality and social change in the Menomini.[25]

Of the many studies of personality in "primitive" societies, very few have achieved Spindler's clarity and precision in maintaining a precise distinction between personality and the sociocultural system. His study design was concerned mainly with discerning and explaining personality differences in several groups of Menomini, differentiated in degree of acculturation. Nevertheless, it also provides a striking example of apparent integration or congruence between the typical role requirements of a sociocultural system and the modal personality pattern of the society's members.

The "classical" form of Menomini culture, before its extreme acculturation in the late period of white contact, is approximated today only as a remnant in a group of the currently least acculturated Menomini living in the relatively isolated community of Zoar. In that community, however, we can see elements of the classical pattern. For example, there is very little centralization of authority; the leaders are noticeably lacking in coercive power and have little interest in attaining it. The most important task of a leader is to express group consensus and to make sure that no individual's feelings are hurt. Interpersonal equality is strongly stressed, and all the folk heroes are extremely democratic. Although being a good hunter is highly valued, hunting attainments are not objects of marked striving. Whatever one's success, it is extremely inappropriate to boast. Indeed, in general, emotional expressiveness is severely controlled, particularly the expression of aggression. Little value is placed on compulsive qualities involving orderliness, regularity, or changing nature, nor are there requirements for these qualities. Little stress or strain is imposed by the individual's statuses. The world is defined as more friendly than hostile, and provision is made for sharing food and in other ways sustaining a kind of oral optimism.

In the light of this brief description of some of the traditional Menomini culture patterns as they have persisted into modern times,

[24] B. Kaplan and T. Plaut, *Personality in a Communal Society*, University of Kansas Publications, 1956.
[25] G. D. Spindler, *Socio-cultural and Psychological Processes in Menomimi Acculturation*, University of California Press, 1955.

it is most revealing to examine the personality patterns revealed by the Rorschach test administered to 17 of the least acculturated Menomini. The test results for this group were highly homogeneous. At the lowest, 58 percent, and on more critical dimensions, 70 percent or more, shared the same characteristics in Rorschach response. In his summary of the Rorschach results for this group, Spindler states the personality type to be:

> . . . highly intratensive, sensitive to the environment but able to maintain equilibrium despite its variations, lacking generally in overt emotional responsiveness and exhibiting a high degree of rational control over it when it does appear, motivated more by biologically oriented "survival" drives than by self-projective imaginatively creative ones, intellectually uncomplicated but adequate in terms of its setting, lacking in rigidity or constriction, without evidence of the usual forms of anxiety, tension, or internal conflict. . . .[26]

Juxtaposition of this personality profile with the institutional features and role requirements of the classical sociocultural system suggests a number of points at which the modal personality pattern articulates significantly with important aspects of the older culture pattern. The low level of emotional responsiveness, the control over emotion, and the sensitivity to interpersonal relations obviously fit well with the cultural requirements for inhibition of aggression, absence of strivings for power, and avoidance of giving offense. At the same time, an appropriate adjustment to the environment and the requirement of skill in hunting is provided by the strength of biologically oriented survival drives. The Menomini cosmology posits the existence of supranatural powers yielding fateful and irrevocable but generally positive outcomes. Their ideology of passive acceptance of benevolent but inscrutable nature articulates with the personality quality of lack of tension, striving, and anxiety. These and similar points strongly suggest that when the culture was in full form, before white contact, many of the qualities which cut across the Menomini sociocultural system were matched by appropriate qualities which cut across the modal personality patterns of Menomini people. We may then assume that in substantial measure the integration of the sociocultural system was supported by an appropriate matching integration in the personality structure of the members of the society.

[26] *Ibid.*, pp. 133-34.

Spindler's study not only suggests the pattern of integration between the classical social structure of the Menomini and what was apparently once the dominant modal personality pattern of the people. It also calls our attention to the effects of social change on character and of character on sociocultural patterns. In Menomini society today one can discern a range of groups based on socioeconomic status and degree of acculturation, from the native-oriented, described above, to a highly acculturated elite group. These groups show important differences in modal personality patterns which have substantial relevance for understanding their status and social adjustment. The highly acculturated elite group has gone farthest in departing from the traditions of the classical culture and in accepting the surrounding white culture. These Menomini live in a style barely distinguishable from that of the white group. It is particularly revealing, therefore, that when the Rorschach protocols of these highly acculturated Menomini were compared with those of a white control group they exhibited no significant differences. It is not clear whether in this case the social change is producing personality adaptation, or whether existing personality types are taking advantage of changed opportunities for mobility. Probably both processes are at work in a complex interaction of personality mode and social structure, producing changes both in the sociocultural system and in the type and distribution of the personalities generated in the community. In any event, it is clear that there are exciting and important implications in such explorations for all students of social stability and change.

Another major point of articulation between psychological and sociological studies is the study of child-rearing. The particular child-rearing disciplines which produce one or another consequence in the adult personality present what is clearly a predominantly psychological problem. It seems to me, however, that the sociologist has an important contribution to make to the question of why the parent does what he does. If child-rearing practices are variable, we can hardly assume the variation to be unrelated to the life situation of the parents and the pressures to which they are subjected. The work of Miller and Swanson [27] on these issues represents a substantial step forward by showing the intimate connection between the occupational setting of the parent,

[27] D. Miller and G. E. Swanson, *Inner Conflict and Defense*, Henry Holt, 1957.

the child-rearing practices he adopts or adapts, and the consequences in the personality of the child. I think it no exaggeration to say that one of the most important clues, and an extraordinarily neglected one, to the means whereby social stress in one generation leads to social change in the next lies in the various ways in which parents raise their children.[28] Unfortunately, I have only enough space to note in passing that here again are major opportunities for the independent but co-ordinate action of personality modes and social structure in fostering social stability or generating social change

Summary and Conclusions

I have argued that sociological analysis—the attempt to understand the structure and functioning of social systems—will often require the use of a general theory of personality and knowledge of the distinctive personality characteristics of participants in the system as a whole or in major subsystems and in particular roles. To many, this may at once suggest that I am proposing a "reduction" of sociological analysis to the presumably more basic level of psychological analysis. I am by no means implying or suggesting this course of action. What is at issue here is not the reduction of one discipline to another but the articulation of the two for certain specific purposes under certain specific conditions.

I have already emphasized that I conceive of the two disciplines as having quite different analytic foci. Let me add that there are many areas of traditional sociological research for which personality theory or knowledge of modal personality patterns would seem to have little or no relevance—for example, most demographic research, a substantial part of urban sociology, and a great many problems in measurement or social mapping, including the mapping of class structures. But if we go beyond the mapping of a class structure to deal with the behavior of members of different classes and the rates, say, of stability in or mobility out of the particular classes, then psychological data may assume great importance in the general model of analysis. This is not to say, however, that the problem reduces itself to personal psychology.

[28] For a pilot study of these processes see A. Inkeles, "Social Change and Social Character: The Role of Parental Mediation," *J. soc. Issues,* 11 (1955), 12-23.

Obviously, in an occupational pyramid with relatively few jobs defined as very desirable and many defined as less desirable, the amount of mobility out of the lower classes is objectively given by the nature of the pyramid. If education of a given level or quality is a prerequisite to attaining certain occupational levels and such education is generally not available in rural areas, the rate of mobility for those of rural residence will be primarily determined by these facts.

Within the framework of such structurally set limits, however, there is a broad area in which other forces have considerable room to operate. For lack of appropriate motivation, those who are otherwise eligible may not use the opportunities for mobility to maximum advantage. Among those who are eligible, some will make the effort, others will not. Of those who strive, some will have the capacity, some will not. Even a cursory glance at the many recent studies stimulated by our national need to discover and train inborn talent will reveal the serious miscalculations we have made by assuming that only objective factors of "opportunity" are important in determining mobility drives. If we are to go beyond the mere statistical charting of mobility rates for different strata to more complex explanatory schemes with predictive power in new situations, we must be able to deal with the personal component—the motivated actor in the situation of social action. The mobility rate for the society is not thus reduced to a matter of mere personal psychology. It remains a social, not a personal, datum.

The same is true of the other aspects of the individual's social context of action. But the action of individuals in any situation are personal, however much they reflect the determining influence of the social environment. And that environment, in turn, can be reflected in individual action only to the extent that it is mediated through the personal system or personality. A full understanding of any social situation and its probable consequences, therefore, assumes a knowledge not only of the main facts about the social structure—the gathering of which is presumably the special province of sociological study—but also of the main facts about the personalities operating in that structure. What is required, therefore, is an integration or coordination of two basic sets of data in a larger explanatory scheme—not a reduction of either mode of analysis to the allegedly more fundamental level of the other.

It may seem unclear wherein what I urge differs substantially from what has long been practiced under the name of social psychology. I therefore hasten to state that I do not regard my position as a departure from social psychology in its classical formulation. On the contrary, I consider it to be highly congruent in spirit and in general orientation, if not in detailed substance, with the early formulations of social psychology, in particular with the approach of such men as W. I. Thomas.

It is much more difficult for me to say how my position relates to that of social psychology as it is practiced today, simply because I find it extremely difficult to understand just what social psychology *is* today. At times it seems to be a vast residual category into which everything not otherwise classifiable is placed. At other times it seems to represent everything which is objectively measured through contact with or response from a subject. Thus ecology, population statistics, and crime rates are all sociology, but the study of opinions and attitudes or of the reasons people move from country to city is social psychology. The study of interaction in small groups is for some mysterious reason almost always treated as social psychology, even though the researcher's interest may be in social-system problems indistinguishable from those dealt with by students of large-scale social systems, who are thought to be "plain" sociologists. That many, indeed most, of these studies contain no reference to any kind of psychological theory and, in fact, seem to be uninformed by any such theory apparently does not disturb those who classify them as social psychology.

Although I do not urge that personality and social structure be considered an area of inquiry distinct from social psychology, I cannot easily reconcile the basic unity of the approach I have urged and the grab-bag generally called social psychology. Nor would I equate the approach I have stressed with much of the work done by psychologically trained social psychologists. In most of their work there is as little systematic use of sociological theory and data as there is of psychological theory and data in the work of sociologists. The confusion might be somewhat reduced if we returned to the earlier term "psycho-social," or "psycho-sociology," while yet preserving the term "social psychology." Then we might designate as social psychology the study of personality, which seeks to explain individual action not only by considering the psychological properties of the person but also by giving systematic attention to sociocultural forces in the individual's action situation. We might designate as psycho-sociology efforts to explain the functioning and change of social systems which not only consider properties of social systems but give systematic consideration to general personality theory or to the modal personalities of the system's participants and their psychological adjustment to the social forces impinging on them. The study of personality and social structure means no more and no less than this.

Bibliography

General (and bibliographic) Sources

Haring, D. G., *Personal Character and Cultural Milieu*, Syracuse University Press, 1949.

Honigmann, John J., *Culture and Personality*, Harper, 1954.

Kluckhohn, C. K., H. A. Murray, and D. M. Schneider, *Personality in Nature, Society, and Culture*, Knopf, 1954.

Sargent, S. S., and M. W. Smith (eds.), *Culture and Personality*, The Viking Fund, 1949.

Theoretical and Methodological Reviews

Barber, B., *Social Stratification*, Harcourt, Brace, 1957, chaps. 11, 12.

Inkeles, A., "Some Sociological Observations on Culture and Personality Studies," in C. K. Kluckhohn, H. A. Murray, and D. M. Schneider, *op. cit.*

————, and D. J. Levinson, "National Character: The Study of Modal Personality and Sociocultural Systems," in G. Lindzey (ed.), *Handbook of Social Psychology*, Vol. II, Addison-Wesley, 1954.

Gorer, G., "National Character: Theory and Practice," in M. Mead and B. Metraux (eds.), *The Study of Culture at a Distance*, University of Chicago Press, 1953.

Kaplan, B., "Personality and Social Structure," in J. Gittler (ed.), *Review of Sociology*, Wiley, forthcoming.

Hallowell, A. I., "Culture, Personality, and Society," in A. L. Kroeber (ed.), *Anthropology Today*, University of Chicago Press, 1953.

Klineberg, O., "A Science of National Character," *J. soc. Psychol.*, 19 (1944), 147-62.

Lindesmith, A. R., and A. L. Strauss, "A Critique of Culture-Personality Writings," *Amer. sociol. Rev.*, 15 (1950), 587-600.

Linton, R., *The Cultural Background of Personality*, Appleton-Century, 1945.

Mead, M., "The Study of National Character," in D. Lerner and H. Lasswell (eds.), *The Policy Sciences*, Stanford University Press, 1951.

Selected Studies

Adorno, T. W., Else Frenkel-Brunswik, D. J. Levinson, and R. N. Sanford, *The Authoritarian Personality*, Harper, 1950.

Benedict, R., *The Chrysanthemum and the Sword*, Houghton-Mifflin, 1946.

Cantril, H., *The Psychology of Social Movements*, Wiley, 1941.

Erikson, Erik, *Childhood and Society*, Norton, 1950.

Freud, S., *Civilization and Its Discontents* (trans. Joan Riviere), Hogarth Press, 1930.

Fromm, E., *Escape From Freedom*, Farrar and Rinehart, 1941.

Glueck, S., and E. Glueck, *Unravelling Juvenile Delinquency*, Commonwealth Fund, 1950.

Henry, A. F., and J. F. Short, *Suicide and Homicide*, Free Press, 1954.

Kaplan, B., and T. Plaut, *Personality in a Communal Society*, University of Kansas Publications, 1956.

Kardiner, A., *The Psychological Frontiers of Society*, Columbia University Press, 1945.

Lewin, K., *Resolving Social Conflicts: Selected Papers on Group Dynamics*, Harper, 1948.

McClelland, D., *et al.*, *The Achievement Motive*, Appleton-Century-Crofts, 1953.

Miller, D., and G. E. Swanson, *Inner Conflict and Defense*, Henry Holt, 1957.

Parsons, T., and R. Bales, *Family, Socialization and Interaction Process*, Free Press, 1955.

Riesman, D., *The Lonely Crowd*, Yale University Press, 1950.

Roe, Anne, *The Psychology of Occupations*, Wiley, 1956.

Stern, G. G., M. I. Stein, and B. S. Bloom, *Methods in Personality Assessment: Human Behavior in Complex Social Situations*, Free Press, 1956.

Whiting, J. W., and I. L. Child, *Child Training and Personality: A Cross-Cultural Study*, Yale University Press, 1953.

12
The Study
of
Consensus

THEODORE M. NEWCOMB

University of Michigan

No one, I suppose, needs to be persuaded that some manner and degree of interpersonal consensus is a necessary condition for social organization, at any level of complexity. Concern with the collective aspects of human life has always, implicitly if not explicitly, connoted concern with its consensual aspects, and, whether or not we regard Auguste Comte as the founder of our discipline, he was neither the first nor the last to note the inseparability of the two.[1] No one has been more explicit about it, I think, than Park and Burgess, the authors of another sociological landmark:

> The continuity and life of a society depend upon its success in transmitting from one generation to the next its folkways, mores, techniques and ideals. From the standpoint of collective behavior, these cultural traits may all be reduced to the one term "consensus." Society viewed abstractly is an organization of individuals; considered concretely it is a complex of organized habits, sentiments, and social attitudes—in short, consensus.[2]

[1] A. Comte, *The Positive Philosophy*, Vol. I, London: Trubner, 1853.
[2] R. E. Park and E. W. Burgess, *Introduction to the Science of Sociology*, 2nd ed., University of Chicago Press, 1924, p. 163.

Although none of my readers needs to be persuaded of these things, I should like to begin by recalling them; if they are truisms, they are not trivial ones.

In 1947, just ten years before this writing, the presidential address delivered before the American Sociological Society by Louis Wirth [3] was devoted to problems of consensus. "I regard the study of consensus," he said in that address, "as the central task of sociology, which is to understand the behavior of men in so far as that behavior is influenced by group life." I am not sure how many of my readers would go that far, nor am I at all sure that I would. My present concerns, at any rate, are somewhat different from those of Wirth in 1947. His address was dominated by the theme of the urgent necessity of creating world consensus in a world which might otherwise destroy itself.

> . . . The subject matter for the cultivation of which society sustains us . . . is the life of man in society, and the heart of that subject matter today is the understanding of the processes through which consensus on a world scale is created. Unless we solve that problem, and solve it in a reasonably satisfactory way soon, there will be no opportunity to work on any of the others on which our hearts and minds are set. [4]

My own concerns are perhaps as microscopic as Wirth's were macroscopic. They spring from a simple and, I hope, reasonable assumption—that any process as dependable and as fundamental as the achievement of consensus on the part of two or more persons must include psychological processes on the part of those persons. These processes, I further assume, occur in orderly manner and should be understood both in their own right and as part of the broader problem of how consensus is achieved, modified, or maintained within human collectivities.

I find it interesting, in passing, to recall that all the great sociological theorists who are usually considered to have shown a special interest in social-psychological questions have, in their several ways, wrestled with the problem of consensus. Tarde looked at consensus

---

[3] L. Wirth, "Consensus and Mass Communication," *Amer. sociol. Rev.,* 13 (1948), 1-15.

[4] *Ibid.,* p. 15.

and "explained" it in terms of imitation.[5] LeBon found "the law of mental unity" at work "as soon as a few individuals are gathered together." [6] For Durkheim, "collective representations" were central to every sociological problem.[7] Cooley, making what seems to me an enormous advance, saw in that apparently most private of all entities, the self, a consensual product.[8] And Mead, in particular, brilliantly illuminated the whole problem by describing it in terms of symbolic interaction, the crucial outcome of which is consensual: "the generalized other." [9]

Thus the problem has by no means been ignored by sociologists with social-psychological interests. Compared with them, however, as with Wirth, my own treatment of the problem is microscopic.

Definitions and Assumptions

Perhaps the reader is wondering how I am defining consensus. At this moment I prefer to say just enough to be reasonably clear, but not so much as to prejudge certain issues by definitional question begging. I mean by the term nothing more or less than the existence, on the part of two or more persons, of similar orientations toward something.

Even though this is the simplest and most general definition that I can think of, it contains at least three words that require further comment. *Orientations,* first, are equivalent to attitudes in the broadest sense of the term, having both cognitive and cathectic components. Like attitudes, they are always toward *something;* orientations are labeled by their objects, which may be any discriminable entity, concrete or abstract. *Similarity* refers to likeness in any aspect or dimension of an orientation; for example, two or more persons may have cognitively similar but cathectically different orientations toward the same object, and if so they are characterized by cognitive consensus with regard to it—even though, in the popular sense of the word, they

[5] G. Tarde, *The Laws of Imitation,* Henry Holt, 1903.

[6] G. LeBon, *The Crowd,* London: T. Fisher Unwin, 1920, p. 48.

[7] E. Durkheim, "Répresentations Individuelles et Répresentations Collectives," *Revue de Métaphysique,* 6, 1898, 274-302.

[8] C. H. Cooley, *Human Nature and the Social Order,* Scribner's, 1902.

[9] G. H. Mead, *Mind, Self and Society* (ed. C. H. Morris), University of Chicago Press, 1934.

are not "in agreement" about it. Cathectic disagreement may actually be enhanced by cognitive consensus about the object of disagreement. And similarity, finally, is not an all-or-none affair, but a matter of degree.

If it is axiomatic that some degree and manner of consensus is a necessary social cement, I suppose it is equally so that the maintenance of consensual states within human collectivities presupposes certain kinds of psychological process on the part of the individuals who achieve or maintain consensus. Hence the proper study of mankind, for social psychologists, should include the psychological processes which are essential to consensuality, and which presumably vary with changes in consensuality.

Let me begin a consideration of those psychological processes by noting the interdependence of consensus and communication. At the simplest level, it seems evident that the most general purpose of communication is to enable the transmitter to share with one or more other persons some information not available, or not certainly available, to the recipient(s) of the message. Under most conditions, one does not transmit information to a person known to have it already, or ask for information (which is transmitting information to the effect that one desires to have other information) which one already possesses. (The apparent exceptions to this generalization have to do, I believe, with confusions about the actual referent of communication. For example, when one seems to be transmitting information to the effect that it is a "good morning," one is probably, in a much more important sense, transmitting information to the effect that the greeter recognizes the greeted and wishes to be courteous to him.)

I find it tempting to defend the very general proposition that, in some degree and in some manner, the actual consequences of communication, as well as the intended ones, are consensus-increasing. At the cognitive level, I believe the proposition to be defensible, but in many instances the nature of the increased consensus is trivial; often, for example, it can only be said that, following the transmission of a message, there is, for a fleeting instant, more consensus than before concerning the transmitter's desire to call the receiver's attention to the referent of the message. In an actuarial sense, however, whether or not in the absolute sense, the proposition is far from trivial. The actual achievement of increased consensus has been experienced by every socialized human being with sufficient regularity to result in a dependable motivation to achieve it. (This is not to assert, of course, that the desire for increased consensus is the whole motivation for communicative behavior; there may, for example, be motivation to deceive.) The rewards of actual consensus in facilitating coordinated activity *vis à vis* a common world are obvious enough; it therefore seems safe to conclude that successful communication is generally rewarding to communicators and that, whether or not they are able to describe the consensual consequences of successful communication, the fact of being rewarded by it results in their acquiring motivation to achieve it.

This conclusion can be stated more effectively, for present purposes, in its negative form. That is, under certain specifiable conditions, a relationship among communicators that is judged by any one of them to be nonconsensual is punishing, stressful, or—as I prefer to say—characterized by strain. Readers who are familiar with the work of Professor Heider [10] will recognize the close parallel between this kind of statement and Heider's more generalized propositions about "cognitive balance and imbalance." His central assumption (somewhat oversimplified) is that when an individual has attitudes toward two objects, cognitive imbalance exists for him if the two objects belong together (by any of several criteria) while his cathectic orientations toward them are opposed—*e.g.,* if he "likes" one of two related objects and "dislikes" the other.

To illustrate, if A likes both B and C but believes that B dislikes C, this constellation is one of imbalance. Or if A likes some of B's traits and dislikes others (all of them obviously belonging together in B), the situation is, again, one of imbalance. (Heider, in fact, has a more formal definition of imbalance than I have presented, nor have I exhausted the possible conditions that constitute imbalance. More recently, Cartwright and Harary [11] have supplemented and formalized Heider's propositions.)

To Heider's notions, to which I am greatly indebted, I have added little beyond the attempt to apply them specifically to the phenomena of communicative behavior. In particular, I have applied them in this way. If two persons, A and B, are in communication about a certain

[10] F. Heider, "Attitudes and Cognitive Organization," *J. Psychol.*, 21 (1946), 107-12.

[11] D. Cartwright and F. Harary, "Structural Balance: A Generalization of Heider's Theory," *Psychol. Rev.*, 63 (1956), 277-93.

object, X (or, for that matter, if either of them is merely thinking about the other in the context of X), then, from A's point of view, B and X belong together, as, from B's point of view, do A and X, for the moment at least and in some degree. (I have elsewhere [12] referred to this phenomenon as one in which A co-orients to B and X.) Under these conditions, if A has a positive cathectic orientation toward B and a negative orientation toward X, and if A judges that B's orientation toward X is positive, the situation is one of imbalance or strain. Hypothetically, the strain of perceived nonconsensus, or discrepancy, serves as an instigation to communication—the process by which, ordinarily, consensus is increased. I say "serves as an instigation" rather than "leads to communication" because there are many possible sources of inhibition of the instigation. Hypothetically, the instigation is a predictable outcome, but whether or not the instigation will lead to overt communication is less predictable.

I must now mention briefly three important qualifiers to this application of Heider's notions. First, there may be persons toward whom the individual is so completely indifferent that no amount of perceived nonconsensus with them would induce any strain in him; on the other hand, perceived nonconsensus with persons who, for almost any reason, are important in the given situation is very likely to be strain inducing. This determinant of strain I shall refer to as strength of attraction.

Secondly, there are many objects of orientation concerning which a perceived discrepancy of orientation would lead, hypothetically, to little or no strain. In particular, if A's cathectic orientation toward X is so feeble as to approach indifference, little strain will be aroused by the perception of discrepancy—even with a B toward whom he is strongly attracted. This parameter, most easily measured in terms of strength of cathexis, I shall refer to as *importance*. And, thirdly, if A perceives no common impact upon both himself and B from the object, there is no reason to anticipate that strain will follow A's perception of discrepancy. For example, it may be very important to A to have lots of cream in his coffee, and he may know that it is equally important to B, whom he very much likes, to have his coffee black. Since, however, the manner in which either drinks his coffee has no conceivable impact upon the other, the object "cream in one's coffee" has

[12] T. M. Newcomb, "An Approach to the Study of Communicative Acts," *Psychol. Rev.*, 60 (1953), 393-404.

no *joint relevance* for both. At the other end of the continuum, a crying baby is likely to have very great joint relevance for both of the parents whose slumber he simultaneously disturbs. Thus there are at least these three additional parameters of strain: strength of attraction, importance, and joint relevance.

My argument, up to this point, can be simply summarized. The consensual states that are so essential to smooth integration within collectivities requires for their maintenance not only overt communicative behavior but also the occurrence of certain psychological processes. The latter are influenced, interdependently, by individual orientations both toward objects of communication and toward fellow communicators (actual or potential), as well as by perceived states of existing consensus among communicators toward objects of communication. Study of these interrelationships is necessary if one is to understand, predict, or control the consensual states of collectivities.

The Development of Consensus by Initial Strangers

One approach to the empirical study of such processes lies in observation of the developmental stages by which a population of strangers proceeds, with continued acquaintance, from initial unstructuredness to differentiation and structure. In any population of more than two persons, behavioral differentiation will emerge following opportunity for continued interaction; that is, differential association and subgroup membership, together with differential norms and consensuses, will predictably occur. It is also predictable, according to the notions that I have been outlining, that differential association will be paralleled by differential consensuses. On first acquaintance, presumably, a group of strangers is characterized by minimal and fluid structuring. As behavioral differentiation begins to emerge—for example, as cliques solidify, and as isolates begin to become conspicuous —the consensuses to which such differentiation corresponds will at first be illusory in some degree—*i.e.,* will be based upon more or less inaccurately perceived states of consensus. Gradually the differentiated subgroups become more fixed; members of some subsets come to spend more time together and to assess one another's attitudes more accurately, while members of other potential subsets spend less time together and do not become more accurate in their assessment of the attitudes of others. They may, indeed, become less accurate, in so far as they are influenced by autistic hostility.

But autisms, we may expect, will also characterize the frequently associating subsets, whose members tend not only to know more about one another as they associate more, and thus to assess one another more accurately, but also to exaggerate the existing degrees of consensus so that, while actual "agreement" becomes higher, it is judged to be even higher than it is. And so, hypothetically, the process of socio-metric differentiation is paralleled by consensual differentiation. Thus some subsets develop cohesiveness characterized by strong mutual attraction of members, by objective consensus regarding important and relevant objects, and by perceived consensus of the same kinds—perceptions which are on the whole accurate but are yet subject to distortion. The consensual contents of the several subsets will presumably be different from, or even opposed to, one another. Simultaneously, some individuals will begin to emerge as isolates, relatively unconnected with any others either by association or by consensus regarding matters important and relevant to them.

I shall go beyond the obvious prediction that some form of group structuring will develop with continuing acquaintance and try to show that, from the foregoing notions, certain predictions can be derived and tested. These predictions concern not only the nature of that structuring but also the positions of specific individuals in the overall structure—positions in the same or different subgroups, and positions as isolates or "leaders."

With the aid of generous grants [13] and of indispensable research assistants, I have been able to recruit two 17-man populations of students who were complete strangers to one another. While they were living for a four-month period in the same student house, for whose management they were responsible, we observed the development from week to week of the kinds of differentiation I have noted. It would scarcely be accurate to assert that every hypothesized prediction was supported at the .001 level, but the general lines of development were quite clearly as I have outlined them.

[13] I am indebted to the Rockefeller Foundation, to the Office of Naval Research, and to the Horace H. Rackham School of Graduate Studies for the support of this research, more detailed and systematic findings of which will be reported elsewhere.

This is not the place to present detailed findings from my own research, but I cannot refrain from offering a brief overview of some contrasts between the very early period of first acquaintance and the period of close acquaintance, four months later, following daily association in a house which provided not only bed and board but also (particularly in the early weeks) the chief source of close acquaintance. The major findings for my two populations were very much alike, and the following comments apply, with only minor exceptions, to both.

First, some findings with regard to consensus about sociometric choices. At the third day of acquaintance, there were many pairs whose members not only selected each other but also made the same second, third, and fourth choices. Apart from the reciprocal choices, this is a state of high consensus with regard to the desirability of other members. It is also a description (almost by definition) of a subgroup. These very early subgroups were determined largely by the accidents of first acquaintance. Roommates (who had been arbitrarily assigned) chose each other, at first almost without exception, and for the most part also gave high rankings to the same other persons. One week later—after ten days of acquaintance—there was noticeably less of this kind of consensus; that is, a subject and his highest ranking choice were less likely than before to give their high choices to the same other persons. Among the initial subgroups, early consensus, based largely upon accidents of contact and propinquity, was giving way to lesser consensus of attitudes toward other house members, as their range of acquaintance increased. This is equivalent to saying that the initial subgroups were already breaking down.

Four months later, consensual subgroups—in the main, quite different from the early ones—had formed again; in many cases, more or less permanent ones had formed by the end of the first month. These later subgroups were less discrete than the first ones; some individuals had membership in more than one of them. Within each of the "final" subgroups there was very high consensus about the relative desirability of all individuals in the total population. The mean rank-order correlations for all pairs of persons within each subgroup (based upon each man's rank-order of all others, excluding the pair members themselves) were in the neighborhood of .8. The comparable correlations for pairs of persons having membership in different subgroups were much lower—mostly nonsignificant statistically, and sometimes negative. Although the criterion for designating a subgroup was not the same as the one used to establish consensus about house members, the subgroups, without exception, were characterized, following a few weeks of acquaintance, by very high consensus with respect to house members as objects of orientation.

What about nonperson objects of orientation? There is reason to expect, *a priori,* that in this particular research setting, in which person-orientation almost necessarily dominated task-orientation, in-group consensus regarding persons would be more conspicuous than that regarding other objects. The latter, nevertheless, was also present. Briefly, there were two conditions under which we were able to demonstrate it: first, by simply counting the number of objects, among a very long and wide-ranging list, on which two or more subjects agreed not only in taking either a favorable or an unfavorable position, but also in having somewhat strong opinions; and, secondly, by considering as objects of orientation highly generalized values, like those of Spranger, which form the basis of the Allport-Vernon test.[14] Indices of either of these kinds of consensus, derived from preacquaintance or very early acquaintance responses, predicted very well to sociometric structuring four months later. The relationship between these varieties of consensus and interpersonal attraction was not a simple linear one; rather, it was such that only pairs of persons who showed very high preacquaintance agreement were likely to have very high indices of association and reciprocal preference much later. This relationship was not apparent on first acquaintance, since it took time for them to explore each other's attitudes. But on final acquaintance, this relationship was marked; of the 21 pairs of persons in three highly cohesive subgroups in one population, more than half had been in the highest fifth of all pairs in degree of consensus on Allport-Vernon Values four months earlier; the statistical significance of the relationship is beyond the .001 level.

It may strike the reader as strange that such measures of initial consensus have such high predictive value for subgroup differentiation so much later but virtually none for contemporary subgrouping during the first or second week. On second thought, of course, this is exactly

[14] See E. Spranger, *Types of Men,* Steckert, 1928; and G. W. Allport and P. E. Vernon, "A Test for Personal Values," *J. abnorm. soc. Psychol.,* 26 (1931), 231-48.

what one would expect; the reverse finding would be mysterious in-deed, since it takes time for people to discover one another's attitudes on a wide range of topics. Since, during the first week or two, the sub-jects knew less about one another's attitudes than the investigators did, the investigators could have made better predictions than the subjects, at this time, as to who would eventually turn up in the same subgroups. (This advantage on our part did not last long, I might add, and doubtless it is just as well that we did not know, at the time, that we had this advantage.)

Drawing upon a rather considerable body of evidence, I believe that something like the following happened as these two populations gradually divided themselves into subgroups and isolates. At first, at-traction relationships among individuals were based largely on super-ficial cues. Pairs of persons between whom attraction was reciprocally high spent a good deal of time together and were able to explore each other's attitudes toward objects of common interest—including, par-ticularly at first, other house members, who were not only important objects but also unexplored ones. If and when relatively high con-sensus on one or more matters of relevance and importance to both persons was discovered, or was created by reciprocal influence, the existing bonds between the two were strengthened. In so far as the developing consensuses included favorable attitudes toward one or more other house members, a subgroup of three or more was at least potentially in the making. In so far as exploration between persons initially attracted to each other failed to develop or to create con-sensuses on matters of importance and relevance to both, the bonds of attraction between them tended to weaken. Most individuals, of course, were involved in this kind of process more or less simultaneously with several other individuals, and our data show that most of the initial exploration had been carried on by the fifth or sixth week, after which subgroup differentiation changed comparatively little.

Before the end of the four-month period, sociometric structuring was rather closely paralleled by consensual structuring. Members of each subgroup tended to agree about one another, about other house members, and about nonperson objects. Sociometric isolates, by the same token, did not "belong," consensually, in any of the subgroups, being more or less consensual with one or more of them in one or more respects, with others of them in other respects, and so on. This con-sensual "homelessness" of the isolates dated in part from deviant preacquaintance attitudes but was also, in part, a consequence of limited association and communication following early states of their isolation. The week-to-week behavior of those who gradually emerged as isolates was characterized throughout by high variability in expressive sociometric preference—as if they were eternally doomed to "shop around" in search for a consensual subgroup—consensual, *inter alia,* about themselves.

As to the nature of the psychological processes involved, perhaps the most illuminating of our data are those having to do with perceptions of consensus. At frequent intervals, subjects made estimates of one another's attitudes toward various objects. For example, each man estimated each other man's degree of attraction toward all other members. These estimates show very clearly that most individuals found it very difficult to believe that their two or three highest choices would not also choose each other. This was true both early and late in their acquaintance—but for different reasons, I believe, at different periods. The early estimates had more of an autistic component and were less accurate. Thus many respondents commented, on the tenth day, that their estimates were little better than guesses. Since vague impressions notoriously are most apt to be swayed by autistic influences, it is not surprising that these early estimates supported the hypotheses regarding strain reduction. The less one really knows about the attitudes of others, the greater the tendency to reduce strain by assuming that those whom one "likes" also "like" each other. Later estimates were more accurate, but by this time the existing state of affairs tended in fact to support the hypotheses regarding strain. That is, the eventual clique formation was actually such that subjects who chose each other also ranked the remaining fifteen members in about the same way; the actual and the autistically desirable had become more nearly coterminous.

From these facts I conclude that the final situation, in which subjects choosing each other tended to resemble each other in choosing the remaining members, was in considerable part determined by the psychological factors revealed by the early, autistic responses—*i.e.,* by strain-reducing forces. The one way in which it is possible for a population to satisfy both the individual-autistic demands and the demands of social reality is to sort itself into subgroups which are in fact characterized by this kind of consensus.

Consensus Needs, Reality Demands, and Subgroup Formation

There is another consequence of the principles of strain and balance which I regard as crucial: the circular tendency to exaggerate existing consensus with persons toward whom attraction is strongly positive, and to increase attraction when consensus is perceived to increase; and the converse tendency for underestimation of consensus and declining attraction to proceed together. Let me offer a single finding to illustrate this strong tendency. There was a correlation of about .7 (roughly the same at all times) between individual indices of general sociometric status ("popularity") and measures of what I can best refer to as "attribution of agreement." That is, on the Spranger Values, for example, the most "popular" persons were also the persons most generally perceived by others as agreeing with others; the most rejected ("unpopular") persons in the same population were perceived by others as at or near the bottom in agreement. The greater the tendency of other members to perceive value consensus with an individual, the higher the sociometric status that they accord him, and vice versa. These perceptions, though exaggerated, tend to parallel the actual situation following acquaintance. Just as in the case of consensus about other persons as objects of orientation, the only way of coming to terms both with consensus needs and with reality needs is to develop subgroups which are in fact highly consensual.

With regard to nonperson objects, it would be possible, of course, to develop consensus on the part of the entire population with no subgroup differentiation. But with regard to consensus about members themselves, this presumably becomes more and more unlikely as population becomes progressively larger than two. One of the basic reasons for this (which I have not time to develop here) is that consensus about members themselves can be achieved only by making no differentiations at all (an unlikely event) or by obtaining the agreement of the members who are ranked lowest that they should in fact be ranked lowest—also improbable. Subgroup differentiation, among other advantages, makes possible a state of affairs in which each subgroup member can participate in consensus about himself.

The end result of the psychologically autistic processes, if not countered by reality-based considerations, would be the formation of completely schismatic subgroups. If only autistic processes were at work, following communication, then the initial discovery of already existing consensus on the part of two or more persons would lead to exaggerated perceptions of consensus, heightened attraction, and more or less exclusive association among themselves, together with just the opposite relationships *vis à vis* other members. But if no such processes were at work, then (under the conditions of my own study, at any rate) relatively little persisting differentiation would take place. If there were no autistic determinants of perceived consensus—*i.e.,* if the accuracy of such perceptions were undiluted by considerations of interpersonal attraction—structural differentiation would be less pronounced and less persistent than we know it to be, in populations like those that I have studied. Structural differentiation would vary from moment to moment, and from situation to situation, as consensuses of immediate significance determined optimal structuring for the moment, without benefit of bias of interpersonal preference, and without "transfer" to one situation of the consequences of consensus in other situations. It is precisely because both sets of forces, the autistic and the realistic, are at work in interaction with each other that problems of theory and research seem so formidable.

Since I have alluded at some length to my own research, I want to make it clear that my consensual data do not account for all the observed variance in sociometric structuring. Even if the present hypotheses were sufficient to account for all the variance, it would not be possible to obtain adequate data to demonstrate it—if for no other reason than that there are too many possible bases for consensus; there is no way of discovering what all of them are, nor could they all be measured. All I wish to imply is that (according to many sets of data, including my own) the principles to which I have referred are so clear and omnipresent that they cannot be ignored. The psychological need to perceive consensus about important and relevant objects is a necessary though not a sufficient condition to account for differential structuring within human populations.

Since the phrase that I have just used—"the psychological need to perceive consensus"—refers to the central notion in this paper, it behooves me to justify its use. In what sense may the consequences of the principles of strain and balance, as outlined above, be regarded as a psychological need? Could not a parsimonious approach to the problems of perceived and actual consensus dispense with psychological determinants and regard findings like those here reported merely as consequences of interaction and realistic coping with the requirements of interaction?

As I have elsewhere insisted,[15] human susceptibility to considerations of strain and balance is a learned outcome of socialization, and in this sense the postulated "need to perceive consensus" is a consequence of social interaction. But this, of course, is not to say that an individual's need to perceive consensus in a given interactional context is an outcome of previous interaction in that same context. The evidence, in fact, points quite the other way. In the research setting here described, the decisive fact is that *as early as the third day* there was as much perceived consensus (under the specified conditions) as on the hundredth day. The latter estimates, of course, were the more accurate, but they were no more influenced by the hypothesized need to perceive consensus than were the earliest judgments, which could hardly have been influenced by interaction in this setting.

Whatever it is that is responsible for individuals' assumptions (under the specified conditions) of greater-than-chance consensuality, this is what I mean by "need for consensus." Apart from the theoretical considerations underlying the notions of strain and balance, two empirical findings lead me to conclude that it is necessary to postulate such a need: (1) Whether early or late in acquaintance, and whether correctly or incorrectly, most individual estimates of existing states of consensus are such as can be accounted for by the postulated need. (2) Interpersonal behavior (selective preference and association) tends to change over time in such ways as to make previously autistic estimates of consensus more nearly realistic; consensus within subgroups tends to be achieved and not merely wished for. Since I do not believe that such changes are "merely accidental," I am forced to conclude that the "need for consensus" is real, because it has real effects—as real as the subgroups whose existence, I believe, is in part accounted for by the need.

Unsolved Problems

As so often happens, the deviations from the predicted outcomes of this study have become quite as interesting as the outcomes that conformed to prediction. Why is it that some pairs of persons—and, less

[15] T. M. Newcomb, "The Prediction of Interpersonal Attraction," *Amer. Psychol.*, 11 (1956), 575-86.

often, triads or even larger sets—remain cohesive in spite of the apparent absence of important and relevant consensuses? Why is it that, as more frequently happens, persons who are in fact consensual on important and relevant matters remain indifferent or even hostile to one another? It is not enough to point out (doubtless correctly) that in the former case there are surely other bases, unknown to the investigator, for consensus; or that, in the latter case, other and unknown bases for nonconsensus outweigh the known bases for consensus. It is not very illuminating to take refuge in unknown factors.

The kinds of research most needed now, I believe, will be much more specifically oriented to a wide range of situations than my own research has been. The only kind of structural differentiation available for study, in my own research setting, was that of preferential association. (This fact tended, I suspect, in some ways to dilute and in others to intensify the predicted relationships between consensual and behavioral differentiation.) In other settings it would be possible to study the consensual bases for hierarchical structuring, for structuring characterized by division of labor independently of stratification, etc. In particular, the study of task-oriented groups (as distinct from those primarily person-oriented, as in my own investigation) would do much to extend our knowledge of the consensual bases for social structuring.

Summary

If, as I assume, the fact of social consensus is important in its own right, then so is an understanding of the psychological processes which underlie the fact. I have selected, as one kind of sociological problem that can be illuminated by the application of certain assumptions concerning the formation of consensus, sociometric structuring within a population large enough to contain several subgroups. The bits of empirical findings that I have presented were selected to suggest the likelihood that structuring within such populations is an outcome of behavioral attempts to create, as social realities, sets of interpersonal relationships that correspond maximally to psychological needs for consensus about important and group-relevant objects. Under the conditions of the study here reported in small part, the observed facts of subgroup structuring can be largely accounted for in terms of a few assumptions about consensual processes.

13
Small-Group Theory and Research ⌒

ROBERT F. BALES
Harvard University

Certainly one of the important problems of any field of research is that of gathering together and keeping accessible to researchers the main body of relevant literature. The field of small-group research is currently in good condition in this respect—so good, happily, that I need not undertake any survey of the literature in this paper, except to indicate the main sources in which surveys can be found. It is interesting to note, however, that none of these main sources is more than five years old.

Cartwright and Zander [1] edited the first major compilation of articles, under the title *Group Dynamics: Research and Theory*, in 1953. A year later, Lindzey's *Handbook of Social Psychology*,[2] appeared. Among several relevant chapters in this book, those by H. H. Kelley and J. W. Thibault, on "Experimental Studies of Group Problem Solving and Process," and by H. W. Riecken and G. C. Homans, on "Psychological Aspects of Social Structure," are especially notable on substantive aspects. The Lindzey volume also contains two excellent surveys of the literature on methodology: a chapter on "Systematic Observa-

[1] D. Cartwright and A. F. Zander (eds.), *Group Dynamics: Research and Theory*, Row, Peterson, 1953.

[2] G. Lindzey (ed.), *Handbook of Social Psychology*, Addison-Wesley, 1954.

tional Techniques," by R. W. Heyns and Ronald Lippitt, and one on "Sociometric Measurement," by Lindzey and E. F. Borgatta. In 1954, Strodtbeck and Hare published an exhaustive bibliography of small-group research from 1900 through 1953 [3] which helped to provide historical perspective on the field. Building on this groundwork, Hare, Borgatta, and Bales published a compilation of papers and a large annotated bibliography in 1955.[4] The bibliography of this work, in turn, formed the basis for a chapter in Gittler's *Review of Sociology*, by the same authors.[5] The latest extension of this work is a book, not yet published, by Hare, which will probably be entitled *Social Interaction, An Analysis of Behavior in Small Groups*. This book, I believe, represents the first attempt to write a rounded treatise on small groups based entirely on empirical studies. One should not review a book before it is published, of course, but it seems to me an encouraging sign of the maturation of the field that empirical studies exist in sufficient variety and depth to make such a venture possible.

If I may make one further remark without trespassing on the territory of a reviewer, I am impressed by the number of studies that build on the work of earlier investigators. I sometimes have the feeling that complaints about the so-called "non-cumulative character of knowledge" in our field refer not so much to the character of knowledge as to our failure to accumulate it. In an important sense, of course, every scientific worker must gather for himself the facts from which he works. But the researcher in small groups today can begin his study immeasurably further along than his colleagues of even five years ago. It may turn out that the distinguishing mark of the last five years of development in this field is the degree of accumulation and consolidation that the literature has undergone.

Nevertheless, as I explore the maze of available studies relevant in one way or another to our present scientific needs, the most insistent need I feel is for synthesis. The very respectable body of studies that we now have has raised my level of aspiration; I am no longer content

[3] F. L. Strodtbeck and A. P. Hare, "Bibliography of Small Group Research (from 1900 through 1953)," *Sociometry*, 17 (1954), 107-78.

[4] A. P. Hare, E. F. Borgatta, and R. F. Bales, *Small Groups, Studies in Social Interaction*, Knopf, 1955.

[5] R. F. Bales, A. P. Hare, and E. F. Borgatta, "Structure and Dynamics of Small Groups: A Review of Four Variables," in J. Gittler (ed.), *Review of Sociology, Analysis of a Decade*, John Wiley, 1957.

merely to discover that "X makes a difference significant at the .05 level if everything else is carefully controlled." I am not even satisfied with an occasional feeling that I "understand," in a general way, most of the things that go on in the groups I happen to know. As scientists, most of us have aspirations that go beyond this feeling of "understanding." What we would really like to be able to do is *predict*. This, of course, is what the layman also expects us to be able to do.

Generally, when the layman thinks of prediction he means prediction about the course of natural events, not about a highly controlled laboratory event. Some laymen, indeed, seem to feel that the scientist should be able to predict without any special information—in other words, to foretell the natural future by a kind of clairvoyance. The scientist, on the other hand, knows that prediction of complex natural events—for example, of the weather—requires access to a very large amount of information which usually must be gathered in very small bits, more or less continuously, from many scattered sources, and compiled and reduced to compact empirical generalizations—all of this before the more abstract part of the scientific theory can be brought to bear. In the case of weather prediction, we can form some idea of the process by thinking of all the scattered weather stations and the many readings of temperature, humidity, wind, and so on summarized in the weather maps that form the factual base for the weather forecaster.

The nearest thing to this kind of publicly exposed, practical, naturalistic prediction I can think of in the social sciences is the prediction of elections by poll. Some aspects of demographic theory perhaps also come close, although the predictions are generally less specific and apply to a longer time span than prediction of elections. In neither of these instances, however, is the theory very complex in the sense that it specifies the relations of a large number of qualitatively different factors in interaction with one another. Sampling theory and straight extrapolation of present trends into the future more or less take the place of behavior theory. The difficulty in making these predictions stems not from the variety of factors involved in the theory but from the large number of geographically separated persons from whom information must be obtained. The measurement made on each person or unit is relatively simple, and the combining process requires little more than simple addition.

But the sort of prediction that would actually make a difference in the practice of the "interpersonal arts" is quite different. (By the "interpersonal arts" I mean the arts of changing motivation and behavior through person-to-person communication—for example, the arts of developing an appropriate and binding group decision, of teaching and learning, of individual psychotherapy, of leading a training group in human relations, of fostering cooperation and morale in a crew or work group.) In such situations, what the therapist, leader, or any other interested participant wants to be able to do is to read the signs that appear in the behavior (his own as well as others)—to diagnose accurately what is going on, predict where it is going, and how it will change if he takes a given action—all of this soon enough for him to intervene and try to change the course of events if he deems it desirable.

It is hardly thinkable that the participant in complex interpersonal situations like these could obtain all the information he would need, or, if he could obtain it, that he could process it fast enough to be able to predict with absolute accuracy. This would be omnipotence, or something very close to it. But much less than absolute accuracy would answer very well. What my values specify as desirable and what I think is probably attainable is some enhancement of the ability to read the signs better than most people now can, and some increase in the ability to do something intelligently experimental about it.

A social participant in a course of events who is in a position to take remedial action can get along with middling-to-poor prediction, as we do at present. But the scientist who can arrange matters so that he can obtain more information on more relevant factors must hope for a corresponding improvement in prediction. To obtain the improvement in prediction, he must be able to calculate the weights of various factors relative to one another under given conditions. It is this sort of synthesis that one misses in the literature. An accumulation of studies does not solve the problem, although it is a necessary step.

I assume that most of my colleagues will agree with the foregoing. But the next point is one on which I must be prepared to lose some friends. It is simply this: I do not believe that the ordinary English language, or any of the special versions of it that we devise for theoretical purposes, will be nearly adequate to the demands of the sort of prediction we are talking about. In fact, from what I can find out, it does not appear that any existing body of mathematics is suited to the task either.

Yet I do not despair entirely. Quite the contrary. I believe that science has recently come into possession of the ideal method of representing the kind of theory we require. The method is computor simulation, and I shall describe it briefly later. But before talking further about this method, let us examine some of the characteristics of the phenomenon to be represented in an attempt to form a more concrete conception of the problem of synthesis that must be solved if naturalistic prediction in interpersonal situations is to be much improved over predictions based purely on common sense

Some Factors in Naturalistic Prediction

In order to obtain a perspective from which we can view a number of factors in behavior, let us suppose that we as scientific theorizers can explore the mind of each member of a group of, say, five persons, engaged in some task. We shall suppose that we have the power to examine in detail everything that goes on in a very small interval of time, or to wait and look back over a long interval. In other words, we shall permit ourselves to substitute hindsight for foresight. We shall also suppose that we have the power to examine the characteristics of the environment from a longer distance in time than that available to the participants. As scientific theorizers, in other words, we should like an omniscient perspective, far beyond that available to any of the group members in their moment-to-moment behavior decisions. They may attempt to maintain such a perspective, but they must do it by symbolic representation of facts that are not available to them.

And now we must admit, of course, that the scientific theorizer does not escape this problem when he tries to predict. As a predictor, the scientific theorizer, like the practical human being he is theorizing about, has to reduce his demands for an omniscient information-gathering apparatus if he wants to predict forward in real time from real information. The trick in improving prediction, since omniscience is so hard to come by, must lie in learning how to get more information, or how to make more and better inferences from what we have, or both, and to do either or both before something else happens. These are the requirements of naturalistic prediction, and all good theory must eventually face up to them. But as a theorizer, the scientific predictor, like the theorizing human being he is predicting about, has to be prepared to think and talk about states of affairs to which he has had no empirical access, as he struggles by symbolic means to construct an omniscient perspective.

For our theorizing, then, let us adopt the omniscient perspective and go ahead without embarrassment. Our problem is to try to form

some concrete idea of the various influences that we would have to synthesize in order to predict interpersonal behavior naturalistically in real
time. Let us begin with the perspective of a given member at a point in
time. Another member has just completed a remark, and the member
who is our point of reference is in the process of thinking about an act
which we propose to predict. Let us imagine at least part of the process
he might go through, basing our construction on experimental findings
in so far as possible.

Somewhere early in the process of thinking about the new act, there
must be some analysis of the character of the act that has just occurred.
A social act has a large number of possible stimulus properties, depending on the kind of analysis the responder gives it. Suppose that the act
were an assertion about some object that forms a part of the task environment of the group. What is asserted about the object may be called
the task content of the remark. One very relevant property of a stimulus
act is the history of its task content. An assertion made for the first time
has a meaning different from that of one made after the content has
acquired a history. As we all know, and as Sherif [6] and others have
demonstrated, groups tend to develop norms. Individual differences in
perceptions—or, at any rate, in verbal statements—tend to moderate
over time. Most group members tend to converge toward a group norm
as they interact and become aware of one another's judgments.

In attempting to predict the reaction of our hypothetical group
member, it is important for us to know whether the statement of task
content to which he is reacting is occurring for the first time, or whether
it has been made and agreed with (or disagreed with) earlier, and, if
so, by how many group members, and of what status. Perhaps the content in question has been prohibited, in effect, by consensus of some
sufficiently large portion of the group, or perhaps it has been authorized,
in effect, by favorable consensus. Still further distinctions might be
drawn, of a similar kind, but perhaps I have already suggested enough
to demonstrate that the task content of an act has definition (or lack
of it) relative to the norms of the group which strongly affects the
probability that our subject will agree (or disagree) with it.

But which way will the effect go? Asch's experiments [7] have drama-
tized the power of tendencies toward conformity. As he has shown, an

[6] M. Sherif, *The Psychology of Social Norms*, Harper, 1936.
[7] S. E. Asch, *Social Psychology*, Prentice-Hall, 1952.

individual may testify against a strikingly obvious sensory experience if all other group members testify against it and the individual believes that he alone has had the experience. On the other hand, not all individuals give in, even under extreme pressure. What kinds do not give in? We know little about this question at present from empirical studies. Perhaps some of these intransigents are persons who feel generally compelled to be in opposition to group norms or authority figures. At any rate, it seems clear in principle that we must know more than how the assertion of task content fits into group norms. We must take into account the fact that our particular subject may have an attitude toward conformity or deviance that will affect the probability of his agreement or disagreement.

Thus far we have not considered whether it makes any difference who made the remark and to whom it was addressed. But presumably these matters make a difference to our subject. Whyte [8] pointed out that the corner boys as well as members of formal organizations observe channels; that is, the same suggestion that will be rejected or ignored if made by a low-status member may be acted upon if made by a high-status member. Many earlier experiments have been devoted to showing that subjects perceive and judge content differently according to their assumptions about the character of the source. A series of studies now in process by Bauer [9] and others is showing that perceptions of and reactions to content are similarly influenced by the expectation of communicating them to a particular audience. We must, in other words, take into account our subject's perception of who made the remark, to whom it was addressed, who he himself is in the socially relevant sense, and to whom he addresses his reply.

We are here faced with the problem of characterizing in some relevant way the various kinds of "who" that the subject may consider, and the grounds on which he identifies them. Surely he must look at their behavior up to the present point and the kind of behavior that others have addressed to them. To some degree, there has been a process of learning, or "object-adaptive cognition," going on. To some degree, each social object is unique, a class of one, an object characterized operationally in terms of the individual's past experience with it. But there

---

[8] W. F. Whyte, *Street Corner Society*, University of Chicago Press, 1943.

[9] R. A. Bauer, personal communication to the author.

are no social objects that are simply this. Any social object, including the self, is to some degree treated as a member of a class, and characteristics of the class are attributed to it. We recognize various types or aspects of this process by such terms as "projection," "displacement," "transference," "identification," "internalization," "taking the role of the other," the "generalized other," "reference groups," "marginality," and "ego involvement." One of the most difficult aspects of our predictive problem will surely be to take into account the fact that the subject has been trained from his earliest childhood in a repertoire of social roles—some which he identifies with the self, others which he treats as ego-alien— and that in varying degrees he imposes this stereotyped repertoire on any current social situation.

Among other factors which predispose the subject to identify a present participant with some particularly important figure from the past are presumably the kind, direction, and amount of emotion the subject has to handle at the time. As the amount rises, the tendency to cast present characters in past roles presumably increases. Overdetermined interpersonal dramas tend to arise under stress, as Redl [10] has described so effectively. But in general we get into very difficult problems of prediction as we try to take strong affect into account. The reasons are well known. Psychoanalysis has emphasized the resourcefulness of the psyche in dealing with strong affect. It will inhibit the affect, repress it, reverse it, counteract it, find indirect outlets for it, and generally transform it and disguise it until the subject himself, to say nothing of our hopeful scientific predictor, has no conscious idea of what is going on.

But there are still other factors. We should not forget that the subject is generally capable of looking twice at the object of cognition, and that, in spite of all obstacles, he may form a judgment of it that will stand the test of time. The characteristics of cognition as a problem-solving process have been receiving renewed attention in the past few years, particularly in the work of Bruner and his associates.[11] And, with the development of large-scale computors, a number of computor experts and behavior theorists have been working furiously to program machines to solve more and more difficult problems in ways that seem

---

[10] F. Redl, "Group Emotion and Leadership," *Psychiatry*, 5 (1942), 573-96.

[11] J. S. Bruner, J. J. Goodnow, and G. A. Austin, *A Study of Thinking*, John Wiley, 1956.

to resemble human cognition. These two developments, one from cognitive experimentation as such and one from computor programing, show considerable similarity and in all likelihood will grow together rapidly. They will surely be involved in future attempts to build predictive models of human behavior and interaction.

The result of cognitive analysis depends on cognitive abilities. These, in turn, can hardly be defined except in relation to the task requirements. If we are to predict successfully, we will have to be able to measure task abilities in relation to task requirements. But task requirements are not easy to describe. Every task is complex to some extent. In spite of something like fifty years of research on individual *versus* group problem-solving, in which many concretely different kinds of task have been used, there is still no very good classification of tasks. Probably one of the most important characteristics of a task object is the degree to which assertions about it can be checked by reference to the physical environment. Festinger [12] and his associates have called this property "physical reality" as opposed to "social reality." A long list of studies could be cited in support of the generalization that as the degree of physical reality of the task object decreases, individuals tend to differ more widely in their initial perceptions or judgments of it, and have more difficulty in coming to consensus about it. However, any such generalization needs to be considerably qualified by other factors—for example, the degree to which major values are involved, the commitment of members to the task, the commitment of members to group solidarity, the urgency of the task, the specificity of the decisions required, and the degree to which the decision will have ulterior consequences.

Let us pause for a moment to consider the factors that have been mentioned as relevant to our prediction problem—the degree to which the assertion of task content conforms or deviates from group norms; the attitude of the subject toward the group norms; the subject's identification of "who" is asserting the content, and "who," in a psychologically relevant sense, he himself is; his attitudes toward the figures in this repertoire of roles; the degree to which emotion aroused in the present situation increases his tendency to construe the present situation in terms of the past; his mechanisms of defense; his cognitive abilities; and the nature of the task in several respects. The list is certainly not

---

[12] L. Festinger, "Theory of Social Comparison Processes," *Hum. Relat.*, 7 (1954), 117-40.

complete, though it touches a good many factors that can be certified as important from experimental or good observational studies. In fact, the most common conclusion of the most common type of study is that factor X is "important"—that is, that it makes a difference significant at the .05 level if everything else is carefully controlled.

But what are the relative weights of the various factors, and in what circumstances? In what time order do they interact, and how complex is this interaction? How can the predictor obtain information about their probable state? Is there any dependable device, test, observation that he can use to obtain the needed information in a naturalistic setting? Unfortunately, in my opinion, researchers have given far too little attention to the building of usable instruments. But even if the predictor had a good instrument with which to obtain information on every factor he believed to be important and had floods of information available from moment to moment, how, in fact, could he put all the data together and come out with a prediction? Especially, how could he do it in time to do any good? These are problems of synthesis.

Thus far we have hardly considered the fact that there is more than one person in any group. If we really wished to predict, we should have to perform a similar analysis for each member in the group. Each of them presumably prepares to react to the assertion of task content with which we began. But only a few are likely to react openly. Someone will be ready to reply before the others, or there may be a brief struggle for the floor which someone wins. Once a member of the group has spoken, many things may change. Is his probability of speaking again increased by practice, decreased by catharsis, or both, or neither? If he says the same thing another member wanted to say, will that other be vicariously satisfied or competitively frustrated? If the person who made the original assertion of task content receives agreement, is he encouraged to go ahead or satisfied to stop? If he receives disagreement, is he discouraged into stopping or provoked to battle? Presumably, if we could synthesize what goes on inside the member we dealt with above, we could proceed similarly with this one. The questions that I have just raised might then appear to be false and unanswerable, except by "It depends."

But on what does "it depend"? One cannot simply say, 'It depends on the individual personality of the person reacting." Why not? Because part of the process that goes on in that individual personality is based upon the external state of affairs—*e.g.,* whether the last act has made it clear that a majority is in favor of the task content in question; whether the last act has changed the present member's conception of "who" the other is, and who he himself is; whether he has been building up frustration for some time and now encounters the final straw; whether the remark of the other has changed his cognitive picture of the object; and so on. None of these circumstantial factors can be predicted solely from a knowledge of his personality. But none can be predicted without a knowledge of his personality either. "Who" member 1 thinks member 2 is depends (partly) on how member 2 has behaved up to that time. But how member 2 has behaved up to that time depends (partly) on "who" he thinks member 1 is. And so on. In situations of this kind, one small event may make a large difference, by starting in motion a given circular reaction rather than some other. To predict the circular reaction, then, one would have to predict the small event, and that, in turn, is the product of a very large number of factors.

What chance does human intuition have to make a synthesis of this sort? The mere thought of trying to use the English language, or any other natural human language, as the instrument for describing and predicting a process like this tires us out before we begin. People do about as well as they can with natural language in the actual process of interacting, and the result is not good enough. Even with more time, I do not think it would be good enough, because nobody would be able to force himself through the brutal repetition that would be necessary.

Computor Simulation as a Means of Synthesis

There are those who believe that more strenuous attempts to apply mathematical methods of formulation will give the desired results. This is a possibility that is only beginning to be explored. For representing the interrelations of a few variables, existing mathematical methods may be appropriate. The sort of synthesis we need, however, calls for large numbers of variables in highly complex conditional relationships to one another. So far as I know, analogue computors are the most appropriate means of representing systems of this sort. There are many kinds of analogue computors; a scale model of an airplane in a wind tunnel is a good example. But if the nature of the variables is well known, it is not necessary to have a physical model. The analogue of the real system can be constructed by arranging (that is, programing) a general-purpose computor so that its parts are related to one another as they are supposed to be in the real system.

One may know enough about a system to construct such a model as a jig-saw puzzle is constructed—bit by bit, in terms of the fit of one small piece to another. One may know enough to do that and still not know how the whole thing will operate when all pieces are in place. That is what the analogue computor will tell him about his model. The computor is capable of any amount of tiresome canvassing of factors, readjustment of one in terms of the other, and so on.

Newell, Simon, and Shaw [13] have already constructed a highly complex computor program that goes about problem-solving in a way that seems similar in many respects to a behaving organism. Subparts of the program investigate the characteristics of the task objects and describe them in such a way that other subparts of the program can deal with the task objects symbolically, as we deal with cognitive descriptions of objects rather than the objects. Various attempted solutions are produced, tried, and rejected or accepted according to success. The program operating at present is a particular example of the more general class which the authors call "complex information-processing systems." In their words:

> We may identify certain characteristics of a system that make it complex:
>
> 1. There is a large number of different kinds of processes, all of which are important, although not necessarily essential, to the performance of the total system;
> 2. The uses of the processes are not fixed and invariable, but are highly contingent upon the outcomes of previous processes and on information received from the environment;
> 3. The same processes are used in many different contexts to accomplish similar functions toward different ends, and this often results in organizations of processes that are hierarchical, iterative, and recursive in nature.

The processes that go on in social interaction certainly answer this description. A small group is, in the exact sense of Newell and Simon's definition, an empirical example of a "complex information-processing

[13] Allen Newell and Herbert A. Simon, "The Logic Theory Machine, A Complex Information Processing System," *IRE Transactions on Information Theory*, Vol. IT-2, No. 3, 1956.

system." I can see no reason in principle for believing that their tactics of synthesizing models of such systems, using the modern large computor as the medium, and of studying empirically the behavior of the operating total system cannot be applied to our problem of synthesis with the aim of naturalistic prediction.

Of course, the goal that I have here called naturalistic prediction is a very ambitious and idealistic one. But we need a vantage point from which we can successfully put into perspective the problems of theory and research of a whole scientific field. The goal we need to visualize should serve not only as an immediately appealing stimulus to the beginning of work but also as an exacting criterion of scientific progress and an indicator of critical problems for further work. To my mind, nothing less than the goal of naturalistic prediction really answers these needs.

IV
Problems in Demographic and Social Structure

14
The Sociology
of Demographic
Behavior

KINGSLEY DAVIS
University of California, Berkeley

Considered as a branch of sociology, the study of population is peculiar. It did not, like the study of stratification or of education, emerge as a specialty within the larger field of sociology as this field progressed. Instead, being older than sociology as a formal discipline, it grew from diverse beginnings in economics, statistics, medicine, and biology; and only gradually did it become more closely identified with sociology. In some countries, such as Japan or Brazil, no such identification has yet occurred. Even where the affiliation with sociology is closest, as in the United States and Britain, the study of population remains one of the most independent of the sociological branches.

In view of the independence of the two fields, one may question the value of considering them together. My opinion, however, is that demographic and sociological analysis have much to contribute to each other, that both fields are most vigorous in countries in which they are closely integrated, and that as yet their mutual value has not been sufficiently realized because of the ethnocentrism still accompanying specialization in the social sciences. Grotesque as it may seem, social scientists identify themselves emotionally with certain points of view, not only as between major disciplines but also as between branches or approaches within the same discipline. Since this "nationalism" has often been attributed—falsely, I believe—to overspecialization, let us begin with problems of specialization in the relation of demography to sociology.

The Dilemma of Specialization

Many of the purely scientific difficulties that arise in the application of sociology to demography, and vice versa, are those that always attend the progress of specialization. It is now impossible for a person to keep up with and contribute to the field of population and at the same time keep abreast of the voluminous literature and variegated techniques of sociology in general. Twenty years ago this was possible, but not now.

The resulting cost is undeniably great. If the two fields are mutually relevant, and if the best way of getting any two fields together is within a single head, a real loss is sustained when this is no longer possible. Team research offers only an inadequate substitute, because an interdisciplinary group of experts often comes out, at least in social science, with a product that is the lowest common denominator, representing the level of that member of the team who knows least about the field being investigated.[1] Other attempts to solve problems of specialization assume, erroneously, that the culprit is specialization itself. Paradoxically, the inevitable costs of specialization can only be minimized, not by trying to reverse the trend toward specialization, even if that were possible, but by encouraging even more of it; for the effect of specialization is to breach scientific boundaries as well as to create them.

Within demography, for example, specialization and scientific progress are proceeding together. Some demographers deal almost exclusively with fertility, others with mortality or migration or a particular country. The effect of such specialization is to give the individual more time for studies that are *outside* demography but yet closely related to his particular specialty. Thus an interest in fertility may be combined with an interest in family structure, or a focus on internal migration

---

[1] This is not a criticism of team research as such, but only of the notion that team research offers a solution to interdisciplinary problems. The main value of team projects, I think, lies in the massing of manpower. Many worthwhile projects in social science are far beyond the capacities of one man, even when the research is confined to one field.

with a concern with urbanization. In this way a whole network of specialties arises (almost as many as there are individuals) which bridge
sociology and demography in numerous ways. Our awareness of this
process is obscured, however, by the tendency to hypostatize "demography" and "sociology." These are not self-contained entities, nor even
integrated bodies of knowledge; they are, like "anthropology" and "economics," congeries of specialties lumped together for linguistic and
administrative convenience. A demographer who is interested in fertility
is better off concentrating on family sociology than on mortality, just
as an economist working on installment credit is better off studying the
sociology of status and role than learning about international trade. The
best way in which to get demography and sociology together, then, is
not to hold conferences or create centers at which "representatives" of
these two presumed kingdoms are forced to get together, but to put as
few barriers as possible in the way of intense specialization.

Demography, Theory, and Scientific Progress

Population analysis includes topics and interests so diverse that, no
matter how they are classified, they barely belong together. The most
central aspect of the field is perhaps *formal demography*, which includes
not only the statistical measurement of a population's growth, its age-sex
structure, and its fertility and mortality, but also the mathematical analysis of the interrelations among these.[2] Since this aspect forms the most
technical and integrated part of population study, we can see why the
entire science is frequently called "demography." [3] Many people who
contribute to the second aspect of population study—*population theory*
—do not contribute to, or even have much understanding of, formal
demography. What is called population theory is usually the verbal

[2] Also included in formal demography, if one wishes, is the statistical
and mathematical treatment of territorial distribution, migration, and marital status in relation to the factors mentioned.

[3] The name "population" is awkward, since it refers to the thing studied rather than to the science proper—like calling physiology "organism"
or botany "plants." Although "demography" is preferable, this term implies
that the purpose is primarily descriptive, whereas the science of population
is highly analytical. The best term would be *demology*, but this is too close
to *demonology*. A further difficulty with *demography* is that, in its adjective
form, it is so close to *democratic* that linotypists generally spell it that way.

interpretation of the causes and consequences of demographic phenomena, a central question being the effect of population growth on the level of living. Almost anyone can try his hand in this sphere, and the less his social-science training the greater his confidence. From such broad theory it is but a step to another aspect of the field—*population policies*—in which the amateur and official as well as the demographer have their say. But there is another part of population analysis that seems detached from all of the others—namely, the study of *population characteristics*. Since the potentially measurable characteristics are numerous and varied, from race, religion, and marital status to birthplace, occupation, income, and education, this branch of the field touches virtually all the social sciences and lacks any intrinsic coherence.

It is, of course, possible to divide the field of population in some other way—for example, by treating mortality, fertility, and migration as subdivisions—but any mode of classifying its branches will show that the science is too heterogeneous to justify a person's specializing in population as a whole. There is no such thing as a complete populationist, any more than there is such a thing as a complete sociologist or a complete economist. Most of the writing on so-called population theory has been done by economists, sociologists, or biologists who have at best a sketchy knowledge of formal demography; and much of the work in systematic demography has been done by statisticians and mathematicians who have scarcely ventured into the wider reaches of population theory. The expert on migration may take little interest in fertility or mortality but devote much attention to nondemographic subjects, such as race relations and minority groups. Finally, inclusion of population characteristics within the total field is largely accidental. Governments, wishing to obtain certain kinds of information, ask the appropriate questions in censuses or other population surveys. Since demographers depend upon censuses for most of their data, and since they are the census experts, they must necessarily be concerned with population characteristics. This gives the demographers access to a body of data crucial to all the social sciences; but, not being supermen, they cannot encompass it all in a fashion satisfactory to the experts in other fields. To the latter, therefore, it often seems that demographers are merely processing or presenting data without interesting themselves in scientific interpretation. The demographers feel, on the other hand, that they rightfully have the task of providing basic information for the use of others as well as themselves.

The frequent accusation that demographers neglect "theory" is matched by the demographers' contempt for facile and purely verbal explanation. Perhaps both sides are right. There can be little doubt that population experts become so habituated to a given body of procedures and categories that their imaginations become limited. Sometimes they resemble carpenters rather than architects, and they seem to be repetitiously nailing together the same pieces. On the other hand, their suspicion of the sociological or economic theorist is often confirmed by the latter's inability to get straight the facts of population that he is presumably explaining. Indeed, so far as can be determined, those theories of population succeed best (survive longest) which have the least to do with empirical evidence. The joker, of course, is the term "theory." In social science this term, instead of meaning the widest body of rigorous reasoning about a set of observed relationships, has come to mean a long stretch of purely verbal analysis. If a publication contains any empirical evidence, particularly of a statistical kind, it is not theory; but if it contains only verbal generalizations, no matter how loosely connected, it is theory.

It is difficult to avoid the conclusion that the major advances in the science of population have come from improvements in the sources of information and in the techniques of analysis, rather than from the broad interpretations. Ironically, the interpretative literature on population probably exceeds by many times (if not in pages, certainly in readers and attention) the amount of empirical publication. The discrepancy was already clear with Malthus. He did not fully understand the progress in systematic demography that had been made by his time; yet it was his work that captured most attention, and it is his work that is still debated today in general population theory. Despite the outpouring of books, pamphlets, and articles on population theory—*Bevoelkerungslehre*—it is hard to cite a single scientific advance since Malthus' day that this literature has contributed to the subject. Perhaps an exception is the concept of the demographic transition, which has proved valuable as a guiding generalization; but the continuing debate on "the population problem," the Marxian criticism of Malthus and the counterattack on Marx, the discussion of "optimum population," the notion of "carrying capacity," etc. have all used up ink and paper disproportionately to their scientific value.

Perhaps the critics are right who say that demographers have neglected theory. If they mean by theory what it has meant up to now, however, the burden of proof is on the critics. Future advance will hardly be made by pretentious attempts to develop general theory or to "integrate" the big "ologies" with demography: it will more likely be made by individuals pursuing particular problems with all the conceptual and empirical tools they can find.

Some New Directions in Population Research

If we select some developments that combine demographic and sociological skills, we must surely refer to the following areas of work: (1) fertility in connection with attitudes and social institutions; (2) population change in relation to social and economic change; (3) the labor force with respect to population structure and social organization; (4) the family with regard to demographic behavior. All four areas ideally have certain features in common. They all involve comparative analysis of different societies, either historically or contemporaneously or both. They all involve a two-way relationship between population and social structure; and they all allow for the study of motives and attitudes and yet permit the application of demographic techniques as an essential part of the analysis.

Before discussing each of these areas of research, let us mention briefly a few less promising subjects. Migration, for example, seemingly offers a favorable ground for combining sociology and demography. In the past, much of American sociology was built upon the problems created by massive immigration. But since the data and techniques for migration are less adequate than those for any other topic in demography, and since the subject is replete with emotional overtones and propaganda, it has lost ground in comparison to other fields of population research. Internal migration, statistically more manageable and emotionally more neutral, has gained in attention compared to international migration, but it is hardly a subject of rapid advance in population study.

A topic that has noticeably lost demographic and sociological attention is "population quality." Interest in this subject waned as cultural and psychic determinism took hold in the social sciences, but the more permanent blow came when progress in genetics removed the subject from lay competence. Most social scientists, including demographers, now leave the complex field of genetics alone, rationalizing their avoidance by saying that heredity has little to do with social phenomena.

A third topic—population forecasts and projections—has receded in interest mainly because of a loss of confidence. Not long ago the view was prevalent, particularly among nondemographers, that demography is a field in which the prediction of future events is especially accurate. As the future came to pass, disillusionment followed.[4] Population projections will continue to be made because future population changes are too important to be ignored. Furthermore, their prescience will surely be improved—primarily, I think, by sociological research on people's intentions regarding reproduction. Forecasts thus represent a live topic from our point of view, but precisely because they draw upon all branches of demographic knowledge, they are not of special sociological interest. From the standpoint of public reaction, it is not likely that the old faith in their accuracy will be regained.

Finally, the subject of mortality occupies a peculiar place in regard to sociology. Its demographic importance is, of course, equal to that of fertility, and the funds spent on research designed to control it (sociological as well as medical) are astronomical compared to those expended on fertility; yet there has been more sociological integration of fertility with demography than of mortality with demography. The reasons for this are not easy to state, but it seems true that motives play a more direct role in the birth rate than in the death rate. Whereas the attitude toward death is monotonously negative (except in suicide), that toward reproduction is positive or negative depending on the circumstances. Also, since death occurs only once to a person whereas reproduction can occur several times, motives with respect to childbearing are influenced by previous childbearing. Further, reproduction necessarily involves social relationships, since it arises out of a sexual connection and sets up a parent-child bond. These differences suggest why it is that the sociological research bearing on mortality is directed more toward health and illness than toward the death rate per se. It has to do with attitudes toward illness, availability of medical care, the sociology of the medical

---

[4] Joseph S. Davis led the critics, but there were others as well—*e.g.*, Palmer C. Putnam, *Energy in the Future*, Van Nostrand, 1953, Chap. 2. For discussion and references, see Harold F. Dorn, "Pitfalls in Population Forecasts and Projections," *J. Amer. stat. Assoc.*, 42 (1952), 304-25; and Kingsley Davis, "Future Population Trends and Their Significance," in *Transactions* of the Eighteenth North American Wildlife Conference, Wildlife Management Institute, 1953, pp. 8-21.

profession, and so on. The social factors actually governing the death rate and the social consequences of different levels of mortality and morbidity have been dealt with less extensively than in the case of fertility. Considerable attention has been devoted to the age structure in its social effects, but the changes in the structure have been due more to variations in fertility than to variations in mortality. In the future, it may be that more sociological attention will be devoted to the social causes and consequences of mortality per se (an interest that certainly deserves cultivating), but we shall reluctantly omit it from the present discussion in favor of fertility.

In any case, we see that the promising topics from a socio-demographic point of view are not those that take demographic information and superimpose, so to speak, a sociological "explanation." They are topics that involve actual research on social structure and attitudes in combination with demographic analysis. The four areas of research listed at the outset are in this sense among the most promising, and therefore they occupy the rest of our discussion.

Fertility in Industrial Societies

Innovations in demography, or in other social sciences, are determined mainly not by the inner development of the science itself but by the impingement of historical events. Thus the study of human fertility in the West was dominated from 1925 to 1945 by two historical trends —the secular decline in the total birth rate which had been particularly rapid from 1915 to 1933, and the class differences in fertility which had increased up to about 1930. Since the first trend produced a drastic change in the age structure, it vitiated crude rates as indicators of demographic processes. This forced demographers to develop and use new analytical tools, such as reproduction rates, intrinsic rates, and stable populations. These were abstractions, saying what *would* happen *if* current age-specific rates *were* continued indefinitely, but they allowed international and other comparisons to be made independently of perturbations in the age structure. Unfortunately, under the influence of the long downward trend in fertility, the abstractions were reified. Both demographers and nondemographers yielded to the temptation to assume that the net reproduction rate described what was *likely* to happen —that a rate, say, of .75 in the 1930's indicated that the population would eventually start declining by something like 25 percent per generation. Furthermore, it was assumed that the principal scientific task was to explain the long decline in fertility. This was normally accomplished by showing how associated trends, such as urbanization, class mobility, and the loss of family functions, had affected reproduction. Indeed, the best explanations were evolved at just about the time when the phenomenon being explained had ceased to exist.

The next event that forced demographers to re-examine their analytical tools and invent new ones was the rise in the birth rate. Beginning in the late 1930's, this rise continued longer and went higher than the experts had thought possible. Yet the same secular trends that had been used to explain declining fertility continued after the upturn. It was clear that demographic theory and technique were defective, that abstractions gave no predictive power, that the most certain thing about reproduction rates was the unreality of their assumptions, that too simplified a view of human reproduction had been followed.

The rise in the birth rate shifted attention from long-run to short-run trends. Since current fertility, whether measured by crude or by refined rates, could shift radically in a few years with business fluctuations or with war or peace, analysts were forced to recognize that the *same* couples could be involved in periods of contrasting fertility. In other words, people can postpone marriage or childbearing at one time and make up for such postponement or even borrow on the future at a later time, depending on the circumstances. One birth is not just like another: a couple's reproduction at the moment is influenced by whether or not they already have children, and how many. Attention therefore turned from current fertility (the reproduction rate during a specified, usually a short, time) to cumulative fertility (the number of children ever born by age of woman and duration of marriage). Whelpton and others began to analyze the reproductive performance of cohorts of women and to study births by birth order, or parity. The result was a more complex and faithful demographic analysis of reproductive behavior than had been used before.

It is logical that the new type of demographic analysis should be combined with the sociological study of attitudes and motives. One pioneer project along this line, undertaken jointly by the Scripps Foundation and the Michigan Survey Research Center, has as its principal aim the improvement of future population estimates by research on reproductive intentions.[5] (Fertility has been the main source of error in population forecasts in industrial countries.) A national sample of about 3,000 white women, some married and aged 18-39 with husband present or in the armed forces, and some single and aged 18-24, are given sixty-minute interviews on their marital and pregnancy history, how many children they expect to have and when, their reasons for the expected number, and how their expectations may be affected by changed conditions. Some of the responses are compared to those on previous polls, and it is hoped that similar surveys can be conducted about every five years, thus providing unprecedented information on shifts in family planning and reproductive attitudes in relation to changing conditions.

The other study, under the auspices of the Milbank Fund and the Office of Population Research, focuses on factors affecting the interval between births and the likelihood of an additional birth after a given number. The initial sample is evidently restricted to couples who have recently had their second child. Follow-up interviews with these couples will occur roughly eighteen and twenty-four months after the first ones.[6] Since the avowed purpose is basic research rather than improvement of population forecasts, the questionnaire is long (242 questions on the pretest schedule) and covers topics varying all the way from purely demographic to purely psychological.

Both studies bring birth order, or parity, into the forefront of investigation. Reproductive motivation is not only a matter of how many children one wants all told, but also a matter of whether a second child is wanted after the first, a third one after a second, and so on. As Mischler and Westoff say, each birth "occurs in and is influenced by a different set of circumstances," and each child alters the family's situa-

[5] P. K. Whelpton, "A Study of the 'Expected' Completed Fertility of a National Sample of White Women," in *Current Research in Human Fertility*, Milbank Fund, 1955, pp. 106-12.

[6] Clyde V. Kiser, "General Objectives and Broad Areas of Interest in a Proposed New Study of Fertility," and Elliot G. Mischler and Charles F. Westoff, "A Proposal for Research on Social Psychological Factors Affecting Fertility: Concepts and Hypotheses," in *Current Research in Human Fertility*, pp. 115-50; Kiser *et al.*, "Development of Plans for a Social-Psychological Study of the Future Fertility of Two-Child Families," *Popul. Stud.*, 10 (1956), 43-52; Westoff *et al.*, "A New Study of American Fertility," *Eugen. Quart.*, 11 (1955), 229-33.

tion "and so affects the probability and timing of future births." [7] Research of this type will increase our knowledge of the factors governing reproductive decisions in industrial societies.

At the risk of seeming utopian, I might mention three addditional lines of investigation which, if carried out, would increase our knowledge of reproduction:

1. *Longitudinal studies that follow the reproductive planning and performance of couples from the inception of marriage to the completion of childbearing*. Ideally, successive panels composed of couples beginning marriage at five-year intervals could be studied. Such a technique would permit the integration of physiological, demographic, and sociological observations with respect to the same couples and would avoid the customary reliance upon retrospective data. Information on the capacity to conceive, to retain the foetus, to achieve a normal parturition, and to nurse the baby would become more detailed and more accurate; and the relation of such phenomena to the process of aging, situations of stress, changes in attitudes, and so on would become clearer.

2. *Interview studies of factors governing the decision to marry*. The circumstances influencing the desire to marry at a given age, to postpone or to hasten marriage, or to forego it altogether play a major role in birth-rate fluctuations. Although the Scripps-Michigan study will obtain some relevant material, the topic has received less investigation than its demographic importance requires.

3. *Replication of studies in different industrial countries*. The tendency to psychologize and thus overlook sociological determinants of reproduction is so strong that precautions are required to avoid it. One precaution is the replication of studies in different countries. This approach, having already proved valuable in studying stratification, should prove helpful in demography as well.

Fertility in Underdeveloped Societies

In the agrarian countries, the event that has forced a revision of population theory and research is the unprecedented decline in the death rate. It has not only speeded up the already fast rate of increase in the world's population but has also transferred the locus of the faster growth from the advanced to the backward nations. The natural increase rate

---

[7] Mischler and Westoff, *op. cit.*, pp. 124-25.

in the latter areas is now approximately twice that in the industrial countries, despite the postwar baby boom in industrial countries.[8]

The poorer countries are leading the population race, however, because of continuing high fertility as well as declining mortality. The question therefore arises as to when and how a decline in the birth rate will set in or be induced. The issue is of practical as well as theoretical importance; three crowded agrarian countries—China, India, and Puerto Rico—are, like Japan, officially encouraging family limitation, and other countries may do so soon.

The problem is the reverse of what it was in the 1930's. Then a number of industrial countries, fearful of eventual population loss, were pursuing or considering policies designed to *raise* the level of fertility, and social research on reproduction was directed to that end. The governments concerned derived little of practical value from the research, but demography received some benefit. In the United States, the Indianapolis study of "social and psychological factors" was begun in 1938, and in Britain the Royal Commission on Population was constituted in 1944 and the basis laid for the Family Census of 1946. Characteristically, these studies were made at just about the time that the main problem they dealt with—insufficient reproduction—was over,[9] and at a time when field-survey techniques were not so well developed as they are today.

With high fertility in underdeveloped countries as the problem, it is not strange that modern interview methods should be applied there to find out about reproductive motives. Nor is it strange that the studies should be conducted with experts, technical assistance, and funds from the Western industrial countries. The surprising thing, however, is that so few countries have as yet been touched by such investigations. India, Puerto Rico, and Jamaica virtually exhaust the list, although other areas will doubtless soon be included.[10] Yet the number of studies made

[8] See Kingsley Davis, "The Amazing Decline of Mortality in Underdeveloped Areas," *Amer. econ. Rev.*, 46 (1956), 305-18.

[9] It should be mentioned that one other issue was influencing demographic research at the time—differential class fertility. This, too, was diminishing by the time the studies got under way.

[10] One of the earliest field surveys, initiated in 1946, was made jointly by the Office of Population Research and the Social Science Research Center of the University of Puerto Rico, reported in Paul K. Hatt, *Backgrounds of Human Fertility in Puerto Rico: A Sociological Study*, Princeton University

is already too large to permit a brief but accurate characterization. All that can be done is to make certain general observations that apply to most but not to all of them.

One observation is that the studies have a practical purpose: they focus on attitudes toward family size in so far as these throw light on the possible use of birth control. This point of departure offers no inher-

---

Press, 1952. Since then a second study by the Center has been made under Reuben Hill's direction, the plans being reported in numerous articles by Hill, Stycos, and Back. A preliminary report based on pilot interviews with a limited number of lower-class Puerto Ricans is found in J. M. Stycos, *Family and Fertility in Puerto Rico*, Columbia University Press, 1955.

The principal surveys in India are: (1) A study undertaken jointly by WHO, the UN, and the Government of India in Mysore State. Initiated in 1951 and concerned chiefly with population growth in relation to socio-economic change, it includes data on fertility attitudes in a sample of about 1,200 couples. The results, already adumbrated in several articles by C. Chandrasekaran, will soon emerge as a book by this author. (2) A series of studies of reproductive attitudes in rural and urban areas of the Deccan, by the Gokhale Institute of Politics and Economics. Among the reports so far are V. M. Dandekar and Kumudini Dandekar, *Survey of Fertility and Mortality in Poona District*, Poona: Gokhale Institute, 1953; and N. V. Sovani and K. Dandekar, *Fertility Survey of Nasik, Kolaba and Satara (North) Districts*, Poona: Gokhale Institute, 1955. (3) William A. Morrison's survey of male and female attitudes toward family planning in a village of Bombay State in 1954. See his "Attitudes of Males Toward Family Planning in a Western Indian Village" and a similar article on females, Milbank Memorial Fund *Quarterly*, 34 (1956), 1-24; 35 (1957), 67-81. (4) A continuing survey of fertility attitudes and family planning in Uttar Pradesh by the J. K. Institute of Sociology and Human Relations at Lucknow University. The first report, after five years of experimental work and observation on the diffusion of birth control, is Baljit Singh, *Five Years of Family Planning in the Countryside*, Lucknow: J. K. Institute, 1958.

In Jamaica the Conservation Foundation has sponsored field studies of fertility attitudes. The results of a pilot intensive-interview analysis of lower-class family structure and reproductive motivation will be available soon in a book by Judith Blake. See her "Family Instability and Reproductive Behavior in Jamaica," in *Current Research in Human Fertility*, pp. 24-41. A more restricted survey but using a larger sample has been conducted by Back and Stycos.

A study which deals with Indonesian villages, emphasizing economic as well as social and psychic factors, has apparently been made. See Nathan

ent sociological disadvantage; on the contrary, it may sharpen the investigation by offering a potential test of accuracy. There is a danger, however, that the limited purpose may keep the investigator from getting behind the so-called attitudes to the institutional patterns and economic settings in which attitudes take shape. Some surveys, for example, have reported expressions of opinion about reproduction and birth control without relating these opinions to the social structure or current conditions of the society in question. The result is a certain amount of ambiguity, for we do not know how well the verbal statements reflect present or future behavior. Since expressed attitudes change readily, a greater knowledge of underlying institutional and conditioning factors should augment the investigator's ability to foresee changes in fertility. Furthermore, the field studies in underdeveloped areas have not made much effort as yet to analyze reproductive decisions in the context of different parities. If this focus is added to the interest in attitudes toward total family size, it may help one to gauge what point in the family cycle is most propitious for birth control or sterilization and to see more clearly how declining childhood mortality affects parental attitudes.

Thinking of themselves as dealing with attitudes and motives and thus as being in a realm called "social psychology," the investigators have sometimes paid lip service to "the role of culture" and "community values" but have actually been technically unaware of social structure. The situation is curious, because generations of sociologists and anthropologists have dealt with social organization in peasant societies, particularly with family and kinship structure. True, much of this material is defective, the information having been obtained from informants or by informal and uncontrolled observation; and much of it stops with the normative system rather than going on to treat actual behavior.[11] Never-

---

Keyfitz, "A Field Study in Population," *Proc. World Popul. Conf.*, 6, 1954 (New York: United Nations, 1955), pp. 313-19.

No attempt is made here to cover the work done on reproductive attitudes among primitive peoples in Africa. The author has the impression that this work, dominated by British anthropologists, has not made much use of modern survey techniques. Nor are the numerous studies in Japan dealt with here. See Irene B. Taeuber, *The Population of Japan*, Princeton University Press, 1958, Chap. 18, pp. 420-23.

[11] I. Schapera asks anthropologists to give more attention to actual as distinct from ideal behavior. It is easy, he says, to get from an informant a statement of what people should do, much harder to find out what they

theless, the connection between social organization and reproductive motivation is too close to be ignored, and it cannot be adequately investigated unless the investigator has a technical knowledge of the subject.[12] Demographic field studies not only have much to gain from the science of family and kinship but also much to contribute to it—provided, of course, that the investigators are aware of the nature of systematic work in that sphere.

An inevitable limitation of field surveys is the brief time they cover. They cannot substitute for historical or statistical studies encompassing long-run changes. With the help of cautiously used retrospective data, they can throw some light on past changes, but this can best be done if the investigators know relevant features of the statistical and social history of the people being studied.

The traits just described, in so far as they characterize the studies in question, are generally associated with a raw-empiricist tendency—the tendency to initiate research either with no explicit hypotheses at all or with hypotheses pulled out of a hat. In such cases, useless information may be gathered while valuable leads are ignored. At worst, the attitudinal possibilities are unconsciously assumed to be similar to those in Western society, or, equally misleading, they are assumed to be of necessity utterly different. Peasant women in Asia, for example, may be asked how many children they would like to have—the question being put without a realization that, under conditions of high mortality, "to have" in the sense of bearing children and "to have" in the sense of having live children growing up in the house are two different things. Or questions may be asked which assume that peasants automatically conform to community values without reference to the particular economic circumstances facing the family. The fallacy of preconceived categories is readily apparent when even the ordinary demographic conceptions are inapplicable. Where most children are born out of wedlock, for example, such concepts as "marital fertility," "age at marriage," and "duration of marriage" are misleading. Where a woman may have chil

---

actually do, especially when the community comprises several thousand people. In the end, he continues, the field worker must use a statistical approach. See "Tswana Conception of Incest," in Meyer Fortes (ed.), *Social Structure,* Clarendon Press, 1949, pp. 105-06.

[12] Judith Blake's work, already cited, will bear out this point. See also her and my article, "Social Structure and Fertility: An Analytic Framework," *Econ. Devel. cult. Change, 4* (1956), 211-35.

dren engendered by several different men and fathered by none in particular, the term "completed family size" is hardly applicable to men and is a misnomer for women. Since demographic concepts are aided in clarity and comparability by their biological aspect, one can see that if they are sometimes inapplicable the same must be true to an even greater degree of attitudinal and motivational categories.

Such difficulties become most apparent at the very moment when least can be done about them—that is, when the field work is completed and the analysis of results has begun. At this moment the investigator must finally ask, or risk having a critic ask, what did the given question mean to the respondents, or why was a now obviously relevant question not asked?

One way of avoiding catastrophes due to hasty and prejudged data collection is to undertake a pilot study in advance of the main survey. This is done by conducting intensive exploratory interviews with a limited number of respondents and subjecting the results to a full-scale qualitative analysis. When the pilot study is completed, the planning of the full survey can be undertaken with the aid of what has been learned about, and *from,* the people concerned.[13] The chief trouble is that the qualitative analysis of the pilot interviews is so time-consuming that it may take from one to three years to complete.

These remarks about surveys of reproductive attitudes in underdeveloped countries do not apply universally or imply that any of the researches is of no value. If space were available, it would be possible to show that these pioneer efforts are beginning to revolutionize our outlook on the sociology of reproduction. No longer is it possible to dismiss the topic by quoting ethnographers to the effect that "these people love children and therefore. . . ." No longer is it permissible to refer sagely to "the strictures of their religion." No longer is sexual motivation to be confused with reproductive motivation. The days when one could go out to a foreign area, "live" among the people, talk to a few

---

[13] A pilot study was made by the Hill project in Puerto Rico and the Conservation Foundation project in Jamaica, but not in the Hatt study in Puerto Rico or the Poona and Mysore studies in India. A pilot study is not a "pretest." The latter is a limited program of preliminary interviewing to test the adequacy of a questionnaire. A true pilot study is designed to let the respondents tell the investigators what is on their minds; hence a rigid questionnaire is avoided.

informants about "what folks do in this culture," and write a book on it that will pass scientific muster are over—at least as far as the study of demographic behavior is concerned.

Population Growth and Social Change

Behind the current interest in fertility in poorer countries lies the oldest problem of population theory—the relation of population growth to human welfare. The form of the question has varied with the times, but in essence it has remained the same. Malthus, starting as a critic of utopian ideology, gradually shifted from the issue of perfectibility to the issue of economic welfare. He could hardly conceive of a permanent rise in the general level of living because of the inevitability of population growth under favorable conditions. Today the question is normally phrased in something like this form: To what extent is economic progress being impeded or enhanced by population growth?

It may be thought that this problem has been worn threadbare, and in a sense it has. But the scientific treatment of it is just beginning, and the fact that most of this treatment is by economists means that a great opportunity awaits the sociologists. Nobody doubts that all aspects of society are involved, as both causes and consequences, in both demographic and economic change. The problem is to develop operational theories that approximate the complexities of the phenomena and to test them by long-run and comparative evidence.

The slowness of sociologists to take up the problem springs partly from their emphasis on field surveys, social psychology, and microsociology, and partly from their reluctance to learn technical demography and economics. Nevertheless, some contemporary sociologists are reviving the subject of social change which so much occupied their predecessors.[14]

The nondemographer often assumes that the only form of population change is a growth or decline in the total number. This causes him to overlook trends in mortality, morbidity, fertility, and migration,

---

[14] Among these are Marion J. Levy, Jr., Reinhard Bendix, S. N. Eisenstadt, and Wilbert E. Moore. Lyle W. Shannon's readings, *Underdeveloped Areas*, Harper, 1957, reveals a lively interest in the sociological aspects of economic development; and the proportion of sociological articles in the journal *Economic Development and Cultural Change* has been high.

which have social consequences independently of their connection with population growth. It also leads him to overlook significant changes in population structure, in spatial distribution, and in group differentials. In fact, to reason solely in terms of population growth or decline is absolutely fruitless so far as social change is concerned. Unless other demographic changes are brought into consideration, one cannot understand population growth itself, much less its significance. Only when all aspects of demographic change are seen as a system can their connections with the rest of the society be understood.

Needless to say, the analysis of long-run demographic change runs into the problem of data scarcity. As we move back into preceding centuries, however, information does not disappear completely, but it becomes scantier, more indirect, and more questionable. American demographers have been inactive in discovering and analyzing historical data. They have left almost untouched nearly forty surveys of population during the American colonial era, and have made little use of local records. There are exceptions, of course,[15] but interest in demographic history has been greater in Europe.[16] A demographer and an archivist in France have gone so far as to prepare a manual on abstracting and utilizing demographic data from parish registers.[17]

[15] Wendell H. Bash, "Differential Fertility in Madison County, New York, 1865," Milbank Memorial Fund *Quart.*, 33 (1955), 161-86; Robert Gutman, "The Birth Statistics of Massachusetts During the Nineteenth Century," *Popul. Stud.*, 10 (1956), 69-94, and "Birth and Death Registration in Massachusetts: I. The Colonial Background, 1639–1800," Milbank *Quart.*, 36 (1958), 58-74; and earlier work by Jaffe and Spengler on fertility. Most of the American work on historical demography has been done by nondemographers, and mainly with reference to Europe or Latin America—*e.g.*, the research of Josiah C. Russell on medieval population, of Sherburne F. Cook and associates on colonial Mexico, and of George Kubler on colonial South America.

[16] See the three-volume work of Roger Mols, *Introduction à la démographie historique des villes d'Europe du XIVe au XVIIIe siècle*, Université de Louvain, 1954; K. H. Connell, *The Population of Ireland, 1750–1845*, Clarendon Press, 1950; Jacques Henripin, *La population canadienne au début du XVIIIe siècle*, Presses Universitaires, 1954; and numerous articles in *Population Studies* (British) and *Population* (French).

[17] Michel Fleury and Louis Henry, *Des registres paroissiaux à l'histoire de la population: Manuel de dépouillement et d'exploitation de l'état civil ancien*, Paris: L'Institut National d'Études Demographiques, 1956.

Although demographers are in such short supply that few can be spared to search for historical statistics, the task cannot be left entirely to nondemographers. Actually, data already published and readily available are not fully utilized. For example, one can determine for a number of countries the approximate dates of crucial changes in the demographic transition,[18] such as the commencement of steady decline and then of rapid decline in mortality, the same points with respect to fertility, the consequent alterations of trend in natural increase, and the gaps in time between these alterations. With information on other aspects of the economy and society (indices of economic development, urbanization, educational achievement, migratory movement) one can translate time into stage of development and thus derive a dynamic model of the interaction between demographic and other changes. The results can be checked by a statistical comparison of contemporary countries in different stages of development.[19]

Examples of the questions that this kind of analysis could answer are these: Has emigration acted in such a way that, when the net outflow was great, it permitted fertility to remain high and hence the period of rapid natural increase to prolong itself exceptionally after mortality began to drop? Does technological change, once it gets started in a country, exercise influences that keep population from growing fast enough to stop technical improvement? Does demographic evolution in the new land settled by northwest Europeans differ from that in Europe itself or in other new lands, such as Latin America?[20] Do the

[18] An account of the demographic transition and some measurable aspects of it will be found in my essay, "The Demographic Consequences of Changes in Productive Technology," in the UNESCO publication, *Social, Economic and Technological Change: A Theoretical Approach* (Paris: International Social Science Council, 1958), pp. 193-227.

[19] A start has been made along these lines, but not as yet with enough appreciation of the range of demographic phenomena or of the basic turning points in the demographic transition. Treatments also tend to be too narrowly tied to economic variables. See Simon Kuznets, "Quantitative Aspects of the Economic Growth of Nations: I. Levels and Variability of Rates of Growth," *Econ. Devel. cult. Change,* 5 (1956), 1-94; Kingsley Davis, "Population and the Further Spread of Industrial Society," *Proc. Amer. phil. Soc.,* 95 (1951), 8-19.

[20] The first question is raised by Gayl Ness, currently a student at the University of California, in comparative historical research on population;

conditions, the culture, or the historical epoch determine the speed of the demographic transition in a particular country or region? How do differences of speed affect the resulting age structure and hence the dependency ratios? Such questions lie at the heart of the new empirical theory of population.

Population, Labor Force, and National Efficiency

The populations inside and outside the labor force, like any other populations, have their own demographic features and their own economic and social traits. Since the size and quality of the labor force are of great importance to a nation, the analysis of these two populations offers an opportunity for bringing sociological and demographic analysis into an integral relation with economic science and national policy.

Let us illustrate by reference to two current national problems: the shortage of scientists and technicians, and the utilization of womanpower in the American labor force. The first problem raises the question of what "shortage" means with respect to an occupational category; but if we assume this query to be answered, the next question is clearly one for research: why has the deficiency arisen, and what steps would be necessary to remedy it? The demographic contribution would include an analysis of the occupational structure of the labor force, of the "population flow" through educational channels, and of occupational mobility in relation to age. The sociological contribution would include juxtaposed study of incentives and public images with reference to occupations, and an analysis of family, school, and economic organization behind these incentives and images. So far, for reasons too complex to discuss here, demographers and sociologists have contributed less than they could to research on this problem. There is yet time, however, because the shortage of highly trained personnel in the United States shows signs of getting worse before it gets better.

This question of scientific shortage merges easily with our second illustrative problem—the handling of womanpower—because we make less use of talented women in the labor force than do some rival nations

---

the second is raised by Everett E. Hagen, "The Process of Economic Development," *Econ. Devel. cult. Change,* 5 (1957), 208; and the third is raised by Kingsley Davis, "Recent Population Trends in the New World," *Annals Amer. Acad. polit. soc. Sci.,* 316 (1958), 2-8.

(notably Russia). In fact, although the greatest disregard of talent is commonly assumed to arise from class and racial inequality, this source of loss is probably less than that involving women. When we consider that female participation in the labor force is a public issue from a purely quantitative point of view as well, we can see the practical importance of research on womanpower.

The scientific aspect of this subject is equally interesting, for here the theory of role conflict and of functional adjustment between separated parts of the institutional system can be tested. The contrast between the requirements of the family and those of the politico-economic order sets up strains that come to a head in the feminine role. The opinion polls reveal the ambivalence of the public attitude by the violent shifts in reaction as conditions change, but the dominant view is disapproval of married women working; yet the actual trend is strongly toward increased employment of married women. The sociological theory offered by Parsons [21] to account for the normative situation runs as follows: Given the independence of the nuclear family, given its spatial separation from work and its personal and diffuse character as opposed to the business world, the division of sex role by which the husband alone enters the occupational sphere is a mechanism that minimizes rivalry within marriage and promotes family solidarity. Precisely because this explanation has great analytical power, it needs to be extended as far as possible in empirical as well as logical directions. Exploration of alternatives that are within but not decided by the theory is possible. For example, since many married women work, even in the United States, and since an even larger proportion do so in some other nations, how much participation can a social system tolerate without reducing the essential family functions? Are institutional mechanisms available that shield the family from the full impact of married-female employment? One such mechanism mentioned in the theory and verifiable from U.S. labor-force data is the greater participation of women in parttime employment and their greater concentration in temporary and dead-end jobs that offer no rivalry with husbands. This adaptation, while giving protection to the family and utilizing feminine talents in parental and household tasks, involves a loss of talents for the economic system. The Soviet Union has pursued a different tack by capturing more female

[21] Talcott Parsons, *Essays in Sociological Theory*, Free Press, 1949, pp. 242-47.

ability for scientific, technical, and medical professions, thus posing the
question of whether the Soviet family is suffering in consequence or
whether remedial mechanisms have been adopted to prevent this from
happening. In addition to such empirical work bearing on aspects of the
Parsonian theory, an effort can be made to derive from the theory certain
implications that would follow from changed conditions. As present-day
industrial society undergoes alterations that are already suggested, how
will these affect the integration of the family and the occupational world
and hence the employment of women?

In any case, the combination of demographic and sociological analysis seems the only way to gain a scientifically satisfying understanding
of the female labor force. The ever more numerous data on female
employment in this and other countries permit statistical analysis of the
differences between working and nonworking married women with respect to such matters as children, family status, husband's occupation and
income, educational achievement; and, for working women, the relation
of these to labor-force characteristics such as full- or parttime work,
length of employment, occupational status, industry. Any theory of the
family or of woman's position today is subject to having some of its
propositions, or derivable propositions, tested against such facts; and
any treatment of the labor force that pretends to predictive or explanatory adequacy cannot ignore sociological data and theory on the social
structure.

Demography and the Family

The demographer's primary interest in the family derives from his
interest in fertility. In addition, as we have just seen, his concern with
the labor force also takes him back to the family, as does his interest in
infant mortality. Such preoccupations are sufficient to bring him to consider most aspects of family structure if he gives reign to his scientific
curiosity. He has the material ready at hand for pursuing such interests,
because censuses and vital statistics contain a wealth of information on
family formation and dissolution, marital status, family composition,
reproductive behavior, and household types. From analyzing such material for demographic purposes it is but a step to analyzing it for understanding the family per se, as illustrated by Paul C. Glick's *American
Families.*[22]

[22] John Wiley, 1957. This is a volume in the Census Monograph Series.

Currently there is, it seems, an increased interaction between sociology and demography with respect to the family, as shown by the work of Glick, Kephart, Jacobson, Monahan, Goode, Jessie Bernard, and others. The result is a renaissance of scientific study in the family field, a revival which promises to gather speed in the next few years. It is worth pointing out, however, that certain obstacles remain. One still encounters in the demographic literature on the family either an unwillingness to attempt any sort of interpretation of data, or the use of what may be called the "irresponsible stop-gap explanation." In the latter case a careful statistical analysis reveals, say, a regularity in the facts. The author seeks to "explain" it, but, having no further data bearing directly on the matter, he feels no particular responsibility for what he says and tosses off a half-truth before going on to the next carefully presented statistical finding. If, instead of pursuing such easy tactics, the demographer would take seriously the task of integrated interpretation, he would not only bring his rich data to bear more effectively upon the science of the family but would also find relationships, or facts, in his data that he cannot otherwise see. On the other side of the fence, family theory is often elaborated by sociologists and anthropologists with little awareness of the evidence which demography could provide. It is a melancholy indication of how far we have yet to go that the Parsonian analysis previously cited makes no reference to the relevant demographic materials, and that Glick, in his *American Families,* makes no reference to Parsons. One would not know that these two men are both members of the same professional group and are dealing with the same phenomenon, the American family.

Demography is peculiarly useful for what one may call the macro-sociology of the family—the comparative study of family structure, the analysis of family change, and the determination of the relation of the family to the rest of the social order. Its usefulness lies both in the theoretical and in the empirical spheres. On the theoretical side, for example, it is worth noting that the explanation of population change is at the same time, in part, an explanation of what is happening in the family with reference to one of the main functions of the family, reproduction. On the empirical side, we know that census-taking and vital registration have become common practices in many countries with contrasting social systems, and that these sources almost invariably call for information on the family, much of it in roughly standard form. Kephart exaggerates only slightly when he says that "a number of

European and Asiatic nations publish census volumes with more family statistics than are contained in our own census reports." [23] His point that this material has been little used for comparative analysis is well taken. Since some countries have census and registration data covering many decades, the opportunity for studying changes in family structure is excellent. Further, the fact that the same sources contain socioeconomic as well as demographic data makes it possible to cross-tabulate family characteristics, on a scale not possible elsewhere, with economic, educational, religious, racial, and other significant traits—thereby providing the richest available evidence on the functional relation of the family to the rest of the social order.

Conclusion

By now it should be clear why the best integration of demography and sociology will not come from erasing their distinctiveness or by reducing specialization. It will come, rather, from increasing the number of specialties that use skills, data, and ideas from both fields. The only undesirable form of specialization is that which divides theory from empirical research. Sometimes, unfortunately, the demographer (who works with statistical data) is thought of, and thinks of himself, as a raw empiricist who knows nothing of and cares little for "theory." On the other hand, the sociological theorist is often so busy interpreting things in words that he fails to acquire the techniques or knowledge necessary for testing his easy generalizations. In demography the older speculative theory is giving way to systematic model-construction and empirically tested generalization. In its broadest context, this theory joins insensibly with, and contributes to, the most fundamental aspect of sociological thought—namely, the bases of survival or extinction of types of societies and types of institutions. Those social mechanisms tend to be strengthened and perpetuated which give rise to the highest rate of natural increase, and those tend to be lost which fail to do so. In this sense, the theory of population is an essential part of the theory of human society.

Although the mutual value of sociology and demography is poten-

[23] W. M. Kephart, "Some Knowns and Unknowns in Family Research: A Sociological Critique," *Marr. Fam. Liv.*, 19 (1957), 10. Illustrating the use of demographic materials to answer sociological questions about the family is Taeuber, *op. cit.*, Chaps. 4-6, 11-13.

tially great, it cannot be realized by trying to join the two "fields" as
wholes but only by pursuing particular scientific interests that draw upon
both. I have tried to illustrate my points, therefore, by selecting four
areas of interest. In each case, it appears that selective integration of
sociological and demographic elements is going forward, albeit with
some hesitation and difficulty. It also appears that in each case the relation between the two broad disciplines, if they can be called such, is a
two-way one. The idea that one provides the "explanations" and the
other the "data" is not true. Each contributes theoretically, technically,
and empirically to the solution of common problems through the work
of people specializing on those problems.

15
Comparative Urban Sociology ⌒

GIDEON SJOBERG
University of Texas

Interest in cross-cultural urban study dates from at least as early as the sixteenth century, when Giovanni Botero's impressionistic work, *The Greatness of Cities*, was first published.[1] In 1899, Adna F. Weber wrote a more specifically sociological treatise, *The Growth of Cities in the Nineteenth Century*,[2] and some two decades later Max Weber composed "Die Stadt."[3] Although these and other works pertaining to comparative urbanism[4] have been available to American urban sociologists for some time, it is only very recently that an appreciable number of sociologists in this country have shown an interest in cities elsewhere in the world. It is increasingly being recog-

[1] Giovanni Botero, "The Greatness of Cities" (trans. Robert Peterson, 1606), in Giovanni Botero, *The Reason of State and The Greatness of Cities*, Routledge and Kegan Paul, 1956.

[2] Adna F. Weber, *The Growth of Cities in the Nineteenth Century*, Macmillan, 1899.

[3] Max Weber, "Die Stadt," *Archiv für Sozialwissenschaft und Sozialpolitik*, 47 (1921), 621-772.

[4] See, for example, Pitirim A. Sorokin, Carle C. Zimmerman, and Charles J. Galpin, *A Systematic Source Book in Rural Sociology*, University of Minnesota Press, 1930.

nized that cities in other societies, whether historical or modern, differ from those in the United States in many facets of their social and ecological organization. Yet, even today, the comparative approach is little used in urban sociology, judging from the paucity of cross-cultural data in textbooks in the field [5] and in articles in sociological journals.

Granted that comparative urban study is still in its formative stages, what are some of the obstacles to further work in this field, and how can these obstacles be overcome? We shall devote special attention to three principal problems: (1) utilizing the existing literature, (2) formulating more adequate theories, and (3) testing hypotheses in a comparative setting.

Utilizing the Existing Literature

The data on many facets of urban life, particularly social organization, are clearly inadequate. Yet considerably more information is at our disposal than most sociologists realize. Among American sociologists, Kingsley Davis is undoubtedly leading the way in synthesizing data on world communities, particularly from a demographic perspective.[6] And studies by the Dotsons, Caplow, Gist, and Eberhard,[7] among others, have added to our knowledge of urban centers in various societies. Nevertheless, sociologists interested in comparative urban studies must reach beyond the confines of their own discipline, and even beyond American social science, for much of their material. Demographers and geographers have amassed considerable information on cities over the world, as have anthropologists. So, too, have historians, econ-

[5] Rose Hum Lee, *The City: Urbanism and Urbanization in Major World Regions*, Lippincott, 1955, purports to take a comparative perspective but falls far short of this goal.

[6] See, for example, Kingsley Davis and Hilda Hertz Golden, "Urbanization and the Development of Pre-Industrial Areas," *Econ. Devel. cult. Change*, 3 (1954), 6-26.

[7] See, for example, Floyd Dotson and Lillian Ota Dotson, "Urban Centralization and Decentralization in Mexico," *Rural Sociol.*, 21 (1956), 41-49; Theodore Caplow, "Urban Structure in France," *Amer. sociol. Rev.*, 17 (1952), 544-49; Noel P. Gist, "The Ecology of Bangalore, India: An East-West Comparison," *Soc. Forces*, 35 (1957), 356-65; and Wolfram Eberhard, "Data on the Structure of the Chinese City in the Pre-Industrial Period," *Econ. Devel. cult. Change*, 4 (1956), 253-68.

omists, and political scientists, as well as governmental officials. All
have contributed to our store of data, if not to theory.

We have relatively few materials on cities in such an area as Latin
America, although in recent years some important studies on urban life
have appeared.[8] For European cities, on the other hand, considerable
information is extant. The historical records containing data on social
structure and ecology are remarkably extensive. As a result, it has been
possible to make detailed diachronic studies of cities such as Toulouse,
France.[9] And recently a number of urban communities in Europe have
been studied with the aid of modern field-work techniques. Bibliographies in *Current Sociology* list works on cities in England, the Scandinavian countries, and France.[10] Less research has been done on present-
day urban centers in eastern and southern Europe.

Much is being written concerning Africa south of the Sahara, most
notably by anthropologists, on the social and ecological organization of
the cities that have recently arisen or are expanding rapidly.[11] The recent
book *Social Implications of Industrialization and Urbanization in Africa
South of the Sahara* [12] assembles the relevant information in convenient
form. It is hoped that this compilation of materials will stimulate greater
use of the research findings on this area. In North Africa, French social scientists have undertaken to describe a number of urban communities.[13] Le Tourneau's work on Fez, Morocco,[14] is of particularly high
quality.

[8] The *Report on the World Social Situation*, United Nations, 1957, pp.
170-92, summarizes some of the work which has been done on cities in
Latin America.

[9] See, for example, Philippe Wolff, *Commerces et Marchands de Toulouse*, Paris: Librairie Plon, 1954; and Jean Coppolani, *Toulouse: Étude de
Géographie Urbaine*, Toulouse: Privat-Didier, 1954.

[10] *Current Sociology*, 4:1, 4 (1955). Also, a good many detailed empirical studies—for example, those on Darmstadt—have recently been published in Germany.

[11] The bibliographies in each issue of the journal *Africa* list, among other
items, many studies on urban life in this area.

[12] *Social Implications of Industrialization and Urbanization in Africa
South of the Sahara*, Paris: UNESCO, 1956.

[13] *Curr. Sociol.*, 4:1 (1955).

[14] Roger Le Tourneau, *Fès: Avant le Protectorat*, Casablanca: Société
Marocaine de Librairie et d'Édition, 1949.

For the Near East, the region in which cities first arose, the historical data are most pertinent in that they permit us to trace urban development over many centuries.[15] Concerning contemporary Near Eastern communities, few research projects have been realized, although additional publications on this area should soon be forthcoming.[16] So, too, for India: a recent UNESCO bibliography lists a number of efforts to describe the structure of urban communities and the impressive social changes transpiring there.[17] We can expect much more relevant research data from India in the years to come—fortunately, for India, with its unique social system, can serve as a crucial test case for numerous theories or hypotheses about urban life. Southeast Asia is a relatively neglected area, although some projects pertinent to urban sociology appear to be under way.[18] Although some research findings exist on cities in Japan, these are typically in the Japanese language, and therefore little of this information reaches the attention of American scholars.[19] This language problem seems to be spreading elsewhere in Asia as well. As nationalism intensifies in this part of the world, more and more social-science research findings (including census data) will be published in non-European languages, thus multiplying the already existing barriers to communication.

The countries of the Communist bloc, both in Asia and in Europe, pose still other obstacles. Not only have American sociologists lacked direct access to these areas, but empirical social science is poorly developed there. However, a concomitant of the increasing industrial-

[15] Much of this material is summarized in Ralph Turner, *The Great Cultural Traditions*, McGraw-Hill, 1941.

[16] Note *Current Research on the Middle East, 1955*, Washington, D. C.: The Middle East Institute, 1956, pp. 96-110.

[17] *Research Information Bulletin: Social Science Projects in Southern Asia*, Calcutta: Research Centre on the Social Implications of Industrialization in Southern Asia, 1956, *passim*. Consider also the studies published by the Gokhale Institute of Politics and Economics and materials appearing in the *Sociological Bulletin*.

[18] *Research Information Bulletin, op. cit.*

[19] Some of the existing materials are cited in Kunio Odaka, "Sociology in Japan: Accommodation of Western Orientations," in Howard Becker and Alvin Boskoff (eds.), *Modern Sociological Theory*, Dryden Press, 1957, Chap. 25.

urbanization in these societies is the need for extensive data concerning many facets of the social order. If industrial cities are to function, a modicum of published factual data about them must be disseminated through the formal educational system, newspapers, and other mass media. Possession of certain basic information is necessary for effective industrial and economic planning.[20] Such materials are being accumulated in Communist societies and, though not systematized and of uneven, and sometimes doubtful, quality, have clear relevance for urban sociology.

A survey of world urban literature leads to the obvious conclusion that many American sociologists are unaware of the vast body of materials at hand—*e.g.*, those collected by city planners in many societies. Sociologists must make greater efforts to catalogue and diffuse the existing urban data and those that are being accumulated. *Current Sociology,* *Sociological Abstracts,* and *Population Index* are valuable adjuncts to our profession, but additional bibliographies with evaluative annotations, collections of readings, and, especially, surveys of the literature for specific regions and problems are imperative.[21] Translations of the key works in lesser known languages would also be valuable. Through such means, the attention of sociologists can be directed to the writings that are of theoretical significance for their research. The pitfalls awaiting those who generalize solely from data on American society are becoming increasingly apparent. If we are to accumulate a sound body of knowledge, we must, somehow, make more use of the findings on urban areas outside the United States. Otherwise the stated scientific goals of sociology will be little more than empty words. Nevertheless, we must view realistically the obstacles to gaining access to comparative data on other societies, for the inaccessibility of certain kinds of data has important bearing upon the testing of hypotheses, a point we shall elaborate later in the discussion.

---

[20] A recent review article by A. Nove, "In Search of Economic Reality," *Soviet Studies,* 9 (1957), 37*ff.*, notes the increased functional demands in the Soviet Union for factual data relating to the economic sphere.

[21] Summary articles for major world regions, such as those that appear in the *Report on the World Social Situation* on Africa south of the Sahara and for Latin America, would greatly facilitate comparative urban sociology.

Formulating More Adequate Theories [22]

It seems clear that a considerable body of factual data exists on cities over the world, although these are deficient concerning numerous facets of urban life and at times of questionable accuracy. Obviously, there is a need for additional descriptive materials. Yet the broader problem of synthesis must not be overlooked. As vast amounts of information accumulate, order can be achieved only by relating these data to some theoretical scheme or schemes.

In recent years there has been a tendency, as Reiss [23] has observed, to study segments of urban social and ecological structure rather than the totality, or else to use the city as a laboratory for testing theories and hypotheses not specifically related to urban sociology. Although this trend will probably continue, a gestalt perspective has much to offer, for it can help us to understand more clearly the relationships among elements of the social structure and between the sociocultural system and the ecological organization.

Urban sociological theorists face, at the outset, the need to clarify and refine many of the basic concepts in the field—*e.g.*, the community, the city, urbanism, urban society, and ecology—for these terms are variously, and often loosely, employed in the literature. However, we shall proceed directly to some of the broader issues involved. Discussed below are four primary theoretical orientations in urban sociology. Each is evaluated in terms of its significance for the comparative study of urban ecology and social organization. The approaches differ according to the variable that is given primacy—the city, cultural values, technology, or power. We do not claim that this classification is exhaustive, but the existing theory and research in the field suggest that these variables are highly significant for explaining the key patterns of urban life. Certainly

[22] Everett C. Hughes, "The Cultural Aspect of Urban Research," in Leonard D. White (ed.), *The State of the Social Sciences*, University of Chicago Press, 1956, pp. 255-68, touches upon the problem of urban theory in light of comparative study. But his essay is much narrower in its scope than the present paper and differs markedly in subject matter.

[23] Albert J. Reiss, Jr., "The Sociology of Urban Life: 1946-1956," in Paul K. Hatt and Albert J. Reiss, Jr. (eds.), *Cities and Society: The Revised Reader in Urban Sociology*, Free Press, 1957, pp. 10-11.

none of them can be dismissed, although in time others, such as demo-graphic factors, may have to be added to the list.

The City as the Key Variable.   The concept of the city as the key variable in urban sociology has been emphasized particularly by sociologists of the Chicago school, as represented first by Park [24] and later by Wirth [25] and Redfield,[26] among others. Their attempts to interpret urban life present a number of difficulties. Their interpretations involving ecology have not articulated well with their efforts to explain social activity. Most writers influenced by Park have examined human ecology within the so-called biotic or subsocial framework. Although interpreted somewhat differently by its proponents, this theory omits the social aspects of human interrelations as a mechanism for explaining ecological patterns and emphasizes such forces as impersonal competition and the "natural environment." Some writers, like Hawley,[27] have interwoven the technological, or economic, variable into the biotic frame of reference. However, the technological variable, a highly significant one, is considered below shorn from this biotic setting. The biotic viewpoint is of little value—especially as an independent variable—in accounting for the ecological patterns that occur among cities over the world. If this theory were valid, world urban centers would display significant consistencies (and differences) independent of cultural values, the power structure, and technology. And this the supporters of the biotic viewpoint have not demonstrated to be the case.

The city, the writer believes, can be taken as an independent variable for explaining some types of ecological pattern; yet this need not commit us to the ideological consequences of a subsocial frame of reference. Certain spatial and temporal patterns seem functionally necessary to the continued existence of an urban community (in contrast to a rural one) and, conversely, the rise of cities makes possible the develop-

[24] Robert E. Park, *Human Communities*, Free Press, 1952.

[25] Louis Wirth, "Urbanism as a Way of Life," *Amer. J. Sociol.*, 44 (1938), 1-24.

[26] Robert Redfield, *The Folk Culture of Yucatan*, University of Chicago Press, 1941.

[27] Amos H. Hawley, *Human Ecology*, Ronald Press, 1950. Although Hawley has shown much more sophistication than earlier writers who employed the biotic framework, he has not resolved the dilemmas inherent in this approach.

ment of specific types of ecological patterns. Unfortunately these problems have not been explored cross-culturally.

Let us examine more specifically Wirth's position that the impact
of the urban community—characterized by size, density, and heterogeneity—is the key determinant of social organization and behavior.[28]
(Redfield postulates heterogeneity and lack of isolation as the key characteristics of the city.[29]) To Wirth, urbanism as a way of life was
typified by secularization, secondary-group associations, increased seg-
mentation of roles, and poorly defined norms. The city was for him a
center of fluidity and of tenuous social relationships. He contrasted
urban centers with rural or folk communities and regarded the traits
developing in the urban milieu as necessary concomitants of a city's
growth, especially with respect to size and density. Wirth and his fol-
lowers considered the "effects" of urban development as distinct and independent from the consequences of cultural values or industrialization,
which they held constant. Ideally, then, all cities, both historical and
contemporary, should display the aforementioned characteristics.

A number of limitations to this approach can be discerned. Some of
these have been noted, explicitly or implicitly, by Axelrod[30] and
Whyte,[31] among others, on the basis of their research in American cities.
One of their primary criticisms of Wirth and others of the Chicago
school is that they have exaggerated, even for the United States, the
degree of secularization and disorganization that supposedly typifies
urban communities. Actually, these critics claim, cities are more highly
organized than they have been assumed to be; many informal networks
of social relationships exist that were overlooked by such early writers as
Zorbaugh.[32] Wirth's failure to see the implications of the bureaucratization of contemporary urban life is also pertinent. His theory is hardly
congruent with the points Whyte sets forth in *The Organization Man*.[33]

[28] Wirth, *loc. cit.*

[29] Redfield, *op. cit.*, p. 344.

[30] Morris Axelrod, "Urban Structure and Social Participation," *Amer.
Sociol. Rev.*, 21 (1956), 13-18.

[31] William F. Whyte, *Street Corner Society*, University of Chicago Press,
1943.

[32] Harvey W. Zorbaugh, *The Gold Coast and the Slum*, University of
Chicago Press, 1929.

[33] William H. Whyte, Jr., *The Organization Man*, Simon and Schuster,
1956.

Clearly, Wirth's writings reflect the ethos of the 1920's and 1930's, a period when many American intellectuals, including sociologists, were attempting to cope with the social strains that had arisen—those of culture conflict due to immigration and, later, those resulting from the Great Depression. The limitations of a gross preoccupation with disorganization are all the more apparent when we attempt to apply the Wirth frame of reference to other cultures. Oscar Lewis has sought to document empirically the point that urbanization in Mexico City is not necessarily accompanied by destruction of the social and moral order.[34] And, indeed, most studies of preindustrial cities support the contention that Wirth and Redfield have overstated their case, that city life can in fact be highly organized.[35]

Another weakness of this orientation, apparent in Redfield's early writings on folk-urban theory [36] as well as in some of the works of other sociologists who have adopted this frame of reference, involves the logic of comparison. Redfield has considered the folk, or primitive, society to be functionally a closed system.[37] The urban community, on the other hand, is only a partial system—it can not survive without the hinterland that supplies it with food and raw materials. In effect, Redfield and other sociologists, by contrasting folk societies with urban communities, have been comparing a whole with a part, a questionable procedure at best. Logically, comparison should be made between folk and urban societies or between rural and urban communities. Such a category as "urban society" may require still further breakdown, inasmuch as some rural-urban differences appear to be valid only for specific types of societies—*e.g.*, for either industrial or preindustrial civilizations. Thus in preindustrial (or feudal) societies, the familial and religious organizations in their most highly developed and integrated forms are urban rather than rural,[38] a fact that contravenes many generalizations

[34] Oscar Lewis, "Urbanization Without Breakdown: A Case Study," *Sci. Mon.*, 75 (1952), 31-41.

[35] Some of these data have been summarized in Gideon Sjoberg, "The Preindustrial City," *Amer. J. Sociol.*, 60 (1955), 438-45.

[36] Redfield, *op. cit.*

[37] Robert Redfield, "The Folk Society," *Amer. J. Sociol.*, 52 (1947), 293-308.

[38] Sjoberg, *loc. cit.*

based solely upon research in the United States. Even in India today rural-urban differences in family size appear to contradict the generalizations set forth in standard textbooks.[39] The fact is that sociologists need to give much more attention to defining the precise limits of their generalizations concerning rural-urban phenomena.

Another criticism concerns the failure of Wirth and sociologists of like mind to recognize that in some contexts the city is influenced by the total sociocultural system of which it is a part and thus is a dependent variable. This failure to view the city as a subsystem has led these writers to overlook some highly significant patterns. They often do not realize that cities may be created purposively or that their ecological or social norms can be determined by institutional structures external to any particular community. Sociologists have perhaps been overly influenced by writers such as Pirenne,[40] who emphasized the social and political independence of the medieval European city, a pattern which seems somewhat unrealistic for that period, even in Western Europe. Some urban centers have historically been politically autonomous, but typically cities, certainly contemporary ones, must be viewed as subsystems which in many ways can be controlled by extracommunity factors (a point developed below in our discussion of social power as the independent variable).

We have been critical of the formulations that consider the city as the key independent variable. Of what value, then, is such an orientation for comparative study? Even though sociologists, in attempting to establish the specific "correlates" of city life, have generalized all too freely from the American scene, we can not summarily reject their approach. For, regardless of the cultural system, urban and rural communities *do* diverge. Throughout history, the city, as the focal point of communication, has been the center for important types of change, not the least of which are those stemming from formalized creative intellectual activity. Indeed, the city seems to provide the necessary conditions for certain kinds of change, including various forms of collective behavior. The positions of Wirth and Redfield are meritorious for their emphasis on the city as a positive force in social change, but the precise role of

[39] K. M. Kapadia, "Rural Family Patterns: A Study in Urban-Rural Relations," *Sociol. Bull.*, 5 (1956), 119.

[40] Henri Pirenne, *Medieval Cities*, Princeton University Press, 1925.

the urban community in this process awaits clearer formulation.[41] More-over, to counterbalance an overemphasis upon disorganization, urban sociologists who view the city as the independent variable should pay greater heed to social organization. After all, urban centers, unlike rural areas, are the focal points of political organization and power and of formal education, and cities typically are regulated by more numerous formal social controls than are rural communities. These structural cor-relates, or functional prerequisites, of urban life must be more care-fully worked out, not just for cities in general but also for those in specific types of societies. Only then will the theoretical approach which considers the city as the key independent variable advance sufficiently to prove useful in comparative urban research. Thus one of the most urgent requirements in urban sociology is a reformulation of the theo-retical approach that takes the city as the independent variable.

Cultural Values as the Key Variable.   A second theoretical per-spective, one that has clashed with the orientation discussed above, seeks to explain urban social and ecological organization in terms of cultural values. A number of sociologists have contributed to the development of this approach. The recent work of Kolb is especially pertinent here.[42] Firey's *Land Use in Central Boston*,[43] the first major effort to analyze the role of values in a city's ecological organization, gave this theoretical orientation perhaps its greatest impetus. Certainly the book has gen-erated a good deal of controversy, despite the fact that social scientists have amassed impressive amounts of data implicitly documenting the point that "value orientations" are a crucial variable in determining a community's land-use patterns. Both Dickinson's *The West European City*[44] and von Grunebaum's discursive essay on Muslim cities[45] rein-

[41] Some progress is being made in this area—*e.g.*, Bert F. Hoselitz, "The Role of Cities in the Economic Growth of Underdeveloped Countries," *J. Polit. Econ.*, 61 (1953), 195-208.

[42] William L. Kolb, "The Social Structure and Function of Cities," *Econ. Devel. and cult. Change*, 3 (1954), 30-46.

[43] Walter Firey, *Land Use in Central Boston*, Harvard University Press, 1947.

[44] Robert E. Dickinson, *The West European City*, Routledge and Kegan Paul, 1951.

[45] G. E. von Grunebaum, *Islam*, American Anthropological Association, Memoir No. 81, 1955, Chap. 8.

force Firey's thesis. As a matter of fact, traditional Muslim cities are particularly revealing for the unique manner in which the religious values order the temporal activities of urban life. For one thing, at regular intervals during the day, the muezzin calls the faithful to prayer, and this to a degree sets the pace for other daily activities. Furthermore, during the month-long ceremony of Ramadan (or Ramazan), people adjust their activities to the religious restrictions that impose strict fasting from sunrise to sunset. Many of the ordinary daily pursuits now take place at night, and various economic enterprises necessarily undergo some curtailment. As suggested earlier, many urban ecologists, particularly those who deny the relevance of values in ecology, have overlooked much comparative data.

Values not only have relevance for land use but also determine in part whether urban centers will arise at all and, once established, whether they will flourish. With respect to the growth of cities, some social orders appear to be more permissive than others. Here Weber's concern with the function of religious values in the development of business enterprise [46] has some indirect implications for urban sociology. Values can also influence a city's size, heterogeneity, and density—key characteristics in most definitions of the city, and the very traits Wirth considered central to the characterization of the city. On this point a recent article by William Whyte [47] is most provocative. Whyte's thesis is that cultural values appear to be responsible for the fact that some people re-establish residence in American urban areas after they have lived for a time in the suburbs, a pattern that affects the size and density of cities. Whyte also treats the implications for urban ecology of the values held by American city planners. In light of the extensive empirical data, it is difficult to understand the objections that have been voiced concerning the cultural approach to ecology.[48] In fact, more systematic

[46] Max Weber, *The Protestant Ethic and the Spirit of Capitalism*, George Allen and Unwin, 1930. *Cf.* Robert N. Bellah, *Tokugawa Religion*, Free Press, 1957.

[47] William H. Whyte, Jr., "Are Cities Un-American?" *Fortune*, 56 (1957), 123-27+.

[48] For the effect of cultural values on planning in other societies, see the relevant articles in *Town Planning Review* and *Urbanisme*. Note, specifically for Poland, Georges Penchenier, "Urbanism: The Psychological Factor," *Landscape*, 5 (1955), 12-18.

studies are needed to point up the implications of values for urban ecology and demography.

Certainly, there can be little quarrel with the notion that values are a critical independent variable in accounting for the differences among urban social structures—*e.g.*, familial, religious, and educational—in various cultures throughout the world. But the precise relationships between values and social structure or between values and ecology in complex societies are most difficult to pinpoint.[49] In industrial-urban orders particularly, the number of truly shared values may be few indeed. Shils [50] has observed that in our society a tenuous relationship exists between the action patterns of numerous individuals and subgroups and the more abstract value system. It is questionable procedure, therefore, to assume any direct correspondence between values and the social or ecological structure of urban centers. The nature of this relationship can be determined only through more detailed theoretical and empirical study on a cross-cultural basis.

Another limitation of this approach is that mere "historicism" may well result from undue emphasis on cultural values. Cultural values as an independent variable are most meaningful when invariant reference points are employed to gauge their impact. Parsons' pattern-variable schema—an elaborate attempt to work out a set of universal reference points—has, despite its limitations, considerable relevance for the comparative study of urban social structure.[51] And sociologists can (and must) isolate still other universal categories that ideally hold for all cities or for special types of cities—*e.g.*, industrial ones. We can then determine how varying cultural values create deviations in these ideal patterns and, in turn, the effect of diverse values on urban life. To a degree, this procedure has been followed in some ecological studies which have demonstrated that certain ideal arrangements that presume the complete dominance of technological or economic factors are distorted by cultural values. The point is that the perspective which gives

[49] In a controversial fashion, E. R. Leach, *Political Systems of Highland Burma*, London: G. Bell and Sons, 1954, challenges the notion that there is any direct tie between cultural values and social structure, even for preliterate societies.

[50] Edward Shils, "Primordial, Personal, Sacred and Civil Ties," *Brit. J. Sociol.*, 8 (1957), 130-45.

[51] Kolb, *loc. cit.*, attempts to apply the pattern-variable schema to the analysis of urban social structure.

pre-eminence to cultural values is not necessarily at odds with the Wirth or Redfield approach or with the technological orientation discussed below, for ideally these latter theoretical perspectives should establish invariant reference points that can be used to "measure" the impact of values upon urban ecology and social structure. Unfortunately, the inter-relationships between these approaches are often not even recognized.

Technology as the Key Variable. A third theoretical perspective in urban sociology conceives of technology as the key variable; here industrialization—that system of production utilizing inanimate sources of energy—is considered a special type of technology. Among sociologists, Ogburn and Hawley in particular have espoused this approach. However, some of the time-honored generalizations in ecology concerning the impact of technology upon the spatial and temporal patterns of cities may not be universal, as the proponents of this view have assumed. Certainly one hesitates to move as far as Ogburn in stating ". . . the placement of city populations, residences, and places of work is singularly a function of local transportation as cities themselves are the creation of long-distance transportation . . ." [52] So, too, Hawley's statement that "The scatter of population about urban centers is a *direct response* to the increased ease of movement" [53] requires qualification. As we suggested above, values other than strictly economic ones can cause distortions in the "ideal patterns" that supposedly should result from the expansion of industrialization. The Dotsons' studies in Mexico,[54] some works on French cities,[55] and Gist's survey of Bangalore, India,[56] indicate that in these areas the suburbanization process has been slow; it has not followed the patterns in American society upon which so many sociologists base their generalizations. Even though certainly some of the means of achieving greater suburbanization are available, many persons prefer to maintain residence in the city—especially in the central area—historically a source of high prestige. These remarks are

[52] William F. Ogburn, "Inventions of Local Transportation and the Patterns of Cities," in Hatt and Reiss, *op. cit.*, p. 281.

[53] Hawley, *op. cit.*, p. 421. Italics supplied.

[54] Floyd Dotson and Lillian Ota Dotson, "Ecological Trends in the City of Guadalajara, Mexico," *Soc. Forces*, 32 (1954), 367-74.

[55] Pierre George *et al.*, *Études sur la Banlieue de Paris*, Paris: Librairie Armand Colin, 1950, Chap. 1.

[56] Gist, *loc. cit.*

not intended to minimize the role of technology in urban ecology; that it is a most significant variable can readily be perceived from a comparison of industrial and preindustrial cities.[57] However, the cross-cultural patterns that arise with the advance of technology, especially industrialization, have not been carefully delineated.

Determining the implications of the technological variable for urban social structure is an even more complex task. A number of problems demand investigation. One involves the differential impact of industrial-urbanization on folk and on feudal social systems. Folk orders like those in Africa, which lack a historical tradition and a well-defined literate elite such as exist in feudal societies (preindustrial civilizations), appear to have considerably less potential than the latter for resisting the effects of industrial-urbanism upon numerous facets of the social structure. The literate elite in feudal orders can at times be a potent force in maintaining a firm link with the past. Another task is to examine the influence of varying levels of technology upon the social patterns of cities. Considerable evidence points to a rather marked distinction between preindustrial and industrial-urban communities with respect to social organization—family, religion, economic life, etc.[58] Even more specifically, we might consider the differential effects of various types, or stages, of industrialization *per se* upon the structure of cities.

The aforementioned issues are related in part to a highly significant question: What kinds of social structure are common to all industrial-urban communities or societies? The structural-functionalists, in their efforts to delineate these structural prerequisites (or what are variously termed structural imperatives, requirements, or necessary conditions), have helped to set the stage for the resolution of this problem. To be sure, some sociologists take issue with certain of the assumptions of structural-functional theory and prefer to speak only of "correlates" of industrial-urbanism.[59] Be that as it may, if we are to see contemporary

[57] Sjoberg, *loc. cit.*

[58] *Ibid.*

[59] There have been several critical essays on structural-functionalism, by Merton, Bredemeier, Barber, and Nagel, among others. We shall not review the controversial aspects of this theory here, except as they relate directly to industrial-urbanization (although obviously our arguments have bearing upon structural-functional theory in general).

American cities in proper perspective, we must attempt to isolate the structural patterns common to all industrial-urban communities or societies. Only then can we determine the extent to which our own patterns are typical of other industrial-urban orders.

Most efforts to establish the structural requirements of an industrial-urban order (which implicitly compare it with the traditional pre-industrial city or with the feudal society of which this city is a part) have cited the need for a large-scale rational economic organization, a fluid class system in which achievement rather than ascription is emphasized, a loosely organized conjugal family system, mass education that stresses science and technology, and extensive mass communication.[60] At the present state of our knowledge, all of these seem essential. But certain difficulties are still to be resolved.

One issue stems, as have problems in other theoretical schemes, from the fact that sociologists may be generalizing all too freely from the United States. The American value orientation appears to accentuate particular traits—*e.g.,* those relating to the conjugal family—in a manner not duplicated in other industrial-urban orders. Greater caution must be exercised in forming generalizations, and these should be documented empirically rather than left to theoretical solution.

Secondly, certain structural requirements of industrial-urbanism, particularly in the areas of religion, power, and ecology, have never been properly investigated. The religious systems associated with industrial-urban communities or societies seem to vary more widely among cultures than other forms of social organization.[61] But what are the limits of this variation? Evidence suggests that religious systems, such as Protestantism, that embrace values which can be divorced from

[60] For analyses of the structural requirements of industrial-urban systems, see, for example, Marion Levy, "Some Sources of the Vulnerability of the Structures of Relatively Nonindustrialized Societies to Those of Highly Industrialized Societies," in Bert F. Hoselitz (ed.), *The Progress of Underdeveloped Areas,* University of Chicago Press, 1952, pp. 113-25; Kingsley Davis, "Social and Demographic Aspects of Economic Development in India," in Simon Kuznets *et al.* (eds.), *Economic Growth: Brazil, India, Japan,* Duke University Press, 1955, pp. 293 ff.

[61] Pertinent here are some of the views of Allan W. Eister, "Religious Institutions in Complex Societies: Difficulties in the Theoretic Specification of Functions," *Amer. sociol. Rev.,* 22 (1957), 387-91, although he neglects comparative data relating to complex societies.

many segments of the social structure are more congruent with industrial-urbanization than religious systems that are clearly dependent for their survival upon a specific type of social structure. This point merits considerable investigation. Moreover, what are the relationships among nationalism, religion, and industrial-urbanization? Although the advent of industrial-urbanism is usually associated with destruction of the traditional religious system, it is also connected with the rise of nationalism and other "secular religions." [62] The structures which support nationalism perform many of the functions of traditional religious systems, especially that concerned with societal integration. In fact, in a number of societies in the early stages of industrialization—*e.g.*, modern Burma—the traditional religious system has become fused with nationalism; this pattern is typical of cities, not of the countryside. Moreover, in the Soviet Union, a rather highly industrial-urbanized system, the traditional religious patterns have to a very great extent been destroyed and replaced by nationalism, coalesced with the new political organization. Thus we must pose the question: What type of religious system is functionally necessary to sustain industrial-urbanism, and to what extent do the structures supporting nationalism serve as a substitute in this situation? And can nationalism or other "secular religions" (such as science, among intellectuals) prove successful over long periods as an integrative force in industrial-urban systems? The answer to this should tell us something about the long-run stability of industrial-urban communities.

A third difficulty in delineating the requirements of industrial-urbanism resides in the fact that in some aspects of social structure there are major divergencies between mature industrial-urban systems and those that are becoming industrialized. Although industrial-urbanization has not yet reached its peak in any society, it seems feasible, for analytical purposes, to consider these two systems separately. The divergent power structures in these societies justify such a dichotomy. It appears that an authoritarian state is more likely to flourish in a social order that is seeking to industrialize and urbanize than in one that has already attained this goal. A feudal society that is attempting to industrialize has within it many conflicting forces; some of the traditional

---

[62] Edwin O. Reischauer, *Wanted: An Asian Policy*, Knopf, 1955, argues that nationalism is functionally necessary to the development of industrialization (and, implicitly, urbanization on a large scale) in Asia.

elements in the social system may actually be quite antagonistic to industrialization. And such a society may labor under the burden of a rapidly expanding population. If it is to marshall its human and natural resources effectively to overcome these obstacles, it may have to develop a powerful state organization. But once a high degree of industrial-urbanization has been achieved, it is doubtful that a small elite can maintain a monopoly of power in a society. This point has recently been touched upon by Djilas,[63] as well as other writers in the popular press. Data indirectly support the contention that, in progressively maturing industrial-urban communities or societies, power tends to become dispersed. Among other factors, the acquisition of increased specialized knowledge by members of the lower ranks of the social hierarchy serves to heighten the importance of these persons and, consequently, their position of power. The increase in such specialists as scientists and industrial managers accentuates this process. It appears that in eastern Europe today increased industrial-urbanism is forcing a realignment in the power structure. From a different perspective, this discussion has relevance for South Africa. It is questionable whether the power elite, the Afrikaner group, can maintain its authoritarian position in the face of expanding industrial-urbanization. For as additional segments of the Native, or Bantu, population acquire more formal education and technical skills, the rigid segregation policy known as apartheid will be more difficult to sustain.[64] This diffusion of power will be heightened by the fact that, because of the labor shortage in South Africa, Bantus must be recruited into skilled occupations if industrial-urbanism is to advance.

Fourthly, in seeking to assess the structural requirements of industrial-urban centers or societies, sociologists must also recognize that certain of these imperatives may be in conflict with others. Actually, many structural-functionalists have exaggerated the degree of harmony existing in social systems. Even a mature industrial-urban order experiences conflicts—*e.g.*, between the "need" for large-scale, rational

---

[63] Milovan Djilas, *The New Class*, Praeger, 1957, *passim*. It is noteworthy that some newspaper columnists—*e.g.*, Joseph Alsop—have displayed greater insight concerning this subject than have sociologists.

[64] See, for example, Leo Kuper, *Passive Resistance in South Africa*, London: Jonathan Cape, 1956, pp. 64*ff.*; and Ellen Hellmann, *Racial Laws versus Economic and Social Forces*, Johannesburg, South African Institute of Race Relations, 1955.

bureaucracies with well-defined hierarchical arrangements and the "need" for a fluid class system and a more equitable distribution of power. Although such bureaucracies may indeed ensure a degree of fluidity in the class structure by selecting personnel primarily on the basis of universalistic criteria, the very fact that hierarchical arrangements (including a well-defined managerial group) obtain is in conflict with the demands for egalitarianism in industrial-urban systems. Even within a bureaucratic organization, a delicate balance must be maintained between the employment of practices that tend toward universalism and those that are more particularistic. This phenomenon helps to account for some of the points of disagreement in sociological literature, for certain writers emphasize the essentiality of certain types of stratification or centralization of power, while others give prominence to the demands for egalitarianism. Although the latter are highly significant in industrial-urban orders, especially as these societies are compared to preindustrial civilizations, some stratification is also necessary. We need much more research and theorizing concerning the contradictory functional requirements of industrial-urban systems over the world, not only in the spheres of stratification and power, but in areas such as family or religious life as well.

Fifthly, there are difficulties in ascertaining the structural requirements, or correlates, of industrial-urban societies that can be traced to sociologists' preoccupation with "closed systems." Consider, for example, the resource base necessary to sustain an industrial-urban order.[65] It is customary in sociological analysis to take nation-state systems as working units. But a frequent error is to assume that these systems function in isolation. Japan and England are prime illustrations of modern social orders that lack in their home territory a sufficient quantity of the resources necessary to sustain a high level of industrial-urbanism. In order to construct a predominantly urban society, these nations have utilized political power to ensure access to raw materials and to establish markets for their finished products. If we accept Barclay's analysis,[66] we can discern how Japan prior to World War II rather consciously employed Taiwan as a tool for establishing and fortifying industrial-

[65] Norton Ginsburg, "Natural Resources and Economic Development," *Annals of the Association of American Geographers, 47* (1957), 197-212.

[66] George W. Barclay, *Colonial Development and Population in Taiwan,* Princeton University Press, 1954, Chap. 2.

urbanism in the homeland. The fact is that although what constitutes "resources" is a function of technology and culture, at any given time these are a scarce commodity and the nation that has access to them is in an advantageous position. Concomitantly, as Japan and England have relinquished control over much of their former resource base, they have lost some of their potential for industrializing and urbanizing. Their industrial-urban centers are now more vulnerable to external decisions— *e.g.*, those by other nations to curtail trade in raw materials and food, on which the stable functioning of city life depends. Definite structural relationships exist between industrial-urbanization and the spatial distribution of a society, and even between industrial-urbanization and "imperialism." Investigation of these and similar correlates of industrial-urban communities or societies can be facilitated if sociologists will avoid viewing social systems as closed. Although some sociologists will contend that interest in problems of this kind is external to the urban field, I would argue to the contrary.

Power as the Key Variable. A fourth frame of reference is the special-interest approach, in which social power is the independent variable. This approach was recently introduced into urban ecology by William Form to explain urban land-use patterns.[67] But it requires elaboration, for Form concentrated upon local community patterns and failed to perceive the value of this scheme for analyzing the growth of cities and urban social organization in general.[68] Moreover, this perspective can be strengthened by relating it to recent formulations in game theory.[69]

The power, or special-interest, approach can be effectively employed on several levels of analysis—local, national, and international. Local power decisions obviously have an impact upon a city's ecology and social structure. Typically, actors are able to achieve a desired goal

[67] William H. Form, "The Place of Social Structure in the Determination of Land Use: Some Implications for a Theory of Urban Ecology," *Soc. Forces*, 32 (1954), 317-23. Form's is a special-interest or power approach, but this necessitates an understanding of social structure, for interest-groups, to be effective, must be organized.

[68] Gideon Sjoberg, "Urban Community Theory and Research: A Partial Evaluation," *Amer. J. Econ. Sociol.*, 14 (1955), 199-206.

[69] R. Duncan Luce and Howard Raiffa, *Games and Decisions*, John Wiley, 1957.

only if they possess the necessary political power. Thus, for example, if a group is to convert a graveyard into a business district or a residential area into a commercial area, it must have sufficient power to overrule the opposition.

A city's ecological and social structure can also be affected by power decisions on the national level. Numerous empirical instances demonstrate how this pattern obtains not only in the United States but in other societies as well. The local ecological patterns of a number of South African cities have been modified as a result of decisions formulated by the national government. There are first of all the pass laws which restrict the movement of Natives, or Bantus, into and within the city. Moreover, in the Union of South Africa large numbers of Natives have in recent years been forcibly evicted from areas near the center of such cities as Johannesburg and relocated in newly created communities quite distant from their place of employment. These and similar acts have been part of a program to reinforce the policy of apartheid, a means by which the European element has sought to maintain its position of dominance.[70] Social planning on the societal level also has repercussions for urban location and growth. In the Soviet Union the course of industrial· urbanization has been strongly influenced by the national government's exercise of power. A number of cities owe their existence to purposive governmental planning. Moreover, the Communist leadership has purposively sought to destroy the traditional peasant way of life as a means of stimulating industrialization and urbanization.[71] The collectivization of farms has made possible the industrialization of agriculture, which in turn has driven numerous peasants no longer needed on the farms into the urban labor force. Collectivization also makes possible more effective governmental controls over the "agricultural surplus" required to support the expanding populace. Consideration of these developments within the power or special-interest frame of reference seems legitimate and necessary.

National power decisions, furthermore, have clear consequences

[70] For background material on recent laws, see Eric A. Walker, *A History of South Africa*, 3rd ed., London: Longmans, Green, 1957. Also "Johannesburg Pushes Apartheid Evacuations," *Christian Science Monitor*, Aug. 29, 1956, p. 6.

[71] Barrington Moore, Jr., *Terror and Progress: USSR*, Harvard University Press, 1954, Chaps. 2, 3.

for the social structure of local urban communities. The U.S. Supreme Court decision relative to segregation in public schools is a case in point. It can hardly be doubted that this action has modified the social structure of many cities. Its effects were indirectly, though dramatically, portrayed in the "Little Rock incident," in which the federal government (as well as the state government of Arkansas) actively intervened in the functioning of this community. Pertinent also are patterns in other societies. In the Soviet Union, for example, the extracommunity governmental organization has, since the Revolution, effected numerous revisions in familial, religious, educational, and economic arrangements on the local level. For example, Khrushchev's decisions leading to a redistribution of bureaucratic power on the national level undoubtedly have modified some of the power alignments in urban centers as well. Unfortunately, sociologists know little about the interplay between the local community and the extracommunity organization.[72]

In the international realm, the motivation for industrial-urbanization in former preindustrial civilizations has stemmed in large degree from the desire of the ruling elite to maintain its power position as well as to enhance its country's role on the world scene. Nowadays social power on the world scene is predicated upon the possession of a large industrial-urban base. Because of external considerations, segments of the elite seek to override the resistances to change that inhere in the traditional social structure. Witness the situation in Japan, where the desire of many members of the ruling group for a place in the global power configuration was a clear-cut impetus to urbanize. In a somewhat similar manner, the struggles for power in the "cold war" of the post-World War II era have accelerated the process of industrial-urbanism in many countries. Of course, total war can result in massive changes in urban social and ecological structures. Moreover, the great industrial powers can, through a variety of policies, stimulate or inhibit urban growth in many "underdeveloped" areas. These issues, which have considerable relevance for the sociology of urban life, remain relatively unexplored.

We have attempted to present an overview of four of the dominant

[72] More studies are needed such as Roland J. Pellegrin and Charles H. Coates, "Absentee-Owned Corporations and Community Power," *Amer. J. Sociol.*, 61 (1956), 413-19, and the study in England by Harold Orlans, *Stevenage*, Routledge and Kegan Paul, 1952.

theoretical orientations (they can hardly be termed full-fledged theories) in the field of urban sociology. What can we conclude? First, a greater effort must be made to clarify the implications of taking either the city, cultural values, technology, or power as the independent variable in attempts to explain certain facets of urban ecology or social structure. It appears that each of these variables can be utilized in several ways and still prove useful. Secondly, the theoretical schemes in question can be worked out satisfactorily only if urban sociologists will pay greater heed to general sociological theory. The emphasis has been upon "fact gathering" to the neglect of broader theoretical issues. Because of this concern with particulars, many cross-cultural problems have been slighted. To isolate similar patterns among different cultures, urban sociologists must operate on a rather abstract level of analysis. Thirdly, the relationships among these four variables (as well as others that might be added) need to be explored; some of these relationships have been suggested here. Actually, the urban social system cannot be understood without considering all these variables. Even here problems arise, for these variables are not of the same "order." Those such as technology and the city appear to differ in some fundamental respects from those of cultural values and power. Nevertheless, a consistent general theory of urbanism, though perhaps unattainable, should be the goal toward which we strive.

Testing Hypotheses in a Comparative Setting

But the question arises: What next? How are urban sociologists to test these theoretical orientations, or hypotheses derived from them, on a comparative basis? Continued urban research in world societies is obviously required. Here, too, the highly empirical nature of much of contemporary urban sociology and the rigorous procedures typically employed in data collection and analysis, though laudable and eminently worthwhile, intensify the problems that already inhere in comparative study. The impediments to effective comparative research are such that a rigorous testing of many hypotheses will in all likelihood not be accomplished to the satisfaction of the strict empiricists in the field.

A rather harsh fact is that a number of research techniques currently in favor in urban sociology are not readily exportable to other cultural settings, since they have been developed to fit a constellation of traits many of which are unique to American cities. Warner's I.S.C.

scale [73] is a case in point. The occupational category therein can be used cross-culturally to evaluate social status or class position, but the categories for income, house type, and dwelling area may have to be sharply modified or even eliminated if the index is to portray realistically the status systems of cities in other cultures (assuming in the first instance that the data are available). For example, at least one writer has observed that dwelling area and, by implication, housing are poor indexes of status in contemporary Russian cities.[74] Similarly, the various segregation indexes, the Shevky-Williams-Bell technique, and perhaps even the Queen and Carpenter urbanism index—all of which have gained enthusiastic approval in many quarters—would require marked alterations before they could be applied, and in some societies they could not be employed at all. Although these procedures have also been targets of criticism, their most obvious defect—their general culture-boundedness—has been overlooked by those sociologists whose perspective ends at the continental shore line. Many of these devices presuppose methods of data-gathering—*e.g.*, the use of census tracts—not necessarily employed in other societies. This is not to deny the utility of these research tools for special purposes, but urban sociologists must be mindful of their limitations for comparative study. Certainly these techniques and procedures must not be allowed to become ends in themselves.

The second point, an extension of the above, is that urban sociologists often must rely upon data collected by persons outside the field, particularly government administrators. As indicated earlier, industrial-urban societies, in order to plan for their development and ensure the maintenance of their organization, must amass various types of data. American urban sociologists have at their disposal a vast body of materials collected by the U.S. Bureau of the Census and by numerous other governmental and private agencies on the local, state, and national levels. Such indispensable information could not be assembled solely by sociologists, with their limited numbers and scanty resources. When

[73] W. Lloyd Warner *et al., Social Class in America: A Manual for Procedure for the Measurement of Social Status*, Science Research Associates, 1949.

[74] Robert A. Feldmesser, "Social Status and Access to Higher Education: A Comparison of the United States and the Soviet Union," *Harvard educ. Rev.*, 27 (1957), 98.

sociologists require data from other cultures, they are still more dependent upon the services of nonsociologists, notably bureaucrats. And these bureaucrats typically do not seek data with an eye to gaining scientifically generalizable information. Instead, they are concerned with providing materials that will help to resolve certain issues confronting their own social system. Even much of the research accomplished by social scientists themselves has been geared to the special requirements of bureaucratic organizations or special-interest groups. Shryock has discussed the pressures exerted on the U.S. Bureau of the Census in its creation of classification schemes such as Standard Metropolitan Areas.[75] Chambers of Commerce vie to have their cities included in the classification, to the extent that the "scientific validity" of this concept may be threatened. On a global scale, the obstacles to attaining comparable empirical data are compounded greatly by a multitude of social pressures. That considerable overlapping does exist—for example, in the types of information obtained from censuses in different social orders—can often be attributed to the fact that industrial-urban societies face similar problems, not necessarily to any special efforts to coordinate the techniques and categories employed in data collection. Although such coordination is greatly to be desired, in actual practice it is most difficult to attain on any broad scale.

A third problem concerns the barriers, formal and informal, to the collection and diffusion of many types of social data. Actually, a number of urban communities in other cultures are closed to first-hand investigation by sociologists, restricting the use, for example, of random-sampling techniques within and among societies. Even in the United States, sociologists cannot probe into all facets of urban life with impunity. Instead they must often rely upon evidence of an indirect nature. Because social-research data can be used to challenge the power structure of a social order, certain areas are "off limits" to social scientists. Moreover, all societies limit the diffusion of data, some more than others. The sensitive sectors vary with the society and the time period, but their existence makes comparative research extremely difficult to formalize.

All this suggests the need for a more realistic approach to hypothesis-testing. Some adaptations in the methodology of scientific inquiry

[75] Henry S. Shryock, Jr., "The Natural History of Standard Metropolitan Areas," *Amer. J. Sociol.*, 63 (1957), 163-70.

as now practiced seem essential. To be sure, by ingenious use of census data from many societies, Kingsley Davis and his associates have examined many aspects of world urbanization, and Inkeles and Rossi [76] have advanced our understanding of the comparative ranking of occupations in various industrial-urban societies by piecing together existing materials on this subject. However, we must recognize the limitations of cross-cultural studies of this kind as well as the fact that even these projects cannot be pursued in many areas. The methodology of comparative inquiry requires rethinking, and urban sociologists can assist in resolving some of the major difficulties. For example, they might purposively select "negative cases": cities or urban societies that can be studied by means of rigorous research designs and that may disprove or set limits to existing hypotheses. And such tools as the ideal or constructed type are more functional than is at times supposed.

We have here surveyed some of the problematics of comparative urban sociology. These issues may loom discouragingly large, and perhaps only partial solutions are possible. Often we may have to be satisfied with "plausible hypotheses" indirectly supported by empirical data. Yet the advantages accruing from utilization of a comparative point of view are manifold. Urban ecological and social structure in America cannot be understood without recourse to comparative sociology. Only through a comparative approach can we separate the general from the particular. Granted that many sociologists must necessarily align themselves with bureaucratic organizations whose concern is the resolution of day-by-day problems in American society, and granted that the major share of research funds will continue to flow in this direction; sociologists nevertheless cannot lose sight of the more general questions implied in the study of urban life. The world is rapidly urbanizing, and knowledge of this process and of the probable end result is vital to science and to society.

[76] Alex Inkeles and Peter H. Rossi, "National Comparisons of Occupational Prestige," *Amer. J. Sociol.*, 61 (1956), 329-39.

16
Trends in
Rural
Sociology

C. ARNOLD ANDERSON
University of Chicago

Rural sociology is one of the oldest branches of
sociology in this country; indeed, it has strong claims to being the senior
branch. This field has been well received by the public, which has a
sentimental attachment to traditional rural life, and during the last
quarter-century there has been fiscal support by Congress. As measured
by formally allocated research time and personnel, rural sociologists
have enjoyed a distinctively favorable position. Unfortunately, this support has entailed administrative and cultural restrictions that have
hampered professional development of the field. Scholarly output has
not improved in quality or in adaptation to the changing society com-
mensurate with this institutionalized recognition. Indeed, the interests
of rural sociologists have changed little during the present century, a
century that has seen major reorientations in other areas of sociology.

The work of rural sociologists may be assessed in terms of four
types of contribution: (1) understanding of the stable and changing
aspects of rural society, (2) conceptual analysis and theoretical constructs of broader application, (3) innovations in research methods, and
(4) assistance in formulating public policy for rural life.[1]

[1] There have been innumerable evaluations of rural sociology by committees and in presidential addresses. For example: *Rural Sociological Adult*

Articulation of rural with general sociology has weakened during the past generation, while other specialties have emerged in response to the growing heterogeneity of American society. The fading of rural-urban distinctions should have brought closer ties. A persisting rural provincialism in both training and personal outlook has handicapped the professional maturation of rural sociologists, who at the same time share most of the defects of other sociologists. On the other hand, rural sociology has avoided some blind alleys because it has remained in close touch with the sector of society in which it is interested. All the more surprising, then, are the gaps in the analysis of problems in the rural domain and the meagerness of contributions to public policy. Evaluation of these developments and of professional traits is an exercise in the sociology of knowledge in which particular attention must be given to the conditions of recruitment and operation imposed by the structure of the agricultural colleges.

The Poverty of Theoretical and Methodological Contributions

An adequate perspective for examining the performance of rural sociology presupposes a parallel scrutiny of general sociology, for absolute judgments are puerile. So broad a discussion would carry us beyond the limits of this paper, which must of necessity be short, assertive, and partial.

During the early years of this century, rural sociology was a major

Education in the United States, Social Science Research Council, n.d.; *The Field of Research in Rural Sociology*, U. S. Department of Agriculture, 1938; C. E. Lively, "Rural Sociology as Applied Science," *Rural Sociol.*, 8 (1943), 331-42; L. Nelson, "Rural Sociology: Dimensions and Horizons," *Rural Sociol.*, 10 (1945), 131-35; R. M. Williams, Jr., "Review of Current Research in Rural Sociology," *Rural Sociol.*, 11 (1946), 103-14; W. A. Anderson, "Rural Sociology as Science," *Rural Sociol.*, 12 (1947), 347-56; B. Youngblood, "Status of Rural Sociological Research in the State Agricultural Experiment Stations," *Rural Sociol.*, 14 (1949), 111-15; C. H. Hamilton, "Some Current Problems in the Development of Rural Sociology," *Rural Sociol.*, 15 (1950), 315-21; W. H. Sewell, "Needed Research in Rural Sociology," *Rural Sociol.*, 15 (1950), 115-30; M. J. Taves and N. Gross, "A Critique of Rural Sociology Research, 1950," *Rural Sociol.*, 17 (1952), 109-18; O. D. Duncan, "Rural Sociology Coming of Age," *Rural Sociol.*, 19 (1954), 1-12; N. Gross, "Review of Current Research on the Sociology of

contributor to the theoretical canon of sociology. In recent years, these contributions have diminished, and much of the work merits the impatient judgment it receives: "fact-finding." It must be emphasized, however, that other sociologists overlook most of the meritorious rural work. A generation ago the ecological measurements and concepts developed by Galpin contributed to the development of the Chicago school as well as to the general literature on the community. Rural field studies were testing grounds for several novel demographic methods. More recently, Schuler and Kaufman have demonstrated the usefulness of the "local informant" technique for the study of stratification.[2] The concepts of the rural-urban continuum and family cycle received their early formulations in rural sociology.

It is no reflection on rural sociologists that they have not been the creators of the more abstruse varieties of theory, for such work does not normally arise from the empirically oriented specialties. At the same time, one observes their failure to develop cross-societal comparisons and to push field studies—on the community, for example—toward adequate generalization. In these field studies, moreover, little use is made of the refined techniques developed by other social scientists. Some of the reasons for this reticence and a few of the steps that might be taken toward a more effective discipline will be discussed below, after a brief review of the trends in the content of rural sociology.

The Changing Focus of Rural Sociology

Rural sociologists have held steadily to their traditional task of investigating the nature of rural society and the social aspects of farm living. Contrasts between metropolitan and village or farm life will not disappear soon, and meanwhile generalizations and methods are

---

Rural Life," *Amer. sociol. Rev.*, 17 (1952), 83-90; H. F. Kaufman, "Rural Sociology, 1945–55," in H. L. Zetterberg (ed.), *Sociology in the United States of America*, Unesco, 1956; W. A. Anderson, *Bibliography of Researches in Rural Sociology*, Cornell University, 1957; T. L. Smith, "Rural Sociology: a Trend Report and Bibliography," *Current Sociol.*, 6:1 (1957); E. de S. Brunner, *The Growth of a Science: A Half-Century of Rural Sociological Research*, Harper, 1957.

[2] E. A. Schuler, "Social and Economic Status in a Louisiana Hills Community," *Rural Sociol.*, 5 (1940), 69-87; H. F. Kaufman, *Prestige Classes in a Rural Community*, Cornell University Press, 1944.

being transplanted to underdeveloped societies. Since rural life is broader than "the sociology of the farm occupation," the field is unlikely to be absorbed by industrial sociology. Moreover, since every aspect of group life is colored by generic features of rural living, other specialties (such as demography or the family) will continue to receive contributions from rural sociology.

The heterogeneous character of the activities of rural sociologists is indicated by the categories used in reporting the 1956 list of federally supported projects. Study of the diffusion of farm practices is of central interest now (with 29 projects) along with the conventional topic of demography (28). Studies of rural groups and of "social participation" remain numerous (21), followed by levels of living (16), studies of public-agency programs (9), of tenure and the labor force (9), of the community (8), of health (6), and of social security (4). This inchoate set of interests reflects the administrative organization of the agricultural college, as will be seen.

Trends in interests can be inferred from the contents of the 21 volumes of the journal *Rural Sociology*. During the 1930's and early 1940's, several topics received attention that are today less frequently emphasized: demography and migration, regionalism and ecology, the church, youth, farm tenure, ethnic groups, and levels of living. Interest in certain other topics has grown: education, suburbanization, the aged, foreign societies, health, and diffusion of technical practices. Areas of more stable interest include the community, social participation, extension work, stratification, housing, rural attitudes, the family, and research methods.

One may observe a distinct lack of interest in a few other topics that would appear to be of central importance for the study of rural society. Little attention is given to the history of rural society. Taylor's work on the history of farm organizations and Smith's examination of the morphology of rural settlements have not aroused their colleagues' interest.[3] Notably lacking, also, is research of direct value to the formulation of rural public policies.

[3] C. C. Taylor, *The Farmer's Movement: 1620–1920*, American Book, 1953; T. L. Smith, *Sociology of Rural Life*, Harper, 1940, Chaps. 10, 11. It would be rewarding to compare the activities of rural sociologists during the past two decades with the projects designed in the Social Science Research Council's "scope and method" series. The evaluations made in *The*

The Recruitment of Rural Sociologists [4]

There are several features of rural sociology that must mystify an outsider until he understands the recruitment of the men in the field. Expansion of employment opportunities has benefited from the formal and even legal recognition given rural sociology in the land-grant-college system. The conditions of employment that are set by the ethos of local administrators and faculties do much to give the field its present complexion. All in all, this privileged legal position is not an unqualified boon.

The training and accomplishments of a prospective appointee receives more than the usual scrutiny. Normally the applicant is expected to have a "rural background," for it is assumed that he cannot otherwise understand rural people. The rural-sociology department must usually share its decision about new members with the academic dean, the director of research, and the director of extension. The department head is often an agricultural economist.

Agricultural colleges have a fraternal, rural atmosphere and their staffs, including sociologists, are markedly ingrown. This land-grant culture influences the recruitment of new men.[5] It also fosters a self-defeating defensiveness against the general sociologists' scorn for the prevailingly applied character of most of the research and impels other sociologists to view the rural group as outsiders.

The temptation to make adverse judgments about rural sociology must be corrected for a particular sampling error. Experiment-station staffs have light teaching loads, and much of their time is budgeted to research. It is comparatively easy to obtain publication of research find-

---

Field of Research in Rural Sociology can be compared with the comments in this section. It may be asked also why the proposals of C. C. Zimmerman, in *Rural Sociological Adult Education in the United States*, pp. 51 f., have been so incompletely realized.

[4] An earlier report is not outdated: T. W. Schultz and L. W. Witt, *Training and Recruiting of Personnel in the Rural Social Sciences*, American Council on Education, 1941.

[5] One therefore finds rural sociologists to be "folksy," to enjoy distinctive sorts of humor, and frequently to be teetotalers. They are more friendly, and they have less of a "cultural" background, than general sociologists. These rural folkways inhibit the formation of the personal cliques that are the bane of most branches of sociology.

ings, and there is pressure to turn out bulletins that will be useful to citizens and extension teachers. As a result, most of the work comes to public attention without having been screened by editors of journals catering to the total profession.

There is, then, a circular process that holds down the quality of rural-sociology staffs. Traditional conceptions of the nature of sociology among administrators, strong in-group attitudes within the agricultural colleges, and stereotypes about the qualities essential for research among farmers all work together to perpetuate a certain type of work and of sociologist. The free-wheeling, anarchic pursuit of new ideas permitted in liberal-arts departments is discouraged in agricultural colleges.[6]

A quarter-century ago, the Social Science Research Council made an effort to overcome these handicaps by subsidizing graduate training for rural sociologists and economists. At the same time, the Council underwrote publication of several "scope and method" handbooks to improve the quality of projects. It would be only fair to say that the recipients of these awards have been the leading men in their field since that time, even though they have been unable to alter the structure of the colleges.

The Administrative Organization of Rural Sociology

Rural sociology is the most explicitly and bureaucratically structured branch of sociology. Although this quasi-legal status and the accompanying public funds have fostered quantitative expansion, the rural sociologists find themselves closely reined by the conditions of this recognition.

Experiment-station projects are numerous, but they are included on the docket of work only after review by faculty committees (often including natural scientists) and approval by administrators.[7] Few mem-

---

[6] It must be pointed out that the criticisms of this branch of sociology can be matched point for point by criticisms of agricultural economics, and many of the causes and the difficulties in resolving them are the same.

[7] Quantitatively at least, administrators today are verbally favorable to expansion of the field, but the lag behind agricultural economics remains large. Rural sociology has only a third as many courses, half as many people doing extension work, and a fourth as many research projects or personnel. The lag is largest in research and least in extension. The federally granted research funds have been a boon to rural sociology, however, even though

bers of these committees have social-science training, and they are strong supporters of "the rural point of view." In about half the states, rural sociology remains a junior partner in a department administered by an agricultural economist. The paper work associated with this organization is voluminous and in some states professors must keep conventional office hours.

As one would anticipate, the men in control in agricultural colleges typically view sociology as an applied subject, readily comprehended by common sense and with a "do good" aim. A considerable share of the projects that are ridiculed by other sociologists are pushed off onto the rural sociologists because the economists do not want them but citizens call for the information.

In addition to resident teaching and research, agricultural colleges are responsible for agricultural extension teaching. This is pitched at the laymen's level, but extension staffs make heavy demands on research workers to implement the programs. Some sociologists participate directly in extension work—which seems to encourage lower standards in other aspects of their work. It is easy to become accustomed to thinking at the lay level, to share localistic sentiments, and to become unduly hospitable toward farm pressure groups.

The tradition of "folksiness" in agricultural colleges, combined with the peculiar administrative structure, inhibits attachment to scholarly standards. It is easier, and sometimes essential, to do the sort of work local colleagues can understand if one is going to gain status. Emphasis on recruiting rural-minded sociologists brings in few men who can resist this atmosphere. These social pressures are reinforced by the generous subsidies to service-oriented research. Although land-grant faculties are less rural today and more strongly oriented toward theoretical work than they were a generation ago, the agricultural college remains a distinctive type of academic organization.

One must acknowledge, however, that this same environment has stimulated no small amount of fundamental research; a perusal of either Brunner's or Anderson's bibliography will demonstrate that some important work has been done on almost any sociological topic. Rural

---

it has received far less than its share and despite the accompanying red tape and bureaucratic prejudices. See *Human Relations in Agriculture and Farm Life: The Status of Rural Sociology in the Land-Grant Colleges*, Chicago: The Farm Foundation, 1950.

sociologists have been spared much of the hair-splitting theorizing and the sterility attendant upon status competition in formulating precious terminological novelties. They have benefited from the "realism" that has always marked the land-grant schools. Rural sociologists must to some extent fit into their local milieu. What the outsider may criticize is that as an organized profession they spend so little time plotting strategy to make the most of their opportunities and to circumvent the local constraints. Given favorable local conditions plus high standards, as at Michigan State University, rural sociologists will produce basic research.

Neglected Opportunities and Unfinished Tasks

One way of attacking the problem of enhancing the contributions of rural sociology is to survey the manifest unexploited opportunities within the present organizational structure. The stability in orientation and interests among rural sociologists, already mentioned, reflects the dominant influence of the land-grant system upon personnel and budgets. In harmony with these conditions, individual rural sociologists and the Rural Sociological Society have acquired certain traits that inhibit rapid reorientation or professional maturation. In the remaining portion of this paper, we attempt simultaneously to support this evaluation and to suggest ways out of the impasse, by pointing out gaps in research programs and failure to develop topics of initial promise.

The Need to Codify and Synthesize. The large amount of work published by rural sociologists and its mixed quality reflect the academic situation in which most of the men have worked. The rich ore buried in the mountain of publications would have been more widely discovered if rural sociologists had possessed a propensity for generalization. Few rural-sociology textbooks, for example, can compare with second-rate ones in general sociology.

Sophisticated designs for specific projects are certainly not lacking. Codification of findings, however, elicits little local acclaim, for it falls between the armchair theorizing scorned by colleagues in the colleges and these colleagues' limited conception of practical research. Innumerable studies have been replicated in several states or nations and at different times. If rural sociologists would draw this material together and abstract the common findings, their reputation with other sociologists would receive a boost. It is no excuse that such writing would have to be done after hours; most sociologists who write have heavy teaching loads.

One research area that is ripe for this consolidation is study of social participation.[8] Although comparable data are to be found in hundreds of rural reports, the broad generalizations on this topic to be found in our journals are written mainly by men in arts departments. From these data new perspectives could be gained on the nature of groups, social stratification, and community integration.

Study of the community has always been central in rural sociology; it was in this area that sustained interest in theory first arose and has persisted longest. Yet Brunner's earlier summary of the work has not been repeated, despite the multiplication of local studies in most states.[9] Similar opportunities lie in the numerous investigations of the farm family, mass communications, and levels of living.

A few men who were signally lacking in this provincialism—and most of them were among the beneficiaries of the fellowship program mentioned earlier—have produced some of the best studies on under-developed societies. A quarter-century ago, Sorokin, Zimmerman, and Galpin published a synthesis of the world literature on rural societies that is unmatched in other branches of sociology.[10] Neither of these two streams of influence has had much impact upon the planning of research in the several experiment stations.

There are rural sociologists in nearly every state working within the common federal-state framework, with numerous coordinating facilities available in the Washington office. There is a ready-made structure for interstate collaboration, apart from the quasi-official struc-

[8] This topic is defined not by its title but by conventions about the data to be collected; it deals with membership and attendance in organizations, the interrelationships of affiliations with various factors, such as income, and relations among various types of participation (formal and informal, religious, civic, etc.).

[9] Some sociologists contend that Williams' studies of a New York community have not been surpassed by any later books. See J. M. Williams, *Our Rural Heritage*, Knopf, 1925; and *The Expansion of Rural Life*, Knopf, 1926. The Cornell rural sociologists have repeated a few local studies and Kolb has repeated the Galpin Wisconsin surveys several times.

[10] P. Sorokin, C. A. Zimmerman, and C. J. Galpin, *Systematic Sourcebook in Rural Sociology*, University of Minnesota Press, 1930–32.

ture of the Rural Sociological Society. These opportunities are seldom utilized to conduct studies on similar topics and with similar methods. When a Division of Farm Population existed in the United States Department of Agriculture, there was readiness to accept its subsidies but reluctance to allow it to coordinate work. During the depression years, the Federal Emergency Relief Program made skillful use of central financing and direction, but the projects were almost exclusively practical in the narrowest sense.

The twin topics of region and ecology offer unique opportunities for interstate collaboration, precisely because regional traits are more discernible among rural people.[11] It would be easy to suggest other types of projects suitable to joint work—*e.g.*, the current French studies on religious practices.

The Need to Follow Through on Pioneer Projects. Examples of pioneering work by rural sociologists have been mentioned. Galpin's village studies were followed by a series directed by Warren Wilson and later by a broader investigation directed by Brunner. It is curious how seldom rural sociologists have restudied these communities. Although they continue to make community studies, the more widely recognized investigations and textbooks are coming from the arts departments. Similarly, the studies of trade areas that threw so much light on rural ecology have been taken over by economists.

If rural sociology has a distinctive rationale, it must lie in relating the traits of rural life to contrasting backgrounds. But if one looks for societal typologies, schemes of community types, or dissection of the rural-urban continuum, he will find that most of the recent writers are identified with other specialties. Studies of the "agricultural ladder," which is a central element in our stratification system, are now in the hands of economists,[12] as are studies relating tenure practices

---

[11] A. R. Mangus, *Rural Regions of the United States*, Works Progress Administration, 1940. Various techniques for quantifying regional delineations have been worked out by several people. The sociologists in the U. S. Department of Agriculture published a useful summary of regional social patterns; see C. C. Taylor *et al.*, *Rural Life in the United States*, Knopf, 1949, Part IV.

[12] Despite broad syntheses by Schuler and a group working with Hoffsommer. E. A. Schuler, *Social Status and Farm Tenure*, U. S. Department of Agriculture, 1938; H. C. Hoffsommer, *Social and Economic Significance of*

and family customs. Rural sociologists continue to publish reports on stratification, but most of the impressive field studies now come from other sociologists. Sanderson and his students worked out some of the earliest studies quantifying case materials on family life; these old studies continue to be quoted, but few rural studies today are feeding into the literature on the family.[13]

One cannot identify any factors intrinsic to rural sociology as a discipline to explain this fading interest in problems of undeniable importance to a science of society. Rather, one must turn to the customs of the land-grant college for an explanation. For a few topics, additional factors can tentatively be identified to explain why the work has fallen into the hands of other disciplines; for example, study of levels of living. On the one hand, rural sociologists have progressively defined this topic so broadly as to identify it with "way of life" and thereby opened it to ethnological techniques in which others are better trained.[14] On the other hand, they have failed to master the refined techniques needed to move beyond the descriptive level, and in this direction economists have taken over.

There are other topics for which it would not be hazardous to predict that failure to use sophisticated tools, even those current in sociology generally, will force rural sociologists to surrender their initial lead. In some of these, the present conception of the problem is scarcely sociological; the question is whether even the sociological aspects will remain in the hands of their originators. Exploration of health attitudes and practices is a timely example. Because few projects in this field root the phenomena in a broader social nexus, people in medicine are likely to master the elementary sociological techniques that have been used thus far and preëmpt the field.

In one area, rural sociologists are definitely breaking new ground today: diffusion of technical practices. Interest in this area stems as much from the practical slant of the colleges as from the importance

---

Land Tenure in the Southwestern States, University of North Carolina Press, 1950.

[13] H. W. Beers, *Measurements of Family Relationships in Farm Families of Central New York*, Cornell University Press, 1934. W. H. Sewell's recent testing of psychogenetic concepts is an exception: "Infant Training and the Personality of the Child," *Amer. J. Sociol.*, 58 (1952), 150-58.

[14] "Sociological Research in Rural Levels and Standards of Living," *Rural Sociol.*, 21 (1956), 183-95.

of the problem for illuminating cultural processes. This may well be the most important topic that rural sociologists have ever studied. It is "realistic" and appeals to farmers, administrators, extension workers, and technologists. It invites application of highly refined methods cutting across all the social sciences: information theory, group dynamics, and others. It is a problem inviting mathematical and not only statistical analysis. The rural sociologists' projects in this area are becoming more acute and penetrating each year, and it is perhaps only a biased view that methods are being refined faster by men from other fields working on this same problem.[15]

The Need to Make More Imaginative Use of Census Data. Federal census procedures have benefited from the field studies of rural sociologists; for example, demonstration of the practicability and importance of the "rural non-farm" population and refinements in migration data. Rural sociologists have been among the most zealous consumers of census data, although in ways that often make questionable use of scarce professional manpower. Many bulletins are merely pedestrian summaries: "Population Trends in . . ." This task should long ago have been turned over to the agricultural journalists on the staff. Otherwise, the census tends to be used mainly to test the character of field samples. Yet it is easy to find more imaginative ways of exploiting the census reports, even without special tabulations, in order to uncover hitherto unnoticed features of the social structure.[16] Given the generous funds for field studies, it should be possible to devise more penetrating combinations of census and survey data than we have yet seen.

The Need to Convert Applied Research into Policy Research. Most of the present service projects do not tax the professional skills

---

[15] No rural sociologist has tested the new approaches to diffusion developed by the Swedish geographer Hägerstrand, although his work is published in English and cited in *Rural Sociology*.

[16] Perhaps the writer may be permitted to cite his own papers in support of his argument on this point! "Inequalities in Schooling in the South," *Amer. J. Sociol.*, 60 (1955), 547-61; "Economic Status Differentials within Southern Agriculture," *Rural Sociol.*, 19 (1954), 50-67; (with M. J. Bowman) "Educational Distributions and Attainment Norms in the United States," *Proc. U. N. World Pop. Conf.*, 1954, Session 27.

of the men conducting them and should long ago have been given over to other agencies, once the routines were set up. If rural sociologists would decline to boil down their findings or to abstract census tables for farm audiences, extension journalists would have found it quite possible to summarize these data, just as they have done with economic data. Naturally, also, an administrator is happy to be spared the trouble of searching a census volume when he conceives no more important work for his sociologists to do.

There are even some research projects giving rise to the suspicion that the rural sociologist is doing the work of someone else; one can rarely infer any considered priority list for the projects under way. The discipline with the least status unfortunately often finds itself saddled with uninteresting projects. This is not to deny the fact that rural sociologists can be invaluable contributors to joint projects, such as a study of health practices. The final result, however, should rise above the level of a public-opinion poll.

A major reason for the frequency with which rural sociologists find their time occupied with routine surveys, one suspects, is that they do not keep a flow of truly sociological projects moving across the desk of the administrator who controls the funds. Education is a salient example of a topic suitable for the application of distinctively sociological concepts and methods. Education plays a central role in developing human resources and in migration and vertical mobility, all of which are important to farm people. Again, despite the dramatic role of farmers' organizations in state and national politics, these groups have been virtually ignored by rural sociologists. The process of cultural urbanization that is so conspicuous in this country, to mention one more example, is receiving little attention.

We recognize today that in a society in which politico-technical processes are dynamic, "applied" research is inextricably mixed with "policy" decisions. This has been emphatically true of the agricultural industry. One may lament this situation, and also the occasional corruption of agricultural economics by such questions, without escaping the necessity of facing up to the questions. Yet, except during the depression years, it would be difficult to find many events on which rural sociologists' research has had even so modest an impact as, for example, work in criminology. Comparison of the two journals, *Rural Sociology* and *Farm Economics,* highlights this observation. Doubtless the financial implications of the economists' work enhances its appeal, and allowance must be made for public resistance to prying into personal topics.

Policy discussion by rural sociologists tends to be unfocused.[17] Their rural background inclines them to favor a large rural population and the rural way of life; their recommendations, accordingly, often merely "buck the trend." But while they are deploring the economists' "economic man," the economist is busily applying social psychology and modernized conceptions of the decision process and becoming a more proficient sociologist.

The agricultural college is dedicated to uniting science with practice "for better rural living," and the rural sociologists work in this sort of college. But this union will be furthered by more rigorous attention to the nature of policy decisions—although no one is so naive as to believe that policy makers are guided only by science. An appropriate policy statement must analyze the existing situation, point out what will happen to the factors in given existing or altered conditions, and total the resultant so that the points to be decided are set forth clearly. In rural sociology, by contrast with agricultural economics, it would be difficult to find any good example of such a policy statement. Even an attempt at this kind of assessment—for example, about social security for farmers—would have constructive effects upon the formulation of research projects. If one is going to think in "applied" terms, one should produce results that will influence the men who make decisions.

Toward a More Professional Science of Rural Sociology. Although I would prefer to juxtapose an imaginative budget of research projects, a prediction of anticipated policy demands, and an evaluation of what the colleges will allow rural sociologists to do, a few simple illustrations must suffice.

The potentialities of regional ecology and regional culture study have been noted. Changes in these phenomena impinge on disputes about school desegregation, on reactions to industrialization, and on tax structures. Inquiries into rural health practices, readjustments in education, studies of technical diffusion, and patterns of communal living all tie into these two broad topics. These are the kinds of ques-

[17] W. H. Sewell, "Needed Research in Rural Sociology," *Rural Sociol.* 15 (1950), 119-21.

tion, to repeat, that are especially suitable for interstate research and policy research. On all these topics the most elaborate research techniques can be brought to bear.

The anomalous position of low-income families in agriculture is again receiving close scrutiny after an interlude of a quarter-century. Here rural sociologists have a chance to gain public support while using their sharpest tools and to expose for us the structure of the new rural society. But if they are to move into this area, they must do more than conduct inventories of family composition and community participation. Here is a fundamental problem, however much it is twisted by political oratory, of role allocation to human resources in the total economy. Perforce, the central analysis must be economic, but that analysis will be sterile without the sociologists' contribution. Any research the sociologist does on this question, if it is going to be heeded by the economists who have the ear of political leaders, must be integrated with the basic framework of economic processes. So far, this broad conception has not been forthcoming from the rural sociologists.[18]

Rural sociology has been maturing, if not in step with its expansion of personnel and funds. The positive signs can readily be found in the bibliographies cited. There are, however, certain adjustments within the profession that would enable it to take the place marked out for it by public grants of status and funds.

A major stimulus would result if the land-grant association were to solicit an assessment by a panel of non-rural sociologists. Such a review, incidentally, would turn up a surprising number of excellences to be brought to the attention of sociologists at large. It would make certain recommendations to the agricultural colleges. Recruitment policies should be altered with the intention of drawing in a larger corps of men who are urban rather than rural in outlook, to diminish

---

[18] The interstate study of farm-management practices and decision-making made some use of sociological advice but was almost exclusively an economists' affair. A subsequent project designed to study "the human factor" in farm management has been revised to focus on "identifying and measuring management performance"—apparently as a reaction to sociological complaints of poaching. But sociologists have not yet developed plans for work on the sociological aspects of the human factor in farm management.

the land-grant-college inbreeding. It would be helpful to protect the weak position of sociology in so bureaucratized a structure by utilizing sociologists in other types of colleges to review proposed projects and publications.

The rural sociologists as an organized association could easily launch some major changes themselves. One constructive move would be to abandon the practice of holding their meetings separately on agricultural campuses. And they could bring general sociologists into their meetings as one way of injecting more theory and analysis into a program that inherently inclines toward the narrowly empirical. They could enlarge the resources provided for the committees occasionally assigned to review current research in order to ensure more comprehensive and penetrating reports. Certainly the possibilities of interstate collaboration in research could be explored more diligently. By corporate action, they could bring more pressure to bear upon their administrators for all these proposals. They could also emphasize the importance of budgeting funds to write up the general results buried in the mountainous files of field data.

When all this is said, and all the special conditions of rural-sociological work are recognized, the fact remains that what is most wrong with rural sociology is equally a blemish on much of the work in other areas of sociology and in other social sciences. Although rural sociology avoids the sterility of rootless theorizing, it is impaled on the other and equally sterile horn of the dilemma: To think without data is easy and exhilarating; to collect data without purpose is easy. More money is needed for hiring men who can think in the context of data. Rural sociology would be well placed to become a leader in such a development if recruitment were broadened and standards of training raised.

Additional References

C. P. Loomis and J. A. Beegle, *Rural Social Systems,* Prentice-Hall, 1950.

J. H. Kolb and E. de S. Brunner, *A Study of Rural Society,* 4th ed., Houghton Mifflin, 1952.

L. Nelson, *Rural Sociology,* American Book, 1948.

M. T. Matthews, *Experience Worlds of Mountain People,* Columbia University Press, 1937.

E. D. Sanderson, *The Rural Community,* Ginn, 1932.

17

The Sociology of Race and Ethnic Relations*

**GEORGE E. SIMPSON AND
J. MILTON YINGER**
Oberlin College

Perhaps in no other area of sociology has the search for an adequate theoretical approach been more arduous than in the field of intergroup relations. The vast variety of situations within which people meet and the long list of variables that affect their interaction have led some writers, in recent years, to suggest that a general science of "race relations" is impossible. They advise that we adopt the more modest goal of a policy science—a series of guidelines to action based on careful research but applicable mainly to specific situations, with full attention to their individual peculiarities. Although we sympathize with the restiveness that comes from a study of the complexity of intergroup relations, we believe it unwise, in this field as in other complex areas of human life, to retreat from the classic goal of science: a series of inter-related propositions, on several levels of generality, that describe the sequence of events (in this case, in intergroup behavior) under certain stated conditions.

During the last half century, scholars have been moving toward

* Portions of this article are to be found also in Simpson and Yinger, *Racial and Cultural Minorities,* rev. ed., Harper, 1958.

this goal with what must seem to be rather great reluctance. Although any picture of "stages" is likely to be overly simple, we can sketch the dominant trends through several periods. In the first stage there were numerous assertions about intergroup, and especially interracial, relations in the name of social science, but many of these were value declarations (not unmixed with facts and some sociological concepts). They relied heavily upon biological terms to prove what today appear to be racist notions. In the second stage, there were important gains in descriptive work, more objective recording of the facts of minority-group life, and some *ad hoc* concepts (relatively unrelated to larger systems of theory). In the third stage, there were serious efforts to relate the analysis of intergroup relations to larger theoretical patterns, a growing interest in research, and even the beginnings of some experimental work. The theoretical schemes were still too limited, however, for they reflected the partial frames of reference of the historian or psychologist or sociologist. In recent years, the study of racial and ethnic relations has begun to be integrated into a slowly developing general theory of human behavior. At least a few specialists are beginning to see that the limits of their knowledge are not the limits of knowledge, that their concepts have abstracted only a part of a complex whole for study. It is the purpose of this paper to discuss a few of the theoretical questions that have emerged at this stage.

Personality and Situational Factors in Prejudice

The problems connected with the development of an adequate theory of intergroup relations are especially apparent in recent research on the personality factors in prejudice. This is a dimension of the field that psychologists have explored most intensively.

Psychologists became interested in the study of intergroup relations, particularly as they are influenced by prejudice, fairly late. When they did enter the field, they brought a much-needed enthusiasm for measurement and for experiment; many of them also brought a conviction that the "individual is the unit of analysis." To them, psychology is the basic science of everything human; culture and interaction are important only as they are reflected in the individual. Dominant theories of personality that conceived of the individual as a more or less self-contained system led readily to studies of "the authoritarian personality"[1] as the basic approach to the analysis of prejudice and discrimination. In the last decade, a great many studies have affirmed that prejudice is fundamentally a manifestation of insecurity and that the prejudiced person is one who is ego-alien—that is, who has repressed many of his own impulses—one who regards life as capricious and threatening, and one who looks upon all human relationships in competitive power terms. Prejudice, moreover, is tied in a functional way to many other personality trends, to particular styles of politics, religion, and sex behavior.

Research along these lines has added a great deal to our understanding of prejudice. It is based, however, on an inadequate theory of personality. We shall not undertake here a methodological critique of *The Authoritarian Personality;* nor shall we describe the numerous studies that have sought to refine the measurement of the variables used and to discover other variables that affect the extent of prejudice.[2]

[1] T. W. Adorno *et al., The Authoritarian Personality,* Harper, 1950.

[2] See, for example, Richard Christie and Marie Jahoda (eds.), *Studies in the Scope and Method of "The Authoritarian Personality,"* Free Press, 1954; Leo Srole, "Social Integration and Certain Corollaries: An Exploratory Study," *Amer. sociol. Rev.,* 21 (1956), 709-16; A. H. Roberts and Milton Rokeach, "Anomie, Authoritarianism, and Prejudice: A Replication," *Amer. J. Sociol.,* 61 (1956), 63-67; Bernard M. Bass, "Authoritarianism or Acquiescence," *J. abnorm. soc. Psychol.,* 51 (1955), 616-23; Roger W. Brown, "A Determinant of the Relationship Between Rigidity and Authoritarianism," *J. abnorm. soc. Psychol.,* 48 (1953), 469-76; Loren J. Chapman and Donald T. Campbell, "Response Set in the F-Scale," *J. abnorm. soc. Psychol.,* 54 (1957), 129-32; Harrison G. Gough, "Studies of Social Intolerance," *J. soc. Psychol.,* 33 (1951), 237-69; Jerome Himmelhoch, "Tolerance and Personality Needs; A Study of the Liberalization of Ethnic Attitudes among Minority Group College Students," *Amer. sociol. Rev.,* 15 (1950), 79-88; Nathan Kogan, "Authoritarianism and Repression," *J. abnorm. soc. Psychol.,* 53 (1956), 34-37; William J. MacKinnon and Richard Centers, "Authoritarianism and Urban Stratification," *Amer. J. Sociol.,* 61 (1956), 610-20; Marian Radke-Yarrow and Bernard Lande, "Personality Correlates of Differential Reaction to Minority Group Belonging," *J. soc. Psychol.,* 38 (1953), 253-72: Patrick L. Sullivan and Joseph Adelson, "Ethnocentrism and Misanthropy," *J. abnorm. soc. Psychol.,* 49 (1954), 246-50; W. D. Wells, Gene Chiaravallo, and Seymour Goldman, "Brothers under the Skin: A Validity Test of the F-Scale," *J. soc. Psychol.,* 45 (1957), 35-40.

Rather, we shall be concerned to ask only how this approach can be brought into the framework of a larger theory of personality.

From our point of view, personality is best conceived, not as a collection of traits, not as a static system, but as process. As process, it can be understood only by analyzing the flow of behavior that comes from the interaction of the individual with the situation. An individual exists or behaves not in a vacuum but always in some situation. Which of the numerous and often contradictory tendencies of which we all are capable will be set in motion cannot be predicted from knowledge of the individual alone. With what reference groups is he most closely identified at the moment? Which of his various potentialities are being encouraged by the existing situation? Which are being blocked? How do the structured aspects of his role channel his behavior? Role is a social concept, designating the expected behavior of a person in a given social relationship. The process of carrying out the functions of shop steward in a union, superintendent of schools, or "courteous customer" does not allow full individual variation to come into play. The roles themselves have some compulsions that influence which of various tendencies the individual will express. Thus personality thought of as process is "field"-determined.

Before we can explain antiminority feelings in terms of a harsh, capricious, and unloving childhood, we must be aware of group structure and of variation in values among the subcultures of a society. If residents of Mississippi have a higher anti-Negro score than those of Minnesota, this does not prove that they are more authoritarian— *i.e.,* more intolerant of ambiguity, more cynical, more rigid, less self-accepting. It may be that they simply express different cultural influences. Differences in agreement with the idea that there are two kinds of people in the world, the weak and the strong, may simply indicate differences in actual experience.[3]

Before we draw personality conclusions from the tendency of one person to select General MacArthur as a hero and another to choose Bertrand Russell, we should be aware of educational differences between the respondents. MacKinnon and Centers found that authoritarianism varied with age, social status, income, and education.[4] Differences in the realities of the situation, in cultural values, in role, in

---

[3] See Christie, in Christie and Jahoda, *op. cit.,* p. 51.

[4] See MacKinnon and Centers, *loc. cit.*

the ways in which different groups use language and respond to the testing process, and other variables are involved. All this is not to say that deep-lying personal insecurity, frustration, guilt, and diffuse hostility are not involved in the origins of prejudice. But before the influence of these factors can be measured, other variables must be controlled. To disregard group membership is to permit all sorts of spurious factors to obscure the relationships on the individual level. The need is for a more adequate theory of personality, one that fully incorporates situational influences. Thinking of personality as process, not as a fixed essence, we are concerned with the way in which it unfolds. The self-other relationships are vital to an adequate theory.

There is now widespread, if not universal, agreement that collective behavior in intergroup relations cannot be explained by what is "in" individuals. Men are role-playing creatures; they act in structured situations; to an important degree, they behave in terms of their obligations and group-defined interests. There is less agreement—yet we think the point is vital—that personality itself may be thought of in interactional terms. A person "is" what he does. To hypothesize some essence previous to the doing is to complicate analysis and make prediction of behavior more difficult.

This point of view does not make the individual a wholly malleable agent of the situation. It is equally inappropriate to hypothesize some fixed structure for the situation (patterns of roles, norms, group interests) as the determining factor in behavior. Situations must also be defined "in process."

Some of these problems are illustrated in this statement by Adorno and his associates:

> Although personality is a product of the social environment of the past, it is not, once it has developed, a mere object of the contemporary environment. What has developed is a *structure* within the individual, something which is capable of self-initiated action upon the social environment and of selection with respect to varied impinging stimuli, something which though always modifiable is frequently very resistant to fundamental change. This conception is necessary to explain consistency of behavior in widely varying situations, to explain the persistence of ideological trends in the face of contradicting facts and radically altered social conditions, to explain why people in the same sociological situation have different or even conflicting views on social issues, and why it is that people whose behavior has been changed

through psychological manipulation lapse into their old ways as soon as the agencies of manipulation are removed.[5]

In so far as this statement emphasizes the need for taking account of personal tendency, it is helpful. It fails to note, however, that we must explain inconsistency as well as consistency (being tolerant of Negroes in one's union but not in one's neighborhood); that an adequate theory must account for changes in ideological trends as well as persistence (many navy officers dedicated to segregation have reversed their judgment on an integrated ship); that persons in the same social situation often *do* have similar views (and what appears to be the "same" situation often proves, on close study, to be a different constellation of group influences); and, finally, that people do not always lapse into their old ways when influencing agencies are removed—and, if they do, it may be because they return to the old pattern of situations.

In our use of the concept, personality is what personality does, and the doing varies with the way in which a situation is defined, the reference group with which the individual identifies at the moment, the sanctions and rewards in a given setting, the roles into which the individual is cast, and the range of tendencies which the individual brings to the situation.

The responses of Japanese-Americans to relocation illustrate the view that personality is a function of situations and tendencies in interaction, not of fixed "traits." The evacuation meant financial disaster to most of the Japanese-Americans; self-government in the camps was limited; salary schedules ranged from $12 to $19 a month; the first-generation Japanese were defined as enemy aliens. In this context, in January 1943, all residents of the relocation centers over 16 years of age were required to declare their loyalty or disloyalty to the United States. Six thousand Japanese-Americans answered "no" to the loyalty question. Grodzins indicates very clearly the ways in which the discriminatory situation affected these results: a declaration of disloyalty was a protest: "We have citizenship and still we are . . . treated just like aliens. So what's the use of talking about citizenship and being loyal citizens?" It was also an indication of family loyalty, an expression of the identity of Nisei with their alien parents who were not

[5] Adorno *et al., op. cit.*, p. 6.

permitted to become citizens and had suffered great economic loss. A declaration of disloyalty was an attempt to find security in a situation that was very threatening.[6] It is important to note that there were great differences in the percentage of persons in the ten relocation centers who declared themselves disloyal (ranging from 8% to 52% of adult males). This range reflects the differences among the centers in social situations—residential conditions, the frequency of change of administration, location of the center, attitudes of governing officials, types of leadership among the Japanese-Americans, etc. Grodzins summarizes the situation as follows:

> Loyalties change as social situation changes and individuals assess previous experience, present plight, and future promise. Loyalty to his nation comes easily if an individual's job and career are secure, if he participates amiably in work and play with colleagues and friends, if he feels accepted and secure, if his relationship to the larger community is not strained. Destroy his career, disrupt his work and play groups, isolate him, persecute him, show your disdain for him, and you plant the seeds of his disaffection. His allegiance will withstand maltreatment. But the multiplication of abuses will weaken his loyalty; and, as abuse continues, loyalty to nation erodes away—the more completely and rapidly if he believes that the government is directly responsible for his difficulties. Loyalty does not thereby disappear. It is transferred to another cause, another group, perhaps another nation.[7]

An interesting test of situational influences on prejudice and discrimination was made in a fashionable suburb in a Northeastern state.[8]

[6] For a discussion of these and other factors involved in the declarations of disloyalty, see Morton Grodzins, "Making Un-Americans," *Amer. J. Sociol.*, 60 (1955), 570-82; and for a general treatise on the meaning of loyalty, see his *The Loyal and Disloyal*, University of Chicago Press, 1956.

[7] Grodzins, "Making Un-Americans," *loc. cit.*, p. 582.

[8] See Bernard Kutner, Carol Wilkins, and P. R. Yarrow, "Verbal Attitudes and Overt Behavior Involving Racial Prejudice," *J. abnorm. soc. Psychol.*, 47 (1952), pp. 649-52. For further examination of situational influences, see Muzafer Sherif and Carolyn Sherif, *Groups in Harmony and Tension*, Harpers 1953; Wilbur Brookover and John Holland, "An Inquiry into the Meaning of Minority Group Attitude Expressions," *Amer. sociol. Rev.*, 17 (1952), 196-202; Alvin Winder, "White Attitudes Toward Negro-White Interaction in a Number of Community Situations," *J. soc. Psychol.*,

Two young white women went into a restaurant and were seated; a
Negro young woman then entered, asked for her party, and was seated
with the white women. This was repeated in ten restaurants, in each
of which they were all served without incident. In two places, the
party attracted some attention. Two weeks later, a letter was sent to
the management of each restaurant requesting a reservation for an
interracial party. In seventeen days, not one of the letters was answered. The managers were then telephoned, with a variety of results:
eight denied having received the letter; five finally gave tentative approval to the party, although each acceptance was qualified in some
way. The next day, each restaurant was called to request reservations
without any mention of the race issue. Ten accepted the reservation
and the eleventh indicated that no reservation was necessary.

Here we have a series of responses to interracial situations: acceptance (the original situation), avoidance (no responses to the
letter), and a variety of improvisations (to the telephone call). Which
represents the "true" attitudes? They all do; they all represent potentialities of individuals involved in certain kinds of situations with
a variety of influences at work. Sometimes it is assumed that the "true"
attitudes, somehow unaffected by a situation, are expressed in paper-
and-pencil tests or interview situations in which persons are asked to
express their feelings toward minority groups. If behavior in another
setting deviates from the verbal description, it is often assumed that
the "true" attitude has been blocked and that the individual will "return to normal" under more usual circumstances. We prefer to state
that the verbalized attitudes are also behavior in a situation—the situation of a paper-and-pencil test or an interview. They express the tendencies of the person that are set in motion in that particular set of
conditions. Other sets of conditions facilitate the expression of different tendencies. They all are part of the personality; they all can be
understood only by studying process, by searching for the conditions
under which a person acts in various ways.

44 (1956), 15-32; J. D. Lohman and D. C. Reitzes, "Note on Race Relations in Mass Society," *Amer. J. Sociol.*, 58 (1952), 240-46; J. D. Lohman
and D. C. Reitzes, "Deliberately Organized Groups and Racial Behavior,"
Amer. sociol. Rev., 19 (1954), 342-44; Lewis M. Killian, "The Effects of
Southern White Workers on Race Relations in Northern Plants," *Amer.
sociol. Rev.*, 17 (1952), 327-31.

Structural-Functional Theory in Sociology and Intergroup Relations

Although an adequate conception of personality is essential to a theory of intergroup relations, analysis at the level of personality alone will result in only incomplete understanding. The study of the influence of social structure on intergroup relations requires the use of a different set of concepts relevant to societal processes. Perhaps the most fruitful perspective on the level of the social system is structural-functional theory in sociology, which can be characterized briefly in these terms: Society is a system of interrelated parts. The processes that go on are relevant to the maintenance of that system. When major changes occur, they are felt throughout the structure; but, oppositely, if changes in one part are not supported by others, their effects can be sharply curtailed. The usefulness of this series of concepts is beginning to be tested in intergroup relations. Perhaps we can illustrate their application by a few comments on desegregation, a process which can be understood only by attention to a number of basic changes in the social system of which the segregated patterns were a part.

Ralph McGill has said that desegregation, to the extent that it is a Southern phenomenon, began with the boll weevil. Lest we give the little devil too much credit, it should be remarked that his attack on cotton was most intense at the same time that a major depression was attacking the economy. Between the two, the one-crop system was dealt a serious blow. The federal government began to give greater encouragement to crop diversification, the mechanization of agriculture increased rapidly, an accelerated movement to urban areas was set in motion, and the pace of industrialization was quickened. Many an ardent segregationist, in fact, was a strong supporter of moves to encourage the location of industry in the South. Had he been an equally ardent student of social organization, he might have been curious about some of the unintended consequences. Urbanization, the beginning of unionization, the upgrading of some Negro workers, the migration of Yankees, the development of an urban middle class, the growing integration with the national economy—all these factors disturbed the existing patterns. Although the South is still less urban than most other areas of the country (43% compared with 59% for the whole country in 1950 and 47% and 64%, respectively, according to the

new census definition), it has been urbanizing more than twice as
rapidly as the rest of the nation since 1900. (The comparative rates of
growth of the urban populations are 436% and 190%.) Half the
Negroes of the South now live in urban areas. The rural South lost
a million Negro residents from 1940 to 1950 alone, of which many
migrated to the North and West, but a large number to Southern
cities as well.

The move to the cities has been accompanied by a rapid increase
in industrial employment. On common indexes of industrial production, the South, since 1930, has increased at a rate about one third
faster than the rest of the nation. This increase, to be sure, is from a
lower base; but the gap is being closed. Per-capita income in the South
was less than half the national average in 1929, but by 1952 it was
two thirds.

What is the significance of these population and income data for
the question of desegregation? Lewis puts the issue as follows:

> The normal economic, political, and social imperatives of urban life
> are such that the Negro in the cities of the South gets an automatic
> increment in his struggle for status and power merely by the fact of
> being there. The urban premium on freedom, impersonality, efficiency
> and profits, voluntary organizations, and participation by representa-
> tion provides for Negroes and whites a new frontier for the shaping
> of a common destiny.[9]

If patterns of segregation were an integral part of the one-crop
plantation economy, we should expect, on the basis of a structural-
functional approach, to find those patterns changing as the system in
which they were embedded changes. That indeed is the case. In an
interesting application of Parsons' concept of the "pattern variables,"
Rubin has described the gradual transformation of some of the plantation area. Obligations are moving from diffusiveness to functional
specificity, for example. The dependence of Negro tenants on the plantation owner in almost every facet of life is slowly giving way in the
face of public-welfare services, hourly pay rates, the increased need
for semiskilled and skilled workers, and, increased shopping in town
stores. There is some decrease in the ascription of status and some
increase in achievement. It is difficult to assign a Negro cowboy or

[9] Hylan Lewis, "Innovations and Trends in the Contemporary Southern Negro Community," *J. soc. Issues,* 10:1 (1954), 24.

skilled cotton-picking-machine operator to a traditional status. Vocational programs in the schools and extension programs for veterans and other adults are beginning to train the workers that the new economy requires. There is also a shift, to mention only one other pattern variable, from collectivity orientation to self-orientation. As Davis has observed, the values of free enterprise and private property have long restricted the full application of "caste" in the South.[10] Now an increasing number of white merchants, real-estate agents, and industrial employers ". . . for rational economic reasons have subordinated white supremacy values to economic gain." [11] The merchant is caught in much sharper cross-pressures than those that affect the plantation owner. He may believe in segregation, but he also believes in customers. As a result, Negroes are beginning to get, even in the Deep South, a minimum of business-oriented courtesy in the use of titles, more nonsegregated service in stores, the right to try on clothing, and the like.

The changes that are occurring, although more extensive in urban areas, are not limited to cities. The social structure of the plantation itself and of parts of the plantation area are changing. Rubin calls this a transition from feudal agrarianism to a factory-in-the-field system. The partial mechanization of cotton production has exerted pressure on portions of the rural population to leave the farms, and this pressure will continue. Mechanization leads to a drastic reduction in the acreage allotted to tenants and to the expansion of the "day crop" and of management personnel. The net decrease in both white and non-white croppers during World War II continued at an accelerated rate in the postwar period. From 1940 to 1950, the number of farms operated by croppers in the South decreased by approximately 195,-000, or 36 percent. Some questions about these changes remain unanswered or only partially answered. For example, what proportions of these former croppers have left farming, have climbed the agricultural ladder, or have become wage laborers on farms? Will the increase in hired labor and the decrease in cropper farming result, as Anderson and Bowman suggest, in the provision of channels of upward mobility

[10] Allison Davis, "Caste, Economy, and Violence," *Amer. J. Sociol.*, 51 (1945), 7-16.

[11] Morton Rubin, "Social and Cultural Change in the Plantation Area," *J. soc. Issues*, 10:1 (1954), 34.

within the employee structure that are missing where accumulated capital was required for advancement? [12] What will be the repercussions of a decreased dependence on the use of child labor in those areas where mechanization has forced a large number of farm families to move to towns and cities? In some Southern counties the average daily school attendance of Negro children has increased markedly, as has enrollment in high schools. Careful studies of the effects of better economic opportunities, both within the Negro community and in the larger community, rates of migration to other areas, and educational desegregation will be needed.

Other changes in the economic aspect of the social system are occurring. For the most part, Southern tradition requires that direct competition in the labor market be limited to "isolated" jobs in which a man works alone (truck driving, gardening, janitoring, etc.). These isolated jobs are also "dead-end" jobs. Since Negro and white workers do not usually work side by side at the same jobs in the South, the employer chooses between using all-white or all-Negro labor in a given set of jobs.[13] However, some employers have modified segregated procedures and have opened new opportunities for Negro workers. Under what conditions are new opportunities opened to Negroes? There is some indication that such opportunities are more likely to be found (1) in newly opened plants, (2) in plants operated in the South by Northern firms, and (3) in plants in which labor unions have pressed for changes in the racial pattern of employment in their contracts. For example, all master contracts of the UPHWA with the Big Four packers now contain nondiscrimination clauses, and desegregation is proceeding in the Cudahy and Armour plants in such Southern cities as Fort Worth, Atlanta, and Birmingham.[14] One observer notes that although the changes in the proportion of Negroes in the South at job levels above service and unskilled labor have not been numerous, "the

[12] C. A. Anderson and M. J. Bowman, *Tenure Changes and the Agricultural Ladder in Southern Agriculture*, University of Kentucky Bulletin 634, June 1955, p. 31.

[13] Donald Dewey, "Negro Employment in Southern Industry," *J. polit. Econ.*, 60 (1952), 285.

[14] John Hope II, "Efforts to Eliminate Racial Discrimination in Industry—with Particular Reference to the South," *J. Negro Educ.*, 23 (1954), 263.

gains in job mobility and income have fermented a disproportionate social mobility within the Negro community itself." [15] Does this conclusion hold for the new Negro middle class throughout the South? Does this response support or undermine Frazier's hypothesis of the "world of make-believe" and the attitude of "play" of the "black bourgeoisie"? [16] These questions deserve careful research.

Contracts which contain nondiscrimination clauses represent devices, other than legislative enactments, judicial decisions, and administrative actions, which are intended to modify economic relationships within the social system. We have referred above to labor contracts which include such provisions. A new type of relationship developed between a labor union and a social-welfare organization when the UAW and the National Urban League signed an agreement in July 1957 calling for the elimination of racial discrimination in plants employing the union's million and a half members. Approximately 20 per cent of the union's members are Negroes. The agreement provides for cooperative action by the Urban League and the UAW's Fair Practices Committee in dealing with cases of discrimination. Hypotheses dealing with the likelihood of further contractual agreements concerning discrimination would have to give attention to type of industry, type of union, type of leadership, region, size, and strength of union, and proportion of minority-group members, among other factors.

Labor organizations may have effects on race relations beyond the plant situation, but it cannot be assumed that persons who show a high degree of acceptance of Negroes on the job will necessarily show a low degree of rejection of Negroes in their home communities.[17] But has anyone really tested Reitzes' proposition that union leaders who wish to influence neighborhood policies may be able to do so by studying the organizational structuring of the community and by showing that nondiscriminatory behavior would serve the individual's interests better than discriminatory behavior? [18]

[15] Lewis, *loc. cit.*, p. 22.

[16] E. Franklin Frazier, *The Black Bourgeoisie*, Free Press, 1957, Chs. 9, 10.

[17] Lohman and Reitzes, "Notes on Race Relations in Mass Society," *loc. cit.*, p. 244.

[18] D. C. Reitzes, "The Role of Organizational Structures: Union *Versus* Neighborhood in a Tension Situation," *J. soc. Issues*, 9:1 (1953), 43-44.

In the approach to desegregation that we are taking, one can perceive a major recurring theme of sociological theory. Here is Sir Henry Maine's idea of the shift from status to contract. Here is an illustration of the perceptiveness of Simmel's work in *Philosophie des Geldes* concerning the influence of a money economy. One need scarcely add that here is much of Tönnies and Weber and Durkheim. Parsons and others who use the structural-functional approach have caught this fundamental orientation and sharpened and refined it in such a way as to make it more readily applicable to such specific research problems as the one with which we are concerned.

If this way of looking at desegregation is helpful, we must be careful not to give our sole attention to the dramatic legal changes of the last decade without full regard for the quiet revolution that is slowly weakening the foundation of the structure of segregation. The multiple forces at work—demographic, economic, international, religious, and many others—are drastically changing the context in which the legal processes take place. Moreover, we cannot assume that desegregation can be understood by studying the South alone. Not only is there segregation in the North, but what goes on in each region is vitally affected by developments in the other regions.

The desegregation process is not automatic or inevitable once the changes we have described begin to transform a society. The speed with which it will occur, the degree of conflict it will cause, the extent to which attitudes will also be transformed, all vary depending upon the presence or absence of organized groups capable of focusing their efforts on the patterns of segregation. In some communities, pressures toward change are supported by a wide range of groups—mayor's committees, church organizations, interracial councils, and the like. In other communities, we find only two sharply contending groups. Such a contrast helps to explain results as widely different as the school-desegregation developments in Louisville and Little Rock. The strategic skills of leaders also affect the speed and direction of change. Have they identified and brought into the planning the groups and persons whose support is vital? Have they identified the sources of most vigorous opposition and taken steps to counter their influence? Shils has suggested that the leaders of "nativist political groups" in the United States have been relatively ineffective because their actions have often been prompted by paranoid tendencies, not by the requirements of effective group organization.[19] This may be true of some of the more violent segregationists today. Others, however, are driven by economic and political interests or by moral convictions. It would be a mistake in this matter to equate Kasper with Senator Byrd.

Because of variations in effective group organization, leadership skill, and other factors, desegregation does not proceed at the same pace even in situations that seem equally ready for it. Without articulate and determined opposition, the structure of segregation can remain for generations, despite a setting favorable for integration.

An aspect of the study of desegregation that continues to require careful analysis is the interpretation of the influence of legal processes. The dogma that law is impotent to change intergroup relations has been sharply challenged by contemporary social science. Yet not so long ago we found it easier to accept a Sumnerian view of things with respect, let us say, to the Eighteenth Amendment. Perhaps something besides hard-headed analysis is involved in both ideas. In the contemporary view, there is sometimes a failure to seek out the conditions under which law is most likely to be effective. Some observers, looking at the question from the perspective of the United States in the mid-twentieth century, a setting in which the legal and administrative approach is effective to some degree, have simply reversed the earlier dogma to affirm that law is the crucial weapon in the fight to improve intergroup relations. The scientific task is to describe the factors involved in the variations of the effectiveness of legal and administrative action. A conception of law as part of a complex social system, functionally interconnected with every other aspect of society, is an appropriate starting point. In terms of action, law can best be described as a "middle strategy." It is unnecessary to wait until everyone in a society is ready for a change before incorporating it into law; yet laws that have little support in other institutional patterns are relatively ineffective.

With reference to the United States, important changes in the social system, some of which we have described, have created a situation in which changes in interracial patterns through political and legal processes can readily proceed. We need mention only a few of the developments of the last decade to illustrate this fact.

The armed forces, noted for their social and political conservatism, have demonstrated the remarkable ability of whites and Negroes to

[19] E. A. Shils, in Christie and Jahoda, *op. cit.*, pp. 45-49.

adjust satisfactorily to new racial relations. Integration in these organizations has meant not only military integration but integration in housing, transportation, education, and recreation as well, within their own communities, both in the United States and overseas.[20] This instance and others, such as the desegregation of schools, swimming pools, parks, and playgrounds, together with police operations in situations of racial tension, show that a clear policy, enunciated unambiguously and administered with firmness by trained personnel, is usually effective. The hypothesis of Lohman and Reitzes is that "in modern mass society the group continues as the essential reality in human behavior, but the relevant and controlling collectivities are, increasingly, deliberately organized interest groups." [21] Among other points, it will be necessary to look for limits and exceptions in testing this hypothesis.

The operations, achievements, and problems of the wartime federal FEPC and the state and municipal FEP agencies are fairly well known. A less-known type of political pressure on economic activity is the recently inaugurated New York program involving industry-wide investigations by the State Committee Against Discrimination to change the policies of industries as a group. In December 1956, the airlines agreed to judge applicants in all categories on the basis of merit, without regard to race, creed, color, or national origin. The effectiveness of such agreements and the results achieved by the President's Committee on Government Contracts (and its predecessor, the Committee on Government Contract Compliance) remain to be tested.

The effects of legal and political forces on intergroup relations are not without complications. Despite nondiscriminatory policies in the publicly assisted redevelopment and urban-renewal programs in six states and four major cities outside these states, an unanticipated consequence of these programs has been the upsetting of racial balance in public-housing projects. Those displaced by redevelopment projects usually have a priority on vacancies in public-housing projects. Two thirds of these relocation families are nonwhites. When such projects

---

[20] See J. C. Evans and D. A. Lane, Jr., "Integration in the Armed Services," *Annals Amer. Acad. polit. soc. Sci.*, 304 (1956), 78-85; Lee Nichols, *Breakthrough on the Color Front*, Random House, 1954; and Eli Ginzberg, *The Negro Potential*, Columbia University Press, 1956, p. 91.

[21] Lohman and Reitzes, "Notes on Race Relations in the Mass Society," *loc. cit.*, pp. 245-46.

become 40- to 60-percent nonwhite, they tend to become predominantly or totally nonwhite. Also, families displaced by redevelopment projects put pressure on transitional neighborhoods by doubling up and improvising conversions, thus threatening integrated neighborhoods.[22] From 1933 to 1948, the federal government itself sanctioned segregated housing under the FHA policy that racial homogeneity was essential to the financial stability of a neighborhood. Since desegregation in housing is highly important to every other aspect of racial and ethnic integration, the consequences of recent efforts to preserve or reduce such desegregation deserve careful study. Will the extension in New York, New Jersey, and Connecticut of the administrative technique of conciliation, which has been used to combat discrimination in employment, to include FHA- and VA-insured construction support and accelerate nondiscrimination in publicly assisted housing? What counter-tendencies will be generated by the migration of whites to all-white suburbs? Will the public-school decision stimulate private-housing developments in separate areas in Southern cities as a means of keeping the schools segregated? Does the trend in the legal logic of the Supreme Court in the past twenty years foreshadow a decision on the constitutionality of racial segregation in publicly assisted housing projects?

Innumerable sociological questions have arisen in connection with public-school desegregation.[23] The close relationship between residential

[22] Robert C. Weaver, "Integration in Public and Private Housing," *Annals Amer. Acad. polit. soc. Sci.*, 304 (1956), 90.

[23] See, for example, C. A. Anderson, "Inequalities in Schooling in the South," *Amer. J. Sociol.*, 60 (1955), 547-61; H. S. Ashmore, *The Negro and the Schools*, University of North Carolina Press, 1954; H. C. Fleming, "Resistance Movements and Racial Desegregation," *Annals Amer. Acad. polit. soc. Sci.*, 304 (1956), 44-52; Herbert Hill and Jack Greenberg, *Citizen's Guide to Desegregation*, Beacon Press, 1955; Charles S. Johnson, "Some Significant Social and Educational Implications of the U.S. Supreme Court's Decision," *J. Negro Educ.*, 23 (1954), 368-69; Guy B. Johnson, "Racial Integration in Southern Higher Education," *Soc. Forces*, 34 (1956), 309-12; Guy B. Johnson, "A Sociologist Looks at Racial Desegregation in the South," *Soc. Forces*, 33 (1954), pp. 1-10; J. M. Nabrit, Jr., "Desegregation and Reason," *Phylon*, 17 (1956), 286-90; J. M. Nabrit, Jr., "Legal Inventions and the Desegregation Process," *Annals Amer. Acad. polit. soc. Sci.*, 304 (1956), 35-43; Irene Osborne and Richard K. Bennett, "Eliminat-

segregation and school segregation forces increased attention upon the former. Regardless of the degree of their truth or falsity, the common apprehensions about desegregation (health, behavior, social contact, lowering of academic standards) will occasion voluminous legislation and litigation, as well as countless other forms of strategy for and against integration. Despite the many techniques devised to resist the Supreme Court decision, our study of the changes taking place in society makes it appear that desegregation is inevitable in the sense that eventually no child will be denied admission to any public school simply because of race. Within a decade there will be a sharp increase in the desegregation of the schools and colleges of the South. The rates and places of desegregation cannot be predicted precisely, of course, but the changes in the structure of which segregation was a part have been too drastic to make its survival likely.

Another instance of the importance of law in race relations is found in the increase in the Negro vote in the South since the Supreme Court's white-primary decision of 1944. Increased voting strength increases the political power of Negroes and hence their ability to get improved civic services, more political appointments and employment in public agencies, and a closer approximation to equality in all matters of civil rights. The implementation of this decision on voting through the years is, and will continue to be, tied to the growing economic strength among Negroes, their educational advance, their migration to the North, where they occupy balance-of-power positions in at least eight states, and other changes. The growth of political power, in turn,

---

ing Educational Segregation in the Nation's Capital, 1951–1955," *Annals Amer. Acad. polit. soc. Sci.*, 304 (1956), 98-108; T. M. Pierce, J. B. Kincheloe, R. E. Moore, G. N. Drewry, and B. E. Carmichael, *White and Negro Schools in the South*, Prentice-Hall, 1955; *Race Relations Law Reporter*, 1-3, *passim*; J. B. Robison, B. Mintz, and S. Rich, *Assault upon Freedom of Association*, American Jewish Congress, 1957; F. B. Routh and P. Anthony, "Southern Resistance Forces," *Phylon*, 18 (1957), 50-58; George E. Simpson and J. Milton Yinger, *Racial and Cultural Minorities*, rev. ed., Harper, 1958, Chs. 19-20; *Southern School News*, 1-4, *passim*; Ernst W. Swanson and John A. Griffin (eds.), *Public Education in the South Today and Tomorrow*, University of North Carolina Press, 1955; Robin M. Williams, Jr., and Margaret W. Ryan (eds.), *Schools in Transition*, University of North Carolina Press, 1954.

influences these developments.[24] Some have questioned whether the role of Negroes in Southern politics can parallel that of the ethnic political organizations of Eastern cities in the nineteenth century, because of the current difficulty of placing Negro candidates on the ticket and the small likelihood that Negroes will eventually merge into the general population, as did the Irish, the Germans, the Italians, and members of other immigrant groups. It is too early to speak with confidence concerning this question, but it deserves our careful attention.

Social-Stratification Theory and Majority-Minority Relations

An area of research closely related to both personality theory and desegregation, yet requiring some separate analysis as well, is the study of social stratification. Knowledge of types of stratification systems, variables affecting the extent of mobility, the interplay of class with lines of division based on race, ethnic group, and religion, and many other aspects of social stratification is essential for the student of majority-minority relations. Here, as elsewhere in this paper, we can only suggest some of the factors involved.

A number of studies have made it clear that social-class standing affects personality development. However, care must be taken in relating personality correlates to social-class position because "the people in any class may vary with respect to their other social roles and because these other roles may have consequences more important for their personalities than do their class positions." [25] Barber points out that middle-class Jews, Protestants, and Catholics may have significantly different personality traits because of their religious and other traditions. Because persons who are of similar class standing but different racial or ethnic origin are socialized in somewhat similar ways, they tend to have some personality characteristics in common. Presumably, their racial and ethnic differences will tend to produce some personality differences. There is need for further probing into the influences of color and nationality, in relation to social stratification, on personality formation.

[24] See H. D. Price, *The Negro and Southern Politics*, New York University Press, 1957; and Margaret Price, "The Negro Voter in the South," *New South* 12:9 (1957).

[25] Bernard Barber, *Social Stratification*, Harcourt, Brace, 1957, p. 317.

But what of the adequacy of the conceptualization of social classes in the study of racial and ethnic relations? We need not enter upon an extended discussion of the applicability of the term *caste* to the American scene. The present writers think that the concept of caste is not appropriate in the analysis of Negro-white relations in the United States; but it is not crucial whether the concept applied is caste, race-caste, caste-like, race-class, or social classes which have varying aspects because of race, culture, and region. Whatever terms are used, differentiation and stratification as related to race require careful study.

The number of classes utilized in investigations of racial and ethnic communities has varied from zero to five, depending upon such matters as the authors' conceptualization of social stratification, the criteria used to define or identify social classes, who does the classifying, and the nature of the communities themselves. In a recent study of an industrial town in South Carolina, Lewis concluded that the Negro community was not a class-organized society. Because he found that "numerically significant groups differentiated on a basis of intimate association or access are not present, and that the people themselves do not in behavior or verbalizations make references to or relate themselves to such prestige collectivities," Lewis concluded that the existing status differences and the changes toward more differentiation indicate an incipient rather than a fully developed class structure. The most significant status cleavage among the people themselves seemed to be that between respectables and nonrespectables.[26]

Earlier studies of rural areas and small towns in the South viewed Negro life in terms of two or three social classes.[27] Three social classes have been reported by Frazier for border and Northern cities, and by Hylan Lewis for the urban South.[28] Drake and Cayton delineate three

[26] Hylan Lewis, *Blackways of Kent,* University of North Carolina Press, 1955, pp. 223-24, 233.

[27] See E. F. Frazier, *The Negro in the United States,* Macmillan, 1949, p. 279; Charles S. Johnson, *Growing Up in the Black Belt,* American Council on Education, 1941, pp. 325-27; Allison W. Davis, B. B. Gardner, and Mary R. Gardner, *Deep South,* University of Chicago Press, 1941.

[28] E. F. Frazier, *Negro Youth at the Crossways,* American Council on Education, 1940, pp. 24-28; Hylan Lewis, "Innovations and Trends in the Contemporary Southern Negro Community," *J. soc. Issues,* 10:1 (1954), 22-24.

main social classes in the Negro society of Chicago, plus an underworld, but the classes are subdivided on the basis of church-centeredness, non-church-centered respectability, and "shadiness." [29] Warner, Junker, and Adams traced four principal Negro classes in the same city, with further subdivisions on the basis of color and respectability.[30] In the urban South, Davis and Dollard thought of Negro society as composed of five classes,[31] and Robert Johnson divided the Negro population of Elmira, N. Y., into five strata on the basis of socioeconomic status: (a) the isolated "elites," (b) the "stable pillars," (c) the "steady industrious" migrants, (d) the working "floaters," and (e) the indigents, seniles, and "winoes." Later, using criteria of sex, age, status, and social participation, he impressionistically placed subgroupings in that community until approximately fifty subworlds were plotted, each "with its own style of behavior, physical locus, pattern of belief, and reference group.[32] On the basis of studies by Lenski, Kenkel, and Hetzler of a New England city, a Middle Western city, and a county-seat village in the Middle West, Cuber and Kenkel question the value of the discrete-classes hypothesis and favor the continuum theory of stratification.[33] Empirical research on stratification within racial and ethnic groups will be useful in evaluating these theories of social stratification.

It seems doubtful that belonging to racial, ethnic, or religious groups is a primary criterion or determinant of position in a system of social stratification. There is no reason to suppose that a member of a given racial, ethnic, or religious group within a society cannot learn to fill any social role found in that society. According to this view, minority-group status "may be, like wealth, a secondary criterion, in the sense that it *may* determine functional role and therefore position

[29] St. Clair Drake and H. R. Cayton, *Black Metropolis*, Harcourt, Brace, and Company, 1945, pp. 522-25.

[30] W. L. Warner, B. H. Junker, and W. A. Adams, *Color and Human Nature*, American Council on Education, 1941, pp. 20-23.

[31] Allison Davis and John Dollard, *Children of Bondage*, American Council on Education, 1940, p. 260.

[32] Robert Johnson, "Negro Reactions to Minority Group Status," in Milton L. Barron (ed.), *American Minorities*, Knopf, 1957, p. 199.

[33] John F. Cuber and William F. Kenkel, *Social Stratification in the United States*, Appleton-Century-Crofts, 1954, pp. 303-09.

in the system of stratification." [34] According to Parsons, the importance of ethnicity in modifying the system of stratification would be expected, in our type of society, to decrease.[35] It is difficult to determine to what extent such a development is actually occurring. There is some evidence to indicate that "the dynamics of the stratification variables hasten the assimilation of white ethnics, whereas they work in contradictory ways with respect to the assimilation of Negroes, for the economic variables are improving their position, whereas the interaction variables are holding them apart." [36] Studies of different groups, regions, and societies are needed to show how affiliation with particular minority groups affects social-stratificational position.

The Influence of Contact on Prejudice

What is to be learned from the study of efforts to reduce prejudice and discrimination? It is a mistake for the scholar to disregard the applied area, for effective work in the reduction of prejudice and discrimination must draw upon, test, and, indeed, can advance strictly theoretical knowledge. Once again, we can illustrate only one aspect of this situation, to indicate the kind of problem that is receiving attention.

There is a considerable body of evidence that "equal-status contact" between members of different groups tends to reduce prejudice. Yet the evidence is not so clear-cut as it seemed a few years ago. The important task of searching out the conditions under which the proposition is true has begun and needs to be carried further. In interviews with nineteen Asian students in the United States, Lambert and Bressler discovered that contact—even when it was courteous and helpful—did not automatically create favorable attitudes. The effects depended not so much on the personalities of the individuals involved as on the total structure of the situation, especially the status conceptions of the two societies. Whenever the Asian students encountered certain "sensitive areas" that involved implications of low status for their culture, even

[34] Barber, *op. cit.*, p. 60.

[35] Talcott Parsons, "A Revised Analytical Approach to the Theory of Social Stratification," in Reinhard Bendix and Seymour M. Lipset (eds.), *Class, Status and Power*, Free Press, 1953, p. 118.

[36] Joseph A. Kahl, *The American Class Structure*, Rinehart, 1957, pp. 247-48.

if the Americans involved were disagreeing with the implications, they tended to respond negatively.[37]

In his study of an interracial adolescent group, Katz found that, despite its liberal and friendly atmosphere, there was the danger that competition for leadership and other inevitable group tensions that have nothing to do with race would be seen as racial in origin and meaning.[38] Mussen found that of 106 white boys in an interracial camp, 28 became significantly less prejudiced in a four-week period, but 27 became significantly more prejudiced. Those who increased in prejudice had more aggressive feelings and needs and more need to defy authority, felt themselves victims of aggression, and were more dissatisfied with the camp.[39]

These and many other studies indicate the need for a more careful description of the conditions under which equal-status contact reduces prejudice. Both personality and social variables influence the results. Secure and insecure persons respond differently; reactions differ depending on the proportion of members from the minority group (when are there so many that a sense of threat to status develops; when are there so few that they may be regarded as "exceptions"). Is the contact voluntary or involuntary? Is its equal-status aspect supported or opposed by other experiences? Are responses the same in a recreational situation as in economic or religious or residential contacts? Is the situation competitive or cooperative? Until we know more about the answers to these and related questions, we can speak only tentatively about the ways in which equal-status contact reduces prejudice.

Conclusion

We have posed more questions than we have answered. Intergroup relations has emerged so recently as a problem for scientific study that

[37] R. D. Lambert and Marvin Bressler, "The Sensitive-Area Complex: A Contribution to the Theory of Guided Culture Contact," *Amer. J. Sociol.,* 60 (1955), 583-92.

[38] Irwin Katz, *Conflict and Harmony in an Adolescent Interracial Group,* New York University Press, 1955.

[39] Paul H. Mussen, "Some Personality and Social Factors Related to Changes in Children's Attitudes Toward Negroes," *J. abnorm. soc. Psychol.,* 45 (1950), 423-41.

we are not yet even asking the questions in a thoroughly sophisticated way. In our judgment, however, the research situation is rapidly improving. We have witnessed in the last several years and will continue to witness in the years ahead the incorporation of the study of racial and ethnic relations into the framework of the social sciences.

∽ 18

Organizational
Analysis ⌒

ALVIN W. GOULDNER
University of Illinois

For the past several decades, various commentators have viewed with increasing alarm the growth of large-scale organizations, the impending bureaucratization of the world, and the rise of the "organization man." Whether for good or for evil, there is little doubt that the spread of the complex, rational organization is one of the characteristics of modern society, distinguishing it from earlier feudal forms.

Immediately upon the heels of the French Revolution, a few thinkers clearly grasped the significance of the modern organization and gave it a special place in the history of sociology. Both sociology and organizational analysis were early formulated in the work of Henri Saint-Simon.[1] Saint-Simon was probably the first to note the rise of modern organizational patterns, identify some of their distinctive features, and insist upon their prime significance for the emerging society. Saint-Simon argued that, in the society of the future, administrative methods would no longer entail coercion or force, and the administrator's authority would no longer be based upon birth or heredity privilege. The authority of the modern administrator, he held, would rest upon his possession of scientific skills and "positive" knowledge.

[1] For an exegesis of Saint-Simon's theories, see Emile Durkheim, *Socialism and Saint-Simon*, A. W. Gouldner (ed.), Antioch Press, 1958. A translation of selections from Saint-Simon's work is found in F. M. H. Markham (ed.) *Henri Comte de Saint-Simon (1760–1825)*, Oxford: Basil Blackwell, 1952.

Saint-Simon also maintained that there was a close connection between the emergence of modern science, or the professions which grew up around it, and the development of cosmopolitanism. He expected the new professions to be cosmopolitan in their orientation, in that their occupant's loyalties would cut across localistic or national groups. Whatever the extravagances of his plans for social reorganization, Saint-Simon saw with a sure intuition that the ground rules of modern society had been deeply altered and that the deliberately conceived and planned organization was to play a new role in the world.

The transition to Saint-Simon's disciple, Auguste Comte, was a fateful one, both for sociology and for organizational analysis. Comte was much less a relativist than Saint-Simon and lacked his mentor's sensitivity to the novel forms of social organization that were emerging. Consequently, in the program which Comte formulated for modern sociology, the significance of the modern organization was unfortunately obscured. Although Comte believed that planned organization should be used in the event of serious threats to the solidarity of society, his deepest conviction was that the "final order which arises spontaneously is always superior to that which human combination had, by anticipation, constructed." [2] The most eulogistic term in Comte's vocabulary was "spontaneous." In Comte's system, therefore, the "natural" and spontaneous maintenance of social order is counterposed invidiously to planned political, legal, or constitutional organization.

It was not until Max Weber formulated his theory of bureaucracy that the distinctive rational-legal characteristics of the modern organization were systematically explored and Saint-Simon's earlier vision was superseded by scholarly codification. What seems, surprisingly, to have been neglected is the convergence between Saint-Simon and Weber in their views concerning the nature of modern organizations and the basic role in them of rationality, science, and technical experts. Both men stressed the significance of expertise and scientific knowledge for the modern organization, and both also perceived the ways in which these new organizations profoundly affected the character of modern society as a whole.

Despite these similarities, there are nevertheless important differences between Weber's work on bureaucracy and that of his predecessor.

---

[2] August Comte, *Early Essays on Social Philosophy* (trans. H. D. Hutton), London; George Routledge and Sons, n.d., p. 325.

402 Demographic and Social Structure

Saint-Simon viewed modern organization as a liberating force, emancipating men from the yoke of tradition and heightening productivity and efficiency. Although Weber acknowledged the efficiency of bureaucracy, he feared that it spelled the destruction of individual personality and subjected it to a dehumanizing regimentation.[3] Moreover, Weber saw more clearly than Saint-Simon and the early positivists that authority in the modern organization cannot rest on science and technology alone. He regarded bureaucracy as a Janus-faced organization. He agreed that it was, on the one side, a form of administration based on knowledge and expertise. However, he also insisted that authority in the modern organization is, in some measure, always dependent upon nonrational elements. Weber held that bureaucracies require some degree of obedience as an end in itself; obedience is due a superior, not merely because of his technical knowledge, but also because of the office he occupies.

Weber did not, however, develop both sides of his theory of bureaucracy equally. Because of his concern with the distinctive features of the modern organization (which derives from his use of ideal type concepts), he tended to neglect bureaucratic authority which rests upon nonrational considerations. Thus his work focuses on bureaucracy primarily as a planned and rational form of administration and is consequently discontinuous with Comte's interest in the spontaneous mechanisms in groups.[4]

Although Weber's view of bureaucracy as involving two sources of authority—authority based on sheer incumbence in office, and au-

[3] The best discussion in English of this aspect of Weber's thinking is in J. P. Mayer, *Max Weber and German Politics*, London: Faber and Faber, 1943. Compare, especially, Weber's polemic against bureaucratization, in his speech of 1909, with William H. Whyte's call to battle against bureaucracy almost a half-century later in *The Organization Man*, Simon and Schuster, 1956. The similarities in their value positions are noteworthy.

[4] I have used Comte as a historical marker with the object of emphasizing his intellectual influence rather than his intellectual originality. It is evident that thinkers prior to Comte held some of the ideas here associated with him. My comments, however, are made in the framework of the history of sociology and the actual continuities within it, rather than in terms of a schematic intellectual history. Of course, theorists after Comte have also stressed many of the same ideas, such as the importance of shared moral beliefs as a basis of social solidarity. Among these modern theorists, Durkheim and his school are well enough known not to require comment here.

thority based on expertise—was never fully developed theoretically, it is nonetheless an empirically astute observation. For the modern bureaucracy seems indeed to be characterized by this split in its mode of viewing and legitimating authority.

Among the issues to which this line of analysis gives rise is the question of the varying conditions conducive to these different modes of authority. In a recent study,[5] I have taken this problem as my central point of departure, presenting the view that bureaucracy is not a single, homogeneous entity but that there are two types of bureaucracy, the representative bureaucracy and the punishment-centered bureaucracy. The representative bureaucracy is, in part, characterized by authority based upon knowledge and expertise. It also entails collaborative or bilateral initiation of the organizational rules by the parties involved; the rules are justified by the participants on the ground that they are means to desired ends, and persuasion and education are used to obtain compliance with them. The punishment-centered bureaucracy is characterized by authority based on incumbency in office, and by the unilateral initiation of organization rules which are enforced through punishments.[6]

The punishment-centered bureaucracy arises "partly because of a dissensus in ends; that is, obedience would tend to be stressed as an end in itself, and authority tends to be legitimated in terms of incumbency in office, when subordinates are ordered to do things divergent from their own ends." This, in effect, expresses a Comtean concern with shared moral beliefs as a basis of group cohesion and solidarity. Moreover, and again in a Comtean manner, this study suggests that one of the latent functions of bureaucratic rules is to provide a managerial indulgency, in the form of withholding application of the rules, which

[5] Alvin W. Gouldner, *Patterns of Industrial Bureaucracy*, Antioch Press, 1954, esp. pp. 15-29 and Chap. 10.

[6] In thus demarcating two types of bureaucracy it is not, of course, my intention to suggest that this is the only way in which concrete organizations may be analyzed or that these are the only two possible types of bureaucracy. Viewed in one way, these comments may be regarded as specifications of two ideal types of bureaucracies, useful for the qualitative comparison of several organizations or in the analysis of different administrative patterns within one organization. Viewed in another light, these comments may be regarded as a "qualitative" factor analysis or as suggestive of hypotheses about dimensions of organizations which might emerge from a factor-analytic research.

reinforces patterns of informal cooperation and spontaneous reciprocities among those involved. The study notes that "by a strange paradox, formal rules gave supervisors something with which they could 'bargain' in order to secure informal cooperation from workers." This effort to conjoin Comte's focus on spontaneous and informal patterns of organization with Weber's emphasis on rationally planned formal organization was intended primarily to call attention to a major problem of organizational analysis, rather than to provide a definitive solution to it.

The nature of the problem may be summarized as follows: During the historical development of organizational analysis, two distinct approaches to the study of complex organizations have emerged in the work of sociologists. One of these, best exemplified by the work of Max Weber, is a conception of the organization in terms of a "rational" model. The other, which can be termed the "natural system" model, ultimately derives from Comte, was later reinforced by Robert Michels, and is now best exemplified in the work of Philip Selznick and Talcott Parsons.

One of the central problems of organizational analysis is to reconcile the divergent implications of these two models and to synthesize a new and more powerful model. In the following pages, I shall attempt to clarify some of the advantages and limitations of each of these models. I shall also discuss certain organizational problems for which I believe a synthesized model would provide a more adequate tool of analysis. Before doing so, however, I shall first attempt to state briefly some of the assumptions involved in the rational and natural-system models.

The Rational Model of Organizational Analysis

In the rational model, the organization is conceived as an "instrument"—that is, as a rationally conceived means to the realization of expressly announced group goals. Its structures are understood as tools deliberately established for the efficient realization of these group purposes. Organizational behavior is thus viewed as consciously and rationally administered, and changes in organizational patterns are viewed as planned devices to improve the level of efficiency. The rational model assumes that decisions are made on the basis of a rational survey of the situation, utilizing certified knowledge, with a deliberate orientation to an expressly codified legal apparatus. The focus is, therefore, on the

legally prescribed structures—*i.e.*, the formally "blueprinted" patterns
—since these are more largely subject to deliberate inspection and rational manipulation.

This model takes account of departures from rationality but often tends to assume that these departures derive from random mistakes, due to ignorance or error in calculation. Fundamentally, the rational model implies a "mechanical" model, in that it views the organization as a structure of manipulable parts, each of which is separately modifiable with a view to enhancing the efficiency of the whole. Individual organizational elements are seen as subject to successful and planned modification, enactable by deliberate decision. The long-range development of the organization as a whole is also regarded as subject to planned control and as capable of being brought into increasing conformity with explicitly held plans and goals.

The Natural-System Model of Organizational Analysis

The natural-system model regards the organization as a "natural whole," or system. The realization of the goals of the system as a whole is but one of several important needs to which the organization is oriented. Its component structures are seen as emergent institutions, which can be understood only in relation to the diverse needs of the total system. The organization, according to this model, strives to survive and to maintain its equilibrium, and this striving may persist even after its explicitly held goals have been successfully attained. This strain toward survival may even on occasion lead to the neglect or distortion of the organization's goals. Whatever the plans of their creators, organizations, say the natural-system theorists, become ends in themselves and possess their own distinctive needs which have to be satisfied. Once established, organizations tend to generate new ends which constrain subsequent decisions and limit the manner in which the nominal group goals can be pursued.

Organizational structures are viewed as spontaneously and homeostatically maintained. Changes in organizational patterns are considered the results of cumulative, unplanned, adaptive responses to threats to the equilibrium of the system as a whole. Responses to problems are thought of as taking the form of crescively developed defense mechanisms and as being importantly shaped by shared values which are deeply internalized in the members. The empirical focus is thus directed to the spontaneously emergent and normatively sanctioned structures in the organization.

The focus is not on deviations from rationality but, rather, on disruptions of organizational equilibrium, and particularly on the mechanisms by which equilibrium is homeostatically maintained. When deviations from planned purposes are considered, they are viewed not so much as due to ignorance or error but as arising from constraints imposed by the existent social structure. In given situations, the ignorance of certain participants may not be considered injurious but functional to the maintenance of the system's equilibrium.

The natural-system model is typically based upon an underlying "organismic" model which stresses the interdependence of the component parts. Planned changes are therefore expected to have ramifying consequences for the whole organizational system. When, as frequently happens, these consequences are unanticipated, they are usually seen as divergent from, and not as supportive of, the planner's intentions. Natural-system theorists tend to regard the organization as a whole as organically "growing," with a "natural history" of its own which is planfully modifiable only at great peril, if at all. Long-range organizational development is thus regarded as an evolution, conforming to "natural laws" rather than to the planner's designs.

The Two Models Compared

Needless to say, these two models are ideal types in the sense that few modern sociologists studying organizations adopt one to the complete exclusion of the other. Nevertheless, as we have mentioned previously, some sociologists tend to stress one model more than the other.

Each of these models has certain characteristic strengths and weaknesses. The rational model, for example, has the indisputable merit of focusing attention on some of the very patterns which distinguish the modern organization, particularly its rationality. At the same time, however, it tends to neglect the manner in which those patterns which the modern organization shares with "natural" groups may also effect behavior within them. The fact is, of course, that the distinguishing characteristics of a bureaucratic organization are not its only characteristics; systematic attention must also be directed to those features of modern organizations, such as the need for loyalty, which they have in common with other types of groups.

The natural-system model, on the other hand, has the merit of focusing attention on the spontaneous and unplanned (that is, "informal") patterns of belief and interaction that arise even within the rationally planned organization. Often, however, the natural-system model tends to neglect the distinctively rational features of the modern organization.

Sometimes both of these models are used in organizational analysis in an eclectic manner; one part of the organization is analyzed in terms of the rational model and another part in terms of the natural-system model. Studies using this approach tend to present the organization as two distinctive parts, running eternally on parallel tracks; many of them fail to work out the manner in which the rational and informal patterns merge into and influence each other. For example, in the Western Electric studies, Roethlisberger and Dickson distinguished between the logics of cost and efficiency, on the one hand, and the logic of sentiment, on the other. They maintain that the former characterizes managerial elites, whereas the latter is distinctive of employee or worker echelons.[7] Warner and Low's study of industrial conflict in Yankee City [8] makes a similar point. These authors regard the managerial group as dominated by the aim of producing "at the lowest possible cost and highest profit," and maintain that advancement is given primarily to those who contribute more to the "efficiency of production." As a result of this dichotomy between the rational and the natural-system models, the nonrational, traditionalistic orientations of management personnel have been obscured and informal organization tends to be examined primarily among lower ranking personnel. Conversely, the rationalistic orientations of lower echelons, at least with respect to their own ends, tends to be treated as a façade for their own underlying nonrational needs.

Applied Social Science and Organizational Analysis

The statement that the natural-system model neglects the distinctive features of the modern organization means, above all, that it tends

[7] F. J. Roethlisberger and W. J. Dickson, with the assistance of H. A. Wright, *Management and the Worker*, Harvard University Press, 1939, p. 565.

[8] W. L. Warner and J. O. Low, *The Social System of the Modern Factory*, Yale University Press, 1947, pp. 172-73.

to minimize the significance of rationally organized structures and patterns of planned adaptation. It tends, for example, to overlook the full implications of the fact that the modern organization meets its own peculiar needs, as well as those which it shares with all groups, in certain distinctive ways. To illustrate: modern organizations systematically evaluate the degree to which their policies are effective; they rationally appraise the relative effectiveness of the various departments within the organization; they conduct market researches and public-opinion studies which keep them in touch with their suppliers and outlets; they select new recruits and evaluate group members through various kinds of psychological tests; they defend policies with the use of research; they wage war against competitors with facts and figures and rationally documented argumentation; and they prepare for unforeseeable contingencies by briefing their administrators with digests of scientifically accumulated "background information." Indeed, these administrators may stake their very authority on what they know or on what knowledge they can purchase. All this is too well known to require further elaboration. There is a question, however, whether its full significance has been appreciated and theoretically assimilated by those using the natural-system model.

One pattern of particular interest to sociologists deserves to be stressed in this connection. In the modern organization, behavioral science has become a kind of working equivalent for, or supplement to, the profit and loss statement; various types of social research have supplanted the bookkeeper's ledgers as bases of rational decision in cases in which pecuniary consequences cannot be calculated. The very rationality of the modern organization has made it increasingly dependent upon the kinds of information that can be supplied by operations or market researchers, opinion pollsters, industrial sociologists, morale surveyors, and group dynamicists.

Although these newer patterns require only a small part of the organization's budget, they have substantial theoretical implications for organizational analysis. For applied social science has, in effect, become one of the planned functional substitutes for the spontaneous adaptive mechanisms by means of which the rational organization responds to external threats, reduces internal disruptions, and controls various forms of social deviance. As such, it merits a place in the theoretical models and the empirical researches of organizational analysts. So far, however, organizational analysts have neglected to include in their researches a systematic study of the uses made of applied social science in the modern organization.

The neglect of applied social science within the organization, as an object of analysis and research, is, however, simply a special instance of a larger lacuna in organizational analysis. Modern organizational analysis by sociologists is overpreoccupied with the spontaneous and unplanned responses which organizations make to stress, and too little concerned with patterns of planned and rational administration. Only a few sociologists, notably Peter Blau, whose study of the use of statistical techniques of personnel rating is a trail-blazing research,[9] have investigated the latter area. Nonetheless, many of the current studies guided by the natural-system model are still fixated on the Comteian level.

In general, the natural-system model tends to induce neglect of the rational structures characterizing the modern organization, of the forces contributing to their growth, as well as of the distinctive ways in which they are maintained. It tends to take as given rather than as problematic such distinctive features of the modern organization as its complex division of labor, its legally formalized codes, its reliance upon professional and technical experts, its utilization of systematic bodies of knowledge, and its rationalistic orientation.

Use of the natural-system model tends to focus the analyst's concern on the forces that undermine the organization's impersonal principles and subvert its formal ends to "narrower" interests, rather than on those that sustain these and bolster the distinctively bureaucratic structures. It tends to lead to a focus on the characteristics that all occupations share, rather than on the distinctive features of the modern professional expert, who utilizes a body of systematized information. Nonetheless, the very rationality of the modern organization, as well as its other typical characteristics, varies in degree, and this very variation is itself in need of explanation.

The natural-system model, which developed in the course of polemics against the rational model, tends to minimize the role of rationality in human affairs and to counterstress the way in which organizational behavior is affected by nonrational norms. Theorists who use this model have typically emphasized the inherent vulnerability of rationally planned action, particularly action directed toward what might

[9] Peter Blau, *The Dynamics of Bureaucracy*, University of Chicago Press, 1955, Chap. 3.

be termed "liberal" goals. From its Comteian inceptions, the natural-system model has been infused with a conservative and antiliberal metaphysical pathos. In Michels' work this was expressed by an emphasis on the organizational constraints that inherently thwart democratic aspirations. But, characteristically, the natural-system theorists have tended to neglect study of the organizational constraints that conduce to the *realization* of democratic values. It is only recently that this line of analysis has been systematically developed by such organizational analysts as Lipset, Trow, and Coleman.[10]

Manifest and Latent Patterns

There is no doubt, however, that the focus of the natural-system model on the spontaneous mechanisms common to all groups has enabled it to make its most important contribution to the study of organizations. This focus has facilitated the discovery and analysis of the so-called informal organization, which tends to be obscured by the rational model. Yet there is a noteworthy ambiguity in the natural-system model concerning the meaning of "informal organization." In other words, although it is clear that the natural-system model directs attention beyond and away from the formally constituted organizational system, there remains a question concerning what it is that the model directs attention toward.

The notion of informal organization is a residual or cafeteria concept of diverse and sprawling contents. Some informal patterns are organizationally unprescribed culture structures—that is, patterns of belief and sentiment; for example, the belief that one should not be a "rate buster." Other informal patterns are organizationally unprescribed social structures; *e.g.*, the cliques that develop among those working near one another. Further, although the term "informal group" is sometimes used to refer to a primary relation, not all informal patterns involve friendly intimacy and closeness. Some may entail personal enmities, feuds, and conflicts.

Informal patterns vary in other significant ways. Some are patterns

[10] S. M. Lipset, M. Trow, and J. Coleman, *Union Democracy*, Free Press, 1956. For an early statement of my own thinking on this problem, see A. W. Gouldner, "Attitudes of 'Progressive' Trade Union Leaders," *Amer. J. Sociol.*, 52 (1947), 389-92.

prescribed by the traditional values in the larger society which are recognized as relevant within the organization; for example, the "no squealing" rules or the special deference which a supervisor may give to an elderly worker. Other informal patterns are prescribed only by the values traditional to a particular organization; for example, the tendency of professors on some campuses to address or refer to one another as "Mr."

Still other informal patterns are not prescribed by any traditional values, either in the larger society or in the particular organization, but largely derive from the competition or conflict for scarce information or goods; for example, the salesman's "personal following," or the congregation of males around their employer's private secretary. It is precisely this last type of informal pattern, which is not normatively prescribed, that characteristically tends to be neglected in the work of the natural-system theorists. Neglect of this pattern accounts in part for the fact that little systematic research has been done on the effects of machinery and office equipment, so characteristic of the modern organization, on social relations within it.

Some of the distinctive characteristics of the modern organization generate peculiar hazards for organizational analysis. In particular, the specialized roles within the organization, having such a high visibility, tend to become a focus of research, and analysis thus tends to become confined to these prescribed and institutionalized roles. This is a hazard to which both the rational and the natural-system models are susceptible, although not equally so. The natural-system theorists, somewhat more astute about this danger, have been concerned about the ways in which the "social" characteristics of personnel may shape organizational policy and behavior. Selznick's study of the TVA is an excellent example of this. Other studies have analyzed the manner in which the ethnic or religious origins of personnel affect their chances of mobility and the allocation of power within the organization.[11] As yet, however, organizational analysts have not incorporated in their theoretical models a

[11] See, for example, Orvis Collins, "Ethnic Behavior in Industry," *Amer. J. Sociol.*, 51 (1946), 293-98; Melville Dalton, "Informal Factors in Career Achievement," *Amer. J. Sociol.*, 56 (1951), 407-15; and E. C. Hughes, "Queries Concerning Industry and Society Growing Out of the Study of Ethnic Relations in Industry," *Amer. sociol. Rev.*, 14 (1949), 211-20.

systematic concern with the way in which the diverse social identities
that people bring into the organization affect organizational behavior.

It is obvious that all people in organizations have a variety of
"latent social identities" [12]—that is, identities which are not culturally
prescribed as relevant to or within rational organizations—and that
these do intrude upon and influence organizational behavior in interesting ways. For example, there is usually something occurring between
people of opposite sexes, even though this is prescribed neither by the
organization's official rules nor by the societal values deemed appropriate for that setting.[13] Yet many sociologists who study factories, offices,
schools, or mental hospitals take little note of the fact that the organizational role-players invariably have a gender around which is built a
latent social identity. One does not have to be a Freudian to insist that
sex makes a difference, even for organizational behavior. (It should be
noted that there is no analytic distinction between giving attention to
the ways in which latent ethnic or religious identities affect organizational behavior and examining the implications of latent sexual identities for organizational patterns.)

The point, then, is that there is a need to distinguish systematically
between those social identities of organization members which are consensually regarded as relevant or legitimate in that setting, and those
identities which are defined as irrelevant or inappropriate to consider
in that context. The manner in which both the manifest and the *latent*
social identities shape organizational behavior requires more attention.
Study of latent identities and roles within organizations promises to be
fruitful because, among other reasons, it provides a lever for approaching problems of organizational tension. For the pressure of the latent
roles on the manifest or formal roles within organizations is a persistent
source of strain on the equilibrium of every organization.

[12] The concepts of latent and manifest organizational identities and
roles is discussed in A. W. Gouldner, "Cosmopolitans and Locals: Toward
an Analysis of Latent Social Roles—I," *Admin. Sci. Quart.*, 2 (1957),
281-306.

[13] Among the perhaps esoteric but still theoretically interesting patterns partly structured by latent sexual identities is the "touch system,"
which regulates interpersonal bodily contacts. See Erving Goffman, "The
Nature of Deference and Demeanor," *Amer. Anthrop.*, 58 (1956), 486-88.

Organizational Tensions

In the following section I want to outline briefly some of the recurrent problems found within the modern organization—particularly those that seem to derive, in part at least, from the interaction of (1) the distinctive traits of the organization as a rational system of administration and (2) the more common needs of the organization as a spontaneously developed social system. My objective is to document the need for a synthesis and reconciliation of the rational and natural-system models. Among these problems are the following:

1. The authority of the modern administrator is characteristically legitimated on the basis of his specialized expertise; that is, administrators are regarded as proper incumbents of office on the basis of what they know about the organization or their professional skills, rather than whom they know. Problems arise, however, when administrators exert control over subordinates whose technical specialities or organizational experience differ from their own. For example, the orders and authority of a plant manager whose experience has been in electronics may be regarded as dubious and may be resisted when it is directed toward subordinates who are expert in chemistry or mechanical engineering. In the modern organization, with its highly specialized division of labor, administrators may know little or nothing of the diverse specializations under their command. How, then, can their authority be legitimated in terms of their specialized knowledge or experience?

There are, of course, various solutions to this problem. One is that, even in highly rational and technically specialized organizations, authority still tends in some measure to be legitimated on strictly legal grounds. That is, those who hold authority are endowed with a measure of imperative control and are authorized to command on the basis of their sheer incumbency in office. Consequently, there are two fundamentally different criteria for the legitimation of authority—authority based on technical knowledge and experience, and authority based on incumbency in office—simultaneously operating in the same organization. One of the deepest tensions in the modern organization, often expressed as a conflict between the line and staff groups,[14] derives from the divergence of these two bases of authority.

---

[14] See Melville Dalton, "Conflicts Between Staff and Line Managerial Officers," *Amer. sociol. Rev.*, 15 (1950), 342-51.

2. Another solution to the problem of exercising authority over unfamiliar specializations involves a self-imposed limitation on the criteria for inspecting and evaluating the performance of subordinates. The superior relinquishes control over the technical procedures which his subordinate uses, presumably giving the subordinate responsibility for these, and focuses instead on the subordinate's success or failure in realizing organizational goals. In short, it is results that count from the superior's standpoint. From the subordinate's standpoint, however, it is not merely results that count but also conformity with what his professional peers commonly regard as the proper technical procedures. Such conformity is a vital condition of the expert's good standing in his professional community and a significant component of his self-image as a competent professional. Consequently, there is usually some tension in the modern organization between the superior's pressure for results and the subordinate expert's insistence on proper technical procedure. This would seem to be an aspect of what Hughes has referred to as the conflict between "client emergency" and "professional routine." [15]

3. A third solution to the problem of legitimating authority over unfamiliar specializations is to define administration as a distinct field in itself, specializing in problems of "human relations." At this level, however, the problem still remains organizationally taxing, since so many line executives regard themselves as "born" experts in human relations. Pressure is therefore exerted to recruit individuals who have specialized training, and hence legitimate credentials, for human-relations work and administration.

Partly for this reason, new fields of administration and management have developed and acquired a strong infusion of social-science skills and theories. Social science, among other relevant disciplines, tends to serve increasingly as a legitimation for the authority of administrators in the modern organization.[16] To this extent, then, events are

[15] For some of Hughes' ideas about organizational analysis see E. C. Hughes, "Work and the Self," in J. H. Rohrer and M. Sherif (eds.), *Social Psychology at the Crossroads*, Harper, 1951.

[16] Current efforts of this sort are discussed in Whyte, *op. cit.* One of the most important stimuli in this direction was the work of Elton Mayo, *The Social Problems of an Industrial Civilization*, Harvard University Press, 1945.

confirming the prophecy of Saint-Simon and other early positivists that the social sciences, as well as the physical sciences, would provide a new pillar of authority in the modern world. This tendency, however, brings internal repercussions in the organization, involving conflicts along generational lines, between the new and old organizational elites. It may be that the mounting public criticism of "scientism" is in part a result of the fact that social science has become implicated in the struggle between entrenched and rising elites and provides a basis for the latter's challenge to the former, as well as of the fact that social scientists write stuffy and jargon-laden prose.

4. Also implicated in the strain between authority based on incumbency in office and authority based on technical knowledge are some of the special problems of recruiting, inspecting, and evaluating the performance of technical experts in the modern organization. Often, not only is the expert's immediate superior unqualified to judge him, but there are only one or a few qualified judges in the entire organization. Even if there are a few, they may be close friends or fierce competitors, whose judgments about one another will, in either event, be unreliable. This means that administrative superiors must depend upon persons outside the organization to select experts or to judge the performances of those already employed.

This, in turn, means that the technical expert himself is often dependent on persons outside his organization to validate his position within it. Consequently, his work must manifest a high degree of concern for the maintenance of technical standards. This not only disposes the expert to resist imperative pressures for "results," coming from his superiors, but it also makes him less vulnerable to control from those within and in command of his organization. In short, the expert's cosmopolitanism is in some measure a matter of constraint.

Thus linked with the outside, the expert is less likely to be regarded as an organization or "company" man. This implies that he is likely to be viewed as less than completely reliable or loyal to the organization. Around this focus, a conflict may develop between the organization's need for loyalty and its need for expertise. In industry, this conflict is commonly expressed as a dilemma between promotion on the basis of seniority—commonly used as an informal index of loyalty —and promotion on the basis of demonstrated skill and competence. Similar strains have been noted between "cosmopolitans" and "locals" —that is, between those who are primarily oriented to their professional specialization and those who are primarily committed to their employing organization.[17] When these organizational types become informally organized into cliques, factional conflicts between the "itinerants" and the "home-guard" may result.[18]

As Simon,[19] Barnard,[20] and others have stressed, every organization requires that its members have some degree of loyalty to it as a distinctive group. On the other hand, the modern organization also has a distinctive need for men with specialized skills and expertise. Both the rational-model and the natural-system-model theorists have tended to overlook the tensions which may arise as a result of efforts to satisfy these divergent needs. Weber, for example, tended to assume that the more expert the personnel, the more efficient the organization, and therefore the greater its stability. Suppose, however, as Saint-Simon asserted long ago, that those who are expert are also more cosmopolitan in outlook and, at the same time, less loyal to their employing organization.[21] In these circumstances, organizational survival may be threatened by a recruiting policy that considers only the candidate's expertise as much as by a policy that regards loyalty as more important than "brains."

Much of W. H. Whyte's recent study of the "organization man" is a discussion of current efforts by industry to attach managerial loyalty to the corporation. This attempt to manufacture organization men is, in effect, an effort to produce a new elite of loyal "locals," whose authority will be legitimated in terms of their human relations skills, thus perhaps counterbalancing the great growth of specialized experts, technicians,

---

[17] For more detailed discussion, see Gouldner, "Cosmopolitans and Locals," *loc. cit.*, and W. G. Bennis *et al.*, "Reference Groups and Loyalties in an Out-Patient Department," *Admin. Sci. Quart.*, 2 (1958), 481-500.

[18] These are analyzed in a study of the nursing profession by Robert W. Habenstein and Edwin A. Christ, *Professionalizer, Traditionalizer, and Utilizer*, University of Missouri, 1955, esp. Chap. 6.

[19] Herbert Simon, *Administrative Behavior*, Macmillan, 1948.

[20] Chester I. Barnard, *Organization and Management*, Harvard University Press, 1948.

[21] Both Whyte's work and my own seem to have converged independently on this same point. See Whyte, *op. cit.*, p. 232, and Gouldner, "Cosmopolitans and Locals," *loc. cit.* Bennis's research, *op. cit.*, also seems to support it, although certain seeming divergences from some of my own conclusions have yet to be clarified.

and engineers who may be more committed to their professions than to the organization.

Tension between the organization's need for loyalty and its need for specialized expertise does not seem to be a peculiarly American phenomenon. It seems likely, for example, to be implicated also in the Russians' periodic outbursts against "cosmopolitanism," in the conflicts between their politically reliable army commissars and their professional military men, as well as in the vagaries of Russian industrial development.[22] In this last connection, it seems noteworthy that some of the earliest Russian purges were directed against engineers and technicians.

There are, in brief, various indications of the existence of tension between an organization's bureaucratic need for expertise and its social-system needs for loyalty; each sets certain limits within which the other may be pursued.

5. Another tension of modern organizations may also be seen as deriving from the relation between its bureaucratic rationality and its social-system imperatives. If the organization is regarded as a natural system, and if its stability, as Parsons contends, depends upon the degree to which the various role players within it conform to one another's expectations, these complementary expectations of the role players will to some degree involve unstated traditional beliefs and values derived during the course of socialization in the larger society.

Often, however, the traditional social values and the distinctively rational bureaucratic values diverge. For example, the bureaucratic premise that organizational authority should be given to those with skill and competence may diverge from traditional values in the environing society which require that authority be vested in older people rather than younger ones, or in males rather than females.[23] Application of the bureaucratic premise in these circumstances may lead to endemic strains in organizations. Here we may note an instance of the tension-inducing pressure which latent social roles can exert on manifest organizational roles.

Furthermore, the primary group, with its traditional values, is usually the first paradigm of group behavior and of "proper" human

[22] Work done by Robert A. Feldmesser at Harvard University would seem to lend substantiation to this.

[23] See William F. Whyte, *Human Relations in the Restaurant Industry*, McGraw-Hill, 1948, esp. p. 75.

Demographic and Social Structure

relations with which the individual becomes familiar. He may then, as Merton has indicated,[24] tend to evaluate secondary groups in terms of primary-group standards and, finding them too impersonal, react with hostility toward the procedures of the organization, criticizing them as "red tape."

The role players in modern organizations must, in some measure, derive their mutual expectations from sources other than the codified rules. Consequently, the stability of their relationship is always to some extent contingent upon the extent to which they conform with one another's informal, traditional, and implicit expectations. However, the very stress in modern organizations upon the formal, legal rules means that the explicit acknowledgment of an expectation frequently becomes the criterion of its legitimacy. Expectations which have not been given explicit acknowledgment, through contractual or other legal enactments, tend to become regarded as liberties which are permissible or even preferred but are not seen as fully obligatory. Consequently, the legitimacy of all merely implied expectations, the traditional supports on which the organization must in part rest, are vulnerable to sudden challenges and disruptions.

This can be stated from a more general perspective. The rationality of the modern organization means that "things can always be made better," that "nothing is sacred," and, consequently, that nothing is unchangeable. Rationality therefore tends to spill over from the administration of inanimate things to the administration of human relations; it invades areas that were hitherto traditionally and informally controlled. This may generate organizational instabilities in several ways: First, the treatment of human beings as instruments may violate cultural norms prescribing that people should be viewed as ends in themselves. It may, therefore, give rise to accusations of manipulation. Secondly, such unceasing drives to rationalize the organization may impair those very spontaneous homeostatic controls that have hitherto contributed to the organization's equilibrium. To the extent that this occurs, the drive toward rational administration creates new problems which then have to be planfully resolved. The drive toward rationality thus becomes self-generative. This process would seem to underlie the

[24] Robert K. Merton, "Bureaucratic Structure and Personality," *Soc. Forces*, 18 (1940), 560-68.

tendency toward "increasing rationalization" in modern society of which both Weber and Karl Mannheim spoke.

The Functional Autonomy of Organizational Parts

There is one limitation on the natural-system model which derives largely from certain unexamined assumptions in the notion of a "system." This has to do with its emphasis on the interdependence of the parts within an organization. (In speaking of an organization's "parts," I refer both to its group structures or roles and to the socialized individuals who are its members.) The natural-system model tends to focus on the organization as a whole, to take the "interdependence" of the parts as a given, and therefore fails to explore systematically the significance of variations in the *degrees* of interdependence.[25]

This problem can be stated in terms of the "functional autonomy" of the parts of a system—*i.e.,* the degree to which any one part is dependent on others for the satisfaction of its needs.[26] Systems in which parts have "high" functional autonomy may be regarded as having a "low" degree of system interdependence; conversely, systems in which parts have "low" functional autonomy have a "high" degree of system interdependence. The concept of functional autonomy directs attention to the fact that *some* parts may survive separation from others, that parts vary in their dependence upon one another, and that their interdependence is not necessarily symmetrical.

It is obvious, for example, that younger children have less functional autonomy than older ones in that they have a lower probability of survival, other things being equal, in the event of their separation from the nuclear family. Within an organizational context, an example of asymmetrical interdependence would be the relation between the production and the public-relations departments of a business firm. If the two are somehow disjoined, the former normally has a higher

[25] *Cf.* Robert K. Merton, *Social Theory and Social Structure,* Free Press, 1957, pp. 25 *et seq.*

[26] For a more detailed discussion of the problem of functional autonomy, see Alvin W. Gouldner, "Reciprocity and Autonomy in Functional Theory," in L. Z. Gross (ed.) *Symposium on Social Theory,* Row, Peterson, 1958.

probability of survival than the latter. That management usually regards the organization as more dependent upon the production department than the public-relations department is evident during times of budgetary crisis, when it is commonly the public-relations rather than the production department that suffers the greatest cutbacks. One crude, rule-of-thumb index of the functional autonomy of an organizational part, at least in a market society, is the extent to which it can obtain independent financing from sources outside of the organization. It would be instructive to examine, within a university, the comparative functional autonomy of, say, its engineering department and its English department from this point of view.

The tendency of the natural-system model, as I have said, is to focus on the system as a whole and to overstate the degree of mutual interdependence and integration among its parts. Conversely, it can be said to neglect the functional autonomy of the parts. One example of this tendency is to be found in Parsons' attempt to define an organization in terms of its orientation to goals.[27] In Parsons' terms, organizations are social systems which are primarily oriented toward the attainment of a specific goal. But an organization as such cannot be said to be oriented toward a goal, except in a merely metaphorical sense, unless it is assumed that its parts possess a much lower degree of functional autonomy than can in fact be observed. The statement that an organization is oriented toward certain goals often means no more than that these are the goals of its top administrators, or that they represent its societal function, which is another matter altogether.

More precise formulation would require specification of the ends of various people, or of the typical ends of different parts or strata, within the organization. Such a specification would indicate that these ends may vary, are not necessarily identical, and may, in fact, be contradictory. The natural-system theorist, however, may tend to neglect this fact because his underemphasis on the functional autonomy of the system parts and his overemphasis on their mutual interdependence sometimes leads him to treat the organization as if it were a complex organism which, as such, is quite capable of having "ends."

Assuming that the organization's parts, no less than the organization as a whole, operate to maintain their boundaries and to remain in

[27] Talcott Parsons, "Suggestions for a Sociological Approach to a Theory of Organization—I," *Admin. Sci. Quart.*, 1 (1956), 63-85.

equilibrium, then the parts should be expected to defend their functional autonomy, or at least some measure of it, from encroachment.
This suggests that a basic source of organizational tension may derive,
on the one hand, from the tendency of the parts to resist encroach-
ments on their functional autonomy and, on the other, from contrary
tendencies of the organization's controlling center to limit or reduce
the functional autonomy of the parts. The widely noted tensions between field offices and main offices, as well as the common organizational oscillation between centralization and decentralization seem to
support this assumption, as do the frequently observed rejection of
"close supervision" [28] and the pressure which almost all role players
exert to maintain some social distance from and freedom from control
by those most crucially concerned with their work.[29]

Mechanisms of Functional Autonomy

Because the natural-system model, as I have mentioned, tends to
focus analysis too narrowly on the ways in which parts are integrated
into the system as a whole, it neglects systematic analysis of the
mechanisms which parts develop to vouchsafe their functional autonomy. One example of these mechanisms is what Goffman has called
"rituals of avoidance.[30] In the modern organization, one of the most

[28] See Daniel Katz and Robert Kahn, "Human Organization and
Worker Motivation," in L. Reed Tripp (ed.), *Industrial Productivity*, Industrial Relations Research Association, 1951.

[29] *Cf.* E. C. Hughes, in Rohrer, *op. cit.* See also Chris Argyris, "The
Individual and the Organization: Some Problems of Mutual Adjustment,"
Admin. Sci. Quart., 2 (1957), 1-24. The reader with philosophical interests will detect that I have in part been dealing with a classic problem
which has been fruitfully analyzed in terms of the distinction between
Apollonian and Dionysian drives in the work of Nietzsche, Cassirer, and,
more recently, Charles Morris. I believe that the empirical sociologist can
still derive much of value, in connection with the present problem, from
a re-examination of their work.

[30] See Goffman, *loc. cit.*, and "Secondary Adjustment in Complex Organizations," a paper presented at the annual meetings of the American
Sociological Society, 1957. Compare also the insightful discussion of the
mechanisms developed by suburbanites to gain relief from group pressures
in W. H. Whyte, Jr., *op. cit.*, p. 390.

common of these is, of course, the "coffee break" (which, needless to say, may involve consumption of other liquids or of none). Only the naive will assume that the sole function of the coffee break is to procure liquid refreshment or will fail to see that its latent function is to get people away from the office.

Mechanisms for the maintenance of functional autonomy may also entail use of various "material props" as devices which both symbolize and constrain a degree of social distance between role players. One case of this occurs in the department-store salesclerk's use of the sales counter as a barrier between herself and the customer.[31] Another interesting example is to be found in W. F. Whyte's analysis of the use of the "spindle" to limit the interaction between waitresses and pantry help in restaurants.[32]

There are many social and culture structures that serve, wittingly or not, to maintain the functional autonomy of the organization's parts; indeed, the point of these remarks is that all major structures can be profitably investigated from this perspective. In the culture structure, for example, norms of privacy, of privileged communication, of confidentiality of information;[33] norms which call for the hoarding of technical knowledge or the guarding of office secrets; norms which deny to "outsiders" the right and competence to judge technical performances—all commonly serve to reinforce the functional autonomy of organizational parts. On the level of social structures, students of "informal" organization have long recognized that cliques function to enable work associates to resist pressures placed upon them by those in formal authority, and that, further, the undertaking of multiple organizational functions often enables a part to resist control from any single quarter. Indeed, one of the basic functions of any system of roles is to limit the control which others may have over a given role player by limiting, either explicitly or implicitly, his obligations to them. Similarly, analysis in terms of "backstage" or "onstage"[34] or

[31] See George F. Lombard, *Behavior in a Selling Group*, Harvard University Graduate School of Business Administration, 1955, p. 185.

[32] *Op. cit.*, p. 75.

[33] See the discussion of "visibility" in Merton, *Social Theory and Social Structure*, esp. pp. 341 *et seq.*

[34] These concepts are discussed fully in Erving Goffman, *Presentation of Self in Everyday Life*, University of Edinburgh Press, 1956.

in terms of "insulation" often implies a concern for the *ecological* mechanisms [35] by means of which an organizational part maintains its functional autonomy.

The central point here is that current natural-system models tend to lose sight of the autonomy of the system parts, of their autonomy strivings and strategies, as well as of the ways in which such strategies may induce tensions among the other segments or within the system as a whole. This oversight, I suggest, derives primarily from the unqualified assumption which is made about the interdependence of organizational parts.

The natural-system model too readily assumes that the structure of the organization serves only to link parts and to provide avenues for controlling and integrating them. However, the structure of complex organizations also serves to maintain and protect the parts from others within the same system, at least in some degree. Thus organizational structure is shaped by a tension between centrifugal and centripetal pressures, limiting as well as imposing control over parts, separating as well as joining them.

The Reciprocities Multiplier

The natural-system-model theorist commonly assumes that the equilibrium of a group depends very greatly on the conforming behavior of group members. More explicitly, and in Parsons' terms, it is held that group equilibrium is a function of the extent to which group members, Ego and Alter, conform with each other's expectations. Before considering the relevance of this equilibrium model for the analysis of bureaucratic organization, I shall examine one of the general empirical assumptions implicit in it.

This model seems to assume that each of a sequence of identical conforming acts will yield either the same or an increasing degree of appreciation or satisfaction and will thus elicit the same or an increasing amount of reward. This may be regarded as an implicit assumption of Parsons' equilibrium model, for, otherwise it is difficult to understand how he can maintain that "the complementarity of role-expectations, once established, is not problematical. . . . No special mechanisms

---

[35] See, for example, Raymond W. Mack, "Ecological Patterns in an Industrial Shop," *Soc. Forces*, 32 (1954), 351-56.

are required for the explanation of the maintenance of complementary interaction-orientation." [36] So far as I am aware, however, no evidence exists to substantiate the crucial assumption that rewarding responses to a series of identical conforming actions will either remain the same or increase. On the contrary, both impressionistic observations and theoretical considerations would lead one to doubt it. Here, as in the previous discussion of system "interdependence," the crux of the matter is a question of degree.

Ego's conforming acts, it must be assumed, always have some consequences for Alter's expectations; expectations are always modified by prior relevant actions. The question, of course, is, modified in what manner? To state it crudely, we would assume that the longer the sequence of Ego's conforming actions, the more likely is Alter to take Ego's conformity for granted. The more Alter takes Ego's conformity for granted, the less appreciative Alter will feel and the less propensity he will have to reward and reciprocate Ego's conforming actions. For example, we would expect workers to feel less gratified when their employer pays them their regular weekly wage then when he does something for them that they do not take for granted, such as providing an unexpected bonus.

The general theoretical point made here is complementary to the point cogently made by Robert Merton when he holds that *some* measure of anomic or nonconforming behavior may be beneficial to group stability.[37] Approaching the problem from the other side, we have held that at some point repeated acts of conformity may induce a strain toward anomic insatiability and group instability, when, in order to maintain the level of reward previously given him, Ego must conform increasingly with Alter's standards. For our analysis suggests that a sequence of identical conforming actions undergoes an inflationary spiral and that later conforming actions are worth less than earlier ones, in terms of the rewards or propensity to reciprocate which they elicit. We cannot assume, therefore, that identical acts of conformity will yield identical increments in group equilibrium. Consequently, it would seem that, unless Parsons' model is revised to include the "special mechanisms" for which he denies the necessity, his generalized model of a social system contains internally induced tendencies toward

[36] Talcott Parsons, *The Social System,* Free Press, 1951, p. 205.
[37] "Bureaucratic Structure and Personality," *loc. cit.,* 182-83.

entropy or disorder, and the factors now assumed to be involved in it are insufficient to maintain the system in an indefinite state of equilibrium.

Basic to this analysis is the assumption that repeated identical acts of conformity modify—*i.e.*, increase or reinforce—the *expectation* of conformity. Conformity is thus taken for granted, and thereby the propensity to reciprocate is weakened. But other factors in addition to sheer repetition can strengthen the expectation of conformity and thus similarly reduce the appreciation or gratitude felt and undermine the propensity to reward the conformer. Among these other factors, I postulate, is the degree to which Alter feels that Ego's conforming actions are imposed upon him, either by situational constraint or by moral obligation. In other words, if Alter feels that a given conforming act has been imposed upon Ego, we would expect Alter to value and reciprocate it less than if he defined Ego's conformity as "voluntary." [38]

Conversely, the more Ego's conforming action is defined by Alter as voluntary, the greater is Alter's tendency to appreciate and reward it. For example, we would expect a woman to respond to a birthday gift from her husband with less appreciation and less propensity to reciprocate than to the same gift given when there was no special occasion calling for it. Stated generally, the degree of appreciation or propensity to reciprocate is hypothesized to be an inverse (or perhaps a negative exponential) function of the degree to which a desired action is perceived as imposed upon the actor. In other words, reciprocity is a function of the degree to which a given act is desired, multiplied by the degree to which the act is perceived as voluntary.

Since these considerations take a very generalized model as their point of departure, it is clear that they should have application to diverse groups, to family interaction no less than to behavior within a modern bureaucracy. Here, however, we can pursue their implications only with respect to the modern bureaucratic organization. What we mean by "bureaucratization" is, in part, the explication of the group member's rights and obligations through the installation of formal rules and regulations. In other words, the more an organization is

---

[38] Research currently being done by Doyle Kent Rice, Richard A. Peterson, and myself is exploring this general problem area, and preliminary indications of our data would seem to substantiate the point made here.

bureaucratized (and this is clearly a variable), the more the conforming behavior of people in the organization will tend to be perceived as imposed upon them by the rules, rather than as voluntary.

This tendency, in turn, may generate a vicious cycle of increasing bureaucratization. That is, the more formal rules there are governing action, the more conforming actions will be devalued in that they will yield smaller increments of appreciation or gratitude which can motivate reciprocity, and the more the rules will be further elaborated and enforced to prevent the decline in motivation from impairing the organization. (It may be that a corollary of this helps to explain the great stability of primary relations: that is, the more vague obligations in primary relations dispose to a greater appreciation of desired and conforming actions.) In the bureaucratic organization, there may, however, be a development of new patterns of "indulgency" based upon the relinquishing of the rules. That is, administrators may voluntarily withhold application of certain formal rules, even though they have a right to apply them. Nonapplication of a rule, when it is not imposed upon or obligatory for the actor, constitutes a "favor" and multiplies the other person's tendency to reciprocate, thus recharging the informal system and making the formal rules less necessary for organizational operation.

To summarize, it has been suggested that a major task confronting organizational analysis is the reconciliation of the rational and natural-system models. What is needed is a single and synthesized model which will at once aid in analyzing the distinctive characteristics of the modern organization as a rational bureaucracy, the characteristics which it shares with other kinds of social systems, and the relationship of these characteristics to one another. I have briefly indicated a number of organizational problems which seem to derive from a conjunction of forces from both these levels. My attention has been focused largely on the natural-system model, because it is the one dominant among sociologists. In effect, this model constitutes a statement of the assumptions which sociologists frequently employ for analysis of diverse kinds of groups, including the modern organization. It becomes apparent, with our discussion of the "reciprocities multiplier," that the further development of organizational analysis is contingent upon the clarification of the basic models of sociological analysis and the verification of the empirical assumptions on which these models rest.

Selected Bibliography

The most thorough bibliography on bureaucracy is to be found in *Reader in Bureaucracy*, edited by Merton *et al.*, cited below. S. N. Eisenstadt is currently preparing another bibliography of relevant materials.

Gouldner, Alvin W., "Cosmopolitans and Locals: Toward an Analysis of Latent Social Roles," *Admin. Sci. Quart.*, 2 (1957–58), 281-306, 444-80.

———, "Metaphysical Pathos and the Theory of Bureaucracy," *Amer. Polit. Sci. Rev.*, 49 (1955), 496-507.

———, *Patterns of Industrial Bureaucracy*, Free Press, 1954.

———, *Wildcat Strike*, Antioch Press, 1954.

———, "Red Tape as a Social Problem," in R. K. Merton *et al* (eds.), *Reader in Bureaucracy*, Free Press, 1952.

———, (ed.), *Studies in Leadership*, Harper, 1950.

Barnard, Chester I., *The Functions of the Executive*, Harvard University Press, 1938.

———, *Organization and Management*, Harvard University Press, 1948.

Bendix, Reinhard, "Bureaucracy: the Problem and Its Setting," *Amer. sociol. Rev.*, 12 (1947), 493-507.

Blau, Peter, *Bureaucracy in Modern Society*, Random House, 1956.

Clark, Burton R., *Adult Education in Transition*, University of California Press, 1956.

Gerth, H. H., and C. W. Mills (eds.), *From Max Weber: Essays in Sociology*, Oxford University Press, 1948.

Gusfield, Joseph R., "The Problem of Generations in an Organizational Structure," *Soc. Forces*, 35 (1957), 323-30.

Leighton, Alexander H., *The Governing of Men*, Princeton University Press, 1946.

Lipset, Seymour M., M. Trow, and J. Coleman, *Union Democracy*, Free Press, 1956.

Merton, Robert K., *et al.* (eds.), *Reader in Bureaucracy*, Free Press, 1952.

Michels, Robert, *Political Parties*, Free Press, 1949.

Parsons, Talcott, "Suggestions for a Sociological Theory of Organization," *Admin. Sci. Quart.*, 1 (1956), 63-85, 225-39.

Selznick, Philip, *Leadership in Administration*, Row, Peterson, 1957.

———, *The Organizational Weapon: A Study of Bolshevik Strategy and Tactics*, McGraw-Hill, 1952.

———, *TVA and the Grass Roots*, University of California Press, 1949.

Simon, Herbert A., *Administrative Behavior*, Macmillan, 1948.

Stanton, Alfred H., and Morris S. Schwartz, *The Mental Hospital*, Basic Books, 1954.

Whyte, William F., *Human Relations in the Restaurant Industry*, McGraw-Hill, 1948.

Whyte, Jr., William H., *The Organization Man*, Simon and Schuster, 1956.

19
Social
Differentiation and
Stratification[1] ⌒

LEONARD BROOM

University of Texas, Austin

Broadly defined, social stratification covers so large a part of sociology that a synoptic assessment would be a major work and a critical assessment in a brief paper would be bad manners.[2] This paper is principally devoted to the pervasive problem of "goodness of fit,"[3] a topic that seems to offer particularly good prospects for

---

[1] The helpfulness of Frances G. Scott is gratefully acknowledged.

[2] Three publications afford general and rather different surveys of the field, but until quite recently there were none at all: Bernard Barber, *Social Stratification*, Harcourt, Brace, 1957; J. A. Kahl, *The American Class Structure*, Rinehart, 1957; and Kurt B. Mayer, *Class and Society*, Doubleday, 1955. For a rich sampler and bibliography, see R. Bendix and S. M. Lipset (eds.), *Class, Status and Power: A Reader in Social Stratification*, Free Press, 1953; and for bibliography, Harold W. Pfautz, "The Current Literature on Social Stratification: Critique and Bibliography," *Amer. J. Sociol.*, 58 (1953), 391-418; and "Social Stratification and Social Mobility," *Curr. Sociol.*, 2:1,4 (1953–54).

[3] An early expression of concern with this problem in the sociological literature is Sumner's notion of a strain toward consistency in the mores. See William Graham Sumner, *Folkways*, Ginn, 1906, esp. "The strain of improvement and consistency," pp. 5-6; "Consistency in the mores," p. 391 and "Inertia and rigidity of the mores," pp. 79-80.

bringing together contemporary studies that have technical virtuosity with the classic interests of the field.

Goodness of fit in stratification may be approached from three major perspectives: (1) status consistency at the level of the individual, (2) the consistency of attributes of the strata, and (3) the relationship between differentiated systems of strata and associated subcultures.

Status Consistency of the Individual

The study of status consistency has claimed an increasing part of the energy and resources of sociologists and deserves to continue to do so. In this topic, the social-psychological and the structural interests of sociology converge. Status consistency is also a field in which practical inferences may be readily recognized—*e.g.*, in problems of socialization and personality formation, in considerations related to mental health because of the hypothesized relationship between conflicting self-definitions and strain, and in problems of role conflict and marginality.

Some provocative recent work has gone under the designation "status crystallization." [4] The term "crystallization" is perhaps not the happiest choice, for it connotes rigidity quite as much as the mutual reinforcement of statuses. One may hypothesize that mutually reinforcing statuses are conducive to stability, but to imply this by assumption burdens the case. To use a term that unintentionally invites the assumption is even more burdensome. The neutral term "status consistency" seems more likely to deserve consensual acceptance.

At this point, status consistency is treated as a positional variable, and the discussion emphasizes the relative ranks of the multiple statuses of people in an attempt to state the problematics more clearly. (Unranked statuses may also be assessed for their consistency, but this would be inappropriate to the study of social stratification.) In any case, for purposes of exploratory inquiry, stratified data probably present the fewest methodological obstacles. The conception allows for analysis of

[4] Gerhard Lenski, "Status Crystallization: A Non-Vertical Dimension of Social Status," *Amer. sociol. Rev.*, 19 (1954), 405-13, and "Social Participation and Status Crystallization," *Amer. sociol. Rev.*, 21 (1956), 458-64; William F. Kenkel, "The Relationship Between Status Consistency and Politico-Economic Attitudes," *Amer. sociol. Rev.*, 21 (1956), 365-68; and Gerhard Lenski, "Comment on Kenkel's Communication," *Amer. sociol. Rev.*, 21 (1956), 368-69.

the consistency or inconsistency of the behaviors invoked by the several statuses. The consistency of cultural values and their functioning within the stratification system are touched upon briefly below.

As a *positional* variable, status consistency may be described by the scores of an individual on a number of ranked attributes. A study of the consistency of these scores can establish, first, how well the attributes and the social roles imputed to their possessors "fit" together and, secondly, how the over-all social position of the individual compares with that of other individuals in the same society. The selected attributes for measurement should be, as far as possible, indicators of positions crucial to the maintenance of social order. By this criterion, Lenski's attributes of occupation, income, education, and ethnicity [5] are well chosen for contemporary American society. In other societies and at other times, different attributes, such as age, degree of nobility, or physical strength, might be required.

Once measured, status consistency, as an independent variable, can be related to a wide range of dependent variables. Persons can be distinguished roughly according to the consistency or inconsistency of their multiple positions (*i.e.,* the presence or manifest lack of "fit"). However, determining an individual's status consistency (or lack of it) does not describe his profile—that is, his location on several ranks or scales. For example, a person's statuses are considered inconsistent if he is "high" on ethnicity and education but "low" on occupation and income; however, his statuses are equally inconsistent if the pattern of these measures is reversed or if they appear in some other order. Variations in profiles are not random, and certain profile variations or profile types are probably crucially important to role conflict, upward mobility, and mental health.

A different but related variable, the individual's awareness or perception of his own status consistency or that of another, is implicit in much of the discussion of status consistency. Failure to make a clear distinction between awareness of position and position itself is a source of confusion. Awareness is a useful conception, but it is, of course, social-psychological rather than positional. It cannot and must not be imputed *a priori* from measures of status consistency, however these

[5] See "Status Crystallization: A Non-Vertical Dimension of Social Status," *op. cit.*; Kenkel, *loc. cit.*, used rankings on occupation, education, rental value of dwelling, and dwelling-area prestige.

measures are arrived at. Awareness of status consistency may be used most profitably as an intervening variable. It invites hypotheses phrased in the following manner: Persons manifesting a given profile of status inconsistencies and being to a given degree *aware* of these inconsistencies will manifest specified attitudes or behaviors. Although one may suspect that consistencies and inconsistencies affect behavior, it should be recognized that many persons live compartmentalized lives and are not aware of or affected by status inconsistency.

It should be re-emphasized that awareness of status consistency cannot be defined operationally in terms of status consistency itself. Awareness of status consistency is an empirical problem, and one that has received little systematic investigation. It is a problem analogous to the stratum-class distinction. In the latter case, one asks if the social aggregates delineated by the observer are merely statistical constructs (strata) or if they have associated properties of identification (class consciousness). It is analytically useful to maintain the distinction between consistency and awareness of consistency. For example, one might hypothesize that individuals with status inconsistencies and a high degree of awareness of these inconsistencies are more likely to be mobile, or at least to aspire to higher status. If this proves to be the case, one would expect such persons frequently to drop out of former voluntary associations and even formal organizations and to become active in new ones.[6]

An additional source of inconsistency lies in variations between observers in the evaluations they accord to an individual's ranked positions. Even those positions defined "objectively" from census-type data may have varying "subjective" evaluations by different observers and, therefore, may profoundly influence the individual awareness discussed above. Statuses that are stratified in the same way by a large part of the population and in which the rankings of individuals show high consensus are likely to be consequential in defining individuals and in affecting their self-definitions. When consensus is lacking, status rank-

[6] This possibility may have been overlooked by Lenski in "Social Participation and Status Crystallization." He attributes low participation to low crystallization. Certainly, awareness of status inconsistency and its intervening effects on upward mobility should be exhaustively assessed before low crystallization *per se* can be taken as the independent variable. One may guess that concomitants of status striving may account for at least part of Lenski's findings.

ings should not be regarded as elements of social order and should be treated neither as parts of a stratification system nor as deserving of consistency analysis.

The Functional Implications of Consistency

In discussing goodness of fit, one should beware of permitting a descriptive attribute to become translated into a normative estimate; that is, a presumptive evaluation of high consistency as "good" and low consistency as "bad" should be avoided. This caveat obtains for the topics covered later in this paper as well as for the status consistency of individuals.

There remains, however, the very real and interesting problem of discovering the points at which bad fit becomes dysfunctional.[7] (The empirical condition is specified because fit is always appropriate to some situation.) For example, an individual with very high status consistency, in a highly mobile society of heterogeneous membership, may be incapable of interacting effectively with individuals who have a diversity of backgrounds. Similarly, an individual with low consistency might encounter strain in a setting in which his interactions are limited to groups composed of individuals of uniform backgrounds. But in a society of high mobility, status inconsistency may free the individual to make relatively effective adaptations. What is called for here is a specification, through empirical study, of the functions of status consistency and inconsistency, as well as of their dysfunctions.

Stratum-Attribute Consistency

Thus far, I have discussed consistency and inconsistency at the level of the individual, and the emphasis has been upon the individual's profile of ranked statuses. Because societies do not comprise a random collection of individuals with randomized profiles, strata exist. Ideal-typically, a stratum is made up of individuals with closely similar profiles. In fact, of course, the strata are statistical constructs in which the variation contributed by individual profiles is averaged out. But even

[7] For an application to small-group performance, see Stuart Adams, "Status Congruency as a Variable in Small Group Performance," *Soc. Forces*, 32 (1953), 16-22.

then, if the stratum is made up of populations of more than one ethnic, national, or racial background, the stratum profile will be found to consist of a number of identifiable profiles that can be statistically abstracted from it. I know of no convenient and precise term to indicate this phenomenon; for want of a better one, I shall use an inconvenient approximate term, *stratum attribute consistency*. This phenomenon is an important aspect of social order.

If a stratification system is made up of strata whose populations are homogeneous, and if the strata are composed of individuals with flat status profiles, one might expect the individuals readily to perceive the strata as distinctive entities and to be aware of their own positions in the hierarchy of strata. Such conditions would contribute to the transformation of a statistically distinguishable stratum into a consciously identifiable class. On the other hand, if a stratum is made up of rather heterogeneous population elements with diverse profiles, it would seem more difficult for positional awareness and class consciousness to develop.[8] The analytic distinction between class and stratum should be apparent. The existence of statistically distinguishable categories (strata) is a necessary but not sufficient condition for the emergence of popularly defined entities comprised of people who are conscious of their location in the strata and who invest that sense of identity with a corporate interest. Shared perceptions and interests must be added to shared hierarchical locations before stratum can become class.

In recent years, there has been a regrettable lack of communication between sociologists concerned with the theory of social stratification and the historical importance of social classes, on the one hand, and specialists in the statistical specification of the properties and distinctive behaviors to be found in social strata. Symptomatically, Bendix and Lipset [9] make the following observation, although certainly more in sorrow than in anger: "On the whole, studies of social stratification in the United States underemphasize both the theoretical and the historical aspects of the problem. . . ."

I suggest that an important body of verified knowledge built up by American sociologists may contribute to an understanding of such classic problems as the growth, persistence, decline, and even nonemer-

---

[8] *Cf.* Morris Rosenberg, "Perceptual Obstacles to Class Consciousness," *Soc. Forces*, 32 (1953), 22-27.

[9] *Op. cit.*, p. 7.

gence of social classes. Perhaps American sociologists have characteristically found strata instead of classes (and I do not know this, I merely guess it) because their findings have precluded the discovery of class. With few exceptions, American researchers have been reluctant to accept *a priori* and have been unable to discover empirically the reality of class in the sense of fully developed, sharply defined strata comprised of individuals who are aware of their positions and are capable of corporate action. The inference of class from a single psychological property or an attitude in a delimited sphere of interest is, of course, inadmissible.

To illustrate stratum attribute consistency I have selected an example that indicates clearly the key elements in the idea, although the statistics in this illustration are cumbersome. I have taken from the Warner-Srole study [10] the diagram showing the positions of eight ethnic groups compared with the "native whites" of Newburyport on three variables (see Fig. 1). Assuming, as Warner and Srole do, that the native whites can be taken as a standard, their mean on the three variables is 100 (by definition), whereas for the ethnic groups it ranges from about 58 for Poles and Russians to 109 for Jews. (This value is the mean of the three measures for each of the ethnic groups.) The logic of using the native whites as a standard is accepted only for heuristic purposes; it cannot be assumed that the native whites are a real entity or that they have the perfect stratum-attribute consistency implied in the figure. If the arbitrariness of the logic is borne in mind, the example can serve well because it is bold and simple.

For no ethnic group do the means of the three variables fall on a straight line. The profiles composed of the three connected points are erratic, but not equally erratic for all the groups. A summary measure of this inconsistency is necessary. It might be useful to compute stratum-attribute consistency as Lenski, Kenkel, and others compute the status consistency of individuals, *i.e.*, to take the square root of the squared deviations from the mean:

$$SC = 100 - \sqrt{\Sigma(X - \overline{X})^2}.$$

Such computation requires at least independent measures of ranked attributes. Census data, of course, would satisfy these conditions. The data

[10] W. Lloyd Warner and Leo Srole, *The Social Systems of American Ethnic Groups*, Yale University Press, 1945, p. 96.

FIGURE 1. CORRECTED STATUS INDICES OF NATIVE AND ETHNIC GROUPS *

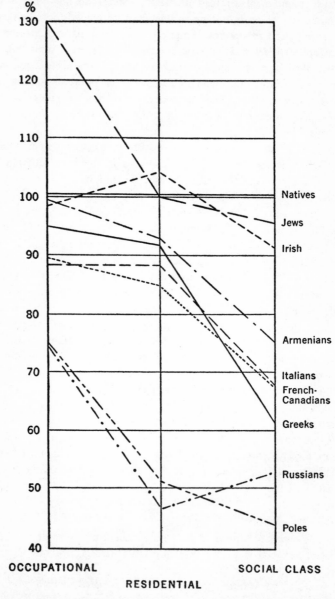

* From W. L. Warner and L. Srole, *The Social Systems of American Ethnic Groups*, Yale University Press, 1945, p. 96.

in Figure 1 do not, but Warner and Srole are not to be held accountable for this; the problem is mine, not theirs.

No doubt more elegant procedures than the one that follows could be devised if the data warranted it and were not already expressed as index numbers, but the logic and the main line of analysis should be clear enough. The observed inconsistency of the positional scores may be described simply by computing separately for each ethnic group the sum of the deviations from the mean, irrespective of sign, and subtracting this result from 100:

$$SAC = 100 - \Sigma |X - \overline{X}|.$$

This inversion of the measure, although mathematically objectionable, is indicated for semantic reasons. Perfect consistency is 100. The Irish are quite consistent, with a score of 87; the Greeks and Jews are most inconsistent, with scores of 59 and 57, respectively (see Table 1). The

TABLE 1. MEAN AND STRATUM-ATTRIBUTE CONSISTENCY SCORES OF EIGHT ETHNIC GROUPS ON THREE VARIABLES *

Ethnic Group	Mean of Status Indices †	Stratum-Attribute Consistency Score
Native Whites	100	100
Irish	98	87
French Canadians	81	75
Italians	81	73
Armenians	89	73
Russians	58	69
Poles	57	63
Greeks	83	59
Jews	109	57

* Computed from Figure 1.
† Mean of three indices (occupation, residence, and "social class").

Jews have a high average status but a low stratum-attribute consistency. The Russians have a low average status and a low attribute consistency. This observation coincides with what is known about the vertical mobility of immigrant populations and with Warner's and Srole's observations in this very work.

A group with an erratic profile would be relatively difficult to incorporate in any existing or emergent class system because its members literally do not know where they belong. Interestingly enough, in the absence of class consciousness, a group with an erratic profile—*i.e.,* low stratum-attribute consistency—might develop a spurious "ethnic consciousness." Ethnicity, in this case, would take its force as much from the strata attributes of a subpopulation as from its distinctive cultural origins, although, to be sure, it is hard to conceive of a group's inventing its existence without some common cultural resources.

The strata attributes of a minority *vis-à-vis* the host population suggest two hypotheses relating to intergroup tension: (1) Tension is correlated with the deviation of the mean attribute score of a minority from that of the host population because such deviation is accompanied by heightened visibility of the minority. For example, when the positions of a minority are visibly higher than those of the host population, the minority may have crystallized against it latent class feelings of the host population. On the other hand, a minority with a low mean score might have its inferior ranking associated with its ethnic identity. Thus ethnicity would become the symbolic focus of invidious evaluations derived from nonethnic contexts. If this takes place, the relatively unstructured phenomenon (tension) would become changed into prejudice held by part or all of the host population and directed at a specific subpopulation.

Assuming contact at the community level, how closely does the minority group correspond to the characteristics of the area? If it fits closely in attributes (other than ethnicity), one may hypothesize less visibility and prejudice.[11] Except in quasi-experimental situations, such as interracial-housing studies, research must cope with the muddy problems of ecological analysis of heterogeneous areas.

The second hypothesis is more elusive: (2) Tension is positively correlated with low attribute consistency—*i.e.,* an erratic subgroup profile. This could be tested concurrently with the first hypothesis. How-

[11] Interracial-housing studies have demonstrated the effect of community contact in reducing prejudice and stereotyping. Although most such studies do not emphasize the relative homogeneity of the residents of public-housing projects on such attributes as income, occupation, and education, housing-authority policy often sets income requirements for eligibility. Thus populations tend to be homogeneous on attributes other than ethnicity. See, for example, Morton Deutsch and Mary Evans Collins, *Interracial Housing, A Psychological Study of a Social Experiment,* University of Minnesota Press, 1951.

ever, the salience of certain elements in the attribute profile rather than
the sheer fact of inconsistency is probably the chief contributor to tension. Some profiles are conducive to visibility and contact; others are
not. If a minority has high income and residential standing accompanied by low education, it will be visible in the "wrong" places, and
individuals will act "above their station." On the other hand, a minority
with high educational standing associated with low residence is probably less likely to be involved in tensional intergroup situations, however
much stress may be developed within minority individuals. The assessment of the contribution of each attribute to the visibility of a minority
and to intergroup tension is a highly researchable topic and might lead
to a typology of prejudice with a situational rather than psychological
or ideological orientation.

Viewed from another perspective, inconsistent strata attributes of
minority populations are diagnostic of the built-in resistances and rigid-
ities in the stratification system. Such profiles tell where various groups
are impeded in their vertical mobility and where their entry is facilitated. Ideal-typically, a new population may be thought of as proceeding at even steps through the status hierarchy, with an advance in education, for example, accompanied by an equivalent advance in housing
or occupation. But such orderly progress almost never occurs, both because new groups bring with them varying skills and aspirations and
because the host society is not even-handed in the way in which it opens
opportunities for progress. Employing the analysis of strata suggested
here, the comparative study of groups of the same origin in different
host countries and in different regions of the same country should reveal
differences in the basic nature of the respective social orders.

Cultural Differentiation

A third aspect of consistency pertains to cultural phenomena associated with the definition and operation of strata. How far the investigator is willing to pursue this topic may depend on how confident he
is of discovering functional interrelations between specific aspects of
the culture and the system of stratification. It is possible but difficult to
imagine a culture that makes no invidious status distinction, that values
each stratum equally, and that calls for similar behavior irrespective of
the hierarchical placement of individuals. (There would then be no
"correlates" of stratification.) In such a culture, the system of stratifica-

tion would be strictly formal and undoubtedly incapable of sustaining itself.

In fact, stratification systems "work" because certain behaviors are deemed more appropriate in one stratum than in another and because positions in the strata are not only differentially ordered but differentially valued. Assuming that in any working system correlations exist between values and behavior, on the one hand, and the system of stratification, on the other, the problem becomes one of assessing the degree of coherence between the values held about and within the several social strata and the tasks apportioned to those strata. If the society has a sharply differentiated division of labor, and if the normative order supports that division of labor by clearly defining roles and by differentially evaluating responsibility and performance, the system will presumably work with relative efficiency. If, for each statistically distinguishable stratum, there were a rather clearly defined cultural subsystem (subculture), the stratum occupant would know what was required of him and what his authentic alternatives were. Such a situation would be conducive to the emergence of social classes, if, indeed, social classes did not already exist.

But if a cultural system does not support the division of labor, if it does not efficiently and realistically describe roles and their appropriate behaviors, strains may be built into the society. A value system may actually be subversive to its associated social order. To take an extreme example, suppose that a culture contained a strong mobility ideology, that the young were exhorted to be dissatisfied with their lot and to strive for higher status at all costs. But suppose that there were a limited number of opportunities for vertical mobility and few provisions for recruitment. The incongruity between culture and society would no doubt be insupportable and in the long run either the mobility ideology would be replaced by a more realistic one or the pattern of mobility would be changed.

The body of knowledge pertaining to subcultural variation according to stratum is less well codified than the data on individual consistency and social strata, but it is not necessarily less amenable to systematic treatment. One possible approach would be to reprocess the store of information accumulated by the public-opinion polls. The purpose of such reprocessing, a massive project indeed, would be to order by strata the responses on a great number of different polls. The summaries would be tabulated by strata and grouped by topic, and orderly arrangements of opinion and valuation should become readily apparent. At the outset it would seem best to pay relatively little attention to the selection of topics polled and greater attention to the criteria of stratification and the nature of the sample. Quite possibly, if the project could be undertaken on a large number of topics, scale analysis would be a useful technique. Such a study could outline the differences among the strata on attitudes and opinions and could measure the degree of consistency on various related topics.

Furthermore, by careful comparison of the responses stratified by the several available criteria of social status, another approach to attribute consistency might be achieved. For example, when the same poll categorizes respondents by both occupation and education, the distributions of responses might be compared. Consistency would be measured by the correlation of responses on two or more rankings. However, material from a considerable number of polls that categorize respondents on at least two measures of socioeconomic status would be needed in order to achieve consequential conclusions.

Summary

These comments are meant to be only suggestive of the hypothesis-generating potentiality of the goodness-of-fit idea. The discussion has approached the large field of social differentiation and stratification from this perspective. I have suggested that it would be advantageous for sociologists to pay special attention to the internal consistency and interrelations of three analytically distinct kinds of phenomena: (1) the statuses of the individual, with emphasis on status consistency and inconsistency; (2) distinguishable strata of social structures, with emphasis on the analysis of the consistency of stratum attributes, variations in profiles by stratum and by subgroups within a stratum, and societal or group functions of stratum consistency and inconsistency; and (3) the cultural correlates of strata.

20
The Study
of
Occupations

EVERETT CHERRINGTON HUGHES
University of Chicago

Any occupation in which people make a living may be studied sociologically. Many have been so studied in recent years, especially those which are undergoing changes in techniques and social organization and in their social and economic standing. Sometimes the study is instigated by those in the occupation; sometimes by people not in it but affected by it. The motive may be immediate practical advantage; it may be greater understanding and general social advantage. Sociology has much to gain from such studies, provided that those who undertake them make and keep a sociological bargain with those who support them and those who allow themselves to be studied. The maximal gain can be reached, however, only when the sociologist keeps clearly in mind his ulterior goal of learning more about social processes in general.

In the following pages, we are frankly preoccupied with this ulterior goal of learning about the nature of society itself from the study of occupations.

The Labor Force

Modern industrial and urban societies and economies, no matter what the political systems under which they operate, are characterized by a wholesale mobilization of people away from traditional and familial activities into more formally organized work activities. These activities are named and categorized in payrolls, organization charts, and union-management contracts, and in income-tax, licensing, and social-security legislation.

In the sense that they work at some times in their lives in this system of things, more people are engaged in occupations than in other kinds of societies and at a greater variety of occupations. In industrial countries, the census more and more serves the end of informing government and business about the actual and potential labor force and about the actuarial problems of providing for people who are not at work, whether because of age, physical condition, lack of the skills needed in a changing technology or simply because they live in the wrong place. Race, sex, marital status, and other characteristics formerly determined civil estate quite directly; now it is work that counts (although it has always been a great determiner of status), and the other characteristics take their importance by virtue of their influence on one's place in the labor force.[1]

It also seems that everyone who is not too young, too old, too sick, or too burdened with household duties is rather expected to have an occupation in the sense indicated. In Soviet Russia, this expectation has become compulsion; a man may not stay away from his work without a doctor's certificate, and the physician who gives such certificates too freely is called on the carpet.[2] In this country, those who look to our national resources have lately added womanpower to the list, not because women did not work in the past and are now expected to do so, but because they have become mobilized away from the household and into the labor force in greater proportion and for longer periods of their lives than previously.[3]

I leave to others the task of counting the occupations in industrial economies and the changing numbers of people engaged in each of them, and the tiresome business of fitting the many occupations into a

---

[1] See Evelyn M. Kitagawa, *The Family as a Unit in the Work Force: A Review of the Literature*, Population Research and Training Center, University of Chicago, 1956.

[2] Mark G. Field, "Structured Strain in the Role of the Soviet Physician," *Amer. J. Sociol.*, 53:5 (1953), 493-502.

[3] National Manpower Council, *Womanpower*, Columbia University Press, 1957.

small enough number of categories to permit crowding them into tables. I can think of no set of categories that has been given such heavy sociological work to do, both theoretical and practical, as those of occupations in census tables. Measures of social stratification and of mobility, both territorial and social, are based upon them, as are international comparisons. They are used as independent variables against which to weigh differences of political opinion, taste, religion, and many other things. One is tempted to ask whether they are equal to the burden; it is a question on which many people are very competently breaking their heads.

Work and Leisure

Oddly enough, at a time when nearly everyone is being drawn into the labor force, the proportion of a man's daily, weekly, annual, and life time that he is expected to devote to work is falling so drastically that the days of leisure in each seven may become nearly equal to the days of work. Already the waking hours spent away from work are, for many people, more than those spent at work, even on working days. At the same time, a new concept has been introduced, that of underemployment. It refers not to hours, weeks, and months of idleness so much as to the supposed underuse of human effort; the standard of efficient use applied is that of an economy which, like ours, provides great amounts of capital per worker and thus allows great per-man-hour production. The underemployed man may put forth great effort, but his product is small. It is as if the famed Protestant ethic had been transferred from the individual to the system; it is the machinery which is supposed to put in seven days a week and almost, if not quite, 52 weeks a year. The machine-tenders can take it easier at work, although they are expected to keep their eyes and ears piously glued to the "media" so that they may keep their consumption up to expectation. For, as G. Tarde said in his *Psychologie économique*,[4] a return to the early evangel, with its belief in the vanity of human desires, would be the death of modern industry.

Although the great masses of people who are occupied are taking it easier, a minority appears to be bound to the tireless wheels of the

---

[4] Paris, 1902, Vol. 1, p. 186. Tarde's chapters on the economic role of desires and beliefs are good reading for those who are working on a theory of consumption and leisure.

machines. Those who manage the machines and the organization required to keep them and their products moving appear to require an extra dose of a certain brand of the Protestant ethic, a brand which does not leave time for prayer or other solitary and idiosyncratic activities. The new distribution of work and leisure in the life of the individual, and as between people in various positions in our society and economy; the new concepts, values, and expectations with respect to them, and to the levels and kinds of effort expected or required of people in the various positions; these are fundamental problems of society and of occupations. The change of balance between work and leisure has given new emphasis and a new turn to studies of leisure. The demand for men of unlimited ambition and drive to fill certain of the positions in our economy of abundance has, in its turn, given a new impulse to studies of social mobility into the higher ranks of management.

The Division of Labor

Division of labor, one of the most fundamental of all social processes, finds one of its most explicit expressions in occupations. The phrase, however, is but a poor term for differentiation of function in a social whole. It is poor because it emphasizes the division and neglects the integration, the relations among the functions so divided or differentiated. All organization of behavior consists of differentiation of function. Economic division of labor is but a special case, or a special aspect of it.

An occupation, in essence, is not some particular set of activities; it is the part of an individual in any ongoing system of activities. The system may be large or small, simple or complex. The ties between the persons in different positions may be close or so distant as not to be social; they may be formal or informal, frequent or rare. The essential is that the occupation is the place ordinarily filled by one person in an organization or complex of efforts and activities. Sociologically speaking, the division of labor is only incidentally technical. It consists, not of ultimate components of skill or of mechanical or mental operations, but of the actual allocation of functions to persons. Individual components of motion or action are combined in ways that sometimes appear fearful and wonderful to a mechanically oriented or rational and detached mind. The logic of the division and combination of activities and functions into occupations and of their allocation to various kinds of people in any system is not to be assumed as given, but is in any case something to be discovered. Likewise, the outward limits of a system of division of labor are not to be assumed but are to be sought out. Analysis of systems whose limits have not been determined can be very deceiving.

Homans [5] has recently emphasized exchange as a basic social process the analysis of which might bring us closer to a sound general theory of social behavior. Although this is not an entirely novel idea, it is an important one and especially pertinent to the analysis of division of labor. Where there is differentiation of function, there is exchange— and exchange not merely of money, goods, or tangible and easily described services. Durkheim's book, let us remember, is entitled *De la division du travail social*—on the division of social labor. And although it may be true that more and more kinds of exchange tend to have an expression in money, it is also true that it is very difficult to keep money exchanges free of other kinds.

One of the problems of the purest markets is to limit exchanges to the purely economic. Glick has recently found this to be so in the market in egg futures.[6] The rules and signals for buying and selling are made explicit so that the dealers will not be able to give private information or to exchange favors on the floor. I mention this case only to emphasize that the division of labor involves many kinds of exchange, many of them not at all apparent, and that several kinds may go on at once. This is true of occupations as well as of those differentiations of functions found in families and other systems of relationship. In many occupations, the exchanges occur on at least two levels. There is exchange between a person and the various others with whom he interacts in his occupational role. It is of this exchange that Henderson wrote in "Physician and Patient as a Social System." [7] It is also described in studies of industrial relations, and especially of the informal relations among people in the same work situation. One must remember, however, that much interaction occurs in formally defined relationships and that much in-

[5] George C. Homans, "Social Behavior as Exchange," *Amer. J. Sociol.*, 53 (1958) 597-606.

[6] Ira O. Glick, "Futures Trading: A Sociological Analysis," unpublished Ph.D. dissertation, University of Chicago, 1957. See also Max Weber, "Die Boerse" (1894), in *Gesammelte Aufsaetze zur Soziologie und Sozialpolitik,* Tuebingen, 1924, pp. 256-322.

[7] L. J. Henderson, "Physician and Patient as a Social System," *N. E. J. Med., 212* (1935), 819-23.

volves persons not in personal contact with one another. The other level is that of exchanges between the occupation and the society in which it occurs; they underlie those characteristic features of certain occupations, license and mandate.

License and Mandate

An occupation consists in part in the implied or explicit *license* that some people claim and are given to carry out certain activities rather different from those of other people and to do so in exchange for money, goods, or services. Generally, if the people in the occupation have any sense of identity and solidarity, they will also claim a *mandate* to define—not merely for themselves, but for others as well—proper conduct with respect to the matters concerned in their work. They also will seek to define and possibly succeed in defining, not merely proper conduct but even modes of thinking and belief for everyone individually and for the body social and politic with respect to some broad area of life which they believe to be in their occupational domain. The license may be merely technical; it may, however, extend to broad areas of behavior and thought. It may include a whole style of life, or it may be confined to carrying out certain technical activities which others may not carry out—at least not officially or for a reward. The mandate may be small and narrow, or the contrary.

License, as an attribute of an occupation, is usually thought of as specific legal permission to pursue the occupation. I am thinking of something broader. Society, by its nature, consists in part of both allowing and expecting some people to do things which other people are not allowed or expected to do. Most occupations—especially those considered professions and those of the underworld—include as part of their being a license to deviate in some measure from some common modes of behavior. Professions, perhaps more than other kinds of occupation, also claim a broad legal, moral, and intellectual mandate. Not only do the practitioners, by virtue of gaining admission to the charmed circle of the profession, individually exercise a license to do things others do not do, but collectively they presume to tell society what is good and right for it in a broad and crucial aspect of life. Indeed, they set the very terms of thinking about it. When such a presumption is granted as legitimate, a profession in the full sense has come into being. The nature and extent of both license and mandate, their relations to each other, and the circumstances and conflicts in which they expand or contract are crucial areas of study, not merely for occupations, but for society itself. Such licenses and mandates are the prime manifestation of the *moral* division of labor—that is, of the processes by which differing moral functions are distributed among the members of society, as individuals and as categories of individuals. These moral functions differ from one another in both kind and measure. Some people seek and get special responsibility for defining values and for establishing and enforcing sanctions over a certain aspect of life; the differentiation of moral and social functions involves both the area of social behavior in question and the degree of responsibility and power.

Since this is the aspect of occupations to which I give most emphasis in this paper, I will illustrate it in a manner which I hope will stimulate discussion and research.

Many occupations cannot be carried out without guilty knowledge. The priest cannot mete out penance without becoming an expert in sin; else how may he know the mortal from the venial? To carry out his mandate to tell people what books they may or may not read and what thoughts and beliefs they must espouse or avoid, he must become a connoisseur of the forbidden. Only a master theologian can think up really subtle heresies; hence Satan is of necessity a fallen angel. A layman would be but an amateur with a blunderbuss where a sharpshooter is wanted. The poor priest, as part of the exchange involved in his license to hear confessions and to absolve and his mandate to tell us what's what, has to convince the lay world that he does not yield to the temptations of his privileged position; he puts on a uniform and lives a celibate existence. These are compensating or counter-deviations from the common way of dressing and living; they would not be admired, or perhaps even tolerated, in people who have no special function to justify them. The priest, in short, has both intellectual and moral leeway, and perhaps must have them if he is to carry out the rest of his license. He carries a burden of guilty knowledge.

The lawyer, the policeman, the physician, the reporter, the scientist, the scholar, the diplomat, the private secretary, all of them must have license to get—and, in some degree, to keep secret—some order of guilty knowledge. It may be guilty in that it is knowledge that a layman would be obliged to reveal, or in that the withholding of it from the public or from authorities compromises the integrity of the man who so withholds it, as in the case of the policeman who keeps connections with the underworld or the diplomat who has useful friends abroad. Most occupations rest upon some bargain about receiving, guarding, and giving out communications. The license to keep this bargain is of the essence of many occupations.

The prototype of all guilty knowledge is, however, a different, potentially shocking, way of looking at things. Every occupation must look relatively at some order of events, objects, or ideas. These things must be classified, seen in comparative light; their behavior must be analyzed and, if possible, predicted. A suitable technical language must be developed in which one may talk to his colleagues about them. This technical, therefore relative, attitude must be adopted toward the very people whom one serves; no profession can operate without license to talk in shocking terms behind the backs of its clients. Sometimes an occupation must adopt this objective, comparative attitude toward things which are very dear to other people or which are the object of absolutely held values and sentiments. I suppose that this ultimate license is the greatest when the people who exercise it, being guardians of precious things, are in a position to do great damage. (No one is in so good a position to steal as the banker.)

Related to the license to think relatively about dear things and absolute values is the license to do dangerous things. I refer not to the danger run by the steeplejack and the men who navigate submarines, for that is danger to themselves. (Even so, there is a certain disposition to pay them off with a license to run slightly amok when the one comes down and the other up to solid ground.) I speak, rather, of the license of the doctor to cut and dose, of the priest to play with men's salvation, of the scientist to split atoms; or simply of the danger that advice given a person may be wrong, or that work done may be unsuccessful or cause damage.

License of all these kinds may lie at the root of that modicum of aggressive suspicion which most laymen feel toward professionals, and of that raging and fanatical anger which burns chronically in some people and which at times becomes popular reaction. Many antivivisectionists, according to Hughes,[8] do not love beasts more but love doctors less, suspecting them of loving some parts of their work too much. It is a chronic protest. Of course there are people who believe that they have suffered injury from incompetent or careless work or that they have

[8] Helen Hughes, "The Compleat Anti-vivisectionist," *Sci. Mon.*, N.Y., 65:6 (1947), 503-07.

been exploited by being acted upon more for the professional's increase of knowledge or income than for their own well-being.

Herein lies the whole question of what the bargain is between those who receive a service and those who give it, and of the circumstances in which it is protested by either party. Of equal or greater sociological significance is the problem of a general questioning of license or mandate. Social unrest often shows itself precisely in such questioning of the prerogatives of the leading professions. In time of crisis, there may arise a general demand for more conformity to lay modes of thought and discourse.

One of the major professional deviations of mind, a form of guilty knowledge, is the objective and relative attitude mentioned above. One order of relativity has to do with time; the professional may see the present in longer perspective. The present may be, for him, more crucial in that it is seen as a link in a causative chain of events; the consequences of present action may be seen as more inevitable, rippling down through time. The emergency, in this sense, may appear greater to the professional than to the layman. In another sense, it appears less crucial, since the professional sees the present situation in comparison with others; it is not unique, and hence the emergency is not so great as laymen see it.

Something like this seems to lie in the attack upon the Supreme Court following its decisions on civil rights and upon professors who insist on freedom to discuss all things in this time of Cold War. They are thought to be playing legal and academic tunes while the Communists plaster us with firebombs. In time of crisis, detachment appears the most perilous deviation of all, hence the one least to be tolerated. Their deviation, in these cases, consists in a drastic reversal of what many laymen consider the urgent as against the less urgent aspects of our situation. And it arises from their license to think in different terms.

Militant religious sects give us an instructive illustration. They ordinarily, in Christianity at least, consist of people convinced that they are all in imminent danger of damnation. So long as they remain militant sects, they are in chronic crisis. It is perhaps not without sociological significance that they do not tolerate a clergy, or much differentiation of function at all. It is as if they sense that professionalizing inevitably brings some detachment, some relative and comparative attitude. In a large society the clergy are generally more ardent than the laity; a sect might almost be defined as a religious group in which the opposite is true. Inquisitions to the contrary, it is probable that the professional clergy tend to be more tolerant than ardent laymen. Although it may seem paradoxical to suggest it, one may seriously ask under what circumstances religious people tolerate a professional clergy.

The typical reform movement is an attempt of laymen to redefine values and to change action about some matter over which some occupation (or group of occupations or faction within an occupation) holds a mandate. The movement may simply push for faster or more drastic action where the profession moves slowly or not at all; it may be a direct attack upon the dominant philosophy of the profession, as in attempts to change the manner of distributing medical care. The power of an occupation to protect its license and to maintain its mandate and the circumstances in which licenses and mandates are attacked, lost, or changed are matters for investigation. (And one must not overlook movements within a profession.) Such work is study of politics in the fundamental sense—that is, in the sense of studying constitutions. For constitutions are the relations between the effective estates which *constitute* the body politic. In our society, some occupations are among the groups which most closely resemble what were once known as estates. While there has been a good deal of study of the political activities of occupational groups, the subject has been somewhat misunderstood as a result of the strong fiction of political neutrality of professions in our society. Of course, a certain license to be politically neutral has been allowed some occupations, but the circumstances and limits of such neutrality are again a matter for study. Special attention should be given to the exchanges implied and to the circumstances, some of which we have mentioned, in which the license is denied, and the ways in which it is violated and subverted, from within or without.

One can think of many variations of license and mandate, and of the relations between them. School teachers in our society have little license to think thoughts that others do not think; they are not even allowed to think the nastier thoughts that others *do* think. Their mandate seems limited to minor matters of pedagogy; it does not include definition of the fundamental issues of what children shall be taught. Educational policy is given into their hands very grudgingly, although they have a good deal of power by default. Mandate by default is itself a matter for study. The underworld, to take another example, has a considerable license to deviate; in fact, members get paid to help respectable people escape the norms of everyday life. But the license is

not openly admitted. The manner in which the people of the underworld find spokesmen and the nature of the exchanges involved have
often been discussed as a pathology of politics. The full circle of exchanges is seldom analyzed with an eye to learning something significant about the very nature of social exchanges. Study of the license of
artists and entertainers could also yield much knowledge concerning the
degrees of conformity possible in a society and the consequences of trying to reduce deviation to something like zero. For these occupations
seem to require, if they are to produce the very things for which society
will give them a living of sorts (or, in some cases, unheard-of opu-
lence), at least some people who deviate widely from the norms more
or less adhered to and firmly espoused by other people. Their license
is, however, periodically in a parlous state, and there seems no guarantee
that it will not, at any moment, be attacked. There has recently been a
case which turns upon whether poetic license includes speaking for an
enemy country in time of war.

Occupations and Social Matrices

If an occupation is a more-or-less standardized one-man's part in
some operating system, it follows that it cannot be described apart from
the whole. A study of occupations, then, becomes in part a study of
the allocation of functions and the consequent composition of any given
occupation.[9]

Although an occupation may conceivably consist of but one activity
in a narrow and mechanical sense, it takes an extremely rationalized organization to keep it so. Most occupations consist of a number, a bundle,
of activities. Some may be bundled together because they require similar skills; others, simply because they can conveniently be done at one
place, or because taken alone they do not occupy a man's full time; still
others, because they are, or seem to be, natural parts of a certain role,
office, or function. The physician's repertoire, for example, includes
technically unrelated activities, bound together by the demands of his

[9] Throughout this paper, but especially in what follows, it would be
hard for me to distinguish what is, at least in some small sense, my own
combining of ideas and what I owe to my colleagues in recent studies,
Howard S. Becker, Blanche Geer, and Anselm Strauss. I am sure that many
of my former students and other colleagues will have reason to think that I
am borrowing liberally from their work.

basic function. Only in those specialties which can be practiced without personal contact with patients can physicians group their activities on strictly technical lines. One might, indeed, try to scale occupations according to the dominance of technical as against role factors in determining combinations of activities.

The extreme of technically rational division and grouping of activities, under conditions of constant and aggressive invention of new machines and forms of organization, would lead to continual destruction and reforming of occupations.[10] The problems of adjusting self-conceptions and social roles in such a case have been much studied lately. The opposite of this would be a system of strongly traditional and entrenched occupations whose activities, whether bound together by technical considerations or not, are considered to belong rightfully and naturally together.

This leads us to the distinction between historic and less historic occupations. An historic occupation is historic, not because its chief activity is an old one but because it has long had a name, a license, and a mandate, a recognized place in the scheme of things. In the extreme case, an historic occupation has a strong sense of identity and continuity; a galaxy of historic founders, innovators, and other heroes, the saints or gods of the trade; and a wealth of remembered historic or legendary events, which justify its present claims. The aspirant to such a trade is expected to acquire a strong sense of belonging to an historic estate, somewhat set off from other men. New occupations, like new families, seek an heroic genealogy to strengthen their claims to license and mandate. Occupations vary greatly in the degree to which they become the master determinants of the social identity, self-conception, and social status of the people in them.

In an occupation which is strongly historic, one would expect the combination of activities also to have a certain historic quality, reinforced by a traditional logic. Historic or not, occupations vary greatly in their autonomy in determining what activities are their duty and prerogatives. One would, however, expect occupations of long standing to

[10] Georges Friedmann has been the leading student of this problem. See his *Où Va le Travail Humain?*, Paris, 1950; *Problèmes Humains du Machinism Industriel*, Paris, 1946; and *Travail en Miettes*, Paris, 1956. He has also written a fundamental criticism called "La thèse de Durkheim et les formes contemporaines de la division du travail," *Cahiers Internationaux de Sociologie*, 19 (1955) 45-58.

resist attempts, especially of outsiders, to determine the content of their work or the rules governing it.

The various activities which make up an occupation are, of course, given varying values both by the people inside and by others. Sometimes the name of the occupation expresses an emphasis upon one rather than other activities; note the use of "preacher," "priest," and "pastor" in referring to clergy of various denominations, and the insistence of some gynecologists upon being called gynecological surgeons. Some one activity may be symbolically valued beyond its importance in the present complex of activities. Changes in technology, economics, and organization may change the balance between the named symbolic activity and others; in extreme cases, the symbolic activity may be lost or dropped from the repertory of the occupation while the name persists.

Nursing is a striking example of such a series of shifts. The word has a certain connotation in the lay mind; it refers to a role and an attitude, but also to certain comforting activities considered consonant with the role. The elaboration of the organization of hospitals, clinics, and public-health agencies, combined with great technological change in medicine and an immense increase in the demand for medical services, has led to a great reshuffling of functions in the whole medical system. Doctors need much more technical help than before; the system also requires much more administrative activity. A host of new occupations has arisen. The physician has passed along many activities to the nurse; the nurse has in turn passed along many of hers to other occupations. The result has been upward mobility of the nurse, since a good number of the new occupations stand below her in the hierarchy and since there are some posts of high prestige, income, and authority to which nurses alone may aspire. But there has been a certain dissociation of the occupation called nursing from the activities traditionally associated with it in the lay mind. The case is not peculiar, but it is so clear cut as to allow sensitive observation.

Every occupation has some history which may in part be described in terms of changes in the bundle of activities, in the values given them, and in the total system of which the occupation is a part. Changes may occur in ownership and control over access to appropriate tools (pulpits, operating rooms, law libraries, stages and properties, Univacs and laboratories), methods of payment and exchange, the formal authority and status systems in which work is done, the terms of entry to the occupation, and competition among individuals, occupations, and whole complexes of goods and services for the patronage of consumers. Of course, these same matters are crucial to study of an occupation at present; but sociologists have to be reminded of the pertinence of history rather more than of present doings.

I hope I have not put so many things into the last few paragraphs that the main points will be overlooked: namely, that the items of activity and social function which make up any occupation are historical products. The composition of an occupation can be understood only in the frame of the pertinent social and institutional complex (which must in turn be discovered, not merely assumed). The allocating and grouping of activities is itself a fundamental social process.

The Work Situation

I should at this point mention work situations as systems of interaction, as the setting of the role-drama of work, in which people of various occupational and lay capacities, involved in differing complexes of *Lebenschancen,* interact in sets of relationships that are social as well as technical. Some of the best work in contemporary sociology [11] is being done in such settings and is giving us new knowledge of reciprocal expectation of role performance, definition of roles, group solidarity, and development and definition of reference groups. We are by this time alerted to the value of work situations as posts for observing the formation of groups and the generation of social rules and sanctions. I am not sure that we are using the findings of such observation vigorously enough in building our theories of social control and of the larger legal and political processes.

A Man and His Work

Let me conclude with some remarks on the individual and his occupation and his career. Career, in the most generic sense, refers to the fate of a man running his life-cycle in a particular society at a particular time. The limitations put upon his choice of occupation by his own peculiarities (sex, race, abilities, class, wealth, access to and motivation for education, and access to knowledge of the system itself)

[11] See Erving Goffman, *Presentation of Self in Society,* University of Chicago Press, 1956.

in interaction with the "times" have been the object of many studies. Not all the problems of logic and method involved in such studies have been adequately attacked or solved.

Occupations vary in their strength as named reference-groups, as the basis for full and lasting self-identification and firm status. They vary also in their demand for full and lasting commitment and in the age and life-phase at which one must decide to enter training for them. Some occupations are more visible to young people than are others, and effective visibility varies also by class and other social circumstances. The inner workings of the best known cannot be seen by outsiders. Add to this the fact of changes in even the most historic occupations, and it is evident that young people must choose their occupations, as they do their wives, largely on faith (if, indeed, they choose at all). The career includes not only the processes and sequences of learning the techniques of the occupation but also the progressive perception of the whole system and of possible places in it and the accompanying changes in conceptions of the work and of one's self in relation to it. A good deal of work is being done on these matters; the phrase *adult socialization* is being applied to some of the processes involved.[12]

The processes are complicated by the fact that some occupations, strong as their symbols of common identity (their license and mandate) may be, are inwardly very heterogeneous. Within medicine, there is wide choice of specialties; each of them is not merely a unit of technical work but a position in the huge and complex system of health institutions. They offer alternative career lines, some of them mutually exclusive from an early stage. These career lines are variously ranked within the profession itself as well as outside; the people in each of them have their own ethos and sometimes their own variant system of relative values concerning many things in medicine. They differ, for example, in their notions of what knowledge and skills should be taught in medical schools. How these factors act upon and are reacted to by students who are in the process of choosing their specialties is

[12] Howard S. Becker and Anselm Strauss, "Careers, Personality, and Adult Socialization," *Amer. J. Sociol.*, 72 (1956), 253-63. See also Robert K. Merton, George Reader, and Patricia Kendall (eds.), *The Student Physician: Introductory Studies in the Sociology of Medical Education*, Harvard University Press, 1957.

discussed in a current paper.[13] A part of the individual's career may be the making of the finer decisions concerning his hoped-for place within an occupational system, the projecting of his self-image in the direction of one rather than others of the available models of mature members of his occupation.

Career involves, at each stage, choices of some rather than other activities in one's economy of effort. A career consists, in one sense, of moving—in time and hence with age—within the institutional system in which the occupation exists. Ordinarily, career is interpreted as progress upward in the system, but a man can make progress in a number of ways. He may become more skillful at the basic activities of the occupation; the increase of skill may be rewarded by increase of income, security, and prestige among his fellows. If his occupation is practiced directly with customers or clients, he may get more of them and better ones. However, progress and advancement also consist in part of change in the proportions of time and effort devoted to various activities, and even in rather complete change of organizational function or role.

Sometimes the greater success is paid for by a complete abandonment of the activities symbolically most closely associated with the occupation, a consequent loss of skill in those activities, and passage from identification with the basic colleagueship to some other. This is a career contingency of much importance to the individual's self-conception. It often creates severe guilt. We might expect the severity of such crises to vary with the sense of commitment and the strength of the colleague-group as a significant other for its members. Some occupations appear intense, others weak and indifferent, in commitment. In some there is a casual attitude toward particular activities and perhaps a full acceptance of the right of employers to determine just what work one shall do. In others, there is a rich culture and a strong sense among the members of being different from other people. There are songs and lore about logging, railroading, and going to sea. In these occupations there are strong feelings about who really shares in the dangers and fate of the group, and who consequently has a right to the name. Jazz musicians, who live life wrong-end-to—for their night

[13] Kurt W. Back and Bernard S. Philips, "Public Health as a Career of Medicine: Specialization within a Profession," paper read at the annual meetings of the American Sociological Society, 1957.

is day, and other people's pleasure is their work—have a similarly strong sense of who is and who is not one of them. Some of the professions also have a sense of identity and a tendency to be self-conscious about who is a true member of the group.

Today, there are great numbers of people in occupations which are, in fact, products of modern industrial and business technology and organization and in which there appears to be little sense of belonging to a closed circle of people with a peculiar fate. The sense of identification of such people with their work, or with classes and categories of people at work, is a matter for study. Many of them are said to be alienated both from their work fellows and from society. Not the least problem of such people is the balance between work and leisure—not merely as proportions of their lifetimes, years, weeks, and days, but in terms of their importance and meaning. This is also, in the broad sense, a problem of career, of a man and his work seen in the perspective of his ongoing life and life chances. We may then think of man and his work, of careers, as an immense area of problems, embracing a great many of the problems of formation of social personality and of adjustment of individuals to their social surroundings. Careers in various occupations are patterned in varying degree. In the narrowest sense, career—as Mannheim wrote—is a predictable course through a bureaucracy.[14] But the patterns, the possible positions and sequences in work systems, themselves change. And each human career is worked out in some particular historical phase. Ours is a rapidly changing phase, which means that careers and career contingencies are changing, too. This gives the study of careers, and of other facets of occupations and work, a certain timeliness and excitement that adds to their basic relevance for study of social and social-psychological processes.

[14] Karl Mannheim, "Ueber das Wesen und die Bedeutung des wirtschaftlichen Erfolgsstrebens," *Archiv fuer Sozialwissenschaft und Sozialpolitik,* 63:3 (1930), 449-512.

V
Selected
Applications
of
Sociology

21
The Study of
Social
Disorganization
and Deviant
Behavior

ALBERT K. COHEN

Indiana University

The most pressing problem in the field of social disorganization and deviant behavior is to define these terms. If we cannot agree on what we are talking about, we cannot agree on what is relevant, much less on what is important.

To constitute a theoretical field, a set of problems and hypotheses must conform to certain criteria. First, all these problems and hypotheses must concern things which are members of the same clearly defined class, in the sense that they are all definable in terms of the presence or absence of the same attributes or in terms of values of the same variables. The task of a theoretical field is to account for the variant possibilities presented by such a conceptual scheme. This is illustrated below in our discussion of Merton and Parsons.

Secondly, the members of such a class must be homogeneous for theoretical purposes. That is, variation within this class must be explainable by a unified system of theory. The various subjects that huddle together under the umbrella of "social disorganization" or "deviant behavior" do not constitute such a class. Either we explain them by theories which are formulated *ad hoc* for each member of the class or we apply to them the general theoretical apparatus of sociology, which is equally relevant to things that fall outside the class.

An important corollary of this criterion is that any definition of a theoretical field is necessarily tentative, because homogeneity for theoretical purposes is a hypothesis that is verified only when a unified theory has actually been evolved to account for the variation in question. Evaluation of any definition of a field, therefore, is more than a matter of semantic criticism; it is a theoretically creative task.

Thirdly, the field must be defined sociologically. Much that travels under the name of sociology of deviant behavior or of social disorganization is psychology—some of it very good psychology, but psychology. For example, Sutherland's theory of differential association,[1] which is widely regarded as preëminently sociological, is not the less psychological because it makes much of the cultural milieu. It is psychological because it addresses itself to the question: How do people become the kind of individuals who commit criminal acts? A sociological question would be: What is it about the structure of social systems that determines the kinds of criminal acts that occur in these systems and the way in which such acts are distributed within the systems? In general, a sociological field is concerned with the structure of interactional systems, not with personalities, and the distribution and articulation of events within those systems.

Deviant Behavior

Definition. We define deviant behavior as behavior which violates institutionalized expectations—that is, expectations which are shared and recognized as legitimate within a social system. The implications of this commonplace definition are not always clearly appreciated.

First, we here define deviant behavior in terms of the relationship of action to institutionalized expectations, not in terms of its relationship to personality structure. Behavior which is psychotic, neurotic, malad-

---

[1] A. K. Cohen, A. R. Lindesmith, and K. F. Schuessler (eds.), *The Sutherland Papers*, Indiana University Press, 1956.

justed, or otherwise pathological from a psychiatric or mental-hygiene point of view is defined in terms of its dependence upon or consequences for personality structure. Therefore, the pathology of personality is not, as such, subject matter for the sociology of deviant behavior.

This is not to say that personality structure is irrelevant to sociology. What goes on in a social system obviously depends upon the personalities it has to work with, so to speak, even if those personalities do not, as such, constitute the system. It does not follow, however, either by definition or as a matter of empirical fact, that the pathology of personalities is any more relevant to deviant behavior than is normality. Much—probably most—deviant behavior is produced by clinically normal people. This would be true, for example, of most illicit sexual behavior. On the other hand, many clinically abnormal people, confronted by sexual temptation and opportunity to which many normal people would succumb, are incapable, in consequence of their pathological anxieties concerning sex, of anything but virtue. In order to build a sociology of deviant behavior, we must always keep as our point of reference deviant behavior, not kinds of people. A major task before us is to get rid of the notion, so pervasive in sociological thinking, that the deviant, the abnormal, the pathological, and, in general, the deplorable always come wrapped in a single package.

A second implication: Since the sociology of deviant behavior is concerned with explaining the departure of behavior from institutionalized expectations, it follows that the sociology of deviant behavior is not the sociology of prostitution plus the sociology of drug addiction plus the sociology of suicide, etc., *in general.* This is so, first, because no behavior is *per se* and universally deviant, and, secondly, because any behavior can be subject matter for many different sociological fields, of which the sociology of deviant behavior is but one. One reason for the undeveloped state of the sociology of deviant behavior is the tendency to focus on a few kinds of behavior that are usually deviant in our society and to study these in a diffuse and encyclopedic way, rather than to concentrate on the theoretical problems inherent in the fact of deviance itself.

A theory of deviant behavior not only must account for the occurrence of deviant behavior; it must also account for its failure to occur, or conformity. In fact, the explanation of one necessarily implies the explanation of the other. Therefore "the sociology of deviant behavior" is elliptical for "the sociology of deviant behavior and conformity"; it includes the explanation of the prevention, reduction, and elimination of deviant behavior.

Merton's well-known paper on "Social Structure and Anomie" [2] and the relevant chapters in Parsons' *The Social System* [3] are deserving of special comment because they are among the few attempts to formulate a general theory of deviant behavior which addresses itself to the generic property of deviance, its variant forms, and their determinants.

AN ILLUSTRATION: MERTON. Merton's typology of modes of individual adaptation is couched in terms of "culture goals" and "institutionalized means," either of which can be accepted or rejected. Any act, whatever its concrete content, can be described in terms of this scheme; what the scheme abstracts from the concrete content is the relationship of the act to the institutionalized value system. Furthermore, "acceptance or rejection of goals" and "acceptance or rejection of means" constitute, in effect, two dichotomous variables; in terms of the values of these variables, we can specify at least five logically possible modes of adaptation to institutionalized expectations, one of which is conformity, the others, distinctive modes of deviance.

What concerns us here is the way in which this scheme illustrates our criterion of a sociological field of deviant behavior. The starting point, let it be noted, is not a definition of deviant behavior, but the specification of two dimensions along which behavior may vary. The class of all points that can be located in these two dimensions defines the full scope of a sociological field which comprehends both conformity and deviant behavior. Furthermore, the varieties of deviant behavior are not described in terms of their unique and incommensurable concrete characteristics but are derived from the logic of the classification itself and stated in terms of the same conceptual scheme. Also, the scheme is a way of classifying actions, not personalities. The widespread use of this scheme testifies to the felt need for such a scheme; the near monopoly it has enjoyed testifies to the paucity of original thinking in this field.

Merton's conceptual scheme, however, although obviously valuable for taxonomic purposes, does not in itself constitute a *theory* of deviant

[2] In Robert K. Merton, *Social Theory and Social Structure*, Free Press, 1957.

[3] Talcott Parsons, *The Social System*, Free Press, 1951, esp. Chap. 7.

behavior–conformity. Such a theory would be a system of propositions which would make it possible to account for the actual choices among the possibilities given by the scheme. The same paper by Merton also contains the beginnings of a theory. Paraphrasing liberally—and Merton is not to be held accountable for this formulation—we suggest that the central idea is socially structured strain, defined as ambivalence relative to institutionalized expectations. This strain or ambivalance arises out of tension or malintegration between culture goals and institutionalized means. This is the general situation which generates deviant motivation. The specific direction of deviant behavior is accounted for, in part, by the relative strength of internalization of goals and means, respectively, and the socially structured availability of alternative means. Of particular note is the fact that strain and the circumstances that determine responses to strain are treated as elements which are variously distributed in the social system and the distribution of which is a function of societal mechanisms.

Note also how Merton's scheme lends itself to the conceptualizing of social control. It would seem that the control of deviant behavior is, by definition, a culture goal. For any given form of deviant behavior, there are institutionally appropriate means of control. In short, the responses to deviant behavior may be conceptualized in terms of the same scheme applied to deviant behavior itself.[4] Whether this extension of Merton's scheme is more than idle play with a sociological toy remains to be seen. It is certain, however, that a sociology of deviant behavior–conformity will have to devise ways of conceptualizing responses to deviant

---

[4] Merton's Conformity would be represented by the use of institutionally expected means in the interest of social control. His Innovation would be represented by disregard of institutionalized limitations on the choice of means—for example, McCarthyism, third-degree methods, wiretapping. Ritualism is a preoccupation with the minutiae of procedure without regard to its effectiveness as a means to an end—legalism, if you will. It would also consist in affirmations and gestures of indignation, by means of which one aligns oneself symbolically with the angels without having to take up cudgels against the devil. Retreatism would take the form of refusal to concern oneself with the fact of deviant behavior or to do anything about it. Lastly, Rebellion would be represented by seduction, so to speak, by the deviant— that is, acceptance of the deviant's goals and substitution of means which support and facilitate his deviant behavior. It might be illustrated by corrupt alliances among police, politicians, and racketeers.

behavior from the standpoint of their relevance to the production or extinction of deviant behavior.

AN ILLUSTRATION: PARSONS. For our present purposes, we shall only point out briefly the ways in which Parsons' work goes beyond Merton's. First, Parsons distinguishes several aspects of the concept "strain" and several ways in which strain may arise.[5] The tension between culture goals and institutionalized means which, for Merton, appears to define strain becomes, for Parsons, a special case of strain. Strain, for Parsons, may take various other forms, including, for example, failure of the actor's expectations concerning himself to correspond to the expectations which others have concerning him, or inability of the actor to make certain institutionally expected object-attachments (*e.g.*, with persons of the opposite sex).

Secondly, although Parsons also formulates a classification of the directions of deviant behavior, based on the same logic as Merton's, he postulates a set of three variables as opposed to Merton's two, and the combinations of these variables yield eight varieties of deviant behavior. The classification is based on the predominance of alienative or conformative need-dispositions within the ambivalent motivational structure, of active or passive orientations, and of concern with social objects —that is, with one's relationships to persons and collectivities—or with normative patterns. It is not possible to present and interpret this classification intelligibly in a brief space. However, it appears to subsume Merton's types under a wider range of alternatives. Merton's "Ritualism," for example, becomes Parsons' "Perfectionistic Observance," the product of conformative dominance, passivity, and focus on normative patterns. On the other hand, Parsons' scheme includes distinctions, such as that between "Perfectionistic Observance" and "Submission" (in which the focus is on social objects), that do not appear in Merton's scheme.

Thirdly, Parsons has given us much more than a taxonomy of deviant behavior–conformity. More than any other person, he has contributed to the clarification of the substantive theoretical problems. I shall make no effort to summarize; suffice it to say that the discussion

[5] Parsons, *op. cit.*, p. 252; Talcott Parsons and Edward A. Shils (eds.), *Toward a General Theory of Action*, Harvard University Press, 1952, pp. 151-52.

which follows is so heavily indebted to him as to preclude detailed acknowledgment, point for point, of my indebtedness.

Deviant Behavior–Conformity as Interaction Process. Deviant behavior and conformity are kinds of behavior that evolve in the course of an interaction process. When we say that deviant behavior is an attempt to reduce strain or to solve a problem of adjustment, we do not mean that an actor finds himself in an awkward spot, considers a number of alternatives, and then makes a choice. The break with the routine and the institutionalized is more typically half-conscious, tentative, and groping. Ambivalence motivates exploratory but noncommittal gestures. The gestures elicit from others responses which tend to reduce the original strain, responses which only make matters worse, responses which signify that further movement in the same direction will receive a cold welcome, or responses which guardedly suggest that alter has problems akin to ego's and would like to explore with ego the possibility of new solutions. Whether incipient deviant behavior is checked before it becomes fully conscious, or becomes explicit and the actors more fully committed in a vicious circle of progressively deviant behavior, accompanied by realignments and coalitions within the system, alter contributes as much to the outcome as ego. In short, the outcome is a cumulative and collective product, and the history of the deviant act is the history of an interactional system, not of the actor who happened to author the act. It follows that research and theory must address themselves to the following questions: What is the detailed structure of this process of progressive commitment? What are the characteristics of the points of no return? What sets in motion the reverse cycles of restoration of conformity? And, implicit in all these questions: In what ways do alter's values affect the course of these processes? In particular, to what kinds of strain is alter subject, and what are the consequences to alter of ego's deviant behavior? When does incipient deviant behavior seduce the ambivalent and lead to deviant coalitions? When does it excite indignation, sanctimony, and hostility? When does it elicit sympathy, emotional support, and nonpunitive efforts to restore ego to conformity?

How, furthermore, does the significance of an event for deviant behavior depend upon the stage of the interaction process? Since the stimulus value of any event depends upon the perspectives on which it impinges, and since the perspectives of participants in a system change with their experience in the system, we cannot say that certain kinds of events or circumstances are pressures for or against deviant behavior without reference to the stage of the interaction process. The rebuke which brings the incipient deviant back into line may further alienate the deviant who is somewhat further advanced. Can we, however, move beyond the platitudinous statement that "the stage of the interaction process makes a difference" and state just what kind of difference it makes under various conditions?

Alternative Responses to Strain.   Deviant behavior is a response to strain, which we have defined as ambivalence relative to institutionalized expectations. Such ambivalence occurs whenever conformity to institutionalized expectations is positively motivated and, at the same time, somehow frustrating or unacceptable. It is probably inherent in the nature of social systems that most of the members are subject to such strain in various degrees. However, most of us conform most of the time. Therefore, deviant behavior is not the only response to strain, and there must be ties to the institutional order that are powerful enough to override deviant motivation most of the time. In other words, social systems must be so organized that deviant behavior tends to produce, more often than not, tensions greater than those produced by conformity. The following discussion of these ties to the institutional order, the restraining forces they exert on deviant behavior, and the possible modes of adaptation in the face of such restraining forces will yield, we think, a systematic formulation of the major theoretical problems of a sociology of deviant behavior.

Let us begin with an example of an individual who is seeking, consciously or unconsciously, to resolve his ambivalence relative to some institutionalized expectation: a doctor considering whether to perform illegal abortions, a police officer debating whether to accept a "cut" from a· brothel keeper, or a person with homosexual inclinations hesitating about yielding to those inclinations. In each case the temptation is attractive but institutionally forbidden.

A satisfactory resolution will have certain characteristics. It will be one which the individual can square with his own moral standards and which is symbolically consistent with the roles in terms of which he defines himself. Thus, overt homosexuality may not only be unacceptable because it is seen as "wrong" and "sinful"; it may also be symbolically inappropriate in the sense that it signifies a denial of manhood. (By the same token, to throw stones at street lights may be "wrong" for boy and man alike. For the latter, however, it is "kid stuff" and threatening to his self-conception as an "adult"; for the former, it serves to validate his claim to being "all boy.")

The adequacy of a response in both these respects depends very much on what have been called the actor's "normative reference groups." It is difficult to be persuaded of the moral rightness of a choice when our judgment does not agree with that of groups which we have come to regard as authoritative with respect to the issue involved. Such reference groups will always be, to some extent, participants in the institutional order. To the degree that this is so, we cannot indulge in behavior that violates their expectations without moral uncertainty, guilt, or ambivalence. Similarly, the symbolism of an act, as of language, depends upon the usages of a community which the actor regards as authoritative in such matters. Thus, whether I consider myself a "square" or a "cat"—assuming that it is important to me whether I am the one or the other—depends upon the role symbolism of what I say and do, and this symbolism is defined by my normative reference groups. The role symbolism that these reference groups confer on institutionally expected behavior will usually, although not necessarily, be congruent with the self-conceptions that the actor is trying to fulfill. Conversely, behavior that violates the institutionally expected is likely to signify roles with which the actor seeks to avoid identification.

One problem for an individual who is confronted with a situation of strain and is consequently tempted to behave in deviant ways is to comes to terms with the moral conceptions and role definitions of his normative reference groups, which, as we have said, are generally ranged on the side of the institutional order. There are three possible resolutions of this problem, one of them conformist, two deviant.

One alternative is for our hypothetical subject to continue to conform, despite continued frustration, because conformity is the only alternative that is morally and symbolically validated by his reference groups. It is probable, as a matter of fact, that most people carry a chronic load of frustration but nevertheless continue to conform because the frustration is easier to bear than moral uncertainty or unfavorable role significance.

A second alternative is for him to break with his reference groups and acknowledge other reference groups, whose norms legitimize deviant solutions and attribute favorable role symbolism to them. This solution may involve "shopping around" to find such reference groups or joining forces with others in the same position to create new reference groups. These processes can be observed in the fields of unethical medical practice, police corruption, and homosexuality. Clearly, we are here talking about processes by means of which subcultures are created and perpetuated. Of these processes we have only the most elementary understanding. The development of a theory of subcultures is a general theoretical problem of the greatest possible import for a sociology of deviant behavior.

A third alternative is for the individual to "go it alone," violating the institutionalized expectations without the legitimation and validation that come from consensus. This would appear to be the most costly and, on current theoretical grounds, the most improbable alternative, but it occurs. In view of the enormous importance attributed to reference-group support by current sociological theory, the conditions under which this response occurs pose a crucial theoretical problem.

The question of whether to conform or not resolves itself, in part, into a choice among these three alternative responses to the problem of what to do about reference-group support in the areas of moral validity and role symbolism. To the extent that this is so, the task of theory is to clarify what is entailed in each of these responses and to account for choices among them.

However, the actor must deal with yet another type of problem, the responses to which take the form of a very similar set of alternatives. This type of problem concerns, not the assessment of morality and meaning, but the objective consequences of the act in terms of the satisfaction or deprivation of the individual's needs or wants. These needs or wants do not exist in pure or disembodied form but are attached or directed to particular objects or classes of objects. Satisfaction consists in acquiring, using, or establishing some sort of relationship to these objects. Some of these needs may be called social-emotional; gratification of needs in this category consists in the establishment of certain kinds of relationships with social objects (persons or collectivities). Those with whom we value such relationships have been called our "status reference groups"—"status," in this context, signifying the whole class of gratifying emotional responses from others.

By definition, satisfaction of social-emotional needs depends upon the responses of others. More specifically, it depends upon the standards and criteria current in the individual's reference groups in terms of which these groups evaluate his personal qualities and conduct. To the degree to which his status reference groups are themselves integrated into the institutional order, the individual's social-emotional security depends upon his conformity to institutionalized expectations, for such conformity is always among the conditions upon which the favorable response is contingent.

In addition to its consequences for gratification-deprivation in the social-emotional area, any act has consequences for the gratification or deprivation of needs and wants attached to nonsocial objects—a residual category commonly called goods and services. These are multitudinous, including food, clothing, shelter, money, drugs and medical care, transportation, and entertainment. Some of these are directly gratifying, some are instrumental to other satisfactions. The important point is that the consequences of an act in terms of want satisfaction depend upon the way in which it articulates with the established systems of interaction through which goods and services are produced and distributed. Families, businesses, fraternal organizations, churches, governmental agencies, and universities are such systems. To obtain the goods and services they offer, the individual must participate in them on their own terms. He must assume responsible roles in these systems and perform them appropriately—that is, in accordance with the institutionalized expectations of the other participants. The systems themselves may generate needs that cannot be legitimately or even illegitimately satisfied within the systems, but this fact does not mean that the individual can lightly turn his back on the systems and refuse to conform to their expectations. For it is characteristic of social systems that through each of them we satisfy not one but many wants. Therefore, the loss of good standing in our family, our neighborhood, or our business community may result in the denial of satisfaction of not one but a whole set of wants. In still another way, therefore, dependence upon the institutional order encourages us to conform, even under conditions of strain.

Again, the question of whether to conform or not resolves itself into a choice among three alternative responses to the problem of what to do about our dependence upon the institutional order for satisfaction of social-emotional and other needs.

First, an individual confronted with this choice may continue to conform rather than risk shame, contumely, loss of love, or the denial or deprivation of goods and services.

Secondly, he can, so to speak, take his business elsewhere. He can seek out or participate in the creation—together with similarly disaffected individuals—of status reference groups which are disposed to reward behavior that would otherwise result in social rejection. To obtain goods and services which he has forfeited by refusal to meet the demands of the institutionalized order, he may participate in or help to create, together with other individuals who stand to profit from such cooperative endeavors, systems which are geared to the satisfaction of illicit wants or which provide mechanisms through which culturally approved wants can be satisfied through illegitimate means.

This second type of response parallels the creation of or participation in subcultures. The subcultural response, however, deals with the problems of meaning and moral validity. The present response deals with the problem of finding or effecting practical arrangements that are capable of gratifying our needs and wants.

A third type of response is to violate the institutionalized expectations and put up with the consequent denial and frustration of needs which can be gratified only through playing a responsible role in a cooperative social concern.

The process of becoming a deviant, therefore, involves coming to terms with a number of problems. A deviant solution which is acceptable on one criterion may not be acceptable on others. Stable deviant solutions usually consist of complex social arrangements that are capable of resolving strain in several areas. Becoming a marihuana user, for example, is a gradual process of induction, step by step, into an elaborate deviant substructure which makes it possible to be a marihuana user and at the same time to cope with all the problems arising out of alienation from the conventional or institutional order.[6] What is it about the structure of the larger society that generates such deviant substructures— and there is a large family of them—and makes it possible for them to survive? What kinds of interactive process produce awareness of, access to, and progressive involvement in such substructures? These are problems generic to the sociology of deviant behavior, not to marihuana use alone.

On the other hand, consider a (somewhat idealized) Skid Row bum who, to all appearances, is isolated and despised, who has lost his self-respect, whose behavior is neither rewarded by response from people whose response he values nor sanctioned by reference groups whose

[6] Howard S. Becker, "Marihuana Use and Social Control," *Soc. Prob.*, 3 (1955), 35-44.

authority he respects, and whose behavior, further, is instrumentally ineffective to the point that even his liquor supply is precarious. In this case, the choice—if the word "choice" is appropriate—seems to be the third alternative. The theory we evolve must be able to make sense of this sort of behavior. To state that deviant behavior and conformity represent resolutions of a threefold dilemma in each of several areas may be a fruitful way of approaching what we are here attempting to explain.

Linkages Among Forms of Deviant Behavior. There is a strong tendency for sociologists to treat the various forms of deviant behavior as somehow interrelated—either as protean symptoms or manifestations of a single underlying pathology, or as cause and consequence of one another.

It is true that varieties of deviant behavior may be linked in a number of ways. Various kinds of deviant behavior—for example, aggressive "acting out" and passive withdrawal—may tend to cluster because they represent different ways of coping with the same situation. One kind of deviant behavior may be instrumental to another—as, for example, in the case of the drug addict who is forced to steal in order to maintain his habit. One kind may be a device for evading the consequences of another; for example, the rapist may be a killer because his victim is his witness. Or again, various kinds of deviant specialties may aid and abet one another. Those who are already involved in deviant behavior exert pressure upon all those who are in a position to affect their operations adversely or to render them services to become their accessories. Thus slot-machine rackets, labor racketeering, political corruption, police graft, and organized gambling tend to encourage one another, to become symbiotically linked, and to come under common control because each serves the interests of the others.

One of the tasks of a sociology of deviant behavior is to classify and elucidate the mechanisms by means of which one kind of deviant behavior generates others. But this is not to say that the sources of deviant behavior are always to be found in the abnormal, the pathological, and the deplorable. They may also be found in the institutionally expected and the sacred. Implicit in the very idea of a system is the fact that whatever is found in it is a function of its total structure. The consequences of any particular feature of a system for deviant behavior or conformity depend not on its moral or hygienic status but on its con-

text. The same strains which help to produce deviant behavior also help
to produce the behavior we most admire and applaud. For example, the
characteristic American belief that a man should "make something of
himself" encourages the hard work, self-discipline, and productivity that
we so much admire; at the same time, it makes failure all the more ego-
involved and humiliating and, if the writer's analysis [7] is correct, helps
to motivate delinquent subcultures in American society. If Kingsley
Davis [8] is correct, the sanctity of the marriage institution and the high
value placed upon female chastity help to explain prostitution as well
as sexual continence. If Chein and Rosenfeld [9] are correct, teen-age
drug use may result from the impact upon a certain kind of personality
of age-graded expectations which motivate other young people to assume the responsibilities of adulthood. Furthermore; much that is deviant can be largely attributed to efforts, some of them nobly motivated,
to control deviant behavior. For example, efforts to prevent the consumption of liquor and narcotics and to prevent gambling have fostered
the growth of large-scale criminal organizations for the provision of
these goods and services, and these organizations in turn have contributed to the corruption of politics and law enforcement. In short,
that which we deplore and that which we cherish are not only part of
the same seamless web; they are actually woven of the same fibers.

Social Disorganization

The sociology of social disorganization is in an even worse state
than the sociology of deviant behavior. Few terms in sociology are defined so variously and obscurely as social disorganization. Values intrude themselves so persistently and insidiously into definition and usage
that the concept is often regarded as a term of evaluation and therefore
unscientific. It is difficult to determine what, if any, is the line of demarcation between social disorganization and deviant behavior. Some sociologists even question whether social disorganization exists and sug-

[7] Albert K. Cohen, *Delinquent Boys, The Culture of the Gang,* Free
Press, 1955.

[8] Kingsley Davis, "The Sociology of Prostitution," *Amer. sociol. Rev.,*
2 (1937), 744-55.

[9] Isidor Chein and Eva Rosenfeld, "Juvenile Narcotics Use," *Law con-
temp. Prob.,* 22 (1957), 59-63.

gest that there are only different kinds of organization. However, we believe that social disorganization can be defined in a way that is value-free, that is independent of the definition of deviant behavior, and that, at the same time, designates a set of crucial theoretical problems. (This definition owes a great deal to a paper by Dr. Harold Garfinkel.[10])

Let us begin by noting what we consider to be some examples of social disorganization. A children's ball game is disrupted when their only ball falls into the creek. A meeting of a learned society is disrupted when some members of the local Chamber of Commerce appear and announce that the room has been reserved for their use during that hour. A military mission is disrupted when the leader is killed and no one steps forward to assume command. In all these situations some activity has been going on and has been disrupted or interrupted. Our task now is to formulate a general definition of an activity or of an interaction system which enables us to mark the boundaries, as it were, between one activity and another, to state whether a particular act is or is not constitutive of a particular activity, and to determine whether an activity is or is not in progress, has or has not been disrupted.

Definition. We shall begin, as does Garfinkel, with the game as our paradigm of an activity or interaction system and show that those characteristics which define organization and disorganization for a game are equally applicable to nongame activities.

THE GAME. In the first place, the names of games are taken from the language of the participants. They designate sets of events which the participants perceive as belonging together and jointly constituting one thing, a certain kind of game. Therefore, to determine whether a particular kind of game is going on, we must use the participants' own criteria for defining that sort of game.

These criteria are given by the rules of the game, which designate certain classes of events and state the standards for assigning events to these classes. All events which can be so classified and only those events are possible game events. Thus a swing that misses and a hit ball that goes out of bounds both fall in the class "strike" in the game "baseball."

---

[10] Harold Garfinkel, "Trust as a Condition of Stable Concerted Action," paper delivered at the annual meetings of the American Sociological Society, 1957.

Game events may include not only actions of the players but also events in the situation of action. For example, the advent of darkness during a baseball game is a game event if it is anticipated by the rules and a class of situations exists to which it is assigned by the rules.

Furthermore—and this is crucial—the rules specify an order among these classes of events; to constitute the game in question, events must conform to that order. Many concretely different sequences may conform to the order of a given kind of game. At a given stage of the game, a player on second base may steal third or stay on second. He may not proceed directly to bat, for this would not be a game event in the game of baseball. Note that the order of events enters into the definition of an event. For example, whether or not hitting a ball out of bounds is a strike depends on how many strikes a batter already has against him.

The rules also provide a criterion for determining whether the game is in progress or has been interrupted. If the "constitutive order of events"—an order conforming to the constitutive rules—is interrupted, the game is interrupted or, as we shall use the word, disorganized. If the game terminates in accordance with the rules of the game—that is, if it culminates in a state of affairs defined by the rules as "the end of the game"—we simply say that the game is over. But if the constitutive order of events is breached at any other point, if the game is neither over nor in progress, it is disorganized. If, for example, a brawl develops in which all the players become involved, the game is disorganized. (A brawl, in turn, can be regarded as a game subject to disorganization on its own terms; for example, police may break up a "rumble.")

DEVIANT BEHAVIOR AND DISORGANIZATION. A property of the rules of the game which is of the most fundamental importance is the fact that these rules are definitional statements. They do not tell us what is the right or the wrong thing to do; they merely tell us whether what we are doing is part of a given game. There are also rules of right conduct, morality, fair play—what we have called institutionalized expectations. But violations of these rules of right conduct, if they are covered by the rules of the game, are themselves game events and need not constitute a breach in the constitutive order of events. It may, for example, be forbidden to step over a certain line, to strike another player, to spit on the ball. If the constitutive rules designate such events as "fouls" or "cheating" and prescribe a penalty, events and penalty are part of the constitutive order. In short, deviant behavior is not defined by the same rules that define game events and therefore does not, merely by virtue of being deviant, constitute disorganization.

This is not to say that deviant behavior may not precipitate disorganization. If a player, in clear violation of the rules of good sportsmanship, stalks off the field and the constitutive rules have failed to anticipate such situations, if the rules prescribe that there shall be a certain number of players on both sides and there are no replacements available, or if the rules are obscure and there is disagreement as to how the situation is to be defined, the resulting situation is, at worst, meaningless and, at best, ambiguous. In any case, it creates at least temporary disorganization. Deviant behavior, therefore, may or may not precipitate disorganization, but it is not *ipso facto* disorganization.

GAMES AND NONGAMES. What we have said of games may be said of the nongame activities of everyday life as well, although the constitutive rules are less likely to be labeled rules and codified, and they may not command the same measure of agreement. The set of constitutive rules of a military operation is the plan of the operation. (Many of its details are provided by an implicit context of army regulations, field manuals, and the subculture of the military unit concerned.) This plan sets forth a sequence of events the fulfillment of which constitutes the operation. In like manner, the operations of a railroad, an industrial organization, a public utility, or a family resolve themselves into sets of recurrent and interlocking activities, each of which is defined by its respective constitutive rules. The range of alternatives possible at any given stage of an activity, and therefore the variety of concrete sequences that are compatible with the constitutive rules, varies from one type of activity to another. The definition of a church service, for example, may require adherence to a rather rigid order of events; the definition of a seminar can be met by a wide range of concretely different sequences.

The matter becomes clearer when we consider how the same set of interactions can be analyzed into different activities. In a basketball game, one of the teams may have a particular strategy, a concerted plan which takes certain contingencies into account and prescribes appropriate action for designated players in the event of those contingencies. Such a strategy has the characteristics of the rules of the game. The order prescribed by the strategy may be breached if the opposing team creates a situation that is not contemplated by the plan. In this case, the execution of the strategy has been disorganized. Nothing has happened, however, that is incompatible with the constitutive rules of basketball; the basketball game, therefore, has not been disorganized. Similarly, the strategy of management or of labor in a collective-bargaining process may be disorganized without disorganizing the collective-bargaining process itself. Again, the disruption of the operations of a commercial firm or even the failure of the firm as a result of unanticipated changes in the market need not imply any interruption in the market as a system defined by its own constitutive rules. It follows, therefore, that in speaking of organization or disorganization we must be careful to specify the game, activity, or interaction system in question.

An activity may consist in an order among lesser or included activities, each of which can be defined in terms of its own constitutive rules and is subject to disorganization on its own terms. Disorganization of one of these included activities, however, may or may not result in disorganization of the constitutive order that defines the more inclusive activity. For example, the operations of one plant of an industrial concern or one unit of a fire department may be disorganized as a result of a natural disaster. If, however, another plant or another unit can be mobilized to do the same job as the disorganized member of the system, there may be no breach of the organization of the larger activity.

Different activities may be interdependent and even interpenetrating in a variety of ways. It is possible to draw up rules for two games to be played simultaneously on the same checkerboard such that every physical event that is a move in one game is a move—that is, a game event—in the other. A winning move in one game may be a losing move in the other, but the continuity of neither game is disorganizing with reference to the other. In a perfectly organized society, all activities would be so organized that every event in one activity would be a possible event in others or would help to create the conditions necessary for the continuity of other activities. As a matter of fact, in every viable social system there must be some approximation to this state of affairs. However, this kind of articulation is always problematical. Every system requires time, space, personnel, and equipment for the unfolding of its constitutive order, but different systems compete for these resources, and the availability of these resources to one system may depend upon their denial to another system to which they are equally necessary. Thus, the execution of a business operation or the very survival of a business may depend, on the one hand, upon the continued orderly functioning—that is, functioning in accordance with their own constitutive rules—of the firms from which it buys and sells and, on the other hand, upon the denial to its competitors of the materials and customers upon which their own operations or survival depend.

CONCLUSION. The foregoing definition of social disorganization is, we think, congruent with usage. In describing military routs and natural disasters—situations in which there is consensus that the word disorganization is relevant—we say that people "freeze," "panic," "flounder," "give up," "run away," "change their plans," or "stand around helplessly." All these behaviors disrupt or at least threaten the constitutive order of the ongoing activity; therefore, they are themselves, or at least they precipitate, disorganization—a fact generally recognized by making these behaviors synonymous with disorganization in ordinary English usage.

Disorganization as we have defined it can occur on a less dramatic scale and with less dramatic consequences in any social setting—in the family, on the job, in the classroom. More than this, in every interaction system, no matter how stable and tranquil, the threat of disorganization, like the threat of deviant behavior, is always present, and the mechanisms for averting it and nipping it in the bud pose a problem that is everywhere relevant. As a matter of fact, our definition of organization as an order of events conforming to a set of constitutive rules implies our definition of disorganization as a breach of that order. The two terms, therefore, define a single field—organization-disorganization— as do conformity and deviant behavior.

The poverty of theory in the area of social disorganization reflects the lack of clarity and agreement with respect to the demarcation of the field. For this reason we have devoted a good deal of space to defining disorganization, to clarifying its relationship to deviant behavior, and to showing how the use of the concept as here defined helps us to analyze more rigorously and, we think, more fruitfully the sequences of behavior that are ordinarily described as "social disorganization." The test of any definition, including that presented here, will lie, of course, in the amenability of the field, as demarcated by that definition, to systematic theory.

The Conditions of Disorganization.   Implicit in any definition of a field is a way of formulating its outstanding problems. The problem of clarifying the conditions under which disorganization occurs can be approached by first asking: What are the preconditions of *organization?* If organization is an order of events conforming to a set of constitutive rules, then organization implies two conditions. First, it presupposes that action unfolds in such a way that, at any stage or phase of the system, the situations that the participants confront and the alternative possibilities of action can be defined by the rules. Secondly, it presupposes that the participants are motivated to "play the game"—that is, to assume the perspectives provided by the rules and to select their actions from the constitutive possibilities designated by the rules. Conversely, disorganization must arise when one or both of these two conditions are not satisfied. First, it arises when the situations that the participants confront cannot be defined as system events or when there is no clear definition of the constitutive possibilities of action. This is a situation of normlessness, anomie, or meaninglessness. Secondly, it arises when the participants are not motivated, when their values, interests, and aims are not integrated with the requirements for continuity of the interaction system.

Localized conditions of anomie or failure of motivation, however, are not, in and of themselves, disorganization. Nor do all events which fall outside the constitutive order necessarily breach that order. For example, an individual soldier may panic and start running about wildly, an event which is not contemplated by the plan and which falls outside the scope of the plan. Yet the loss or defection of one soldier may not affect the orderly development called for by the plan. By contrast, however, the failure of one battery in one radio, if that radio is the only means of communication with a command center, may result in complete confusion and disorganization. In the absence of instructions, the situation and the behavior it calls for from each participant cannot be defined. There is a general state of anomie and a complete breach of the constitutive order.

The broader systemic repercussions of an event depend upon the way in which it is articulated with the rest of the system. Local conditions of anomie or failure of motivation may spread, involving more and more areas of the system, until they reach a vital spot and destroy the minimal conditions necessary for the continuity of the events called for by the plan. On the other hand, systems may have mechanisms for walling off the affected areas so that contagion cannot spread to involve those events that are definitive of the constitutive order. Systems may have mechanisms for restoring organization—for example, by sending in replacements for confused, incompetent, or disaffected personnel—or for reinforcing motivation by bringing powerful sanctions to bear. Systems may have alternative arrangements for producing certain events that are necessary for the constitutive order, which arrangements go into effect when some segment of the system breaks down. All these mechanisms, in turn, depend upon mechanisms for gathering and transmitting information so that incipient or threatening disorganization can be spotted and the appropriate steps taken to halt or avert it.

Anomie and Failure of Motivation. Anomie and failure of motivation are of such central importance to a theory of disorganization that certain additional comments are called for. Anomie may take a number of forms: confrontation by a situation for which there are no relevant rules, vagueness or ambiguity of the relevant rules, or lack of consensus on which rules are relevant and on the interpretation of rules. However, anomie depends not only on the structure of the set of constitutive rules but also on the situations which the system encounters. No set of rules covers all the situations which might conceivably arise. The fact that the rules do not cover certain conceivable situations spells anomie *only if those situations do in fact arise.* Control of anomie, therefore, may depend on one of two conditions. On the one hand, given the situation, it depends upon the existence and clarity of the relevant rules. On the other hand, given the rules, it depends upon the extent to which the system, in interaction with its environment, generates situations for which the constitutive rules provide definitions. This implies that a system capable of maintaining organization only under a narrowly limited set of conditions may nonetheless be very durable, provided that it has sufficient control over its environment to guarantee to itself the conditions it requires, or that some other system, through *its* functioning, can guarantee those conditions. The "wisdom of the body" in maintaining the constancy of its "internal environment" is an appropriate analogy.

One other property which a system of rules may possess should be noted. When a given situation may be defined in more than one way— that is, when there is more than one relevant rule—the rules themselves may specify priorities among rules or other criteria for resolving the ambiguity. When situations are ambiguous or meaningless, the rules may provide rules for making rules—for example, by designating leaders whose definitions are, by the rules, authoritative and valid for all participants.

The theoretical problems implied in failure of motivation and in mechanisms for averting that failure also need clarification. Here we shall limit ourselves to some observations on institutional elements in motivation.

Deviant behavior and conformity, we have said, are not definitive of disorganization and organization. This is not to say that moral considerations are not highly relevant to organization and disorganization through the part they play in motivation. It is difficult to conceive of a system in which the incentive to assume one's role and play one's part in accordance with the constitutive rules does not require, to some extent at least, the backing of a sense of moral obligation and the assumption that others also feel morally bound. Hobbes' Leviathan, the most impressive attempt to conceive such a system, is empirically impossible.

However, a sense of moral obligation is only one factor in motivation. Presumably, even a Nazi concentration camp could not function without some moral discipline among the jailers themselves, but the stability and viability of its constitutive order do not presuppose that the prisoners share the moral sentiments of their jailers. The relevant question for a theory of social disorganization, therefore, is this: How does the relative importance of different types of motivation—for example, moral obligation, force, and coercion—vary wth the type of system, the sector within the system, and the situation within which the system functions?

But the relationship between motivation and conformity to institutionalized expectations is more subtle than this. There may well be situations in which deviant behavior is organizing and conformity disorganizing. Under certain conditions, choice of the institutionally sanctioned constitutive possibility may lead to organizational breakdown, and choice of an institutionally condemned alternative can alone avert this breakdown. For example, the procurement of certain supplies may be essential for the continuity of a certain activity. This procurement may be regulated by certain institutionalized expectations which, under the range of conditions ordinarily encountered, serve their purpose quite well. Under other conditions, however, conformity to these institutionally prescribed procedures will not work or will result in fatal delays in procurement. What used to be called "moonlight requisitioning" in the Army was at times the only method of procurement compatible with the execution of a mission or even the routine functioning of some operation. Too delicate a G. I. conscience was destructive of organization.

There is much more to be said about motivation, but our object is only to indicate in a general way the complexity of the relationship of motivation, and especially institutional elements in motivation, to social organization and disorganization, and the nature of the problems to be explored.

Related Concepts. In the foregoing, we have implied a number of theoretical problems that have a recognized place in sociology: the problem of order, the functional prerequisites of social systems, the conditions of homeostasis, of equilibrium, of boundary maintenance. We shall resist the temptation to discuss at length these concepts and the distinctions among them. It should be pointed out, however, that all of them imply a conception of a social system as a structure of interaction which, despite the buffetings of the environment and internal stresses, manages to preserve certain characteristics. This property is sometimes defined as the ability of the system to maintain constancy with respect to some concrete feature or with respect to the relationships among certain parts of the system or with respect to a direction of movement or change—in other words, the continued adherence of the system to some pattern or model which defines that particular system. One such model is the set of constitutive rules that define, for the participants in the system, the kind of activity in which they are engaged.

All these concepts imply, further, a particular approach to social systems—one that regards them as mechanisms for their own perpetuation. They imply formulation of the problems that systems must solve in order to secure their own viability; they imply classification of the structural features of systems from the standpoint of the part they play in enabling the system to adhere to the model which defines it; they imply classification and analysis of the mechanisms by means of which systems detect conditions that threaten their viability or constancy in some particular respect and meet and counter these threats; and they imply the study of the conditions under which systems break down. These problems exist and are recognized, they constitute a distinct and coherent problem area, and they are implied by our definition of organization-disorganization.

Bibliography

Becker, Howard S., "Marihuana Use and Social Control," *Soc. Prob.* (1955), 35-44.

Cohen, Albert K., *Delinquent Boys, The Culture of the Gang*, Free Press, 1955.

———, Alfred R. Lindesmith, and Karl F. Schuessler (eds.), *The Sutherland Papers*, Indiana University Press, 1956.

Faris, Robert E. L., *Social Disorganization*, Ronald Press, 1955.

Garfinkel, Harold, "Trust as a Condition of Stable Concerted Action," paper delivered at the annual meetings of the American Sociological Society, 1957.

Merton, Robert K., *Social Theory and Social Structure*, Free Press, 1957.

Parsons, Talcott, *The Social System*, Free Press, 1951.

Thomas, William I., and Florian Znaniecki, *The Polish Peasant in Europe and America*, Richard G. Badger, 1918.

22
The Sociology
of Mental
Illness

JOHN A. CLAUSEN
National Institute of Mental Health

A discussion of the problematics and current prospects of a field of sociological inquiry which is in process of being defined is likely to entail a wider ranging review of past work than would be required in a discussion of a field with a well-defined substantive or theoretical core. This is especially to be anticipated when the field of inquiry has emerged partly as a consequence of the pressures of a social problem. The present chapter does not attempt a systematic review of the sociology of mental health and illness; it does offer a rough definition of the field, and it examines some of the problems of theory and research and some of the promising hypotheses now emerging in two subareas—study of the role of social and cultural factors in etiology, and study of the societal response to mental illness.

The Sociology of Mental Health and Illness: A Definition

Any attempt to define the sociology of mental health and illness runs into the difficulty that the designation of behaviors as manifestations of mental health or illness seems to be largely peculiar to our own culture and epoch.[1] Mental illness of one type or another occurs among all peoples, but cultural definitions of the specific problems involved vary tremendously and bear little resemblance to psychiatric definitions. Psychiatric knowledge and the mental-health movement are social products, certainly subject to study; but they do not give us an adequate basis for defining a field of sociological inquiry which would extend beyond the limits of Western culture. A valid definition of such a field must, then, be composite, covering a variety of behavioral phenomena ("illness" and reaction patterns) which are only partially culture-bound and a variety of social responses and institutional forms which may be lacking in some cultures and tremendously elaborated in others. The sociology of mental illness, roughly defined, is the study of the social norms and processes which have a marked bearing upon the production or course of various forms of psychic disturbance (especially as such disturbance impairs the individual's ability to carry out usual roles), or which govern the ways in which disturbed persons are perceived, defined, and dealt with during and after phases of acute disturbance. This definition encompasses the great bulk of sociological research on correlates of the incidence of mental illness and on the mental hospital, but at the same time it covers a much wider scope. Social interest in lack of psychic disturbance—*i.e.*, in "positive mental health"—is, of course, not excluded.

The medical designations of various mental illnesses are social facts. That is, they are the basis for patterned responses to the persons so designated. In some instances they are based upon facts of science. The same behaviors to which psychiatrists attach diagnoses may be given other labels, not related to any body of scientific knowledge. Such designations are no less social facts. One task for sociologists is to help discern the meaning and functions of the designations used in various cultural groups and by various categories of persons. Another is to relate the probability that an individual will be labeled mentally ill or deviant by virtue of psychic disturbance to his membership in a particular part of the social structure, or to his having had particular kinds of social experiences. Thus research in this field must deal with be-

[1] H. Warren Dunham, in "Social Psychiatry," *Amer. sociol. Rev.*, 13 (1955), 183-97, discusses the problem of finding an appropriate designation for this area of sociological interest and traces the sequence of terms used at the annual meetings of the American Sociological Society.

haviors which may be understood partly in terms of underlying psycho-logical or physiological processes and partly in terms of the social defi-nitions attaching to the behavioral manifestations.

Regardless of whether the various disorders which are lumped to-gether under the rubric "mental illness" do in fact constitute biological disease entities or are actually socially and psychologically patterned modes of adapting to stress, the resultant behaviors must be considered maladaptive in one sense or another. In studying the effects of mental illness upon society, one may be concerned with impairment of func-tioning as a consequence of a specific mental illness or of all mental illness. The inclusion of all mental diseases and disorders in a single category in this instance poses no great difficulty. In attempting to delineate the role of social factors in etiology, however, one needs not only to distinguish clearly among diseases but also to draw upon the most sophisticated clinical formulations as a basis for planning the re-search approach. A relatively neglected area of research is the diag-nostic process itself. Such research may be a prerequisite to progress in the delineation of social and cultural factors in etiology.

Social and Cultural Factors in Etiology

Perhaps nothing has emerged more clearly from the research of the past decade than the evidence that the relationship between social factors and mental illness is vastly more complex than most of us had assumed. Few of the correlations that seemed clear-cut in early studies have been unequivocally confirmed in subsequent work.

The oft-questioned yet oft-reiterated hypothesis that the com-plexity and stress of modern life has markedly increased the incidence of institutionalization for mental illness was demonstrated to be highly dubious, if not untenable, by Goldhamer and Marshall.[2] On the basis of data on the symptomatology of persons institutionalized in jails and almshouses as well as in hospitals in Massachusetts, they were able to compute age-specific rates of psychosis by decades over the better part of a century. Below age 50 there was no evidence of a rise in rates over this period.

The hypothesis that persons living in a *gemeinschaftliche* social

[2] Herbert Goldhamer and Andrew Marshall, *Psychosis and Civilization*, Free Press, 1953.

system are less prone to mental illness than those living in a more heterogeneous, segmented urban society received a similar body blow from the study of the Hutterites by Eaton and Weil.[3] Combining the use of informants with more intensive case finding in a few communities, they established the fact that psychotic manifestations among the Hutterites had a relative frequency slightly above the level revealed for Baltimore by Lemkau and his associates [4] and slightly lower than the rate of hospitalization for mental illness in New York State.

Eaton and Weil did not apply their case-finding approach to communities in New York, so one cannot say with assurance that the incidence of psychotic disorders in the two populations is closely similar. Likewise, although Goldhamer and Marshall demonstrated that the incidence of confinement for mental illness in Massachusetts in 1840 was roughly comparable to that in 1940, they could not, of course, demonstrate that the ratio of cases confined to those not confined was the same for the two periods. This is not meant as criticism of the two studies. My point is, rather, that, although they challenge with considerable authority hypotheses which had high acceptance among many social scientists, these studies do not establish that the populations compared are even roughly similar, much less identical, in the true incidence of mental illness. The very fact that manifestations of mental illness are defined and dealt with differently in two populations or at two different times makes it exceedingly difficult to establish the relative frequencies of clinically comparable disorders.

Perhaps the most impressively consistent correlation found in epidemiological studies is the inverse relationship between social status and rates of schizophrenia, especially in larger cities. This was first clearly established in the ecological research of Faris and Dunham, corroborated by nearly all the succeeding ecological studies, attested to by an analysis of Selective Service data in Massachusetts, and most recently affirmed by Hollingshead and Redlich in New Haven and by the Cornell Medical School staff in New York.[5] These several sets of rela-

[3] Joseph Eaton and Robert Weil, *Culture and Mental Disorders*, Free Press, 1955.

[4] Paul Lemkau *et al.*, "Mental Hygiene Problems in an Urban District," *Mental Hygiene*, 25 (1941), 624-46; 26 (1942), 100-19.

[5] See, for example, Robert E. L. Faris and H. Warren Dunham, *Mental Disorders in Urban Areas*, University of Chicago Press, 1939; Clarence W. Schroeder, "Mental Disorders in Cities," *Amer. J. Sociol.*, 48 (1942), 40-48;

tively consistent data have, however, been interpreted in a variety of frames of reference. Faris and Dunham focused their interpretative hypotheses upon the conditions of social interaction, and especially upon social isolation, in the areas with the highest rates of schizophrenia. Hollingshead and Redlich have not yet elaborated their interpretations but have emphasized the subcultural aspects of social class and the effects of striving for social mobility.

One somewhat discordant note in the chorus of findings on socioeconomic status and schizophrenia comes from the research carried out by Kohn and Clausen in Hagerstown, Maryland.[6] We found no evidence of an inverse relationship between rates of schizophrenia and socioeconomic status, regardless of whether ecological or occupational categories were used as the index of status. Moreover, a cursory review of the literature suggests that the correlations between social status and schizophrenia are higher in the largest cities than in medium-sized cities. It seems likely that the social-psychological significance of social-status differentials depends in part on the larger social framework within which they have been evolved or laid down. Also, the amounts of mental illness *produced* within strata may be obscured somewhat by differential migration from rural areas and smaller cities to the larger cities. That mental illness and spatial mobility tend to be related seems well established. Several studies suggest that mobility is more often a reflection of the schizoid personality or of adjustment difficulties in the community of origin than it is a causal factor in mental illness.[7] Nevertheless, it is a factor which constantly plagues efforts to relate incidence of mental illness to social origins.

Robert E. Clark, "Psychoses, Income, and Occupational Prestige," *Amer. J. Sociol.*, 54 (1949), 433-40; August B. Hollingshead and Frederick C. Redlich, "Social Stratification and Psychiatric Disorders," *Amer. sociol. Rev.*, 18 (1953), 163-69.

[6] J. A. Clausen and M. L. Kohn, "The Relation of Schizophrenia to the Social Structure of a Small City," paper presented at the annual meeting of the American Association for the Advancement of Science, New York, Dec. 1956.

[7] A conclusive answer to this question would require longitudinal data of a sort nowhere available and not likely to become available for a long time. For a recent review of past research and a careful analysis of new data, see Benjamin Malzberg and Everett S. Lee, *Migration and Mental Disease*, Social Science Research Council, 1956.

Data from the several studies which have examined the relationship between *social* mobility and schizophrenia have been amazingly lacking in consistency. "Drift" from higher to lower status, accompanying the early stages of illness, might help to account for the high percentage of cases of treated schizophrenia found in the lower socioeconomic strata. Gerard and Houston attribute a substantial portion of the concentration of schizophrenics in census tracts of lower socioeconomic status in Worcester to the fact that the schizophrenics hospitalized from these tracts tended to be drifters from other cities.[8] Schwartz found earlier that schizophrenic patients had experienced a decline in status before they were hospitalized.[9] And Lystad has recently reported that schizophrenics from New Orleans were more often downward mobile, relative to parental status, than were their controls.[10] But Hollingshead and Redlich found New Haven schizophrenics to have been upward mobile to a greater extent than were their controls, and at least two other recent studies have shown no decline in social status on the part of schizophrenics.[11]

It is not necessary to cite more of the literature to indicate that we have many inconclusive findings. The variation in correlations from one setting to another suggests either that the variables or clusters of variables singled out are relevant to mental illness in some settings but not in others, or that they are merely occasional correlates of mental illness.

The foregoing discussion has hinted at two major sets of research problems: (1) problems of defining and ascertaining the incidence of mental illness in any population (entailing consideration of conceptions of pathology, criteria of classification, and their indices or means of application to the population); and (2) problems of conceptualizing

[8] Donald L. Gerard and Lester G. Houston, "Family Setting and the Social Ecology of Schizophrenia," *Psychiat. Quart. 27* (1953), 90-101.

[9] Morris S. Schwartz, "The Economic and Spatial Mobility of Paranoid Schizophrenics and Manic-Depressives," unpublished Master's thesis, University of Chicago, 1946.

[10] Mary H. Lystad, "Social Mobility Among Selected Groups of Schizophrenic Patients," *Amer. sociol. Rev., 22* (1957), 288-92.

[11] Hollingshead and Redlich, *loc. cit.;* Clausen and Kohn, *loc. cit.;* Rema Lapouse, Mary A. Monk, and Milton Terris, "The Drift Hypothesis and Socioeconomic Differentials in Schizophrenia," *Amer. J. Pub. Health, 46* (1956), 978-86.

and assessing social and cultural variables and processes that are believed to be directly related to the production of psychic disturbance or mental illness. Both sets of problems are complicated by the fact that mental illness occurs within a social matrix and is recognized and responded to in ways greatly influenced by the social context. Further, the research task requires competence in handling certain concepts and techniques which are not so much sociological as epidemiological, yet which must be used properly if defensible inferences are to be made.

The Assessment and Classification of Mental Illness. Any study which attempts to assess the frequency of mental illness in a population rests upon (1) a set of criteria as to what constitutes mental illness and (2) periodic access to the population in order to apply the criteria or, failing this, a specified means of bringing to attention persons to whom the criteria apply. Two types of measures of frequency of illness are commonly used in morbidity studies: incidence and prevalence. Incidence is defined as the number of new cases of a disorder per unit of population occurring within a stated period of time—*e.g.*, in a given community, 50 persons per 100,000 "developed a mental illness" within a given year. Prevalence is the number of cases of a disorder that are extant at a given time—*e.g.*, on July 1, 1957, the community had 500 mentally ill persons per 100,000 of population. It will be apparent that the relationship of incidence to prevalence depends upon the duration of illness. A disorder which has the same incidence in population A as in population B but which lasts twice as long in A, will be twice as prevalent in A as in B. As a possible clue to etiology, one wants data on incidence, not on prevalence.

The concepts incidence and prevalence are readily applied to illnesses that have a clearly defined onset and course. They are less readily applied to mental illness. The study of neurotic or psychotic behaviors poses a problem to researchers similar to that which confronts students of delinquency: when does a person first become ill (or delinquent), and when does he cease to be ill (or delinquent)? The problem derives partly from the nature of the phenomenon, partly from the fact that a variety of factors influence the subject's coming under surveillance for classification, and partly from the perspective of the classifier.

Let us briefly consider the indices of incidence and the equivalent indices of prevalence that have been used in past studies. We start with those which tend to reflect maximal impairment and hence greatest restriction of classification:

1. Hospitalization for the first time in a public or private mental hospital, with a specified diagnosis of mental illness. (For prevalence, the equivalent index most often used is being in a mental hospital as of a given date.) Note that this incidence index assumes that the time of hospitalization reflects the onset of disease and that only the first admission represents a new illness; subsequent admissions are regarded as recurrences of the same illness. The equivalent prevalence index assumes, however, that persons not in the hospital on a given date are not ill as of that date. Most of the ecological and occupational studies of mental illness have used first admissions to mental hospitals as an index of incidence.

2. Treatment in an out-patient or in-patient psychiatric facility during a stated period of time. (For prevalence, the index used is the number of persons officially under treatment as of a given date.) The assumptions here are similar to those for hospitalization. A notable use of this prevalence index was in the New Haven studies of Hollingshead and Redlich.

3. Persons in a given population who reportedly first displayed during a given period symptoms which a qualified diagnostician would classify as evidence of a specified mental illness. (A comparable index of prevalence would be persons who, as of a given date, reportedly showed such symptoms.) An index of this sort was used by Eaton and Weil in their study of mental illness among the Hutterites.

In the last analysis, all these indices imply an operational definition of mental illness as diagnosis by a qualified psychiatrist. The indices differ in respect to the circumstances that influence the probability that a clinician will have an opportunity to make a diagnosis—the circumstances that bring the person to a hospital or to out-patient treatment or to the attention of an informant.

Periodic psychiatric examination of all members of the population might seem to be the most satisfactory basis for assessing psychiatric status, but it is not likely to be feasible for a long time to come. The cost and difficulty of recruiting and training a psychiatric staff which could examine sufficiently large samples of the population to yield stable rates of serious mental illness would be tremendous, even in the light of currently available research funds. Further, there are attitudinal barriers to such an approach. Relatively few psychiatrists feel comfortable about examining persons who have not sought help and to whom services are not to be offered even if, in the psychiatrist's opinion, they are needed. Public attitudes toward seeking or accepting a proferred psychiatric examination pose an even more serious difficulty. Most people regard mental quirks in themselves or members of their family as something to be concealed, not exposed. Consequently, those persons who are most likely to be designated as "cases" are often the most reluctant to undergo psychiatric examination. Small-scale efforts to examine specified samples suggest that the refusal rate sometimes runs as high as 40 percent. In attempts to locate cases of severe mental illness—a phenomenon that occurs in a very small proportion of persons in a year—even a 10-percent refusal rate would make systematic estimation virtually impossible. As we shall see shortly, there are other sources of difficulty in classifications based on psychiatric examinations.

One approach to systematic assessment of a population combines a relatively structured interview or test of a large sample with psychiatric examination of a subsample. The difficulty here is that data from such interviews and tests generally do not permit the use of standard psychiatric classifications. As a consequence, each team tends to use different categories and criteria. One may list symptoms, another may assess degree of impairment, and a third may rely on a clinician's judgment of the subjects' need for therapy as a basis for rating severity of disturbance. Such classifications usually entail a good bit of clinical judgment, often influenced by theoretical preconceptions that are not widely shared.

For all the unreliability of application of the standard diagnostic nomenclature, it is a set of categories which are learned by all qualified clinicians and for which criteria of assignment and differentiation have been elaborated in some detail. It represents the results of a great deal of clinical experience and persistent efforts to find disease entities and to differentiate types of reaction. Unfortunately, the standard nomenclature is designed for classifying full-blown pathology. There is no evidence that high reliability of diagnosis can be achieved in the early stages of illness. Indeed, the frequency with which changes are made in provisional diagnoses given when the patient is admitted to a mental hospital suggests that a period of observation is often necessary to check on the course of the disturbance. Therefore, few clinicians feel any enthusiasm for assigning a diagnostic label to persons about whom their information is limited.

There is another side of this problem which further complicates classification through psychiatric examination or screening. Every community has some members who are regarded by their fellow citizens as "queer," "mean," "shy," "offensive," and the like. Many of these persons would be diagnosed by a psychiatrist as neurotic and some as psychotic, even though other community members may not regard them as mentally ill. It is not unlikely that many persons whose social background is grossly divergent from that of the psychiatrist (*e.g.*, lower-class persons) will be seen as sicker than those whose attitudes and behaviors are closer to the psychiatrist's own outlook. Haase has shown that the use by psychologists of projective tests, standardized on the middle class, is subject to the same bias.[12] Unless and until there are valid tests for the diagnosis of schizophrenia and other mental illnesses, studies of so-called true prevalence must deal with biases in clinical classification due to subcultural perspectives, just as studies of treated prevalence must deal with biases of community and professional response. We need, then, to know both professional diagnoses and the peer and family responses to members of populations under study. How do members of various subcultures label and attempt to deal with males and females at various age levels who are suffering from such diverse conditions as simple retarded depression, delusions of persecution, and anxiety states? And what are the consequences of such responses to the symptoms of mental illness?

Thus the researcher faces something of a dilemma in seeking adequate data. If he wishes reasonably well-diagnosed cases, he must, by and large, work with patients who are hospitalized or under treatment, recognizing that they constitute only a part of the total group suffering from a given illness. If, on the other hand, he wishes to approximate a total count of disturbed persons in some limited group, he must expect less reliable diagnoses. One solution might be to try both approaches and compare the characteristics of the cases selected. Another would be to study much more thoroughly than has been done how some ill persons in the community become patients while others do not.

To explain, in part, the differential distribution of rates of hospitalization found by Faris and Dunham, Owen suggested that mentally ill persons are perceived and dealt with differently in different

---

[12] William Haase, *Rorschach Diagnosis, Socio-Economic Class and Examiner Bias*, unpublished doctoral dissertation, New York University, 1955.

settings.[13] Thus far, no one has demonstrated that the areas of the city and segments of the population with the highest rates of hospitalization are characterized by a higher degree of recognition of mental illness than are other areas. Several studies suggest that, if anything, the reverse is true. There is substantial documentation, however, of the fact that the social status of the mentally ill person tends to influence the perception by his family and others of the nature of his problem, their modes of dealing with him prior to his entering medical-psychiatric channels, and the kinds of service offered to him by psychiatric clinics or hospitals.[14] Few would contend that the statistics generated by classifying persons according to social status and psychological state at the time of entrance into treatment settings constitute an adequate record of the relationship between the social environment and the biosocial process of illness.

Tolerance (or any other response to forms of deviant behavior) may in the last analysis determine not only who is brought to treatment, but whether or not the person needs to be hospitalized. In our own research on the families of mental patients, we have encountered instances in which an accepting and nurturant wife has been able to sustain a schizophrenic spouse for five to ten years before symptomatic manifestations in the work situation caused him to be brought to treatment. In other instances, we have seen the utter rejection of a husband within a few days or even hours of his manifesting far less deviant symptomatology. The latter instances are often followed by a period of acting out which brings the patient to the hospital and a regime of isolation and control which leaves its own imprint upon his personality.

The Search for Significant Sociological Variables. We noted above the variability in correlations between gross sociological indices—social class, type of residential area, occupation—and rates of hospital-

[13] M. B. Owen, "Alternative Hypotheses for the Evaluation of Faris and Dunham's Results," *Amer. J. Sociol.*, 47 (1941), 48-51.

[14] See, for example, Edwin Lemert, *Social Pathology*, McGraw-Hill, 1951, Chap. 11, "Mental Disorders and the Insane"; Jerome K. Meyers and Leslie Schaffer, "Social Stratification and Psychiatric Practice: A Study of an Outpatient Clinic," *Amer. sociol. Rev.*, 19 (1954), 307-10; and John A. Clausen and Marian R. Yarrow, "Paths to the Mental Hospital," *J. soc. Issues*, 11:4 (1955), 25-32.

ized mental illness. Even where there has been a relatively high degree of consistency among research results, as in the case of ecological studies, interpretation is difficult. In attempting to interpret in an etiological framework any observed difference in the incidences of treated or psychiatrically observed mental illness between two population segments (whether these be social classes, ethnic groups, or subcultures), the crucial question is: Do some discernible aspects of life processes in one of these segments give rise to more cases of mental illness than are produced in the other? Or, restated, if the two subcultures do differ in the amounts of mental illness produced, what are the specific social and cultural variables or constellations of variables involved, and how do they exercise their effect? [15]

The answer to this question requires a more intensive analysis of the life histories of ill persons than can possibly be achieved in broad studies of incidence. It also requires a frame of reference for seeking and organizing types of data which seem relevant on the basis of clinical experience, theoretical formulations, and previous research. Further, in my own opinion, such a frame of reference can no longer ignore the findings of genetic research and studies of physiological reactions to stress. It may be fruitful to consider one such frame of reference, not as a proposed model, but as an example of a general point of view toward etiology and its study. The same point of view, interestingly enough, is emerging in other conceptualizations.

The conceptual framework used by the epidemiologist in the study of mass disease has general applicability to diseases that are not, strictly speaking, communicable. The epidemiologist John Gordon characterizes communicable disease as "the interaction of a triad; the members of which are a host, with man the primary concern, an agent of disease, and lastly the intricate complex of environment." [16] He notes that causation is a product of all three components, although one factor or another usually dominates. The agent of disease may be a germ, a toxin, a deficiency (*e.g.*, nutritional), or an extreme overload upon the organ-

[15] Oddly enough, sociologists have, until very recently, all but ignored research in the psychological significance of aspects of social class, leaving the field largely to psychologists, psychiatrists, and anthropologists.

[16] John E. Gordon, "The Newer Epidemiology," in *Tomorrow's Horizon in Public Health*, Transactions of the 1950 Conference of the Public Health Assn. of New York City, 1950, p. 22.

ism. The host contributes to causation through both inherent character-istics (anatomic, physiologic, developmental) and acquired immunities or vulnerabilities. The environment, as characterized by the epidemiologist, includes the physical, biological, and social milieus as these influence the interaction of agent and host.

The value of such a conceptual framework is that it helps the epidemiologist to avoid the fallacy of assuming monistic "causes" and to focus on the search for significant relationships. The designs of many studies seeking to relate sociological variables to mental illness have not been oriented by systematic or holistic theories of personality development or of psychopathology. Personality reflects the interplay between constitutional and experiential factors, usually in a series of environments. It is not to be characterized in terms of membership in a given social class or residence in a given area, even though these may leave their stamp. Dominant modes of orienting perceptions, responding to social stimuli, and initiating action tend to be organized in infancy. Although they are subject to change thereafter, they usually have a high degree of continuity. Certain relationships and experiences in infancy may indeed be so frequently linked to subsequent development of pathology as to be designated etiological factors for such pathology. Even here, however, it is clear that such factors are only a part of etiology. When we come to later experiences—to the forging of identity and to confrontations of adult responsibility—certain typical stresses may serve to expose vulnerabilities and to precipitate mental illness, but it is far more difficult to isolate variables to which, by themselves, etiological significance can be ascribed.

The task, then, is to seek clues to the etiology of disease all along the life process—in social patternings or sequences of experiences that go with particular positions in the social system and that result in impairments, vulnerabilities, and predispositions to break down under certain types of stress. This task is made much more difficult by the fact that the investigator can learn of the early social experience of mental patients only through retrospective reporting, largely by persons for whom the relationships reported on are fraught with feelings of ambivalence and anxiety. To obtain reliable and valid data in these circumstances is exceedingly difficult but by no means impossible.

Relatively small steps are required. For example, one useful step would be to ascertain the effects of major status changes upon recollection and reporting of early experience. Almost certainly, severe mental illness distorts the recollections not only of the patient but of those closest to him. In part, this distortion is due to changes in relationships brought about by the illness; the social framework of memory is itself modified. In part, it may be due to changes in the patient's self-concept and to the re-evaluation by others of past events in the light of subsequent developments. The systematic collection of data on changes in relationships, expectations, and life patterns before, during, and after periods of mental disturbance, as perceived by the patient and by various persons around him, would be a valuable aid to conceptualization. Especially valuable would be the analysis of the histories of persons who had been included in family or personality studies prior to the onset of illness.

The foregoing discussion may seem unduly discouraging; many of us have a zest for tackling major issues and considerable impatience with projects which cannot be conclusively designed before a multitude of limited-aim studies have been made. Fortunately, however, many studies with limited aims with respect to mental health and illness can make solid contributions to basic sociological knowledge.

Let me give a few examples of researches which seek to illuminate linkages between social and psychiatric phenomena and which show some convergence of aims and results. (Many others, equally significant, could be cited; the present selection is based largely on personal interest.) In a study made at Hagerstown, interviews were conducted with former schizophrenic patients and their matched controls to compare their reports of childhood experiences and family relationships.[17] Like several other studies, this one found that schizophrenics were more likely than controls to report that their mothers had been the sources of dominant authority, for them, in the family. Further analysis, which rested upon very small numbers of cases, suggested that the difference between schizophrenics and controls was substantially greater at the higher status levels (indexed by occupation) than at lower status levels. That is, the higher status controls differed more often from the schizophrenic patients with whom they were paired in reporting a weak authority role for the mother. At lower status levels, both schizophrenics and controls tended to report a relatively strong authority role for the mother.

[17] Melvin L. Kohn and John A. Clausen, "Parental Authority Behavior and Schizophrenia," *Amer. J. Orthopsychiat.*, 26 (1956), 297-313.

These data suggest a possible link between schizophrenia and parental authority behavior for the higher status patients but show no significant relationship for lower status patients. Yet the prevailing authority structure among lower status controls is more similar to that among higher status schizophrenics than to that of higher status controls!

Obviously, the authority structure of the parental family is only a very small part of the social framework of personality development. We have reason to believe, from the work of Ruesch[18] and from further fragmentary data of our own, that specification of the affectional ties and identifications of child and parents would greatly affect the meaning of parental-authority relations for boys and girls. But adequate characterization along these dimensions proved much more difficult than did characterization of authority relations, and the small number of cases available for analysis made it impossible to draw any conclusions.

A next step, then, is to seek more adequate data on the relationships among social status, authority relations, affection, and identification in the general population. Can we document the ways in which personality development is significantly and systematically affected by social status through the interaction of certain aspects of family structure and functioning? Miller and Swanson, the late Andrew Henry, and others have been demonstrating that we can. The problem falls within the province of social psychology, as do many of the significant research problems in the sociology of mental health.

The research of King and Henry,[19] as part of the larger program directed by Funkenstein at Harvard, goes a step beyond the Hagerstown findings. This research deals primarily with the responses of normal persons to experimentally induced stress. The stress situation entailed acute frustration with little opportunity to cope in any way that would alleviate tension. Typical responses were anger expressed toward the experimenters, anger turned inward, anxiety, and no emotional expression. King and Henry found that the subjects who reported the father

[18] See Jurgen Ruesch *et al.*, *Duodenal Ulcer*, University of California Press, 1948.

[19] Stanley H. King and Andrew F. Henry, "Aggression and Cardiovascular Reactions Related to Parental Control over Behavior," *J. abnorm. soc. Psychol.*, 50 (1955), 206-10.

as the principal disciplinarian and also as stern in discipline tended to respond to stress with anger directed outward and with a cardiovascular reaction similar to that produced by an injection of nor-epinephrine. Those whose mothers were reported as the dominant disciplinarian and whose fathers were mild in discipline tended more often to respond to stress with anger directed inward or with anxiety and with epinephrine-like cardiovascular reactions.

The subjects of this research were all Harvard students—a rather homogeneous group by most sociological criteria. Yet even within this lofty stratum, there were differences in typical psychological and physiological response associated with social status, as indexed by whether or not the subject was at least a fifth-generation American.[20] Here, then, is further evidence that the responses of the organism are linked with very pervasive aspects of social structure. Working toward specification of the linkage can make more sophisticated etiological hypotheses available for testing.

A number of theoretical formulations are emerging which give promise of clarifying linkages. Bateson and his associates have formulated a theory of schizophrenia based upon distortions in communication.[21] The nub of this theory is the "double-bind," which occurs when an individual involved in an intense relationship receives two orders of "messages," one contradicting the other, and is unable to clarify the basis of the discrepancy. The double-bind situation seems often to be imposed by mothers who cannot tolerate an intimate relationship with their child but who cannot accept their own feelings in this regard. It seems to be especially devastating in instances in which a strong father figure, who might help the child to discriminate messages, is lacking.

Wynne has independently developed a somewhat similar theory.[22] He has observed the extent to which the families of schizophrenics attempt to maintain an illusion of complementarity that does not in fact exist, denying differences and directing joint efforts toward achieving what Wynne calls "pseudo-mutuality."

[20] Daniel H. Funkenstein, Stanley H. King, and Margaret Drolette, *Mastery of Stress*, Harvard University Press, 1957, pp. 149-50.

[21] Gregory Bateson *et al.*, "Towards a Theory of Schizophrenia," *Behavioral Science*, 1 (1956), 251-64.

[22] Lyman Wynne *et al.*, "Pseudo-mutuality in the Family Relations of Schizophrenics," *Psychiatry*, 21 (1958), 205-20.

These theories have been derived from studies of schizophrenics and their families after they have accommodated themselves, in one way or another, to the fact of illness. The processes observed in the families of schizophrenics under treatment may be resultants of the families' experiences with the illness rather than factors of etiological significance. In some instances, indeed, it appears that the conditions under which the families are studied may themselves accentuate the relational tendencies to which attention is being called. The test of these theories requires work with normal families from a variety of backgrounds, in a variety of observational settings. Does the double-bind situation occur more often in working-class families or in middle-class families? Is it more common in families which have a high expectancy of schizophrenia on genetic grounds than in families free of schizophrenia for several generations? The answers to these questions and others relating to linkages between the social and the psychological sphere will not immediately illuminate the etiology of schizophrenia; yet, in my opinion, a great deal of very basic work has to be done on such questions before any major break-through on the behavioral-science aspect of schizophrenia can be achieved. Much of this work has to be interdisciplinary. Moreover, the sociologist who participates in it cannot be simply a technician or a graduate student in pursuit of a Ph.D. More adequate theory building will require the most acute observation and analysis of the social dimensions and their interactions.

Social Response to Mental Illness

The second general problem area that I wish to touch upon is an aspect of this question: How do sociocultural modes of defining and dealing with the forms of individual psychic disturbance (those forms of deviant behavior that psychiatrists call mental illness) influence the course and consequences of the deviance? The mental-health movement has directed much effort toward changing attitudes toward mental illness, especially stressing the fact that the deviant behaviors of the mentally disturbed *are* reflections of illness. These efforts seem to have been only superficially effective, according to the findings of recent research on public attitudes and knowledge. It seems fair to say that in many instances they have been based only superficially on real knowledge of the prevailing cultural orientations and the functions they serve. One major study, directed by Shirley Star for NORC, has brought home very forcefully the fact that to most American adults, mental illness means violent, unpredictable behavior, to be dealt with by confinement in a mental hospital.[23]

Elaine and John Cumming, in a study of community response to an intensive mental-health education program, have analyzed the functional significance of public attitudes toward mental illness. They characterize the social response to mental illness as

> . . . first, denial of mental illness; second, isolation of the affected person in a hospital where mental illness can no longer be denied, with concomitant rationalization of this isolation with beliefs that the hospital is a wonderful place, capable of curing mental illness, if it can be cured at all, which is doubtful; and finally, insulation of the whole vexing problem by a secondary denial that a problem exists insofar as it needs solving by ordinary citizens.[24]

Evidence of the pattern of isolation and denial comes from many sources. Of all the voluntary organizations dealing with major health problems, the mental-health associations seem to have the greatest difficulty in raising funds. The discrepancy between the demeanor of most patients in mental hospitals and the popular stereotype is highlighted when one talks to the families of mental patients. When a close relative is hospitalized, many members of the family come to see, for the first time, that most patients, especially in admission services, are not the raving maniacs they had expected. Yet for all but the closest relatives of patients, a visit to the hospital is somehow too painful to manage.

Studies of the ways in which families tend to interpret the early phases of illness—normalizing, denying, or ascribing the problem to situational factors, physical health, or character weakness—support the Cummings' thesis.[25] Even after their husbands have been hospitalized, many wives cannot accept the diagnosis of mental illness. Upon the husbands' return home, residual manifestations of their psychic disturbances are often again seen as meanness, weakness, or laziness. This

[23] Shirley Star, "The Place of Psychiatry in Popular Thinking," paper presented at the meeting of the American Association for Public Opinion Research, Washington, D. C., May 1957.

[24] Elaine Cumming and John Cumming, *Closed Ranks: An Experiment in Mental Health Education,* Harvard University Press, 1957, pp. 122-23.

[25] See, for example, Marian R. Yarrow *et al.*, "The Psychological Meaning of Mental Illness in the Family," *J. soc. Issues, 11*:4 (1955), 12-25.

situation may be deplored by those who wish to accord to the patient the full privileges of the "sick role," but it sometimes facilitates the resumption of normal functioning.

On this point, military experience in dealing with psychotic breakdown in World War II and in the Korean War is instructive. During the North African and Sicilian campaigns, psychiatric casualties were evacuated to a neuropsychiatric hospital at Bizerte. Glass reports:

> Although patients were received at this hospital within 24 to 48 hours after their breakdown, a disappointing number, approximately 15 percent, were salvaged for combat duty. . . . Any therapy, including usual interview methods that sought to uncover basic emotional conflicts or attempted to relate current behavior and symptoms with past personality patterns, seemingly provided patients with logical reasons for their combat failure. The insights obtained by even such mild depth therapy readily convinced the patient and often his therapist that the limit of combat endurance had been reached as proved by vulnerable personality traits.[26]

When patients were subsequently treated in the combat zone, using only superficial techniques such as ventilation, reassurance, persuasion, and suggestion, a much higher rate of returns to combat was achieved. Maintaining ties with their outfits and preserving a conception of themselves as somehow able to cope seem to have given many men the strength to do exactly that. Neurotic reactions are patently responsive to such social definitions, and there is suggestive evidence that psychotic reactions may be subject to a measure of control in similar ways. In any event, the behavioral manifestations and interpersonal consequences of severe mental disorder seem sufficiently different from those of physical illness to ensure that the mentally ill will *not* easily be accorded the sick role. Even psychiatrists and nurses, who *do* subscribe to the view that mental disorder is to be treated as illness, tend in their casual remarks to use "mental illness" as a devaluing term. A good deal of research is needed to learn under what circumstances withholding the label "mental illness" may lead to more effective coping than would combining labeling and therapy.

Recent research on the institution which is the end-point of our chief mode of response to mental illness—the mental hospital—has

---

[26] Albert J. Glass, "Psychotherapy in the Combat Zone," in *Symposium on Stress*, Army Medical Service Graduate School, Washington, D. C., 1953.

been impressive in quantity and in the quality of its contribution to sociological knowledge. Studies of mental hospitals highlight the ways in which informal social organization arises to meet the need for stable expectations and goals when formal structures fail to provide them. The very fact that mental illness is manifested in the disruption of normal relationships and expectations has long intrigued sociologists with the search for residuals of sociability. Recent research suggests that there are more than residuals; even withdrawn and deteriorated patients participate in maintaining certain types of patterned interaction. Indeed, it appears that some of the behaviors ascribed to hospital patients as signs of mental illness might as reasonably be regarded as responses to the hospital itself.

Recent Mental-Hospital Studies

The mental hospital may be characterized as a social establishment designed for the custody and care of persons who have exhibited a degree of mental disturbance which makes it difficult, dangerous, or inconvenient to incorporate them into normal family and community living arrangements. The public mental hospital is a legal repository for such persons, on the one hand, and a medical institution for treatment and care of patients, on the other. Studies of small private mental hospitals, operated for profit or as a part of a university training center, have attested to the prevalence of communication difficulties between patients and staff and among staff members and have emphasized the importance of the social organization of the hospital for the achievement of therapeutic aims.[27] The most recent studies of larger public mental hospitals highlight the great discrepancy between the hospital that is publicly presented as a medical institution and the operating custodial establishment.

The rigid authority structure of the large mental hospital, the great status differentials between categories of personnel, the nontherapeutic attitudes of most attendants, and the discrepancies between formal and informal social structure have been noted by previous investigators.

---

[27] The gist of previous research is summarized in Alfred Stanton and Morris Schwartz, *The Mental Hospital*, Basic Books, 1954, which itself provides one of the major contributions to the field.

Belknap has documented all these for "Southern State Hospital." [28] But he has gone much further in showing how the hospital operates smoothly on minimal resources. Perhaps most impressive is his characterization of "the attendant system." The hospital's formal organization has defined an impossible span of control for the ward physician. His medical-legal responsibilities and the paper work involved leave him almost no time for ward supervision. The resulting gap has been filled by the attendant system, with its set of behavior controls, its ideology, and its informal training systems. For the patients, not only such privileges as freedom of the grounds, but access to the ward physician and consideration for discharge rest upon conformity with the attendant system. The attendants translate insubordination into the "professional" terms "disturbed" or "excited," thereby gaining a medical sanction for the system.

Erving Goffman has noted many of the same tendencies in another large hospital, despite the fact that the medical framework in the hospital he studied is much stronger and the medical culture relatively more dominant.[29] He has focused on the process by which the patient is incorporated into the hospital community and on the characteristics of that community as a "total institution" for the patients. He notes that for the patient the full meaning of being in the hospital does not exist apart from the special meaning of "getting out." Commitment to a large public mental hospital leads to a stripping of customary supports; in Goffman's terms, following admission, the "self is systematically, if often unintentionally, mortified." The authority structure gives any staff member the right to discipline any member of the inmate class. Corrective sanctions are directed toward a multitude of items of conduct which are not subject to regulations on the outside; at the same time, permissive attitudes are taken toward many forms of deviance which would bring sanctions outside. Here again, the privilege system, with its supports, sanctions, and the secondary adjustments to which it gives rise, tends to influence treatment and release. As Goffman notes, for many patients, the chief problem to be dealt with is not their men-

[28] Ivan Belknap, *Human Problems of a State Mental Hospital*, McGraw-Hill, 1956.

[29] Erving Goffman, "On the Characteristics of Total Institutions," in *Symposium on Preventive and Social Psychiatry*, Govt. Printing Office, Washington, 1958.

tal illness; it is how they can survive, psychologically, in the mental hospital.

It is probably fair to say that as yet we have only rather crude hunches concerning the total impact of the hospital on various types of patients. Studies of smaller hospitals which have endeavored to become therapeutic communities rather than custodial institutions suggest that the amount of acute disturbance and of withdrawal can be reduced by paying more attention to the interpersonal needs of patients and attendants.[30] We have only the most rudimentary data on the meaning of the hospital experience for subsequent life in the community.

Several sociologists have been working very closely with psychiatrists in attempting to assess the therapeutic strengths and weaknesses of various types of hospital staff organization. Schwartz has been concerned with staff training for milieu therapy in this country and Rapaport with sociotherapy at the Belmont Hospital in England.[31] Milieu therapy and sociotherapy are concepts forged in the recognition that interpersonal relationships in the hospital ward and the kind of self-concept that is permitted or encouraged by the hospital staff throughout the day can critically influence the course of the patient's illness. This recognition has been achieved by a number of psychiatrists, yet it has inherent in it a source of ultimate tension. If the social organizational or interactional model is the critical model for therapy, where should the power reside in the planning and development of treatment services? This question is not yet pressing for an answer. Much more research is needed to establish whether the premises underlying milieu therapy can be validated in terms of the restoration of patients to effective life in the community. The design and conceptualization of the research, and perhaps the achievement of more effective designs for the treatment setting, require the skills of the social scientist. Whether these skills will best be provided by social scientists sophisticated in the clinical realm or by clinical personnel trained in social science is a matter for time to decide.

When the sociologist becomes concerned not merely with describ-

[30] See, for example, Maxwell Jones, *The Therapeutic Community*, Basic Books, 1953. Also Milton Greenblatt *et al.*, *From Custodial to Therapeutic Patient Care in Mental Hospitals*, Russell Sage Foundation, 1955.

[31] Robert N. Rapaport, "Oscillations and Sociotherapy," *Hum. Relat.*, 9:3 (1956), 357-74.

ing an operating social system but also with participating in the design of interventions to achieve stated objectives, he treads on dangerous ground. This is not, I think, because the study of interventions is any less basic or valuable than the study of existing structures. Experimental designs can be a source of knowledge that cannot be achieved in any other way. The danger lies in the realm of premises and criteria. Broader perspectives than those of the clinician, or at least different perspectives—sociological perspectives—need to be maintained. The demands of community living may not require the ultimate of therapeutic effectiveness as judged by the clinician. A variety of criteria need to be examined relative to the effectiveness of the therapeutic regime.

Lest this discourse take on too much of a sermonizing tone, it may be observed that the social scientist often has the role of helping to make explicit to the clinician what the latter's premises are. What kinds of relationship are to exist between the therapeutic milieu (often extremely permissive in orientation toward deviance) and the larger institution or community within which it is contained? There is the dilemma that while the patient cannot safely be left in the community while he is acutely disturbed, his restoration to the community may be hastened if he has access to it as soon as possible. Risks are involved and sanctions may be invoked not only against the patient but against the treatment service. Considerations of staff organization, the creation or emergence of new role categories for staff, sources of support and of limit setting for patients—these are matters that call for explicit definition within a conceptual framework. These are some of the areas of concern of sociologists working within milieu-therapy programs. Each formulation calls for analysis not only of the static structure but also of the stresses, strains, and modifications that occur over the long course of treatment for disturbed patients.

Postscript

This paper by no means exhausts the subjects that might have been treated under the same title. It might have dealt with issues raised by recent research on social isolation and anomie. It might have attempted to explore the problems and promises of research on cross-cultural aspects of the sociology of mental illness, especially with reference to the cultural patterning of syndromes and to the social roles accorded the mentally ill. The current preoccupation in some circles of American society with "positive mental health" as perhaps the ultimate value would afford a basis for examining a quite different set of problems. There are many limbs on the tree of the sociology of mental health. Indeed, only time can tell whether we have a single tree or an enclave of varied species.

23
Criminological
Research

MARSHALL B. CLINARD
University of Wisconsin

Criminologists are by no means confined to the field of sociology, although the fact that sociologists have written nearly all the textbooks in this area might give this impression. Much research and publication, both here and abroad, is being done by psychiatrists, psychoanalysts, and others with a nonsociological approach.[1] The controversy between the theoretical position of the nonsociologists, which emphasizes personality-trait structures, early family environment, or the physical constitutions of the individual, and that of the sociologists, which emphasizes subcultural norms and an area of group interaction larger than the family, has not been reconciled. Much sociological writing has been devoted to revealing theoretical and methodological errors in psychiatrically and psychoanalytically oriented research. Psychiatrists and psychoanalysts, on the other hand, seldom refer to sociological research, either because they are unfamiliar with it or because they choose to ignore it.

In the sections which follow, we shall evaluate two important general sociological theories, as well as the problem of differential response. We shall then discuss the importance of studying situational factors, some conceptual problems involved in delinquent and criminal typology, and the need for small-group research on delinquent groups. Concluding sections will deal with the relation of the concept of crime

---

[1] Much criminological research in other parts of the world is done by law professors, and criminology is frequently offered in the law schools.

to criminological research, the sociology of corrections, and the administration of criminal justice, and, finally, the need for a comparative criminology.

The Theory of Differential Association

Two of the most widely quoted general theories of criminality advanced by sociologists are differential association and anomie. Sutherland's proposition that criminal behavior is learned and is a product of differential association with criminal and noncriminal norms has been quoted time and again by sociologists, as has his view that differential association varies in terms of priority, frequency, continuity, and intensity.[2] More specifically, his theory involves the following propositions:

1. Criminal behavior is learned.
2. Criminal behavior is learned in interaction with other persons in a process of communication.
3. The principal part of the learning of criminal behavior occurs within intimate personal groups.
4. When criminal behavior is learned, the learning includes (a) techniques of committing the crime, which are sometimes very complicated, sometimes very simple; (b) the specific direction of motives, drives, rationalizations, and attitudes.
5. The specific direction of motives and drives is learned from definitions of the legal codes as favorable or unfavorable.
6. A person becomes delinquent because of an excess of definitions favorable to violation of law over definitions unfavorable to violation of law.
7. Differential associations may vary in frequency, duration, priority, and intensity.
8. The process of learning criminal behavior by association with criminal and anti-criminal patterns involves all of the mechanisms that are involved in any other learning.
9. While criminal behavior is an expression of general needs and values, it is not explained by those general needs and values since noncriminal behavior is an expression of the same needs and values.[3]

[2] Edwin H. Sutherland, *Principles of Criminology*, 3rd and 4th ed., Lippincott, 1939 and 1947. The fifth edition, published in 1955, was revised by Donald R. Cressey after Sutherland's death.

[3] Selected quotations from Edwin H. Sutherland and Donald R. Cressey, *Principles of Criminology*, 5th ed., Lippincott, 1955, pp. 77-79.

What Sutherland continually referred to as a general theory which needed testing has unfortunately become, to many sociologists, an established fact. Testing the theory is difficult methodologically. As Sheldon Glueck has recently indicated, no one has actually counted in a study of offenders those definitions of situations which were favorable to law and those which were unfavorable to law and shown that the former have been greater in most cases of delinquency and crime.[4] Glueck has also pointed out the inconsistency of suggesting that the explanation of criminality is a matter of a numerical excess of criminal norms and, at the same time, of the duration, priority, and intensity of association with such norms.

Although there is much in the general frame of reference of differential association that is sociologically sound, it is extremely doubtful that such a broad theory can explain all criminal offenders. In fact, Sutherland himself made this unlikely when, in the fourth revision of his text, he dropped the logical qualification "systematic criminal careers" from his propositions, leaving the implicit assumption that they applied to all criminal offenders. Thus, although a theory of differential association may explain the behavior of the professional, organized, ordinary criminal and certain types of delinquent, it is probably inadequate as an explanation of the occasional, adventitious, and non-career types of offender. Using a group of institutionalized delinquent boys and girls, Short[5] found a relation between several measures of differential association and male delinquency, although he did not find much relation between these measures and female delinquency. Unfortunately, he did not use a control group. Studies by Cressey, Lemert, and Clinard,[6] among others have indicated that the theory by itself is

[4] Sheldon Glueck, "Theory and Fact in Criminology," *Brit. J. Delinqu.*, 7 (1956).

[5] James F. Short, Jr., "Differential Association and Delinquency," *Soc. Problems*, 4 (1957), 233-39. This article contains a brief questionnaire for testing the theory of differential association. Ball found that delinquent boys feel that there is a greater prevalence of stealing than nondelinquent boys and he has explained this as related to differential association. John C. Ball, "Delinquent and Non-Delinquent Attitudes Toward the Prevalence of Stealing," *J. crim. Law Criminol. Pol. Sci.*, 48 (1957), 259-75.

[6] Donald R. Cressey, "Application and Verification of the Differential Association Theory," *J. crim. Law Criminol.*, 43 (1952), 43-52; Edwin M. Lemert, "An Isolation and Closure Theory of Naive Check Forgery," *J. crim.*

inadequate in explaining certain types of noncareer property offenders. If more extensive studies were made of murder and other personal offenses, and such offenses as nonprofessional shoplifting, these limitations might be found even greater.

Certainly Sutherland's propositions need refinement. Cressey [7] has suggested, for example, that, since it is impossible to observe all prior associations, the differential-association theory needs to be reduced to a learning theory rather than a mathematical ratio of criminal and noncriminal associations. Caldwell [8] feels that the theory is an oversimplification of the process of learning. Weinberg [9] has criticized the fact that the learning theory is based upon a rational psychology in which alternatives of behavior are regarded in terms of quantity and rational deliberation. He also feels that the theory of personality is deficient in that:

> . . . the dynamisms as to why [an individual] selected or did not select a singular organization of attitudes and meanings were not explained adequately, and, in some instances, were not considered necessary for explanation. Hence singular motives, meanings, and aspirations of the criminal were muted in these descriptions in order to emphasize the shared behavior of the criminal as a cultural participant.[10]

The recent publication of *The Sutherland Papers* [11] has made available several previously unpublished articles in which Sutherland not only traces in detail the development of the differential-association theory but, like the true scientist he was, shows that he himself raised several severe criticisms of his own theory. Among them were the possibility that not all criminal behavior is learned; some crimes, he suggested, might be invented by the individual, some may be "partially a function of opportunities to commit specific classes of crime such as embezzlement, bank robbery or illicit heterosexual intercourse," some may be related to the intensity of need in certain situations, and, finally,

---

Law Criminol. Pol. Sci., 44 (1953), 296-307; and Marshall B. Clinard, *The Black Market: A Study of White Collar Crime*, Rinehart, 1952.

[7] Cressey, *loc. cit.*, 51-52.

[8] Robert G. Caldwell, *Criminology*, Ronald Press, 1956, p. 183.

[9] S. Kirson Weinberg, "Theories of Criminality and Problems of Prediction," *J. crim. Law Criminol. Pol. Sci.*, 45 (1954), 413.

[10] *Ibid.*

[11] Albert Cohen, Alfred Lindesmith, and Karl Schuessler, *The Sutherland Papers*, Indiana University Press, 1956, pp. 30-41.

some may arise from a process of alternative choices in a situation, one of which was a crime. Although Sutherland argued against each of these possibilities, his arguments do not always appear to be convincing and certainly need research.

Recently Glaser has suggested the concept of differential identification as a modification of Sutherland's theory.[12] This will be discussed in a later section on the problem of differential response. The importance of rationalizations has been stressed by Sykes and Matza [13] as a crucial component of Sutherland's "definitions favorable to the violation of law." Techniques of neutralization, as they have termed them, involve rationalizations through which a juvenile may come to regard certain illegal actions as not delinquent. According to them, "Much delinquency is based on what is essentially an unrecognized extension of defenses to crimes, in the form of justifications for deviance that are seen as valid by the delinquent but not by the legal system or society at large." [14] The juvenile becomes delinquent through learning these techniques of neutralization rather than primarily through learning the norms and values of a subculture opposed to the larger society. Among these rationalizations are the denial of responsibility, the denial of injury, the denial of the victim, the condemnation of the condemners, and the appeal to higher loyalties.

Anomie, Class Structure, and Delinquent Behavior

Several years ago, Merton suggested that a condition of anomie accounted for various forms of deviant behavior in a society.[15] Recently he has developed this idea more specifically in relation to juvenile delinquency.[16] Broadly stated, his idea is that crime and delinquency grow

[12] Daniel Glaser, "Criminality Theories and Behavioral Images," *Amer. J. Sociol.*, 61 (1956), 433-45.

[13] Gresham M. Sykes and David Matza, "Techniques of Neutralization: A Theory of Delinquency," *Amer. sociol. Rev.*, 22 (1957), 664-70.

[14] *Ibid.*, p. 666.

[15] Robert K. Merton, *Social Theory and Social Structure*, Free Press, 1949, rev. ed., 1957, pp. 131-94.

[16] Helen L. Witmer and Ruth Kotinsky (eds.), *New Perspectives for Research on Juvenile Delinquency*, U. S. Department of Health, Welfare, and Education, 1955. This is a transcription of a conference on juvenile delinquency in which Merton was a participant.

out of a contradiction between the culture and the social structure and between ends in the form of cultural values and the means which the social structure provides for achieving them. In American culture, for example, the ends are symbols of status based on the possession and display of economic goods. But such goods are not available to everyone. This contradiction results in a breakdown of the pattern of complying with legal and social norms in order to obtain the objectives.

Although the theoretical statement of anomie has been widely quoted, until it is related more precisely to empirical evidence it will probably have little research value. Theoretically it sounds like a plausible and sociologically sophisticated explanation for certain types of adult stealing, particularly professional stealing, but as an explanation of all delinquent and criminal behavior it has several limitations. It can hardly explain crime in societies in which highly "esteemed goals" are not thought of as available to everyone—*i.e.,* in which ascribed rather than achieved goals predominate. On the other hand, anomie does not explain why in our society, where status generally is achieved and where most lower-class males desire material possessions, the majority do not go beyond such institutionalized means as work to obtain them. Finally, as Cohen has indicated,[17] it does not explain the nonutilitarian and even destructive nature of much delinquency and some crime.

Cohen has recently stated a theory of gang delinquency which has a general approach similar to Merton's anomie but considerably more specific.[18] He has suggested that the emergence of subcultures, such as delinquent gangs, is the product of the "existence, in effective interaction with one another, of a number of actors with similar problems of adjustment." [19] Delinquent gangs, he suggests, arise as a consequence of the class structure of American society. Delinquent-gang behavior is a product of group solutions to the status problems, needs, and frustrations of the American lower-class system in a world of predominantly middle-class values and virtues.

This is a provocative theory, and evidence is marshalled from vari-

[17] Albert K. Cohen, *Delinquent Boys: The Culture of the Gang,* Free Press, 1955, p. 36.

[18] His theory is limited to delinquency committed by gangs and is not a theory of delinquency in general.

[19] Cohen, *op. cit.,* p. 59.

ous other sources to support it. Yet, although Hollingshead [20] and others have certainly indicated that the norms of adolescents vary greatly by social class, the specific hypothesis that delinquent cultures arise out of a form of class conflict has as yet not been actually tested by Cohen or anyone else. Testing such a hypothesis would be extremely difficult since it involves class motivations which are implied but not necessarily explicit in the lives of delinquent boys. More than likely, it will be found too comprehensive an explanation. Lower-class delinquent gangs, rather than functioning always as a protest against middle-class values, probably function also to satisfy more simple needs, such as adventure, excitement, protection against other gangs, racial, ethnic, and religious identification, and dislike for the police. If delinquency serves as a "protest" against anything, it is probably against the older peer group of adults. The norms of teenagers and adults often clash in an urban world. The world of adults, including those of the working class, largely restricts the adolescent's full participation in society, through compulsory schooling, work restrictions, and restrictions on membership in adult groups or in such activities as going to taverns or voting. The types of conventional recreation provided for teenagers by adults is often not sufficiently exciting. Cohen's theory, moreover, seems an inadequate explanation for delinquency or delinquent gangs in societies where status tends to be ascribed and where there is less "class conflict."

Despite these criticisms, the general theory of anomie and the more specific statement of Cohen need widespread application and testing. Both represent significant attempts to apply basic sociological theory to delinquent and criminal behavior.

The Problem of Differential Response

The question of why some persons who are exposed to illegal norms are affected by them while others are not is the most crucial issue in criminology. In the past, the explanation would probably have been heredity, subnormal intelligence, or poverty. Today differential response is explained on the grounds that the criminal is a mesomorph,

---

[20] See, for example, August B. Hollingshead, *Elmtown's Youth*, John Wiley, 1949.

is insecure emotionally, or has some other trait difficulty. Psychoanalysts have offered a framework of guilt complexes and an unrepressed Id to explain why some become criminal.

Most sociologists have disagreed with these contentions and have been successful in disproving many of them. On the other hand, the sociologists themselves can offer little concrete explanation for the fact that some persons who are exposed to delinquent and criminal norms become deviant while others do not. Consequently, as Reckless [21] has aptly stated, we probably know far more today about what does not cause crime than about what causes it. An examination of any criminology text would support this statement.

Certain social-psychological concepts may turn out to be useful in answering this question, at least for the group type of property offender. They include, particularly, self-conception and differential identification. A recent sociological study [22] has suggested differences in self-conception as the reason that certain children residing in a delinquency area do not become delinquents. After a study of 125 "good boys" and 108 potential delinquents in this area, the authors concluded, "Conception of self and others is the differential response component that helps to explain why some succumb and others do not, why some gravitate toward socially unacceptable patterns of behavior and others veer away from them." [23] Additional research in this direction may furnish valuable insights into why so many middle- and upperclass boys do not engage in delinquency and may help to explain the differential response patterns of adults, including white-collar workers, to criminal norms.

Differential identification as a research tool means, according to Glaser, that "a person pursues criminal behavior to the extent that he

[21] Walter Reckless, *The Crime Problem*, Appleton-Century-Crofts, 1950, p. 19.

[22] Walter C. Reckless, Simon Dinitz, and Ellen Murray, "Self-Concept as an Insulator against Delinquency," *Amer. sociol. Rev.*, 21 (1956), 744-46; Walter C. Reckless, Simon Dinitz, and Ellen Murray, "The 'Good Boy' in a High Delinquency Area," *J. crim. Law Criminol. pol. Sci.*, 48 (1957), 18-25; and Walter C. Reckless, Simon Dinitz, and Barbara Kay, "Self-Component in Potential Delinquency and Non-Delinquency," *Amer. sociol. Rev.*, 22 (1957), 566-70.

[23] Reckless, Dinitz, and Kay, *loc. cit.*, 570.

identifies himself with real or imaginary persons from whose perspective his criminal behavior seems acceptable." [24] As a theory, it emphasizes social interaction in which there is a choice of models and also interaction on the part of the individual with himself in rationalizing his behavior.

> This focus makes differential identification theory integrative, in that it provides a criterion of the relevance, for each individual case of criminality, of economic conditions, prior frustrations, learned moral creeds, group participation, or other features of an individual's life. These features are relevant to the extent that they can be shown to affect the choice of the other from whose perspective the individual views his own behavior. The explanation of criminal behavior on the basis of its imperfect correlation with any single variable of life-situations, if presented without specifying the intervening identification, evokes only a disconnected image of the relationship between the life-situation and the criminal behavior.[25]

Another possibility is that in some types of delinquency and crime certain personality traits may play a significant role, not independently, but as part of a total behavioral configuration. It is generally agreed that personality consists not only of attitudes and roles but of personality-trait structures, or what Sapir termed general reaction patterns. Consequently, the relation of traits to criminal behavior cannot be summarily dismissed. Even Sutherland stated that the relation of personality trait structures to criminal behavior had not been solved and that it was the "most important and crucial question in criminological theory." [26]

[24] Glaser, *op. cit.* Also see Nelson N. Foote, "Identification as the Basis for a Theory of Motivation," *Amer. sociol. Rev.,* 16 (1951), 14-21.

[25] Glaser, *op. cit.,* p. 440.

[26] Cohen, Lindesmith, and Schuessler, *op. cit.,* p. 25. In fact, to ascertain more clearly the relation of personality traits and cultural patterns, Sutherland suggested a lengthy list of intriguing research projects, including a study of the personality traits of members of the criminal caste of India, of persons committing kleptomania or pyromania, of "black sheep" in middle-class families, and of persons committing crimes under the influence of alcohol. As yet most of these studies have not been made. See Edwin H. Sutherland, "The Relation Between Personal Traits and Associational Patterns," in Walter C. Reckless, *The Etiology of Delinquent and Criminal Behavior,* Social Science Research Council, Bulletin No. 50 (1943), 131-37.

Any sociologist examining the case records of criminal psychiatrists will find cases, particularly those involving personal offenses, in which the unusual and often bizarre personality traits of the individual appear to have been important factors in his criminal or delinquent behavior. The existence of such cases, no matter how small in number they may be, means that the personality makeup of the individual cannot be discounted completely.

Unfortunately, some sociologists have assumed that the negative findings reported by Schuessler and Cressey [27] have virtually terminated the discussion. These investigators examined all the studies of the personality traits of offenders and nonoffenders that had been made up to 1950, a total of 113. According to their criteria, 42 percent showed comparisons in favor of the noncriminals and the rest were indeterminate. Their conclusion was a cautious one: "The doubtful validity of many of the obtained differences as well as the lack of consistency in the combined results make it impossible to conclude from these data that criminality and personality traits are associated."

Several criticisms of this finding can be made. First, the studies on which the conclusions are based used thirty different personality tests, some of them long since out of date. Secondly, few of the studies made up to the time of this analysis employed the relatively sophisticated MMPI test, which is now widely used. Some of the more recent work by Hathaway and Monachesi,[28] among others, appear to have differentiated in part between some groups of delinquents and non-delinquents, and it is possible that these findings will be supported in the future by even more sophisticated personality tests. At least more attempts to test the relationship need to be made. Thirdly, although the studies evaluated by Schuessler and Cressey viewed personality traits as separate entities, the traits may be more closely related to some syndromes of behavior or types of criminal behavior than to others. Reiss,[29] for example, has presented evidence that certain types of de-

[27] Karl F. Schuessler and Donald R. Cressey, "Personality Characteristics of Criminals," *Amer. J. Sociol.,* 55 (1950), 476-84.

[28] See, for example, Starke R. Hathaway and Elio Monachesi, *Analyzing and Predicting Juvenile Delinquency with the MMPI,* University of Minnesota Press, 1953; and Hathaway and Monachesi, "The Personalities of Pre-delinquent Boys," *J. crim. Law criminol. pol. Sci.,* 48 (1957), 259-74.

[29] Albert J. Reiss, "Social Correlates of Psychological Types of Delinquency," *Amer. sociol. Rev.,* 17 (1952), 710-18.

linquent personalities are associated with certain social correlates or factors. Hewitt and Jenkins [30] have isolated certain types of psychological characteristics of delinquents and have shown how these syndromes may be related to the nature of the delinquents' antisocial behavior.

Situational Factors in Delinquency and Crime

As W. I. Thomas [31] indicated years ago, every individual has to assess or define a situation in terms of his values and motives and those of others. Often in choosing between alternatives, he must exclude certain actions. In a given situation, the role behavior he selects may be legally appropriate; on the other hand, it may turn out to be illegal. In this choice, the individual must consider both the total life situation and the interaction with the ongoing immediate situation, which he has to define selectively.[32]

Contemporary criminological theory needs to give more consideration to the *situation* in which delinquent or criminal acts arise.[33] In too many studies, almost the entire theoretical emphasis is on the personality traits or attitudes of the offender. Even with a knowledge of the genesis of such personality components, one must still study the immediate situation out of which the delinquency and crime arose. The act as well as the actor must be considered.[34]

Such an emphasis would take us far beyond a static examination of the personality traits and attitudes of the offender into an area of situational analysis. Analyses of the situations out of which crimes

[30] L. E. Hewitt and R. L. Jenkins, *Fundamental Patterns of Maladjustment: The Dynamics of the Origin*, State of Illinois, 1946.

[31] William I. Thomas and Florian Znaniecki, *The Polish Peasant in Europe and America*, Knopf, 1927, pp. 1847-49; and William I. Thomas, *The Unadjusted Girl*, Little, Brown, 1957, p. 42.

[32] See Lowell J. Carr, *Situational Analysis*, Harper, 1948, pp. 12-13. As MacIver has put it, the situation that a person "assesses is one that he has selectively defined, in terms of his experience, his habit of response, his intellectual grasp and his emotional engrossment in it." Robert MacIver, *Social Causation*, Ginn, 1942, p. 296.

[33] Psychiatrists have generally shown more interest than sociologists in considering crucial situational factors in delinquency and crime.

[34] See George H. Mead, *The Philosophy of the Act*, University of Chicago Press, 1938.

or delinquent acts arise might shed light on the problem of why knowledge of a given person's traits and attitudes does not always enable us to predict whether he will or will not perform a delinquent or criminal act in a given situation.[35] In discussing this issue, Reckless has stated:

> Somewhere in the concatenation of weaknesses and strengths of the individual (the internal components), the impact of the confronting situation, and the inability or ability of the surrounding social order to absorb this impact for the individual lies the riddle of crime and delinquency causation. The S [situation] needs an I [individual], and I needs an S. Those who overemphasize the one to the exclusion of the other are probably myopic. As a matter of fact, we do not know what the I really is without the S, and we do not know what the S is without the I.[36]

Both the theory and the research of criminology must be more concerned with those immediate situations which may incite certain individuals to delinquency and crime. Certainly, many potentially delinquent or criminal persons do not engage in delinquent or criminal acts simply because a delinquency- or crime-producing situation never arises. The importance of the situation in criminological research has been indicated by Cressey [37] in his work on trust violators, who, he found, have a nonsharable financial problem and an opportunity to violate their trust. In his theory of "closure," Lemert [38] has suggested that "naive" check forgery (*i.e.*, by persons who are unsophisticated in crime) arises from a number of situational factors in which there is isolation from others and in which behavior alternatives other than forgery are restricted.

Studies of juvenile vandalism by Clinard and Wade [39] have

[35] In selecting personnel for intelligence work during World War II, one of the difficulties was the later development of certain situations to which the individual's response could not be predicted on the basis of prior knowledge of personality. The OSS Assessment Staff, *Assessment of Men*, Rinehart, 1948.

[36] Reckless, *The Crime Problem*, p. 80.

[37] Donald R. Cressey, *Other People's Money*, Free Press, 1953.

[38] Lemert, *loc. cit.*

[39] Marshall B. Clinard and Andrew L. Wade, "Toward the Delineation of Vandalism as a Sub-Type in Juvenile Delinquency," *J. crim. Law Criminol. pol. Sci.*, 48 (1958), 493-99.

shown the importance of situation-induced events in producing malicious destruction of property. Likewise, von Hentig, in his significant volume *The Criminal and His Victim*,[40] has shown in many ways how even the behavior of the victim may explain a criminal act. This is certainly true in many sex cases, confidence games, and even murder and assault cases. Wolfgang's recent study of criminal homicide [41] found that one fourth of the cases were actually precipitated by the victims. The victim of a sex offense may have offered provocative inducements, and the victim of the confidence game may himself have been attempting larceny. The sexually aroused male may become violent and commit a sex offense; an argument between two persons may get out of hand and result in violence. As von Hentig has put it:

> Most crimes leave us with an unknown lawbreaker and a known victim. . . . Through this type of knowledge [of victim and situation] we would learn a lot, too, in the realm of prevention; recognizing potential victims, potential injurious situations and such material as would tend to complement the dangerous perpetrator-victim relationship.[42]

Similarly, the Danish criminologist Hurwitz has recently devoted considerable discussion to criminality-producing situations, which he regards as an important part of the criminal act.[43] He distinguishes between inner and outer situations, dynamic and static situation factors, chosen and unchosen situations, and what he terms "dangerous situations."

Delinquent and Criminal Typology

Increased interest is being shown in the classification of the behavioral aspects of delinquent and criminal offenders. This approach

[40] Hans von Hentig, *The Criminal and His Victim,* Yale University Press, 1948.

[41] Marvin E. Wolfgang, "Victim-Precipitated Criminal Homicide," *J. crim. Law Criminol. pol. Sci.,* 48 (1957), 1-11.

[42] Hentig, *op. cit.,* p. 387.

[43] Stephan Hurwitz, *Criminology* (trans. Elsie Giering), London: George Allen & Unwin, 1952, pp. 359-68. Such research has been done on situations producing, for example, the onset of manic-depressive psychoses. Thomas Rennie, "Prognosis in Manic-Depressive Psychoses," *Amer. J. Psychiat.,* 98 (1942), 801-14.

was emphasized by early criminologists, particularly Enrico Ferri. Analyzing types of offenders means studying behavior systems in crime and the way in which they arise.

The distinguishing features of a criminal behavior system include the social roles the offender plays, the degree of his identification with crime, his conception of himself as a criminal, his patterns of association with others who are criminals or noncriminals, his continuation and progression in crime, the way in which he commits offenses, the relation of his behavior to his personality traits, and the degree to which criminal behavior has become part of his total life organization.[44] Criminal behavior in such an approach is considered a product of social interaction in which the behavior of an individual has meaning only in relation to that of other persons. Moreover, behavioral systems enable us to view the criminal act as an ongoing process rather than a static entity. The relation of human nature to a criminal act is preserved.

The interest in criminal behavior systems represents in part an attempt to avoid legal categories and give a more sociological interpretation to criminal behavior. In this connection, Bianchi, a Dutch criminologist, has recently pointed out that the wide use today of the term "criminal behavior" rather than "criminal" has important implications.[45] The former term, he feels, enables criminologists to consider crime as a problem of human behavior and to avoid a strictly legal conception of crime and normative judgments about the act.

The sociological analysis of criminal behavior systems differs sharply from the typological classifications of most psychiatrists and clinical psychologists. The latter largely utilize broad psychiatric syndromes of personality traits, often with a single personality-trait syndrome applying to a variety of criminal careers differing in both the nature and the seriousness of the criminal activity. Consequently, personality-trait syndromes by themselves may have little meaning for distinguishing either types of criminal careers or the behavior of criminals from noncriminals.

The study of behavior systems in crime differs also from the sta-

---

[44] Marshall B. Clinard, *Sociology of Deviant Behavior*, Rinehart, 1957, pp. 200-21.

[45] H. Bianchi, *Position and Subject-Matter of Criminology*, Amsterdam: North-Holland Publishing Co., 1956, p. 164.

tistical manipulation of a group of factors in the hope that a theory will develop from the accumulations of a large number of facts. Although the latter approach has characterized much of the Gluecks' research [46]—they are even proud of their eclecticism—there is little evidence that such random experimentation has produced much result in the physical sciences. The past has shown the unprofitable nature of such a shotgun approach to research on human behavior.

Various general types of criminal patterns are being worked out, and this represents a profitable area for future criminological research. Such general types can be distinguished as individual and career criminals. More specific behavior systems are the criminally insane, occasional, habitual petty, white collar, ordinary, organized, and professional. Subtypes include trust violators and "naive" check forgers. This research is being reflected increasingly in the typological organization of criminology texts. As Bloch has written:

> This type of research insight, in its recognition of the integral unity of behavior patterns, whether they be law-abiding or law-breaking, suggests the importance of discovering *types of operations and types of criminal operators*. Thus, we are slowly moving into an area where we may tentatively begin to develop a "typology" of delinquency and crime, i.e., a classification of integrated behavior-forms which characterize certain types of criminally-prone individuals, as well as recognizable environmental configurations which produce and are related to such personalities. [47]

According to Cressey, [48] as we have mentioned, the behavior of trust violators, such as embezzlers, is characterized by (1) the presence of a financial problem which they consider non-sharable; (2) the opportunity to violate a trusted position and the knowledge of how to violate it; and (3) the acceptance of verbalizations or rationalizations which enable them to reconcile their conception of themselves as a trusted person with their misuse of entrusted funds or property.

[46] Glueck, *op. cit.*, p. 108. Also see Sheldon Glueck and Eleanor Glueck, *Unraveling Juvenile Delinquency*, Harvard University Press, 1950, and *Physique and Delinquency*, Harper, 1956.

[47] Herbert A. Bloch, "Crime Causation: Research and Its Application," *Federal Probation*, 21 (1957), 19.

[48] Cressey, *Other People's Money.*

Lemert's theory of "naive" check forgery as a behavior system [49] recognizes the existence of certain qualities in the individual as well as in the situation out of which the offense develops. He feels that forgery cannot be explained in terms of emotional conflict or differential association. Rather, he suggests that the forger is either a person with normal characteristics, except for a certain degree of isolation from others, or a person isolated from others owing to a certain situation. Such a person is confronted with a crisis in which money is needed quickly as a solution to a problem. He may actually be in need of money or he may define the situation in these terms. Finally, in forgery a process of closure takes place in which the person excludes alternatives other than writing a bad check. Social-psychologically, this represents suspension of the normal self and role-taking under the stress of the crisis and the situation of social isolation. In some cases, aggression also enters into the process.

Much more research must be done in working out behavior systems in other areas, particularly murder, assault, and sex offenses, in which most of the research has been done by psychiatrists and psychologists.[50] Within recent years, sociologists have written a few books and a number of articles in this area. Weinberg, for example, has recently published a book on incest behavior.[51] Homosexuality is an offense which needs particular study by sociologists because of implied subcultural factors. One sociologist has severely criticized the loose use of the concept of compulsive crimes by psychiatrists and psychoanalysts and has suggested an alternative explanation.[52] Sociologists have been associated with major surveys of sex offenders in New Jersey and Michigan.[53] There is considerable evidence that the nature of sex behavior

[49] Lemert, *loc. cit.* He is now working on a book on forgery and some of the material cited is from a personal communication.

[50] See, for example, Albert Ellis and Ralph Brancale, *The Psychology of Sex Offenders,* Charles C. Thomas, 1956. It is hoped that there will also be some day a book with the title of "Sociology of Sex Offenders."

[51] S. Kirson Weinberg, *Incest Behavior,* Citadel Press, 1955. Also see the discussion of sex offenders in John L. Gillin, *The Wisconsin Prisoner,* University of Wisconsin Press, 1946.

[52] Donald R. Cressey, "The Differential Association Theory and Compulsive Crime," *J. crim. Law Criminol. pol. Sci., 44* (1954), 29-41.

[53] *The Habitual Sex Offender,* Report and Recommendations of the Commission on the Habitual Sex Offender as formulated by Paul W. Tappan,

(producing)

varies greatly by social class. Commenting on sexual offenses in Michigan, the report stated that when some lower-class rural families move from the South into more urban, middle-class areas in the North, certain types of sexual behavior which previously were tolerated or approved become sex offenses.

A number of years ago, Brearly [54] pointed out the extreme differences in the homicide rates of various regions of the United States, indicating the presence of subcultural definitions in the use of violence. Bullock's more recent study [55] is an example of the need for additional research in this area in order to discover the social correlates of homicide. In this study, he found that 87 percent of all murders in Houston occur in four areas near the center of the city, populated chiefly by Negroes and Spanish Americans. In 87 percent of the cases, the victim and the murderer had known each other. The violence of disputes in this area was a reflection of the norms of interpersonal relations of that area. As Sutherland once so aptly put it, when truck drivers get intoxicated, they fight; college professors in a similar situation talk more than usual.

A typological approach to delinquency would also enable investigators to concentrate upon problems of limited scope and to deal with manageable groups characterized by relatively homogeneous behavior.[56] Some of the difficulties in predicting and controlling delinquency probably result from limited typological research on juveniles. To understand delinquency fully, it is necessary to study the various career patterns and types of offenses of delinquents. An important question is why a given delinquent engages in a particular act rather than in another form of delinquency, although some delinquents may be involved in several forms of delinquent behavior. Those who commit petty theft or sex offenses should be compared with vandals, for example, much as delinquents who have committed auto theft rather than burglary have been studied.

Technical Consultant (Trenton: State of New Jersey, 1950) and *Report of the Governor's Study Commission on the Deviated Criminal Sex Offender* (Lansing: State of Michigan Printing Office, 1951).

[54] H. C. Brearley, *Homicide in the United States,* University of North Carolina Press, 1932.

[55] Henry Allen Bullock, "Urban Homicide in Theory and Fact," *J. crim. Law Criminol. pol. Sci.,* 45 (1955), 565-75.

[56] Clinard and Wade, *op. cit.*

The study of criminal behavior systems requires the continued use in sociology of personal documents, particularly the life history, and of intensive interviewing. It may be that other areas of sociology will wish to concentrate on the dissection of human behavior into a series of detached and isolated statistical variables, a technique which many sociologists consider the only scientifically sophisticated research method. Criminology, it is hoped, will also continue to use some of the research techniques that keep human behavior understandable, whole, and intact. In American criminological literature there is a long list of impressive contributions of this type, including such volumes as *The Jack Roller* and *The Professional Thief*.[57]

Small-Group Research and the Gang

When the sociologist is pressed for an explanation of stealing and vandalism, he is likely to attribute them to the offender's association with delinquent companions, particularly gangs. He will cite statistics showing the number of offenders who had associates when arrested, even though such figures obviously do not indicate why a particular individual happened to select certain associates while others did not. If textbooks on delinquency and crime are an indication, more than likely he will offer as the only proof of this theory Thrasher's classic study of *The Gang*,[58] done in the 1920's; life histories of gang offenders published by Shaw and McKay;[59] and a very limited number of more recent studies.

The theory employed and the level of proof offered in many of these studies would be considered superficial today. The design of many early studies was complicated by the fact that the delinquents in the samples were largely children of second-generation immigrants,

[57] Clifford R. Shaw, *The Jack Roller*, University of Chicago Press, 1930; Edwin H. Sutherland, *The Professional Thief*, University of Chicago Press, 1937.

[58] Frederick M. Thrasher, *The Gang*, University of Chicago Press, 1927. Also see the revised second edition, 1936.

[59] Shaw, *op. cit.*; Clifford R. Shaw, *The Natural History of a Delinquent Career*, University of Chicago Press, 1931; and Clifford R. Shaw, Henry D. McKay, and James F. McDonald, *Brothers in Crime*, University of Chicago Press, 1938.

from families which had experienced extensive culture conflict and which were extremely poor. In addition, nearly all the delinquents studied came from areas of high delinquency in large cities. Under these conditions, it is no mystery why sociological theories in the field of delinquency and crime have not been more widely accepted.

This does not mean that the general hypotheses advanced in these early studies are not sound. Rather, it means that additional studies need to be made of the role of companions and delinquent gangs using more sophisticated concepts and techniques, such as are now being employed in the study of small groups generally.[60] The delinquent gang is a natural small group in the sense that the relations are face to face and there is intimate knowledge of each person present. An examination of the bibliography of small-group research reveals few studies in this area.[61] The wider use of sociometric techniques reporting the choice of each member of a group in relation to others would enable us to study gang leadership and understand how decisions are reached by a gang that differ from those normally reached by individual members. Finding out the negative choices of gang members and the choices of non-gang members might enable us to come closer to answering the question of why there is differential response. As an example of a related technique not involving member choice, Whyte, in *Street-Corner Society,*[62] was able to construct by observation a sociogram of the relations of members of the Morton Street gang.

Small-group research on delinquent gangs should emphasize the communication process in the group and the way in which the gang becomes a reference group to the members. More specifically, knowledge is needed about the following matters:

1. How and under what conditions are groups formed, and what is the effect on gang formation of social class, age, race, ethnic and religious background, and residential propinquity?

[60] See, for example, Allan W. Eister, "Basic Continuities in the Study of Small Groups," in Howard Becker and Alvin Boskoff (eds.), *Modern Sociological Theory,* Dryden Press, 1957, pp. 305-39.

[61] Fred L. Strodtbeck and A. Paul Hare, "Bibliography of Small Group Research," *Sociometry,* 17 (1954), 107-93.

[62] William Foote Whyte, *Street Corner Society,* University of Chicago Press, 1943.

2. Out of a certain potential universe of delinquents, why do some and not others associate with a delinquent gang? What, if any, is the relation of personality needs to association?

3. What factors account for the size and structure of gangs?

4. How do gangs influence their members, and what directions do they take? (For example, vandalism committed at one time by a gang may far exceed that committed on another occasion. The nature of the interactional process in a gang or gangs appears to set definite limits to destructive behavior. Without such limits the possible activities of delinquents could probably be boundless.)

5. What specifically is the influence of group leaders on others in the gang?

6. How are group goals and norms decided, and how is morale maintained?

7. What group pressures are exerted to conform, and what variations from the group are permitted? How are roles developed in a gang?

8. What is the effect on a gang of the neighborhood? Of a more urban setting?

Studies of such delinquent groups in middle-class communities, suburban areas, and cities and rural areas of various sizes and types are needed. With this information, sociologists could move far beyond mere generalities to specific knowledge of the effect of gangs on members. Undoubtedly it will be found that gangs can be typed according to differences in structure and function. Moreover, more detailed research on gangs may help us to integrate some psychiatric thinking with sociology. For example, gangs that commit particularly violent and brutal offenses may have a member with a disturbed or sadistic personality who, because of his position of leadership, exercises undue influence on other members of the gang, causing them to become involved in offenses which they would not ordinarily commit.

The Concept "Crime" and Criminological Research

One of the chief interests of contemporary American criminology has been the clarification of the nature of crime for research purposes. This has been a signal contribution, for upon the definition of the behavior called "crime" rests the definition of the criminal offender. In his paper on "White Collar Criminality," Sutherland [63] suggested in

[63] Edwin H. Sutherland, "White-Collar Criminality," *Amer. sociol. Rev.*, 5 (1940), 1-13.

1940 that the definition of a crime, for research purposes, should be broadened to include socially injurious acts punished in any way by the state, through administrative, civil, or criminal laws. Since then, discussions by Sutherland, Tappan, Clinard, Hartung, Cressey, Aubert, Jeffery, Robert Caldwell, and many others have been illuminating even if they have not resulted in consensus.[64] It has been stressed, on the one hand, that bias arises when criminological research is restricted to the criminal law; on the other hand, others have emphasized the greater stigma and more rigorous procedures of the criminal law.[65]

More basic than this issue is whether criminology should be concerned with studying all delinquency and crime or only those acts which involve important social values or represent a high degree of resistance potential on the part of members of society.[66] Probably no single theory or theories could explain such diverse criminal acts as refusing to register for Selective Service, perjury, nonsupport, drug addiction, criminal negligence, drunken driving, embezzlement, statutory rape, homosexuality, murder, and armed robbery. In parts of the American South and the Union of South Africa, it is a crime to violate the segregation laws.[67] More thought should be given to the type of analysis Mannheim has suggested in *Criminal Justice and Social*

[64] For a more comprehensive discussion of this issue, see Marshall B. Clinard, "Sociologists and American Criminology," *J. crim. Law Criminol.*, 41 (1951), 549-77.

[65] On the latter basis, Robert Caldwell, for example, has recently stated that "no person is any kind of criminal until he has been properly adjudicated as such in the criminal courts" (*op. cit.*, p. 68). Also see Caldwell, "A Re-examination of the Concept of White-Collar Crime," *Federal Probation*, 22 (1958), 30-36. Cressey has suggested a compromise by the combination of various legal definitions into more meaningful sociological entities. Donald R. Cressey, "Criminological Research and the Definition of Crimes," *Amer. J. Sociol.*, 56 (1951), 546-52.

[66] See Thorsten Sellin, *Culture Conflict and Crime*, Social Science Research Council, Bulletin No. 41, 1938.

[67] C. Vann Woodward, *The Strange Career of Jim Crow*, Oxford University Press, 1957; and Robert C. Williamson, "Crime in South Africa: Some Aspects of Causes and Treatment," *J. crim. Law Criminol. pol. Sci.*, 48 (1957), 185-93.

Reconstruction,[68] in which he sought to clarify the relation of social values and antisocial behavior to criminal law and criminology. He suggested that criminal law and criminology be concerned only with the values of the protection of human life, protection of sexual and family life, protection of property, protection against the power of property, and protection of labor and against labor.

The response of various groups in the social structure to violations of various legal norms is another important issue. Legal norms forbidding certain kinds of behavior are supported by nearly all segments of a society, the behavior in question being regarded as inimical to group welfare; norms involved in other laws may have support only from certain groups. Such illegal behavior as murder, kidnapping, sexual abuse of young children, and incest are generally strongly disapproved. Other behavior that is disapproved legally, such as gambling, may have less public disapproval.

Aubert [69] has indicated that white-collar crime differs from ordinary crime in the methods of dealing with it, the status of the offender, the tolerance of the public, and the social support of offenders. In a highly differentiated society, the ambivalence of average citizens, businessmen, and lawyers toward white-collar crime reflects structural conflicts in social roles and the change in the larger social system. Sutherland once put this idea in other words: "The demand of law arises out of the conflicts in cultures, and because there is conflict in cultures, the law is not effective as a deterrent upon other groups that did not at first demand the law." [70] Additional studies should give us some idea of the conditions which lead to the definition of behavior as criminal and of the way in which legal norms intersect and are integrated with the norms of other institutional structures.[71]

[68] Hermann Mannheim, *Criminal Justice and Social Reconstruction,* Oxford University Press, 1946; and Hermann Mannheim, *Group Problems in Crime and Punishment,* London: Routledge and Kegan Paul, 1955.

[69] Vilhelm Aubert, "White-Collar Crime and Social Structure," *Amer. J. Sociol.,* 58 (1952), 263-71.

[70] Cohen, Lindesmith, and Schuessler, *op. cit.,* p. 108.

[71] See Clarence R. Jeffery, "The Structure of American Criminological Thinking," *J. crim. Law Criminol. pol. Sci.* (1956), 670-72.

The Sociology of Corrections and the Administration of Criminal Justice

The fact that few sociologists have the clinical experience of psychiatrists, psychoanalysts, and psychologists has largely limited their active participation in programs in the field of corrections, other than those in research or teaching.[72] Most sociologists either have had little opportunity to do clinical work or wish to consider themselves "pure scientists," unsullied by applied considerations. Because of this, and the fact that the advice of sociologists has not often been sought, both the frame of reference in contemporary correctional practice and the implementation of this frame of reference through theory or research have been, by and large, drawn from psychiatric and psychoanalytic sources. Sociologists, despite their long tenure in criminology, have, on the whole, had little to do with the policy formulation of correctional practices.

Ten to twenty years ago there was widespread interest among sociologists in predicting recidivism, through studies of violation rates of offenders on probation and parole.[73] Eventually this research area became bogged down in issues of techniques and questions of validation, and few follow-up studies were made. Part of the difficulty lay in a preoccupation with techniques rather than with the application to prediction of a general theory of human or criminal behavior. The items used in the prediction scores generally had little relation to basic criminological theories, and in most cases the predictive items represented a static rather than a dynamic relation to the ongoing process of adjustment to legal norms.[74]

[72] Several sociology departments in the United States are now offering training programs in the field of corrections.

[73] For a more recent study and survey of the literature, see Lloyd E. Ohlin, *Selection for Parole,* Russell Sage Foundation, 1951. Also see Hermann Mannheim and Leslie T. Wilkins, *Prediction Methods in Relation to Borstal Training,* London: Her Majesty's Stationery Office, 1955.

[74] Weinberg, "Theories of Criminality and Problems of Prediction," *loc. cit.* As Ohlin has indicated, "One of the most difficult problems in this field from a methodological standpoint concerns the problem of predictive stability. It has been demonstrated that parole predictions are soon outmoded by changes in parole conditions encountered by the parolee on his release. . . .

In the area of corrections, prediction studies have been partially supplanted by renewed interest in the social systems of prisons. This correctional research represents an expansion of the important pioneer studies by such sociologists as Donald Clemmer and Hans Riemer.[75] These new studies involve the application of such concepts as clique formation, self-conception, and role conflicts among inmates and, at the administrative level, of problems of function, power, and communication. In particular, recent studies have analyzed the relation of social organization to social change in correctional institutions. This work has had its counterparts in sociological studies of industry and of mental hospitals. It should result in significant contributions, not only to criminology, but to general sociological theory as well.

There have been few treatment programs involving applications of criminological theory derived from sociology.[76] Cressey has suggested how the theory of differential association might be applied in correctional programs.[77] Institutional treatment of offenders seems also to have differential effects depending on a number of undefined variables. Some persons are undoubtedly unaffected by "prisonization" in any significant way; others are probably improved; it is suspected that the majority are adversely affected. More definitive studies are needed to determine the differential effect of such experience. Through the study of criminal behavior systems and the development of typological classifications, it may be possible, for example, for sociologists to assist in developing more effective treatment programs based on the type of offender.

Methods are required for adjusting the prediction to take account of the changes that occur in parole conditions with the passage of time." Lloyd E. Ohlin, *Sociology and the Field of Corrections*, Russell Sage Foundation, 1956, 44.

[75] Donald Clemmer, *The Prison Community*, Christopher Press, 1940, reprinted by Rinehart, 1958; and Hans Reimer, "Socialization in the Prison Community," *Proc. Amer. Prison Assoc.*, 1937, 152-53. In order to make this study, Reimer, a sociologist, voluntarily committed himself to prison.

[76] One of the few exceptions has been the Highfields experiment. See Lloyd W. McCorkle, Albert Elias, and F. Lovell Bixby, *The Highfields Story*, Henry Holt, 1958. Also see H. Ashley Weeks, "Preliminary Evaluation of the Highfields Project," *Amer. sociolo. Rev.*, 18 (1953), 280-87.

[77] Donald R. Cressey, "Changing Criminals: The Application of the Theory of Differential Association," *Amer. J. Sociol.*, 61 (1955), 116.

Other broad areas in the administration of criminal justice require the application of sociological theory and concepts including studies of the police and court administration. They involve the actual as opposed to the formal structure of the police and judicial administration. The administration of criminal justice appears to affect the attitudes and self-conception of many offenders, but why it affects some offenders and not others needs additional research. Newman, for example, has studied the nature of, and the inmates' conception of, the informal bargaining process that goes on in felony convictions.[78] A broader study might be made of the inmates' conception of "justice" and how it differs from that of other interested groups in a society.

The Need for a Comparative Criminology

Much American criminological research and the generalizations derived from it may turn out to be limited to American society rather than applicable universally. Many European writers have suggested, for example, that most of the American findings about criminal behavior are limited to American society because of the extensiveness of culture conflict and the frequent horizontal and vertical mobility in the United States, and the fact that extensive immigration has disturbed the social stability of the country. Such research findings would still be applicable elsewhere, however, provided that the conditions, factors, or variables discovered were found to apply to other societies.

There is limited evidence that certain types of crime are associated with the characteristics of a particular national culture. A few countries, such as Finland, Puerto Rico, and Ceylon, have a high murder or assault rate.[79] Others, such as Sweden and Great Britain, have comparatively low rates. While the Swedish auto theft rate is high, the incidence of robbery is low. The United States appears to have an extremely high armed-robbery rate.

[78] Donald R. Newman, "Pleading Guilty for Considerations: A Study of Bargain Justice," *J. crim. Law Criminol. pol. Sci.*, 46 (1956), 780-90.

[79] Veli Verkko, *Homicides and Suicides in Finland and Their Dependence on National Character*, G. E. C. Gads Forlag, 1951; Jaime Toro-Calder, "Personal Crime in Puerto Rico," unpublished M. A. thesis, University of Wisconsin, 1950; and Murray A. Straus and Jacqueline H. Straus, "Suicide, Homicide and Social Structure in Ceylon," *Amer. J. Sociol.*, 58 (1952), 461-69.

534 — Selected Applications of Sociology

Whereas the physical sciences have developed their theoretical knowledge through numerous repetitions of an experiment under different conditions, the science of criminology has been built on studies whose findings are far too often restricted to a particular sample, culture, or period of time. To develop an adequate science of criminology, more comparative studies are needed, using theories and procedures derived from one society and applied as precisely as possible to another. A really universal generalization requires the repetition of similar studies by different persons in a similar way on samples differing in time and place.[80]

A major difficulty in developing a comparative science of criminology has been the fact that the type of data considered important in one discipline or in one country may not be collected by another discipline or country. This was recognized in the resolutions adopted in 1955 at the First United Nations Congress on the Prevention of Crime and the Treatment of Delinquents. These resolutions included the statement, "Through cooperation between researchers from different countries, it may be possible to develop a highly promising new fields of comparative criminology based on researchers employing standard definitions and techniques." This statement implies, although it does not specifically suggest, the development of standard interview schedules which could be employed by persons in various disciplines and in different countries in gathering data about various types of delinquents or criminals. Such a standard procedure has been followed in intelligence tests. The same personality tests have often been used by persons in different disciplines and countries. Perhaps a group of American criminologists could begin by devising such an instrument.

American criminologists cannot claim that their findings have universal significance if they ignore or fail to reconcile the findings of other societies or other disciplines. While the incorporation of European research has not been conspicuous in most American criminology texts, the Danish criminologist Stephan Hurwitz has recently attempted to integrate the findings of European and American criminologists. His *Criminology*,[81] which has been translated into English,

[80] Marshall B. Clinard, "Research Frontiers in Criminology," *Brit. J. Delinqu.*, 7 (1956), 113-14.

[81] Hurwitz, *op. cit.* Also see Howard Jones, *Crime and the Penal System: A Textbook of Criminology*, University Tutorial Press, 1956.

brings the English-speaking criminologist into contact with a great deal of European, particularly Scandinavian, research in criminology. Any attempt at an international science of criminology may prove impossible at this time, however, because of the widely divergent conceptions of the nature of human behavior. Because sociology and social psychology are in general poorly developed outside the United States, there are often serious communication difficulties among researchers in criminology, for, as Michael and Adler [82] pointed out long ago, the science of criminology rests inevitably on developments in sociology and psychology.

Selected Bibliography

Aubert, Vilhelm, "White-Collar Crime and Social Structure," *Amer. J. Sociol.*, 58 (1952), 263-71.

Bloch, Herbert A., "Crime Causation: Research and Its Application," *Federal Probation*, 21 (1957), 11-20.

Bullock, Henry Allen, "Urban Homicide in Theory and Fact," *J. crim. Law Criminol. pol. Sci.*, 45 (1955), 565-75.

Clinard, Marshall B., "Research Frontiers in Criminology," *Brit. J. Delinqu.*, 7 (1956), 110-22.

———, "Sociologists and American Criminology," *J. crim. Law Criminol.*, 41 (1951), 549-77.

———, "Sociology of Delinquency and Crime," in Joseph B. Gittler (ed.), *Review of Sociology: Analysis of a Decade*, John Wiley, 1957.

Cohen, Albert K., *Delinquent Boys: The Culture of the Gang*, Free Press, 1955.

———, Alfred Lindesmith, and Karl Schuessler, *The Sutherland Papers*, Indiana University Press, 1956.

Cressey, Donald R., "Changing Criminals: The Application of the Theory of Differential Association," *Amer. J. Sociol.*, 61 (1955), 112-18.

———, *Other People's Money*, Free Press, 1953.

Glaser, Daniel, "Criminality Theories and Behavioral Images," *Amer. J. Sociol.*, 61 (1956), 433-45.

Glueck, Sheldon, "Theory and Fact in Criminology," *Brit. J. Delinqu.*, 7 (1956), 92-109.

Hentig, Hans von, *The Criminal and His Victim*, Yale University Press, 1948.

[82] Jerome Michael and Mortimer Adler, *Crime, Law and Social Science*, Harcourt, Brace, 1933.

Hathaway, Starke, and Elio Monachesi, *Analyzing and Predicting Juvenile Delinquency with the MMPI*, University of Minnesota Press, 1953.

Hurwitz, Stephan, *Criminology* (trans. Elsie Giering), London: George Allan & Unwin, 1952.

Lemert, Edwin M., "An Isolation and Closure Theory of Naive Check Forgery," *J. crim. Law Criminol. pol. Sci.*, 44 (1953), 296-307.

Mannheim, Hermann, *Criminal Justice and Social Reconstruction*, Oxford University Press, 1946.

Merton, Robert K., *Social Theory and Social Structure*, rev. ed., Free Press, 1957.

Ohlin, Lloyd E., *Sociology and the Field of Corrections*, Russell Sage Foundation, 1956.

Reckless, Walter C., *The Crime Problem*, 2nd ed., Appleton-Century-Crofts, 1955.

————, Simon Dinitz, and Barbara Kay, "Self-Component in Potential Delinquency and Non-Delinquency," *Amer. sociol. Rev.*, 22 (1957), 566-70.

Reiss, Albert J., "Social Correlates of Psychological Types of Delinquency," *Amer. sociol. Rev.*, 17 (1952), 710-18.

Schuessler, Karl F., and Donald R. Cressey, "Personality Characteristics of Criminals," *Amer. J. Sociol.*, 55 (1950), 476-84.

Sellin, Thorsten, *Culture Conflict and Crime*, Social Science Research Council, Bulletin No. 41, 1938.

Sutherland, Edwin H., and Donald R. Cressey, *Principles of Criminology*, 5th ed., Lippincott, 1955.

Weinberg, S. Kirson, *Incest Behavior*, Citadel Press, 1955.

24

Mass Communication and the Social System[1]

JOHN W. RILEY, JR., AND
MATILDA WHITE RILEY

Rutgers University

A great deal has been written about the millions of messages directed to mass audiences by advertisers, educators, government officials, preachers, entertainers, and propagandists. To date, however, the precise nature and effects of mass communication are little understood, despite the burgeoning of research approaches and the multiplication of empirical findings. Only some of the answers have been found to such questions as: Does mass communication serve to

[1] This paper was written in connection with projects supported in part by a research grant M-926 from the National Institute of Mental Health of the National Institutes of Health, Public Health Service and in part by the Research Council of Rutgers University. To both sources of support the authors are greatly indebted. Valuable comments were made on an earlier version of this manuscript by Robert K. Merton, Talcott Parsons, Wilbur Schramm, Wellman J. Warner, David Wallace, and Winston White, as well as by our working associates, Richard Cohn, Robert Gutman, Grace D. Hooper, and Mary E. Moore.

change basic values and beliefs, or does it dictate only minor decisions of thought and deed? And, whatever its effects, how does it achieve them? What is the process whereby a communication to the many may in some fashion arouse, persuade, or change?

This paper sets forth the development of a sociological view of mass communication as the most pressing need facing students in this field. Such a view would fit together the many messages and the manifold individual reactions to them within an integrated social structure and process. It would be formulated as a working model which organizes the available pieces of substantive knowledge in terms of the relevant theories of social systems. The model would state present assumptions in their relationship to one another. It would then be tested through further research, revised, and specified in greater detail.

We do not presume to develop such a model here. We do, however, propose to sketch some of its major elements and to identify certain strands of ongoing research and related theory which bid fair to contribute to its future development. In the first section of this paper, we shall outline the traditional approach to mass communication, which has been largely concerned with the content of the communicated message and the responses of isolated individuals, and which has succeeded in part, but only in part, in explaining the wide variability of these responses. In the following sections, we shall outline, step by step, the gradually emerging sociological extensions of this traditional view and point out a few gaps in thinking and research which seem to demand attention, dealing in turn with the recipient of the mass-communicated message, the communicator, and, finally, with their mutual relationship within an over-all social system. Without attempting either a full review of the literature or rounded estimates of individual studies, we shall use selected theories and research reports to illustrate the sociological view.

Communicator and Recipient: A Traditional View

Much of the traditional research on mass communication focuses on the movement of a message from the communicator to the recipient and on the recipient's response to this message as a stimulus. It emphasizes the communicator's direct efforts to persuade, the content of the message itself, the audience as a "mass" of unrelated recipients. It serves as the detailed elaboration of principles broadly enunciated by Aristotle and treated as doctrine over the ages:

> ... Since rhetoric exists to *affect* the giving of decisions ... the orator must not only try to make the *argument* of his speech demonstrative and worthy of belief; he must also make his *own character* look right and put his *hearers*, who are to decide, into the right frame of mind.[2]

Since this traditional view provides the firm center from which other approaches are largely extensions, we shall rehearse its general character, following Lasswell's much-quoted formulation of the main elements involved: *"Who says what in which channel to whom with what effect?"* [3]

The *who* in this scheme has been dealt with in research which describes various kinds of mass communicators in terms of their training or their social and personality characteristics.[4] Another line of research has focused on who the communicator is as he is perceived by the audience: on the consequences of revealing or not revealing to the audience his true identity, on the relative credibility of different communicators as sources, and on the importance of such credibility to the long-term effectiveness of the message.[5]

The *what* of the Lasswell scheme, the message itself, has commanded wide research attention. Much as Max Weber earlier analyzed the ethic of Protestantism and the spirit of capitalism,[6] modern scholars are abstracting the essence of the mass communication, classifying sub-

[2] *Rhetoric* (trans. W. Rhys Roberts), Clarendon Press, Book II, pp. 1377b-22 ff. Emphasis added.

[3] Harold D. Lasswell, "The Structure and Function of Communication in Society," in Lyman Bryson (ed.), *The Communication of Ideas*, Institute for Religious and Social Studies, 1948, p. 37. We are attempting here to isolate only the primary emphasis of this traditional approach. Lasswell himself counterbalances this emphasis when he says, "We are less interested in dividing up the act of communication than in viewing the act as a whole in relation to the entire social process" (p. 38).

[4] See, for example, Leo C. Rosten, *The Washington Correspondents*, Harcourt, Brace, 1937.

[5] See, for example, Carl I. Hovland, Irving L. Janis, and Harold H. Kelley, *Communication and Persuasion*, Yale University Press, 1953.

[6] Max Weber, *The Protestant Ethic and the Spirit of Capitalism* (trans. Talcott Parsons), Scribner's, 1930.

ject matter in various ways, counting the themes or symbols, analyzing the rhetorical devices and the underlying popular appeals.[7] Berelson and Salter, for example, have discovered that popular magazine stories, while espousing the doctrine of racial and religious equality, actually tend to reflect the contemporary stereotypes of minorities.[8] Wolfenstein and Leites have found through content analysis that "the hero of the American films happily survives the conflicts of love and hate which have so often been fatal for dramatic heroes of other times and places." [9] A study of radio daytime serials by Warner and Henry shows that "the basic and primary theme is that good and noble women who are wives and mothers are invincible within their own arena of life, the American family." [10]

Other studies have dealt with the relationship between message and audience. A program of research at Yale, for example, indicates that strong fear appeals tend to be less effective than mild ones, and that messages which explicitly carry conclusions are generally more effective than messages which stimulate the audience to draw its own conclusions.[11] Readership research has traditionally classified magazine content first in terms of reading behavior—whether the reader noticed the piece, started to read it, read through to the end, liked it—and only then examined the editorial characteristics to see how the layout or the symbols used in the presentation or the development of the subject matter may have evoked such reader responses.[12]

Research on *channels* has included numerous statistical analyses of the coverage of the various mass media: counts of radio and tele-

[7] See the general treatment by Bernard Berelson, *Content Analysis in Communication Research,* Free Press, 1952.

[8] Bernard Berelson and Patricia Salter, "Majority and Minority Americans: An Analysis of Magazine Fiction," *Pub. Opin. Quart., 10* (1946), 168-90.

[9] Martha Wolfenstein and Nathan Leites, "An Analysis of Themes and Plots in Motion Pictures," *Annals Amer. Acad. polit. soc. Sci., 254* (1947), 48.

[10] W. Lloyd Warner and William E. Henry, "The Radio Daytime Serial: A Symbolic Analysis," *Genet. Psychol. Monog., 37* (1948), 62.

[11] Hovland *et al., op. cit.,* esp. Chaps. 3 and 4.

[12] Although most of these studies are unpublished, a commonly used method is described in Matilda White (Riley) and Hans Zeisel, "Reading Indices," *J. Marketing,* Oct. 1941.

vision outlets and receiving sets, newspaper and magazine circulations, motion pictures produced, theater seating capacities, and the like.[13] But most studies go beyond the channels themselves, showing the relationship between channels and audience. A typical finding, as reported by Lazarsfeld, controverts the popular assumption of a competitive scramble for audiences among the several media. Lazarsfeld found that the audiences in fact overlap to a marked extent: that movie-goers are also radio listeners, magazine readers are also television fans, and nearly all of these at least look at one or more newspapers fairly regularly. Thus a person who has read *Gone with the Wind* is likely to see the motion picture based on the book; and a person who has seen the picture is likely subsequently to read the book.[14]

In regard to the *whom* in the Lasswell formula, a vast effort has long been under way (though frequently unpublished by its sponsors) to discover who receives the communicated message. The audience survey, as it early became standardized within the communications industry, describes the audience in terms of various characteristics. For example, Beville's 1940 report on radio states that the audience "is composed of many 'cells' which can be stratified not only by economic group but also by geographic region, community size and character, family size and composition."[15] More recently, Hovland and his collaborators have gone far beyond such simple classifications, tackling, for example, the problem of individual differences in persuasibility among audience members. A typical finding is that persons with low self-esteem are more easily persuaded by a communication than persons with a higher sense of self-esteem.[16]

Audience research is concerned with program audiences, of course, as well as with media audiences. For years, continuous "ratings" have

[13] A UNESCO report on *World Communication* (Paris, 1951), cites such findings on a world-wide basis.

[14] Paul F. Lazarsfeld, "Communication Research," in W. Dennis (ed.), *Current Trends in Social Psychology*, University of Pittsburgh Press, 1949, pp. 245 *ff*.

[15] H. M. J. Beville, Jr., "The ABCD's of Radio Audiences," *Pub. Opin. Quart.*, 5 (1940), 196. These "cells" are not unlike Aristotle's classification, in Chap. 12 of the *Rhetoric*, of the members of the audience according to youth, prime of life, and old age; and birth, wealth, and power.

[16] Hovland *et al.*, *op. cit.*, pp. 184 *ff*. The question of "self-selected" audiences, as contrasted with "captive" audiences, is discussed below.

been kept, in this country and in England, of the audience sizes for radio and television shows. Descriptive studies characterize the people in the audiences for specific programs or types of programs. In Herzog's analysis of daytime serials, for example, listeners and non-listeners are compared in respect to the usual demographic characteristics, and also in respect to social participation, range of intellectual interests, concern with public affairs, degree of self-assurance, and reported extent of worrying. Interestingly enough, in this case no systematic or conclusive differences were found between those who elect to listen to soapbox dramas and those who do not.[17]

Finally, much research has been brought to bear on the *effects* of the communication. A few studies report spectacular effects. Cantril, for example, has described the panic pursuant upon Orson Welles's radio dramatization of H. G. Wells' "War of the Worlds," which depicts an imaginary invasion from Mars.[18] Merton has investigated a Kate Smith radio marathon which sold some 39 million dollars' worth of war bonds.[19] By contrast, however, a great deal of communication has been found to yield vague or inconsistent effects, or even to produce a "boomerang" response in direct opposition to the intent of the communicator. The evidence is now clear that a movie designed to persuade does not always cause the expected change in attitude; nor does an advertisement invariably result in increased purchase of the product. Effect analysis demonstrates that there is no direct and simple relationship between communication and effect. Such analysis serves, however, to raise for further research many important questions about the nature of this relationship.[20]

The questions raised by effect analysis suggest the need for certain

[17] Herta Herzog, "Motivations and Gratifications of Daily. Serial Listeners," in Paul F. Lazarsfeld and Frank Stanton (eds.), *Radio Research 1942–43*, Duell, Sloan and Pearce, 1944.

[18] Hadley Cantril *et al.*, *The Invasion from Mars*, Princeton University Press, 1940.

[19] Robert K. Merton, Marjorie Fiske, and Alberta Curtis, *Mass Persuasion: The Social Psychology of a War Bond Drive*, Harper, 1946.

[20] See, for example, Joseph T. Klapper, "What We Know About the Effects of Mass Communication: The Brink of Hope," *Pub. Opin. Quart.*, 21:4 (1957–58), 457. See also Klapper's excellent survey of the literature, *The Effects of Mass Media*, Bureau of Applied Social Research, 1949, which is soon to be brought up to date and published in book form.

extensions of the traditional approach, which, in its more extreme versions, has focused exclusively on the simple act of communication, from source to audience. Often implicit in it are notions of a communicator concerned only with sending his message and making it as persuasive as possible and a recipient, alone in his ivory tower, coming to a decision—often purely rational [21]—about how to act upon the message. The very simplicity of such a scheme makes it an effective framework for both survey research and laboratory experiment. Investigators using this approach have amassed (and will continue to amass) a wealth of information. Yet the traditional view does not take fully into account ongoing processes of social interaction of which the single communicative act is merely one component. Nor does it take into full account those psychological processes which, although they may be going on within the individual recipient quite apart from any particular communication, may nevertheless markedly affect his reaction to it.[22] Extensions of this view in both the sociological and the psychological directions seem necessary if the mass-communications process is to be explained more adequately or its outcome predicted more accurately.

The Recipient Himself

Before turning to the sociological analysis of the communicative act, let us consider briefly the body of research which has gradually

[21] The philosophy implied in the "propaganda of truth" conducted by the United States during World War II is an example. And Lasswell writes that the communication process "is efficient to the degree that rational judgments are facilitated" (*op. cit.*, p. 46).

[22] As Lazarsfeld and Merton pointed out in 1943, "Propaganda will not produce the expected response unless its content corresponds to the psychological wants of the audience" (Robert K. Merton, *Social Theory and Social Structure*, rev., Free Press, 1957, p. 519). A few years later, Berelson expanded on this point:

. . . Effects upon the audience do not follow directly from and in correspondence with the intent of the communicator or the content of the communication. The predispositions of the reader or listener are deeply involved in the situation, and may operate to block or modify the intended effect or even to set up a boomerang effect.

(Bernard Berelson, "Communications and Public Opinion," in Wilbur Schramm [ed.], *Communications in Modern Society*, University of Illinois Press, 1948, pp. 183-84.)

been supplementing and modifying the traditional approach by probing into the predispositions and psychological processes of the recipient. As we shall see, this research also contributes to a sociological view, since it points up the importance of the social context of the recipient.

Motivations. One line of research analyzes the motivations for the mass-communications response or the gratifications obtained.[23] Berelson, for example, observing readers at a time when a delivery strike deprived them of their daily newspapers, suggested that the newspaper "serves as a source of security in a disturbing world." [24] A study by Wolfe and Fiske shows that comic books may be a source of ego development, at least for normal children.[25] A study by Herzog finds that for many women daytime-serial listening serves to answer some of their everyday problems and to suggest appropriate patterns of behavior.[26] And Waples and his associates conclude that the more closely a topic fits the personal problems of the reader, the greater will be its appeal.[27]

Audience Self-selection. Another set of studies, stemming in large part from Lazarsfeld's early work,[28] deals with the principles of audience self-selection. A person, whenever he is free to do so, chooses to read certain messages or listen to certain programs, and not to others. In general, whether he is aware of it or not, he listens to what he wants to hear and reads messages in support of what he wants to

[23] Commercial studies of the individual recipient are drawing widely on the psychological and psychiatric literature. For a popular discussion of "motivation research," "subthreshold effects," and the like, see Vance Packard, *The Hidden Persuaders*, David McKay, 1957.

[24] Bernard Berelson, "What 'Missing the Newspaper' Means," in Paul F. Lazarsfeld and Frank Stanton (eds.), *Communications Research, 1948–49*, Harper, 1949.

[25] Katherine M. Wolfe and Marjorie Fiske, "Why They Read Comics," in Lazarsfeld and Stanton (eds.), *Communications Research, 1948–49*.

[26] *Op. cit.*

[27] Douglas Waples, Bernard Berelson, and Franklyn Bradshaw, *What Reading Does to People*, University of Chicago Press, 1940.

[28] As early as 1940, he noted, for example, that "the radio program selects its audience before it affects it . . ." (Paul F. Lazarsfeld, *Radio and the Printed Page*, Duell, Sloan and Pearce, 1940, p. 134).

believe. Thus Robinson, in his study of the farmer, suggests that "Radio is ineffective in changing rural opinions . . . because rural people generally will not listen to opinions with which they seriously disagree." [29] The voting-behavior studies show that, while political campaigns are generally available, actual exposure is consistently partisan.[30] In a report on the U.S. Treasury's 1944 distribution of free tickets to a documentary film on the war, Cartwright remarks that "the people who attended the movie were the ones whose behavior was already closest to that encouraged by the movie." [31]

Perception. Once an individual has decided to read or listen to the message, he may proceed (usually below the level of awareness) to select certain parts of it for special attention, often distorting them, and meanwhile overlooking (or, as Simmel said, "overhearing" [32]) other parts entirely. The substantial literature on perception and cognition [33] makes it quite clear that the human organism does not simply hear or see or touch "what is there"; on the contrary, it perceives (within the limits of the stimulus situation) what it wants to perceive.

[29] William S. Robinson, "Radio Comes to the Farmer," in Paul F. Lazarsfeld and Frank Stanton (eds.), *Radio Research 1941,* Duell, Sloan and Pearce, 1941, p. 267.

[30] Paul F. Lazarsfeld, Bernard Berelson, and Hazel Gaudet, *The People's Choice,* 2nd ed., Columbia University Press, 1948, p. 37.

[31] Dorwin Cartwright, "Some Principles of Mass Persuasion," *Hum. Relat.,* 2 (1949), 257.

[32] Kurt H. Wolff, *The Sociology of Georg Simmel,* Free Press, 1950, p. 311.

[33] See esp. Floyd H. Allport, *Theories of Perception and the Concept of Structure,* John Wiley, 1955. The work of Felix Heider is also basically important to our sociological approach, esp. "Social Perception and Phenomenal Causality," *Psychol. Rev.,* 51 (1944), 358-74, and "Attitudes and Cognitive Organization," *J. Psychol.,* 21 (1946), 107-12. For a recent general theory, see Leon Festinger, *A Theory of Cognitive Dissonance,* Row, Peterson, 1957. See also Aristotle: "When people are feeling friendly and placable, they think one sort of thing; when they are feeling angry or hostile, they think either something totally different or the same thing with a different intensity; when they feel friendly to the man who comes before them for judgment, they regard him as having done little wrong, if any; when they feel hostile, they take the opposite view" (*Rhetoric,* II, pp. 1377*b*-

In this way, perceptions are adjusted to fit the needs, values, emotions, and past experiences of the individual. Hungry men, for example, tend to perceive food stimuli more readily than men who have just eaten; poor children are more apt than rich children to overestimate the size of coins; prejudiced readers tend to avoid those portions of communicated messages which encourage tolerance; and persons in different cultures typically attribute different meanings to identical messages. In short, the recipient of a message may ignore or misinterpret those parts of the message (or those aspects of the communicator himself) which do not conform to his interests and tastes, or which tend to disorganize or threaten his other perceptions and the decisions which he has previously made. On the other hand, he may pay special heed to those parts of the message which seem to reinforce his point of view, fit in with his likes and dislikes, or organize materials already in his mind.

Allport and Postman, in their well-known study of rumor, investigate some of these processes.[34] They recount the anecdote about a Chinese tourist in Maine who, just before the Japanese surrender in 1945, seeking a pleasant view, asked the way to the hilltop. Within an hour, the rumor spread that a Japanese spy had climbed the hill and was taking photographs of the area. Investigation showed, of course, that the rumor had spread among residents imbued with the importance of the war, a desire to protect America, hatred of the Japanese, and suspicion of foreigners in general. The researchers classified the processes which gradually shaped the form of the message in terms of "leveling," or the omission of certain facts; "sharpening," or the emphasis on certain other facts; and "assimilation," or the incorporation of certain facts into the available frame of reference.

Such studies are clearly basic to a psychological understanding of mass-communication behavior. Continuing research in this direction may be expected to round out present knowledge of the individual recipient's tendencies to read the message selectively, to distort it, to accept or reject it, and to act upon it as he does.

Implications for a Sociological View. These studies seem, in one of their aspects, especially relevant to a broader sociological understand-

[34] G. W. Allport and Leo Postman, *The Psychology of Rumor*, Henry Holt, 1947, pp. 134*ff.*

ing of mass communication. Experiments conducted by Sherif [35] and Asch [36] point to certain possible connections between perception and the perceiver's relationship to the social structure. These experiments show that individuals asked to make judgments severally in a group (about the apparent movement of a spot of light or the relative length of fairly equal lines) tend to agree with the judgments of the others in the group, whether or not they are objectively right. The group consensus may provide a standard or frame of reference for the individual judgments.

But the others in the group need not be on the scene to guide or to reinforce the individual's perception. Indeed, his perceptions of a message and his responses to it are often strikingly similar to those of his family, his friends, and the members of other groups which are significant to him—quite apart from whether the members of these groups receive the message together with him or have a chance to discuss it with one another or with him. According to the theories to be discussed in the next section, this agreement occurs in large part because of the continuing interplay between the individual and these significant groups. He shares many of his experiences with them. He has learned from them many of his basic ideas and beliefs about what is true, or aesthetically appropriate, or morally right. And these very experiences and values tend, as we have just seen, to govern what he perceives and how he perceives it. Thus it appears that mass communications tend to reach the target individual as a member of various groups which are important to him.

The Recipient and His Primary Groups

A considerable store of theory, often summarized under the heading of reference-group theory, is at hand to describe recipients as members of groups. As set down by such scholars as Sherif, New-

[35] Muzafer Sherif, "A Study of Some Social Factors in Perception," *Arch. Psychol.*, 1935, No. 187.

[36] S. E. Asch, "Studies in the Principles of Judgments and Attitudes: II. Determination of Judgments by Group and Ego Standards," *J. soc. Psychol.*, 12 (1940), 433-65.

548 *Selected Applications of Sociology*

comb, Merton, and others,[37] this theory "centers on the processes through which men relate themselves to groups and refer their behavior to the values of these groups." [38] Not only do the groups provide a standard against which the individual may evaluate himself and others; more importantly, the individual's family, his community, his workmates—all of his significant "primary" groups—teach him their values and shape his values in line with theirs. During the course of his lifetime, he makes his own many of the central values of these others; the others come to constitute for him, in Mead's term, an "inner forum" before which he privately debates alternatives. Moreover, in the course of daily interaction, whenever he conforms in his acts or expressions of opinion to the values of his associates, these others are likely to approve and reward; and when he fails to conform, they may disapprove, bringing negative sanctions to bear. Hence, he often conforms in order to win approval or (in Veblen's telling irony) to gain "an increment of good repute."

Selected Applications. Such theories are beginning to be applied to problems of mass communications. The traditional approach, as we have pointed out, has long found it fruitful to classify individuals in terms of their location in different parts of the country or different types of communities or in terms of their socioeconomic status within the larger society. In addition to this, it is now increasingly recognized that, if the recipient's values are indeed shaped in part by the primary groups to which he belongs or aspires, then his perception of a message and his response to it may be better understood in terms of his relationship to these groups and to their values. As part of the Yale program of research, Kelley and Volkart set up an experiment in which an outside adult speaker at several Boy Scout meetings criticized the Scout emphasis on the values of camping and woodcraft and

[37] Muzafer Sherif, *An Outline of Social Psychology,* Harper, 1948; Theodore M. Newcomb, *Social Psychology,* Dryden, 1950; Robert K. Merton and Alice S. Kitt, "Contributions to the Theory of Reference Group Behavior," in Robert K. Merton and Paul F. Lazarsfeld (eds.), *Continuities in Social Research: Studies in the Scope and Methods of "The American Soldier,"* Free Press, 1950, pp. 40-105.

[38] Merton and Kitt, *op. cit.,* pp. 41-42.

advocated various urban activities instead. Attitude tests conducted among the boys before and after this speech suggest that the boys who were most strongly motivated to retain their membership in the Boy Scouts were the most resistant to a communication which ran counter to the standards of the group.[39] In another study, Festinger, Riecken, and Schachter observed the members of a religious sect at a time when they expected that the earth would be destroyed and only "believers" would be saved. Even though the prophesied event failed to occur, those who received support from others of the faithful (unlike members who faced the crisis alone) tended to regard the failure merely as a slight miscalculation and not as disconfirmation of their essential belief.[40]

Some Rutgers research illustrates an application of reference-group theory to the receipt of quite another kind of message—one which, made up of fiction or fantasy, is not explicitly designed to persuade, although it may nevertheless exert considerable influence. An exploratory study of children's mass-media preferences suggests that the individual's integration into a significant group may affect both his choice of materials to read or listen to and his interpretation of media content. In this study, children who were not disposed to talk extensively with friends—and who doubtless felt the strain of exclusion from the peer group—were found to express relatively high interest in stories which foster fantasies of aggression or escape. They were more apt than high communicators to like radio and television programs characterized by action and violence or comic books about animals, such as Bugs Bunny, which they regarded as "a rascal," "lazy," "happy-go-lucky," and likely to "get away with it." Even when the excluded child and the integrated child are exposed to the same media material, the content may serve a different function for the two. In describing such a radio program as "The Lone Ranger," the low communicators typically used terms like "scary," "creepy," "hard to get out of your mind when you go to sleep"; the high com-

[39] Harold H. Kelley and Edmund H. Volkart, "The Resistance to Change of Group-Anchored Attitudes," *Amer. sociol. Rev.*, 17 (1952), 453-65.

[40] Leon Festinger, Henry W. Riecken, and Stanley Schachter, *When Prophecy Fails*, University of Minnesota Press, 1956.

municators tended to couple exposure to this program with "playing guns" with their friends subsequently.[41]

Another piece of related research develops the hypothesis that media preferences may be associated, not only with the individual's disposition to communicate with the members of the group (parents, in this instance), but also with his agreement with their values. A sample of adolescent boys in New Jersey high schools were asked which of a list of topics they "like best to read about or listen to" in the mass media. The first step in the analysis again compared high and low communicators. The proportion of boys who named "news" as a desired topic was as follows:

	Degree of communication with parents	
	Low	High
Percent who like to read or listen to news	50	65
Total respondents = 100%	(755)	(357)

This finding is consistent with the notion that the boys' media behavior tends to conform to the expectations of their middle-class parents, even when these significant others are not immediately present to exert control.

Moreover, when the boys were subdivided according to the degree to which their own aspirations (classified in terms of their responses to a series of vignettes embodying selected values of concern to adolescents) conformed to the expectations of parents or peers, the results were as follows: [42]

[41] Matilda White Riley and John W. Riley, Jr., "A Sociological Approach to Communications Research," *Pub. Opin. Quart,* 15 (1951), 445-60. See also Matilda White Riley and Samuel H. Flowerman, "Group Relations as a Variable in Communications Research," *Amer. sociol. Rev.,* 16 (1951), 174-80.

[42] This measure of agreement will be reported in further detail in an article now in preparation by the Rutgers Research Group.

	Degree of communication with parents			
	Low		High	
Predominant agreement with	Peers	Parents	Peers	Parents
Percent who like to read or listen to news	47	55	58	70
Total respondents = 100%	(433)	(322)	(155)	(202)

Thus it appears that a boy's selection of media materials in line with probable parental expectations is related to his predominant agreement with parental values, as well as to his disposition to interact with his parents as persons.

Consequences for Primary-Group Structure. One outcome of individual tendencies to adopt a group as a source of guidance and orientation is the development of a considerable degree of homogeneity in attitudes and values among the group members. (The implementation of these values is often differentiated, of course, according to some "division of labor" among the individual roles.) Newcomb, starting from sociological theory, on the one hand, and the work of Heider, on the other, has developed a theory to account for such homogeneity, explaining how group members, as they interact and talk among themselves, feel rewarded when their attitudes coincide, and thus tend to influence one another to arrive at similar attitudes.[43] And Festinger states a set of hypotheses, developed from a wide variety of empirical experiments in the Lewinian tradition, which indicate in some detail how discrepancies in group opinion lead to pressures toward uniformity—or, failing this, toward extrusion of dissident members from the group. He suggests, for example, that the amount of change in an individual's opinion resulting from the attempts of the other members to persuade him will

—increase as the pressure toward uniformity in the group increases;
—increase as the strength of the resultant force to remain in the group increases for the recipient;

[43] Theodore M. Newcomb, "An Approach to the Study of Communicative Acts," *Psychol. Rev.*, 60 (1953), 393-404.

—decrease in the degree to which the opinions and attitudes involved are anchored in other group memberships or serve important need-satisfying functions for the person.[44]

Conflicting Reference Groups. This mention of "other group memberships" leads to the highly important point that the individual belongs and refers, not just to one group, but to many. The expectations of such groups may reinforce one another, so that he uses them jointly as a reference. If their values conflict, however, he is in a "role conflict," or under "cross-pressure." Studies of voting behavior have shown that cross-pressured individuals, who sometimes vacillate and even withdraw from making any decisions at all, are also apt to change their vote intentions during the course of the campaign.[45]

Toward a Sociological View. These few examples suggest how this use of reference-group theory is beginning to discover the social structure which underlies and tends to integrate the great diversity of individual perceptions of and responses to the mass-communicated message. It becomes apparent that the consumer faced with a baffling array of brands, the voter choosing between political courses with unknown consequences, and the entertainment-seeker with untold possibilities on his television dial make choices which are not based primarily on the inherent merits of the object chosen—no matter how persuasively these merits may have been advertised to them. It further appears that these choices are widely affected, not alone by the choice object itself or by advertising and propaganda about it, but also by other people. The individual often decides to purchase or to vote or to look at television programs *with* trusted other people, rather than *for* a particular brand or candidate or program. Thus his reactions are not random relative to the reactions of these others. His perceptions and his responses form part of a pattern of interactions and mutual orientations among all the members of the group.

By focusing on the recipient's place within such a pattern, reference-group theory points the way toward an extension of the tra-

[44] Leon Festinger, "Informal Social Communication," *Psychol. Rev.*, 57 (1950), 271-82.

[45] See, for example, Bernard R. Berelson, Paul F. Lazarsfeld, and William N. McPhee, *Voting: A Study of Opinion Formation in a Presidential Campaign*, University of Chicago Press, 1954, p. 148, *passim*.

ditional approach in the direction of a larger sociological view. Figure 1 begins to suggest the nature of this emerging view. The arrow from C (the communicator) to R (the recipient) indicates the traditional focus. The sociological approach makes its first contribution to the model by taking into account the connections between R and the many primary groups with which he interacts, which shape his values, sanction his behavior, and, accordingly, impinge upon his role as a recipient in relation to C.

FIGURE 1

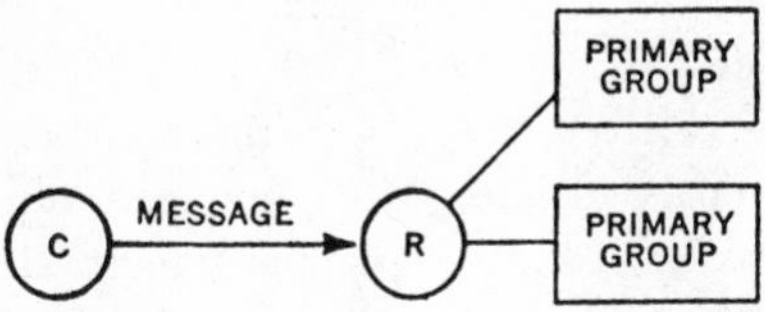

Some Further Problems. Yet, the use of this reference-group concept in research has scarcely begun. The beginnings are sufficient, however, to raise a number of fairly clear-cut questions for further study. Merton, in his detailed analysis of work on reference groups and social structure, has done a great deal to clarify the general problems at hand.[46] With specific reference to the field of mass communications, we can identify some of the types of question that seem to require attention at this time, such as: How is the recipient's reaction to a mass communication related to his membership (or coveted membership) in a *single* primary group? How does this reaction vary, on the one hand, with his positive or negative feelings toward the members of this group and, on the other hand, with his agreement or disagreement with their values? How does it vary with his status in the group and the particular role he is expected to perform? How does his reference group seem to affect his reactions to different types of communication—those intended to inform, persuade, and commit him to action, and those intended merely to entertain and provide him with food for fantasy? Moreover (a far more complicated question), how does he respond when he must react to a message in multiple roles as a member of conflicting reference groups? How does his reaction vary with the relative significance of these groups to him, with the

[46] *Social Theory and Social Structure*, Chap. 9. See also Merton and Kitt, *op. cit.*

relative degree of his positive or negative feelings toward them, and so on?

Much of the methodological framework is already at hand for research on such questions. Yet, since the notion of reference group is a subtle one, often implying a mechanism which operates below the awareness of the recipient, new measurements and new experimental controls will have to be worked out.

Answers to such questions should go far toward locating the recipient in the social structure, but they will serve primarily to locate him in relation only to his diverse primary groups.[47] They cannot in themselves fully describe the structure within which mass-communicated messages are received, for, just as the audience is not composed of discrete individuals, neither is it composed of discrete primary groups. These smaller, solidary groupings must also be viewed in their interdependence with one another and as belonging to some still more inclusive system. By analogy, the economist does not (cannot) account for depressions merely by studying the personal inefficiency of given individuals or the reduced incentives for wage-earning in given families. Nor did Durkheim account for societal differences in the suicide rate as exclusively a function of personal motivation or of family integration. In both instances, the relevant theory also invokes wider structures and longer-term changes which include and also transcend the individual or the primary group as such.

The Recipient and the Larger Social Structure

Concomitant with such studies of the individual recipient and his primary groups, a quite different and less developed line of research has begun to explore the more inclusive structure of social organizations and institutions which surrounds the recipient. For, if the recipient's role is affected by the values and goals of his diverse primary groups, how do these groups themselves derive such values and goals? How are the primary groups related to one another? How are they integrated within the more embracing social structure and process?

[47] The reference-group approach is not by definition limited to primary groups; it applies also to larger, more distant social groupings, as the next section indicates. As effective reference groups, however, the primary groups, with which the individual is most closely associated, seem to have the most compelling hold upon him.

Because this larger structure transcends both the individual and his primary groups, many of the pertinent studies have their major focus, not on R (as in most reference-group research), but on the structure itself. That is, they do not start with the individual recipient and work outward through his primary groups, hoping thereby to piece together the complex network within which these groups are intertwined and interdependent. Instead, they start with the larger structure, examining first the relationships of the primary groups to the larger structure and to one another, and finally seeking the recipient's place within the whole. (Ultimately, these two complementary approaches should dovetail.)

Studies of Formal Organizations. A number of studies in other fields illustrate the fruitfulness of this focus on the structure itself. The classic Western Electric investigations, for example, deal with the industrial plant as a social system made up of interrelated parts. This system is composed of a technical organization and a human organization, each of which affects the other. The human organization, in turn, is subdivided into formal and informal social organizations. Within such a system, research observations indicate the processes through which the informal groupings of friends and coworkers may function either to support or to detract from the formal organization's goal of efficient productivity.[48] In a somewhat similar fashion, studies of the combat behavior of American troops in World War II examine the formal organization which achieves its goals by ordering men to fight, and within this the informal organizations of friends which, because of the common threat, shared ideals of manliness, and the like, reinforce the goals of the formal system. As Williams and Smith conclude, "Affective ties binding the group together were important in keeping men in combat because, among other reasons, the group through its formal organization was inextricably committed to the fight: anything that tied the individual to the group therefore kept him in combat."[49]

[48] See, for example, F. J. Roethlisberger and William J. Dickson, *Management and the Worker*, Harvard University Press, 1940.

[49] Robin M. Williams, Jr., and M. Brewster Smith, "General Characteristics of Ground Combat," in Samuel A. Stouffer *et al.* (eds.), *The American Soldier, Studies in Social Psychology in World War II*, Vol. II, Princeton University Press, 1949, p. 100.

A Study of Propaganda. The prototype of studies of this type in the mass-communication field is perhaps the evaluation by Shils and Janowitz of the impact of propaganda by the Western Allies on the fighting effectiveness of the German Army in World War II.[50] Contrary to earlier views of propaganda as a panacea, their findings did not reveal that the invocation of adverse political, ideological, and cultural symbols produced any sweeping disaffection or collapse in military morale. Nor did they reveal that the extraordinary tenacity of the *Wehrmacht* was due primarily to the political convictions of the German soldier—to his direct attachment to the Nazi system itself as a reference group, as it were. They showed, rather, that his resistance to Allied propaganda and his sustained motivation to fight rested upon the persistence of the primary-group structure of the component units of the army. These analysts concluded that only when the primary groups themselves start to dissolve does propaganda (and then only certain kinds of propaganda) facilitate disintegration.

This study merits careful attention, since it seems to illustrate an important, but little exploited, approach to the study of the social structure within which mass communications are received. In order to account for the stability of the Army and its resistance to propaganda against its norms, Shils and Janowitz began with an investigation of the basic military organization and its relationship to the system of primary groups. They examined the process by which the goals of the larger bureaucratic structure were met by the functioning of smaller groups of friends, suggesting a number of linkages between the Army and these smaller groups. For example, membership in the informal social group was seen to coincide roughly with membership in the military squad. Both the larger structure and the primary group are exposed to the same external danger and share the same ideal of soldierly honor. The small but hard core of Nazis, as well as the paternally protective NCO's and junior officers, served as mediators, or linking persons, between the primary group and the Army. Moreover, the larger system was observed to exercise various controls over the smaller. Not only did the *Wehrmacht* exert authority through its officers, it also deliberately manipulated various factors affecting small-

[50] Edward A. Shils and Morris Janowitz, "Cohesion and Disintegration in the Wehrmacht in World War II," *Pub. Opin. Quart.*, 12 (1948), 280-315.

group solidarity. For example, it maintained in the same units men who had gone through a victory together and who shared the same recollections. It warned deserters of severe sanctions. It prevented family groups from weakening its own hold on the men by issuing strict injunctions against references to family deprivations in letters to the front. At the same time, it encouraged letters which would re-duce the men's anxieties about their families and give the supple-mentary affection which the army unit could not provide.

Within this social structure and ongoing social process, Shils and Janowitz examined the ties between the individual soldier and his group of friends and finally analyzed the fundamental indifference of the troops to the millions of Allied leaflets and the continuous Allied broadcasts. Small wonder that the German soldier, bound to his fel-lows by spatial proximity, intimate association, and the military or-ganization itself, paid little heed to Allied propaganda (even when he believed it) which exhorted him to desert his friends or abandon their goals! It is in this sense that R's response may be understood: first in terms of his primary groups, and secondly in terms of the larger organization in which these groups are implanted.

Primary and Secondary Reference Groups. Studies with this structural focus ultimately lead back, of course, to the individual re-cipient of the message and his reference groups. (They deal with the same problem as reference-group studies, merely approaching it from another level.) In general, the relevant studies of the recipient tend to distinguish between his relationships to the larger, secondary sys-tem and to his primary groups. Thus the worker's productivity is viewed as the outcome of his relationships both to the formal struc-ture of the plant and to his fellow workers. The individual soldier's willingness to fight is explainable both through his relationship to the army and through his affectional ties to his buddies and his unwilling-ness to let them down. (Of course, this is merely a re-emphasis of an old insight: as early as the first Christian century, Tacitus, in the *Germania,* explained the bravery of the barbarian hordes through the presence of their families with them on the battlefield.)

The findings of such studies seem to converge in emphasizing the great importance of the primary reference group within the larger reference system. A study of the reasons given by refugees for fleeing the Communist regime in North Korea reports, for example, that "the ideological repugnance to communism . . . runs a poor second to the more impelling consideration that the system has marked a member of the family for liquidation or imprisonment." [51] Accordingly, it seems that the recipient of a mass-communicated message is rarely reached directly in his role as an anonymous and isolated member of a bureaucracy or of a mass society. His receipt of this message is, rather, "mediated" through the close, informal groupings to which he also belongs.

Studies of Election Campaigns. If studies like the one by Shils and Janowitz seem to be successful in dealing with this important problem of the relations between the recipient and the environing social structure as it bears upon his role in the mass-communication process, their success is doubtless due in part to their use of a type of social structure which is manageable in research. The military structure, as well as the structure of the industrial plant, has a clearly specified formal organization which affords a firm framework within which primary groups may be located and communications traced. Moreover, an army or a factory, although it may be large, is by no means so unwieldy for the researcher as a whole society. How, indeed, is the researcher to cope with larger, less explicitly formulated social structures, or with the whole society? If he does recognize that the voting public, for example, or the market for a consumer product, is not an atomistic "mass," how is he to determine what its structure is, so that he can observe the process of mass communication within it?

Some work on the voter—the recipient of the political campaign message—might suggest the general character of a sociological approach to the political structure. In the noteworthy last chapter of *Voting,* Berelson, Lazarsfeld, and McPhee write:

> After examining the detailed data on how individuals misperceive political reality or respond to irrelevant social influences, one wonders how a democracy ever solves its political problems. But when one considers the data in a broader perspective—how huge segments of the society adapt to political conditions affecting them or how the political system adjusts itself to changing conditions over long periods of time

[51] John W. Riley, Jr., Wilbur Schramm, and Frederick W. Williams, "Flight from Communism: A Report on Korean Refugees," *Pub. Opin. Quart.,* 15 (1951), 277.

—he cannot fail to be impressed with the total result. . . . This suggests that . . . what are undervalued are certain collective properties that reside in the electorate as a whole and in the political and social system in which it functions.[52]

Such "collective properties of the electorate," as propounded and empirically exemplified by these authors, have been elaborated by Parsons in line with his more general theory.[53] He suggests how the primary (or "solidary") groups and the larger political system fit together in a state of mutual interdependence. For example, members of families, friends, occupational and class associates, and fellow members of ethnic and religious groups, all tend to vote in a rather homogeneous fashion. Beyond this, all these groups are caught up in the encompassing political organization. That is to say, the conglomerate of the primary groups is no mere hodge-podge; the groups are, rather, structured in such fashion that each tends to be traditionally aligned with one party or the other. Thus:

. . . at the bottom the process is dependent on the statistical outcome of millions of individual acts. . . . [But] the attachment of the individual to his solidary associations as a voting reference builds the society up in a series of graduated steps to units which can be meaningfully related to the important issues of the day, the realistic alternatives facing the political system as a system. As a structure of political integration the top of this structure is the two national parties.

If small-group homogeneity of political opinion—or of response to political exhortations—provides the individual with social support and the group with harmony, Parsons (in line with the authors of *Voting*) shows how it also fulfills one of the necessary conditions for the successful operation of the democratic two-party system in this country. The fact that people vote as members of groups, and that groups themselves tend to remain stable, ensures a fairly stable division of the electorate into two major parties—thus maintaining the system and thereby providing a balance between the conservatism of the right and the demand of the left for change.

[52] *Op. cit.*, pp. 311-12.
[53] Talcott Parsons, " 'Voting' and the Equilibrium of the American Political System," in Eugene Burdick and Arthur Brodbeck (eds.), *American Voting Behavior*, Free Press, 1959. See also the related discussion in the chapter by Parsons in the present volume.

At the same time, if this political cleavage goes too far, it results in civil war. A second condition of the effective operation of the system is that it remain integrated. This condition is fulfilled only in part by a supraparty loyalty to the government as a whole. In part also it is fulfilled by the fact that the solidary groups are not entirely homogeneous politically—there is a modicum of political division within them. Parsons illustrates this from the point of view of an individual voter: "My fellow union member . . . who is intending to vote Republican . . . is in general a pretty decent guy. I just can't see how all people who hold his views can be so terrible as the party orators say they are." Accordingly, since not *all* the members of a group always vote alike, their common group membership holds them together and prevents any drastic political division from developing between them." [54]

In the third place, the political system cannot operate effectively without a degree of flexibility: from time to time the opposition party must have a chance to win, and there must be opportunity for new goals to be attained. This condition is met by the fact that a certain proportion of voters do not remain loyal, but shift their party allegiance. This shifting arises, not only because entire groups change their alignment, but also in large part because of the cross-pressures placed on individuals by groups with conflicting party allegiance.

If, on the basis of such leads as these, a clearer model of the larger system is developed, within which primary groups are organized and the individual voter responds to campaigns, this would appear to have important further implications for an understanding of mass communication. The voting studies show, for example, that exposure to election campaigns through the mass media not only seems to heighten the interest of voters but also strengthens the relative importance of political, as compared with social, factors in this interest. [55] Thus the influence of a campaign (reinforced by the influence of the opinion leaders) is to line voters up behind one candidate or the other and at the same time to inhibit any concern over

[54] For an earlier discussion of propaganda and consensus versus heterogeneity in the audience, see Robert K. Merton and Paul F. Lazarsfeld, "Studies in Radio and Film Propaganda," in Merton, *Social Theory and Social Structure*, pp. 509-28.

[55] See Berelson, Lazarsfeld, and McPhee, *op. cit.*, pp. 34, 252.

the specific and particularistic demands of their smaller social groupings; the apparent effect, that is, is toward two-party integration of
the political system in this country, rather than toward a fragmenta-
tion along primary-group lines.[56]

Toward a Sociological View. Such scattered empirical findings,
together with such developing theory, begin to specify the place in the
working model of the individual recipient, as he is attached to primary
groups which are, in turn, systematically related to the larger structure
("by diverse patterns of ties," as Shils puts it in a recent paper).[57] The
processes which occur among individuals within primary groups contribute to the functioning of the more inclusive process; and conversely,
the individual's actions tend to be channelled not only by his relationship to his significant reference groups but also by the alignments of
these reference groups within the larger structure. Thus, it appears that
mass-communicated messages reach individuals whose group members and group references themselves have determinate interrelationships. In Figure 2, which shows this further elaboration of the developing sociological view, the circle represents the larger social structure within which R's smaller groupings tend to be integrated and
patterned with reference to one another.

FIGURE 2

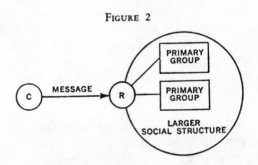

Some Further Problems. For the present, however, a great
many challenging and basic questions remain to be answered. If the

[56] It might be instructive to test this model against the situation in
other countries—for example, France.

[57] Edward A. Shils, "Primordial, Personal, Sacred and Civil Ties," *Brit.
J. Sociol.*, 8 (1957), 135.

"collective properties of the electorate" have been isolated and formulated as a theoretical model, can similar models be formulated of the larger structures within which the consumer responds to advertising, or the student to teaching? How can such models be clarified through further theoretical analysis and tested through further research? If it has been demonstrated that much can be learned by observing the effects of mass communication within a formal structure, would not similar structures lend themselves to observation and experiment in order to test, revise, and supplement the earlier findings? Or, returning to the individual recipient, what more can be learned about his relationship to his primary groups as contrasted with his relationship to the larger structure? Under what conditions does the primary group appear to be the more effective of the two in guiding his response?

In order to answer such questions, further advances in available research methods seem also to be required. The major research unit, in studies of a social system, may be either the system or the individual within it. Using a system approach, the Western Electric investigations indicate the feasibility of experimentation in the study of corporate structures; the *Wehrmacht* analysis shows the advantages of focusing on a system which is at a critical point of rapid process or change. Yet this major research focus on the system often presents difficulties. Shils and Janowitz solve these problems by supplementing the data obtained from individuals with "captured enemy documents, statements of recaptured Allied military personnel, and the reports of combat observers." [58] In view of the patent value of documents and the testimony of "experts" in system analysis, the development of rigorous procedures for the use of such materials would appear highly desirable.

The alternative method consists of collecting and fitting together data about individual members within the structure. But such a method often requires that established procedures of sampling individuals give way to the study of *all* the individuals within the group in order to uncover the crucial bonds in the network of interrelationships.[59] Moreover, once the individual data have been ob-

[58] *Op. cit.*, p. 282.

[59] See, for example, George A. Lundberg and Margaret Lawsing, "The Sociography of Some Community Relations," *Amer. sociol. Rev.*, 2 (1937),

tained, they cannot merely be aggregated. Here the usual group measures using the mean and variance of individual responses may lose their applicability. Statistics based on the assumption of independent individual data are often inappropriate. New methods of measurement and analysis are needed which will fit together data about individuals so as to represent the integrated pattern for the group.[60]

As appropriate methods are developed, some answers will be found to the basic questions about the pressure upon the recipient of the environing social structure and process. These answers will certainly point to the inadequacies of any model of mass communication which takes a sociological view only of the receipt of the communication, of the social structure surrounding the recipient. The communication process clearly has ramifications beyond the individual recipient and his structure. This process includes, of course, the communicator as well as the recipient. And the communicator too, whether individual or organized group, is located within a structure of social relationships.

The Communicator

A vast literature deals with the relationship between the communicator and his social environment. Countless analyses of the creative writer or artist treat him as the product of his historical epoch or of his family setting.[61] Treatises from Milton's *Areopagitica* to Schramm's re-

---

318-35. Some of the critical findings (such as that one sociometric star was attached to a single other person—a "power-behind-the-throne") might have been obscured if only a sample of the community had been used. See also the important article by Harry Alpert, "Some Observations on the Sociology of Sampling," *Soc. Forces*, 31:1 (1952), 30-33, which emphasizes "the importance of introducing considerations of social structure into the development of sampling designs for surveys involving social organizations" (p. 31).

[60] For an extended discussion of this problem, see Matilda White Riley, John W. Riley, Jr., Jackson Toby, *et al.*, *Sociological Studies in Scale Analysis*, Rutgers University Press, 1954, esp. Part III. See also John W. Riley, Jr., Matilda White Riley, Richard Cohn, and Jackson Toby, "Comment on Strodtbeck's Review of 'Scale Analysis,'" in J. L. Moreno (ed.), *Sociometry and the Science of Man*, Beacon House, 1956.

[61] For a recent discussion, see the chapter in the present volume by James Barnett.

cent *Responsibility in Mass Communication* [62] have discussed such topics as formal censorship *vs.* self-regulation, the monopoly of channels by groups in selected economic positions, and the social pressures toward the commercialization of mass-produced art. Like the recipient, the communicator has a cognitive structure through which he screens his perceptions and choices; he too has personal friends and reference groups; he too is part of a larger social structure made up of business concerns or manufacturers' associations or labor or farm or veterans' groups.

The Social Structure Surrounding the Communicator. A model of the social structure as it affects the initiator of mass communications is implied within the venerable tradition of the sociology of knowledge. This field of inquiry, which deals with "the entire gamut of cultural products (ideas, ideologies, juristic and ethical beliefs, philosophy, science, technology)" seeks: ". . . the social determinants of the intellectual's [the communicator's] perspectives, how he came to hold his ideas. . . . The student of mass communications, on the other hand, has almost from the beginning been concerned primarily with the *impact* of the mass media *upon* the audiences. . . . The one centers on the source, the other on the result." [63] In his paradigm for the classification of the many findings already existent in this field, Merton's list of the "social bases for mental productions" might well be used to indicate the major group affiliations and structural contexts which affect the behavior of the mass communicator. [64]

Although Merton's own studies in the sociology of science illustrate the fruitfulness of this approach, which has the special asset of reaching back into the historical past, there have been few explicit attempts to utilize in systematic field research such a model of the communicator's place within the social structure. A few case studies, such

[62] Wilbur Schramm, Harper, 1957.

[63] Merton, *Social Theory and Social Structure*, pp. 439*ff.*, 450, 456.

[64] This list includes "social position, class, generation, occupational role, mode of production, group structures (university, bureaucracy, academies, sects, political parties), 'historical situation,' interests, society, ethnic affiliation, social mobility, power structure, social processes (competition, conflict, etc.)" (*Ibid.*, p. 460).

as those of the movie-makers by Rosten or Powdermaker,[65] tie output to the communicator's place in a social system, but work on the whole has been scattered.

Of possible relevance for an understanding of the mass communicator are various studies dealing with communicative behavior as a form of control in groups. Williams, for example, in a summary of research on disaster,[66] describes the process by which the larger system of a community, confronted by a flood or a tornado, fails to communicate to the populace the information which is needed for proper control. No adequate communication processes or channels exist in the crisis to control the unprecedented flow of supplies and manpower, to prevent traffic congestion, to distribute patients to hospitals, and the like. At the same time, as private citizens rush in to rescue relatives and friends, primary-group communications tend to increase. Urgent personal messages are relayed, not merely by word-of-mouth, but also through emergency private use of the community's communications channels. Although this may prove functional for the immediate rescue and welfare task, it interferes with communication at the community level, resulting in confusion. Thus the private communicator seems temporarily to usurp the role of the large-system communicator. In this way, Williams locates this large-system communicator within a social structure, much as Shils and Janowitz locate the recipient within the cohesive organization of the *Wehrmacht*.

Feedback to the Communicator. To be sure, community communications of the sort investigated by Williams are not limited to mass communications; a good deal of direct response from the recipient, or "feedback," is possible in such situations. Yet the very emphasis of the findings upon the importance of the flow of communication, *to* as well as *from* the communicator, underscores the significance of the restrictions on feedback within the mass-communication process. Williams'

[65] Leo C. Rosten, *Hollywood: the Movie Colony, the Movie Makers,* Harcourt, Brace, 1941; Hortense Powdermaker, *Hollywood the Dream Factory,* Little, Brown, 1950.

[66] Harry B. Williams, "Communication and Control in Disaster: An Interpretation," paper delivered at the annual meetings of the American Sociological Society, 1957.

analysis, for example, building on the work of Homans [67] and on modern "communication theory," [68] stresses the need of the community system itself for feedback information about the outcome of its previous messages, which would indicate what its next steps should be in attempting to control the environment. Thus, one of the major impairments wrought in the communication system by disaster is the cutting off of the communicator's own sources of information.

Observations of much smaller groups, such as a street-corner gang or a problem-solving group in a laboratory, seem also to imply that the function of the chief communicator or leader is not only to initiate but also to receive a large share of the interpersonal communication. Bales, for example, has found that, as the size of the task group increases from three to eight men, the top man tends to initiate a larger and larger share of the total communication, and also to address more and more of his remarks to the group as a whole rather than to specific individuals. Thus one might say that the largest of his small groups begins to approximate an audience being addressed by a mass communicator. Interestingly enough, Bales concludes:

> If the situation is one in which *inter*-action is expected by the participators, however, there would seem to be a ceiling on the amount of participation for the top man. . . . Even if the top man is initiating most of the action, he still has to expect that he will receive a "feedback of reactions," of both a positive and a negative sort, that will tend to equal the amount of action he initiates.[69]

In the study of mass communications, however, relatively little explicit attention has been paid to this element of feedback to the communicator. Yet even here, a degree of feedback clearly tends to exist—scant, indirect, and obscure though it may be. Some kind of reciprocal channel is needed if the communicator is to learn whether and how his message was received, if he is to have any basis for sending further messages. Perhaps the mass response may consist merely of in-

[67] George C. Homans, *The Human Group*, Harcourt, Brace, 1950, esp. pp. 461-62.

[68] See Claude Shannon and Warren Weaver, *The Mathematical Theory of Communication*, University of Illinois Press, 1949.

[69] Robert F. Bales, "Some Uniformities of Behavior in Small Social Systems," in Guy E. Swanson, Theodore M. Newcomb, and Eugene L. Hartley (eds.), *Readings in Social Psychology*, Henry Holt, 1952, p. 155.

creased listening to the program, or increased purchase of the product advertised, or reduction of the enemy's will to fight in line with a psychological warfare message. To be sure, advertisers give careful scrutiny to resultant sales, just as actors, editors, and presidents pay strict heed to their fan mail; [70] but more research seems needed on the impact of such scrutiny upon the communicator. For, as the Hartleys point out, "If the communication is at all successful, the audience responds in some way, and its response affects future communications." [71]

Toward a Sociological View. Thus the communicator emerges as part of a larger pattern, sending his messages in accordance with the expectations and actions of other persons and groups within the same system. As a political communicator, he may act with reference to the other members of his party and the other citizens in his community; as a copy writer, he may act as an employee of an advertising agency sponsored by a particular manufacturing client. Figure 3 adds to the developing sociological model by suggesting schematically the social structure within which the communicator, as well as the recipient, is placed. Moreover, the two-directional arrows connecting C's structure

FIGURE 3

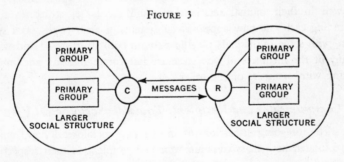

with R's indicate that the communicator is always acting (with more or less conscious intent) in relation to the recipient and to the recipient's probable response. In Mead's words, the effective speaker: ". . . assumes the attitude of the other individual as well as calling it out in the other. He himself is in the role of the other person whom

[70] See, for example, Leila Sussmann, "FDR and the White House Mail," *Pub. Opin. Quart.*, 20 (1956), 5-16.

[71] Eugene L. Hartley and Ruth E. Hartley, *Fundamentals of Social Psychology*, Knopf, 1952, p. 31.

he is so exciting and influencing. It is through taking this role of the other that he is able to come back on himself and so direct his own process of communication." [72]

Some Further Problems. Further study is needed, however, if the social role of the mass communicator is to be thoroughly understood. Codification of findings from the sociology of knowledge in application to this field has scarcely begun. Few empirical studies attempt to explicate the total social structure surrounding the sender, in line with Blumer's suggestion that the outstanding leader and top-level propagandist (in a social movement, for example) must be located in relation to "the vast structure of agitation on lower levels—the community agitators, the neighborhood organizers, the local officials, the zealots among the rank and file, the average party member discussing his views with friends, acquaintances, relatives, and fellow workers." [73]

Moreover, this discussion of the communicator, with its implication of the interactive character of even the mass-communication process, underscores the impossibility of conceptualizing any single element in the process apart from all the others. As the recipient tends to respond to the communicator, communicator and recipient must be viewed in their mutual relationship. And the larger structures surrounding each one now appear as subsystems of an over-all social system, with some individuals playing parts in both structures,[74] and with many of the members of one structure intercommunicating and interacting with members of the other.

Communicator and Recipient: Toward a Sociological View

The foregoing discussions of an emerging sociological view, which have located both mass communicator and recipient in their respective

[72] George H. Mead, *Mind, Self, and Society,* University of Chicago Press, 1934, p. 254. See also Cottrell's similar stress on the necessity of taking the roles of segments of the audience in Nelson N. Foote and Leonard S. Cottrell, Jr., *Identity and Interpersonal Competence,* University of Chicago Press, 1955.

[73] Herbert Blumer, "Collective Behavior," in Joseph B. Gittler (ed.), *Review of Sociology,* John Wiley, 1957, p. 148.

[74] Of course, in extreme cases, the two structures may be relatively unconnected, as when the communicator belongs to the state department of one country and broadcasts to citizens of a foreign and alien country.

social groupings, lead us back to the relationship between C and R and to the process of mass communication itself. In the first section of this paper, we scrutinized the traditional view of this relationship, with its tendency to atomize the audience and to isolate the communicated message from the social process as a whole. If we re-examine this relationship in light of the developing sociological model, several further aspects seem to emerge clearly.

First, communicator and recipient are now seen as interdependent; their relationship no longer fits the one-way who-to-whom notion.

Secondly, with rare exceptions, this relationship does not consist of a single communication which potentially elicits only a single reply. Any given communication is, rather, one link in a chain of communications which extends over time. This chain, of course, is by no means limited to a simple personal relationship between C and R exclusively, in which C beams his message to R and R replies directly. When the communication is sent by a publishing house, a film studio, or a broadcasting network, there is, as Schramm puts it, "very little *direct* feedback from the receiver to the sender. The destination . . . will very seldom talk back to the radio network or write a letter to the editor." [75] Much of the C-R relationship is, rather, indirect, proliferating through the other members and groups to which C and R belong, so that the message is transmitted from individuals in C's groups to individuals in R's groups who in turn reply.

Thirdly, each of these individuals has a definite position in the social structure. This does not mean merely that C's role in the process, as well as R's, tends to be affected by its social context. Beyond this, these several positions are related to one another within the social system. Thus the several communications which flow from one individual or group to another appear no longer as random or unrelated acts but as elements in a total pattern of ongoing interaction.

Theoretical Specification of the Model. A good deal of theory and a number of research approaches seem already to be available for use in filling in the further details of such a model of the indirect, interactive, proliferated relationship between mass communicator and audience. Parsons, for example, lays the groundwork on which a com-

[75] Wilbur Schramm, *The Process and Effects of Mass Communication,* University of Illinois Press, 1954, p. 19.

munication theory might be built in both the economic and the political fields.[76] He shows a parallelism between these two fields which should be useful in developing a general model for mass communication in all fields. Within his schemes of interchange between firms and household, and between political parties and public, communication—often in the form of mass communication—undoubtedly enters wherever persuasion seems necessary. Thus there are attempts on the part of firms to persuade households to purchase goods and to provide labor services, while members of households directly or indirectly attempt to persuade firms to pay higher wages or to produce more desirable goods. Similarly, representatives of political parties exhort the public to support their leaders and their specific decisions, while members of the public put pressure behind certain policies and demand more effective leadership.

This initiation of communication by the public to the policy-makers (as distinct from mere feedback) has been explicated in a recent article by Cohen, among others. Consistent with our emphasis on the systemic character of the social environment surrounding the recipient (who in turn acts as communicator), he says: "The kinds of political behavior engaged in by specific groups among the articulate public seem to be partly traceable to some rather stable factors which are internal to such groups, and which are mostly unaffected by kaleidoscopic changes in policy issue or political alignment." [77] Thus, whereas homogeneous groups can agree rather easily on the measures to be advocated in messages to Congressmen or to the Executive, more heterogeneous groups are slower to come to any operational consensus and so impose restrictions on the communications addressed by their spokesmen.

Codification of Available Knowledge. Although considerable theory is at hand for a two-way mass-communication model, the matching substantive information seems to require much codification, as well as supplementation through further research. In the economic sphere, for

[76] For the former, see Talcott Parsons and Neil J. Smelser, *Economy and Society, A Study in the Integration of Economic and Social Theory,* Free Press, 1956. For the latter, see " 'Voting' and the Equilibrium of the American Political System," *loc. cit.*

[77] Bernard C. Cohen, "Political Communication on the Japanese Peace Settlement," *Pub. Opin. Quart.*, Spring 20 (1956) 27-38.

example, much mass communication might be said to operate practically on the basis of just such a model as we propose, a model in which C's groups and R's interact and are parts of a larger system with determinate relationships. Marketing at its best, for example, regards the consumer as a member of a household, a socioeconomic class, a region. It takes the response of the consumer into account through analysis of audience and sales statistics by regions and over time. By conducting surveys, it provides channels through which consumers may initiate requests for new or improved products. It utilizes wage and cost-of-living indices, recognizing that payments by producers provide buying power for consumers. And yet, although marketers have almost certainly had much experience with the interactive C-R model,[78] little of the substance of this experience has been set down. A good deal of the knowledge being acquired is not being fed into the academic disciplines which build theories and conduct basic research on mass communication. What seems needed here (as guarded secrets lose their competitive timeliness) is a sociological re-analysis of selected commercial cases in which mass communication may be observed as an element in an interactive, ongoing process between producer and consumer.

Content Analysis. Quite another approach to the C-R relationship utilizes the content of communication in order to make inferences about the nature of the ongoing interaction. Here again, small-group research uncovers findings about interpersonal communication which have possible relevance for the mass-communication system. (It often seems instructive to use the small group as a basis for comparison in studying the larger system, with its complex structure and its restrictions on reciprocal action. In this way, it may be possible to discover how mass communication differs from face-to-face conversation, or to specify the conditions under which these differences may be functional or dysfunctional for the system. Moreover, since the small group lends itself as a system to observation, its study suggests modes and procedures of analysis which may be adaptable to large-system research.)

In a relevant set of small-group studies, Bales has developed a distinction between "instrumental" communication, in which instructions are given or information conveyed, and "expressive" communica-

[78] See, for example, Hans Zeisel (ed.), *The Frontiers of Market Research*, Harper, forthcoming.

572 Selected Applications of Sociology

tion, through which tensions are released and group solidarity restored. He suggests that the processs of interpersonal communication consists of instrumental acts, through which the group may pursue its goals but which place strains upon its members, alternating with expressive acts, which ease such strains and tend to re-establish the equilibrium. A proper balance between instrumental and expressive activity seems necessary to the maintenance of the system. Bales also has found that two kinds of "leaders" are likely to emerge in each small task group to take care of these two functions: a social-emotional, expressive leader, or "popular" man, and an instrumental leader, who guides the group and provides ideas for it.[79]

Sutton and his associates deal with this same problem of intercommunication in a study of the American business creed, which illustrates another approach at the level of the large system and a quite different method of content analysis.[80] The public messages issued by business leaders are seen, on the one hand, to form a "patterned reaction to the patterned strains of a social role" (p. 307)—to emanate from C as a member of business and other groups. On the other hand, those businessmen who receive these messages use them as a guide to action. The ideology, as the authors point out (p. 383), serves to promote solidarity among the divergent elements of the business community. Presumably R, receiving the messages as a member of his groups, demands (perhaps even participates in) further communication of similar sort. Thus the given set of messages under study appear as merely one link in a chain of continuing interactions. This example typifies the adaptation of content analysis to the tracing of the broader processes of interactive communication—as the ideas of some people influence other people, who in turn exert further influence, through the course of historical time.

The Recipient as Active Participant. Research might also study the individual roles of C and R in communication conceived as an interactive process. Communication in general is ordinarily defined by so-

[79] Robert F. Bales, "The Equilibrium Problem in Small Groups," in Talcott Parsons, Robert F. Bales, and Edward A. Shils, *Working Papers in the Theory of Action*, Free Press, 1953, pp. 111-61.

[80] Francis X. Sutton, Seymour E. Harris, Carl Kayser, and James Tobin, *The American Business Creed*, Harvard University Press, 1956, pp. 305ff. See also pp. 271-73.

ciologists as a form of interaction between two or more persons. According to Davis, for example, one person first infers from the behavior of another the idea or feeling that the other is trying to convey. He then responds, not to the behavior as such, but to the inferred idea or feeling. The other person in turn reacts to this response in terms of the idea or feeling—the meaning—behind it.[81]

In line with this general definition of communication, our earlier discussion of C has indicated that the flow of communication to the mass communicator (as well as from him) may be functional for the process. Does the model also require that the recipient send messages as well as accept them? Are there any indications, for example, that his active participation may likewise contribute to the effectiveness of the process? A number of loosely related studies seem to provide certain clues here. There is some experimental evidence, for example, that the recipient is more apt to be influenced by a message when he is given a role as an active communicator. Lewin has demonstrated that group discussion may be more effective than one-way lectures in changing food habits.[82] Coch and French found higher production rates and less quitting and aggression among factory employees when job and rate changes were discussed through group participation rather than announced through lectures.[83] Hovland reports a finding which might be interpreted to mean that persuasion is enhanced when the recipient participates, even indirectly, by handing on the message: as the researchers say, "When exposure . . . is held constant, individuals who are required to verbalize the communication aloud to others will tend to be more influenced than those who are passively exposed." [84]

Other researches shed further light on the interactive role of the recipient by describing his feelings in various small-group situations. Bavelas shows, for example, in task groups set up to communicate in writing through prescribed channels, that persons in relatively isolated positions are less satisfied with their roles than more centrally located

[81] Kingsley Davis, *Human Society,* Macmillan, 1949, pp. 149-50.

[82] Kurt Lewin, "Studies in Group Decision," in Dorwin Cartwright and Alvin Zander (eds.), *Group Dynamics: Research and Theory,* Row, Peterson, 1953, pp. 287-301.

[83] Lester Coch and John R. P. French, Jr., "Overcoming Resistance to Change," *Hum. Relat., 1* (1948), 512-32.

[84] Hovland *et al., Communication and Persuasion,* p. 278.

persons.[85] A recent review of small-group research reports that "apparently one-way communication prevents not only expressive catharsis, but also the opportunity for building new understandings and norms by which the members manage their social relationships and their process of communication." [86]

It may be that the receiver responds more readily to a mass communication if he is given even the illusion of participation. In Aristotle's view of Greek tragedy, the actors, through their "imitation of the universal," allow the spectators to identify directly with the interaction on the stage. In this sense, the basis for *katharsis* becomes a kind of pseudo-participation by the spectators. Merton's analysis of Kate Smith's remarkable success in selling war bonds perhaps implies that the listener perceives the radio performance as a mutual relationship in which, as it were, "Kate is wearing herself out in this marathon broadcast because she expects me to purchase—if I fail to buy bonds, she will be disappointed—but if I do buy, she'll see the sales figures mounting and will express her pleasure over the radio—her pleasure, in turn, will make me feel that I did the right thing."

The Paths of Communication. Still another approach to the mass-communication process traces the course along which information or influence flows from one person and group to another. Dodd has developed a model for studying the many successive steps in the process whereby the original recipients of a mass-communicated message, or "knowers," might be expected to tell others, who in turn become "knowers" and tell still others, and so on.[87]

[85] Alex Bavelas, "Communication Patterns in Task-Oriented Groups," in Daniel Lerner and Harold D. Lasswell (eds.), *The Policy Sciences*, Stanford University Press, 1951.

[86] Robert F. Bales, A. Paul Hare, and Edgar F. Borgatta, "Structure and Dynamics of Small Groups: A Review of Four Variables," in Gittler, *op. cit.*, p. 404.

[87] Stuart C. Dodd, "Diffusion Is Predictable," *Amer. sociol. Rev.*, 20 (1955), 392-401. See also Delbert C. Miller, "A Research Note on Mass Communication," *Amer. sociol. Rev.*, 10 (1945), 691-94; and Otto N. Larsen and Richard J. Hill, "Mass Media and Interpersonal Communication in the Diffusion of a News Event," *Amer. sociol. Rev.*, 19 (1954), 426-33. For a recent diffusion study which contains an excellent overview of the litera-

Of central importance here is the series of studies conducted by Lazarsfeld and his associates which traces the flow of influence (on voting behavior, purchasing, movie selection, and the like) through the social structure within which the recipient is imbedded.[88] Katz, for example, speaks of the "networks of interconnected individuals through which mass communications are channeled," thus replacing the traditional image of the audience as "a mass of disconnected individuals hooked up to the media but not to each other." [89] These studies investigate a "two-step flow of influence" from the mass communicator through the "opinion leader" to the other members of the group. Merton elaborates this notion of opinion leaders as recipients, comparing the mass-media exposure of "local influentials," who are the center of the web of primary-group relationships within the community, and "cosmopolitan influentials," who serve as the connecting links between the community and the outside world.[90] Such studies point to the ultimate sociological view of the mass-media audience as a composite of recipients who are related to one another, and whose responses are patterned in terms of these relationships.[91]

---

ture, see Melvin L. DeFleur and Otto N. Larsen, *The Flow of Information: An Experiment in Mass Communication*, Harper, 1958.

[88] Lazarsfeld, Berelson, and Gaudet, *op. cit.*; Berelson, Lazarsfeld, and McPhee, *op. cit.*; Elihu Katz and Paul F. Lazarsfeld, *Personal Influence: The Part Played by People in the Flow of Mass Communications*, Free Press, 1955.

[89] Elihu Katz, "The Two-Step Flow of Communication: An Up-to-date Report on an Hypothesis," *Pub. Opin. Quart., 21* (1957), 61. This article provides an excellent overview of this line of activity.

[90] Robert K. Merton, "Patterns of Influence: A Study of Interpersonal Influence and Communications Behavior in a Local Community," in Lazarsfeld and Stanton (eds.), *Communications Research, 1948–49*, pp. 180-219. Cf. Shils' "diverse patterns of ties" to the larger structure, as mentioned above.

[91] This understanding of the function of networks of interpersonal relationships for the flow of influence seems to have been set forth originally by Moreno. As early as 1934, he wrote that "news, gossip, ideas [and so on] . . . pass . . . through the networks. . . . It is through these channels that people affect [and] educate . . . one another. . . . These networks are the kitchens of public opinion." (J. L. Moreno, *Who Shall Survive?*, Nervous and Mental Disease Publishing Company, 1934, pp. 262-65.)

In spite of the enormous difficulties of piecing together the social structure from data obtained from cross-section population samples,[92] a great many findings have emerged from this research which contribute to a sociological view. For example, the paths along which influence flows are found to extend within, rather than across, the lines of socio-economic status in the larger community.[93] Moreover, although opinion leaders are generally more exposed than others to the mass media, even "most opinion leaders are primarily affected not by the communication media but by still other people." [94]

A study of this kind typically deals with a particular content as it flows along the path from communicator to opinion leader to any given other individual (R) who is at the receiving end—and here the study ends. Presumably this same path ultimately winds back, however indirectly, to the original communicator. To trace this return path would mean shifting the research focus, since this path undoubtedly carries different content—a positive or negative response, for example, or a question, as in the small-group studies. It is to be hoped that future research on the paths of communication will examine these two-directional aspects further. Such research would come close to utilizing the full dynamic sociological model of the intercommunication between members of C's groupings and of R's.

Mass Communication and the Social System. Figure 4 shows the two interdependent structures of C and of R as aspects of the same wide society and the same secular trend, which is represented by the oval boundary which encompasses them both.[95] The several arrows indicate

[92] Another Columbia study attempts to overcome some of these difficulties by using all, rather than a sample, of the members of the group. This seems feasible in cases like this one where the group is manageably small. James Coleman, Elihu Katz, and Herbert Menzel, "The Diffusion of an Innovation Among Physicians," *Sociometry, 20* (1957), 253-70.

[93] Katz and Lazarsfeld, *op. cit.*

[94] Katz, *op. cit.*, p. 77.

[95] Cf. Mead's early statement that: "The process of communication cannot be set up as something that exists by itself, or as a presupposition of the social process. On the contrary, the social process is presupposed in order to render thought and communication possible" (*op. cit.*, p. 260). Cooley defines communication as the "mechanism through which human relations exist" (Charles H. Cooley, *Social Organization,* Scribner's, 1937, p. 61).

the flow of communication back and forth among the several members of these interdependent structures. Within such an all-embracing system, the mass-communications process is now seen as a component of the larger social process, both affecting it and being in turn affected by it.

FIGURE 4

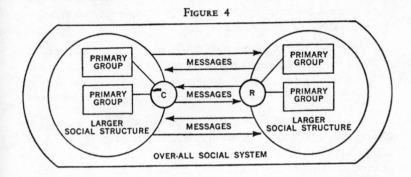

The Need for a Working Model. An understanding of the socio-logical processes through which mass communications take effect thus seems to require the formulation of a working model, based on codification of the empirical findings which are available in several fields, and on application of the relevant theory. In light of such a model, the problems still at hand may be defined. Further studies of these problems may then progress concurrently, so as to throw light on different aspects and from different points of view. The present preliminary sketch suggests that the final list of problems may include such questions as:

How does the mass-communication process fit into the larger social process? At what points is its flow supplemented by the flow of personal communication, for example, or by the transfer of money or goods, or by the movement of people? What functions does mass communication perform for the social system as a whole?

What existing bodies of experience might effectively be codified and brought to bear on the model from the economic, political, and other fields in which mass communication looms large?

What findings from the studies of small groups and personal com-

And Park speaks of it as spinning "a web of custom and mutual expectations which binds together social entities" (Robert E. Park, "Reflections on Communication and Culture," *Amer. J. Sociol.*, 44 [1939], 191).

munication have relevance for an understanding of mass communication? For example, does the apparent small-group balance between instrumental and expressive content imply that, even when the primary purpose of a mass communication is to persuade, there may be resultant strains and tensions unless the communicator provides some form of relief (as through alternating from an instrumental to an expressive role)?

How can various research procedures (including methods of cross-cultural and historical analysis, as well as survey and sociometric techniques) be adapted and systematized for use in the study of mass communication in social systems?

Each finding from further research on such problems, although in itself partial and incomplete, should have its proper place within the unified scheme of the model. Ultimately, in so far as the several findings fit together, mass communication may indeed be viewed as an integral part of the social system.

25
Sociology
as a Teaching
Enterprise

CHARLES H. PAGE
Smith College

This discussion is a consideration of issues which
I believe to be of strategic relevance to the teaching enterprise of sociology, neglecting altogether the important subject of instructional tactics.
Here the principal concern is with certain characteristics of sociology
itself, as they affect the status of sociology in colleges and complicate
the problems of its teaching representatives.

These remarks are not intended to praise, defend, or castigate sociology, although criticism by nonsociologists is a significant matter to be
faced. But most sociologists would agree that the time was reached some
years ago when defensive and offensive postures should be dropped, in
the classroom and elsewhere, in favor of the main tasks of teaching and
research.

The persistence of such postures, however, warrants examination,
for they are not only a frequently annoying feature of sociology in
académe but, together with other patterns to be discussed, they are social
(as well as psychological) phenomena rarely studied by sociologists
themselves. Neglect of this subject is itself an interesting question, especially in view of the large and growing literature in occupational sociology. If sociologists have much to say about managers and ministers,
prostitutes and pugilists, trainmen and jazzmen, warriors and watch-
makers, they are silent about themselves—although, of course, others are

not. Not many, perhaps, would encourage sociologists to imitate the models of psychoanalysis and the ministry, professions in which intense self-investigation is no doubt essential, but the lack of a *sociology* of sociology and sociologists is regrettable.

There are leads, to be sure, some of them stimulated by the European heritage of *Wissenssoziologie*—for example, Florian Znaneicki's *The Social Role of the Man of Knowledge,* published in 1940. In 1942, Logan Wilson's *The Academic Man* provided a study by a sociologist of the college teacher, and recently, in *Constraint and Variety in American Education,* David Riesman has written perceptively about various aspects of the college-teaching enterprise. Useful as they are for the study of academic life, however, these contributions contain only clues for the analysis of the teaching sociologist at work.[1]

This paper merely raises a few of the many questions that might be pursued in such a study of sociological man and his academic environment.[2] Nevertheless, the aim is to depict some major problems encountered by sociologists themselves, by their students and colleagues, and

[1] Willard Waller had collected an enormous amount of material about teachers of sociology during the ten years or so before his untimely death in 1945, as part of a projected full-scale study of sociologists in the United States. Unfortunately, neither his material nor his analytical brilliance is available.

[2] Among the questions which are neglected or merely mentioned in this paper are the "jargon problem" and the low esteem of much sociological writing. The former, I believe, is essentially a tactical matter at the teaching level; in any event, both sociologists and their critics find the specialized terminology of sociology a favorite theme—the literature is extensive but unimportant. The frequent charge that sociological writing is generally undistinguished or worse raises a more important issue for teachers of sociology, especially for those whose "latent social roles" include that of competitor for good students. (The distinction between manifest and latent social roles is developed by Alvin G. Gouldner in "Cosmopolitans and Locals: Toward an Analysis of Latent Social Roles," *Admin. Sci. Quart.,* 2 [1957]. The competitive role of the teaching sociologist is discussed in the final section of this paper.) The "soft flesh of stylistic ornamentation" and "concern with the literary graces" are misplaced, according to Robert K. Merton, in a discipline of scientific aspiration; yet felicity of expression, happy metaphor, and wit mark Merton's own works to a degree unusual in current sociological writing. (See Merton's *Social Theory and Social Structure,* Free Press, 1949, p. 14.)

by educational policy-makers, particularly in colleges of liberal arts. The discussion follows four categories: sociological imperialism; the alliance of sociology with science, the humanities, and social reform; marginality; and sociology's student audience and academic rivals.

Sociological Imperialism

A repeated charge against sociology is that it invades or seeks to invade other scholarly domains.[3] This imperialistic bent may be construed as unseemly arrogance, as naiveté about the demands of scholarship and the general body of established knowledge, or as evidence that sociology in its many-sided quest substitutes thin inclusiveness for solid substance. In this form, each of these charges is a canard, as the record shows, but the history and performance of sociology also give the imperialistic accusation a certain plausibility.

Sociology began as an invader of other fields, especially in the hands of those mighty advocates of a synthetic social science, Comte, Spencer, and Ward. The works of Comte and Spencer, accomplished in the relative freedom of the nonacademic world, imply that sociologists should know every science; Spencer's own system encompasses all of nature, including human society, in both its structural and its dynamic manifestations. Ward's efforts were almost as staggering; on entering teaching, late in his career, he startled his colleagues and students at Brown University by announcing his course in sociology as a survey of all human knowledge.[4] With such men as these, sociology got off to an extraordinarily ambitious start as a venture in intellectual inclusiveness. Heretofore only philosophers—and fools—had attempted so much.

These early giants were philosophers, of course, and men of erudition. But they were not fools. At the very least, they established the possibilities of scientific investigation of social structure and change and

---

[3] Other disciplines, to be sure, are sometimes accused of "imperialism"; see, for example, Calvin W. Stillman, "Academic Imperialism and Its Resolution: The Case of Economics and Anthropology," *Amer. Scient.*, 43 (1955), 77-88. The concern here, however, is with the intrinsic characteristics of sociology (and, to some extent, of cultural anthropology) that encourage this charge.

[4] See Samuel Chugerman, *Lester F. Ward, The American Aristotle*, Duke University Press, 1939, pp. 35-36.

the advantages to be derived from studying society as an interrelated whole. But the exponents of a synthetic sociology, although lavish with all-embracing systems, apt illustrations, and intriguing speculations, added little to confirmed knowledge and produced few tested or testable propositions about society. These tasks were faced by men of another generation—Durkheim and Weber, for example—who gave up the synthetic view in favor of the relatively modest pursuit of precisely defined questions about the role of group life in human affairs and more specific problems of components and relationships in the changing social order. This shift in orientation and greater specification of scholarly effort brought important substance to the field, as well as methodological innovations that continue to preoccupy sociologists and others as well.

In spite of these changes, however, the image of sociology as all-embracing in its aspirations has persisted, and for understandable reasons. For the successors of Durkheim and Weber today, while rejecting a synthetic or inclusive view of sociology, nevertheless employ an approach that often seems to have imperialistic implications. These stem largely from two features, each of which makes sociologists appear to graze in the other fellow's field.

One feature is the way in which sociologists define their central data: as social relationships or social action or group phenomena. Whichever conception is stresssed, their focus—the selective interest—carries them (though by a unique road) into already preëmpted areas of scholarship and teaching. Thus, in explaining to students that "as sociologists we are interested . . . in social relationships not because they are economic or political or religious, but because they are at the same time *social*" and in stressing that "in all else he does, man relates himself to man," sociologists are apt also to warn against the danger of confusing this *focus* with a foolish effort "to study everything that happens 'in society' or under social conditions." [5] But this caution, while signifying a modesty of intention, hardly gainsays the fact that social relationships and social action pervade all institutional and group life, every type of community, informal and formal activities—indeed, areas as diverse and numerous as the human scene provides. To beginners and outsiders, then, the study of social relationships or social action *as such*—and not-

[5] R. M. MacIver and C. H. Page, *Society: An Introductory Analysis*, Rinehart, 1949, p. vi.

withstanding such tidy paradigmatic explanations as Sorokin's [6]—often seems a global and timeless pursuit, unlimited by scholarly conventions.

The relational, interactional, or group focus, moreover, encourages the growth of an ever-increasing number of "sociologies." Thus, like other developed fields, sociology has many subdivisions; there are sociologies of industry, occupations, city life, small groups, deviant behavior, religion, art, and so on.[7] And as specialization advances, as data and theory accumulate, multiplication gains apace, reinforcing the view of sociology as an imperialistic enterprise. The wide-ranging focus and specialization both help in turn to strengthen another image: sociology as a field spread far too thin. All sociologists who have taught introductory courses—or who have examined textbooks designed for such courses [8]—can anticipate this reaction on the part of newcomers to the subject.

[6] P. A. Sorokin, *Society, Culture, and Personality*, Harper, 1947, pp. 6-18; reprinted in L. Wilson and W. L. Kolb (eds.), *Sociological Analysis*, Harcourt, Brace, 1949, pp. 16-30.

[7] For brief discussions of several of the "sociologies" of current importance in this country, see Hans L. Zetterberg (ed.), *Sociology in the United States of America*, Paris: UNESCO, 1956, esp. pp. 43-130.

[8] The thinness, sometimes approaching stark superficiality, of textbooks designed for the introductory course (with a few notable exceptions) is in part a consequence of the authors' understandable effort to "cover the field," an effort that requires wide stretching. But there are other factors at work here, including the propensity of many publishers and some sociologists to seek popularity with intellectually inferior wares in the manner of vendors of much of "popular culture"; the pressure exerted by publishers upon young sociologists to write "student-oriented"—which all too often means watered-down—textbooks (see, *e.g.*, Henry F. Thoma, "Good Morning, Professor, Want to Write a Textbook?" *College English*, 19:2 [1957]); and the related fact that many introductory textbooks are written by relatively immature sociologists or by textbook specialists, whose efforts often appear to be based upon other textbooks (a circularity of feeble, if not vicious, intellectual consequences) and written according to market-tested formulae.

Textbook authorship and performance in general sociology are complex matters which deserve study. One might begin with the observation that of the 20 presidents of the American Sociological Society between 1921 and 1940, 14 have written introductory textbooks, but only one of the 10 between 1948 and 1957. These figures, however, should not obscure the probability that an increasing percentage of teachers are sufficiently well trained

Sociological imperialism is abetted, or often seems to be, by a second and closely related feature of its approach, namely the holistic and functional emphasis which sociology shares with much of anthropology.[9] The use of a semi-organic model and the stress upon functional inter-relationships within whole social and cultural systems are of ancient pedigree but continue today, carrying various implications for both social theory and social practice. But here the significant point is that this orientation (as well as its definition of subject matter) thrusts sociology into areas of human activity and cultural production which have long been viewed as the reservations of established disciplines: political science, economics, literary analysis, and so on. Indeed, when the dynamic aspects of the functional model are in the foreground (currently an all-too-infrequent occurrence), sociologists appear as poachers in the grounds of the mightiest of all, the historians.

Historians, to be sure, cast an even wider net than sociologists, woven of countless subdivisions, each of which has its experts who are apt to view their specializations as restricted scholarly territories.[10] Moreover, whether they are highly specialized or have broader interests, his-

---

to make effective use of books of intellectual merit; some publishers are beginning to recognize this situation by encouraging such textbooks. For many years, the overworked and educationally limited *teacher* was the publisher's primary target, not the student, whose presumed difficulties and deficiencies long served as an excuse for inferior textbooks.

[9] Anthropologists, unlike sociologists, confined their studies for many years to small, remote peoples, of interest to no one except explorers, missionaries, colonial exploiters, and readers of anthropological monographs. The functional-holistic approach was employed in many of these studies, notably by Malinowski and Radcliffe-Brown. Moreover, anthropologists were free "to put all social science to work on the functionally related whole of a single culture" (Robert S. Lynd, *Knowledge for What?* Princeton University Press, 1939, p. 14)—without stepping on toes except those of the "primitives" themselves. Today, however, they study the natives of Jonesville, Old City, Hollywood, Homestead, etc., joining ranks with sociologists, not only in the direction of their interests and methodology, but in entering the preserves of other disciplines. They now face the implications of their traditional claim to represent *the* "science of man."

[10] Some of the consequences of this restriction, especially those stemming from the failure of many historians to make use of sociological methods, are ably discussed by S. M. Lipset in "A Sociologist Looks at History," *Pacif. sociol. Rev.*, 1 (1958), 13-17.

torians are under no strong pressure to explicate their theory. But as the "official" scribes and interpreters of the human record, historians, along with representatives of other traditional fields, are prone to suspect inclusive implications of the sociological approach. Students are exposed to these suspicions, which thus represent an important problem for the teaching sociologist. He may meet this problem by ignoring it, of course, but neither this tactic nor any other should be permitted to reduce his awareness of the situation itself or be used so as to abet the sociologist's insularity in the academic world. Imperialism carries heavy responsibilities.

Science, Humanity, Social Reform

A second set of problems for the teacher stems from sociology's entente with science, the humanities, and social reform. Here, again, the founders of sociology, living in an age when rationality, science, and progress seemed so closely interlinked, established an alliance that has persisted, notwithstanding shifts in leadership and periodic disavowels. Thus, if Comte strove for both a science of society and a better social world, if Marx's "scientific" socialism was a mode of analysis that presumably would help to bring about justice and freedom, so those oft-professed allies of brute fact, Spencer and Sumner, were deeply concerned with moral and ethical questions. Such questions were faced by most of the European contributors, while in the United States they preoccupied a host of sociologists, many of ministerial background.[11] Although this source of sociological personnel has all but dried up, social reformism has by no means disappeared, and sociology itself is used by some of its practitioners—and viewed by many outsiders—as a kind of secular version of an older and currently less fashionable concern with Christian ethics. Insiders themselves, even when dressed in the most austere trappings of science, are by no means immune to either

[11] See, *e.g.*, R. C. Hinkle and G. J. Hinkle, *The Development of Modern Sociology*, Random House, 1954, esp. pp. 1-4, 12-14. In Chaps. 1 and 2 of this volume, the reformistic and scientific aspects of American sociology are clearly sketched, while the humanistic component is suggested by the authors' discussion of neo-positivism and social-action theory in Chap. 3. For a treatment of the scientific-humanistic controversy as it is reflected in methodological issues, by an exponent of the humanistic position, see George Simpson, *Man and Society*, Random House, 1954, Chaps. 4, 6.

the ameliorative tradition or the reformistic challenge. As a British scholar puts it, "In nearly every sociologist there lurks a social reformer, less ambitious but today more practical than Comte." [12]

The identification of sociology with social reform, however, distresses many, if not most, sociologists in this country. Professional and scholarly sensibilities are disturbed when schools of long and noble tradition—for example, Harvard until 1931, Amherst and Williams still—in excluding the subject from the curriculum sometimes explain that sociology is an appropriate study only for young women who may be active in community improvement or who, as amateurs or professionals, may enter social work.[13] Even more irritating is the propensity of the press to refer to deceased philanthropists as "sociologists," thereby linking Rockefeller and Ford with Durkheim and Weber. While these distortions may afford amusement, they are but extreme cases of a persistent and pervasive view of sociology as an ameliorative enterprise.

This view, fairly widespread in academic faculties and among college students, draws many of the latter to classes in sociology, where it functions, moreover, to induce disenchantment when students confront extreme advocacy of a *disinterested* science of social life. Here is a problem for teachers, especially for those who fail to make clear that many sociological scholars of stature conceive of their discipline as scientific, certainly, but nevertheless directly involved in human betterment.

This dual interest, of course, has always marked the social sciences: Adam Smith, we have long been reminded, was a moral philosopher. But the combination of traditional concern with reform and the currently conspicuous efforts to hitch their wagon to the star of science provokes mixed reactions and perplexities among sociologists themselves at times, and frequently among critics and students of sociology.

This situation is further complicated, especially at the college level, by another (and closely related) long-standing division within sociology: between the strictly positivistic and the humanistic conceptions of the field. The first, stressing operationalism and quantification and minimizing or denying a unique quality in human conduct, allies

---

[12] Donald G. MacRae, "Social Theory: Retrospect and Prospect," *Brit. J. Sociol.*, 8:2 (1957), 104.

[13] Note the contrast between the United States and Great Britain, where social work remains the principal vocational goal of most students who concentrate in sociology.

sociology with the biological and physical sciences and rules out flirtations, let alone marriages, with the humanities. The opposing view, in violation of this scientistic taboo, moves sociology in the humanistic direction by conceiving of man as "a goal-seeking, value-creating being . . . distinguished by his capacity to impute meanings to events, objects, and people," [14] and of society and its laws as the product of distinctly human strivings and understandings, of man's successes and failures. The proponents of the latter conception do not, of course, reject the scientific study of social life, but their understanding of the sociological task—in research, writing, and teaching—tends to link them with the humanities. The primary aim of their opponents, "neo-positivists" and others, is unblemished scientific status.[15] Here is a controversy rife with confusion for nonsociological academic folk, whose bewilderment is brought about by a field that sometimes appears to strive to be at once scientific fish, humanistic flesh, and reformistic fowl.

Marginality

These three features of sociology, together with its susceptibility to imperialistic interpretation, contribute to the marginal position of sociology in the academic scheme of things.[16] As teachers, sociologists are marginal men, working in the border areas of other fields and, in their own, shuttling between the solid but often slim lessons of scientific accomplishment and the shakier but exciting questions of application and humane concern. This marginal status is reinforced, moreover, by sociology's preëmption, in the course of its growth, of areas unclaimed by other disciplines. In teaching such leftovers of traditional scholar-

[14] Harry Alpert, "Robert M. MacIver's Contributions to Sociological Theory," in Morroe Berger, Theodore Abel, and Charles H. Page (eds.), *Freedom and Control in Modern Society*, Van Nostrand, 1954, p. 290.

[15] For extreme statements of neo-positivistic and humanistic views, see, respectively, George A. Lundberg, *Foundations of Sociology*, Macmillan, 1939, Part I; and George Simpson, *Science as Morality*, Humanist Press, 1953. Most teaching sociologists, I believe, stand somewhere between these polar positions and many perhaps waver between them. This seems to be the case with some exponents of the currently popular "functionalism" whose empirical emphasis does not always conceal their humanistic—and at times reformistic—bent.

[16] MacRae, *op. cit.*, discusses some aspects of the marginality of sociology and sociologists, especially in Great Britain.

ship as the ubiquitous course in marriage and the family, the curricular
grab-bag of "social problems," and the mushrooming offerings in "human relations" and "small groups," for example, sociologists are often
viewed as *arrivistes*. And, like those of other prosperous newcomers,
both the source and the use of their academic wealth arouse suspicion
and, at times, alarm.

Marginality accounts in part for the diversity of ways in which
sociologists perform their teaching roles: as defenders of the scientific
faith, as "inside dopesters" of social life in general, as relentless pur-
suers of empirical data, as retailers of sweeping theoretical systems, as
free-wheeling commentators on fields other than their own, as demon-
strators and salesmen of "group dynamics," as disinterested social analysts, as concerned social critics. This incomplete listing has no invidious
intent, for each of these role-types and various combinations of them
may be found among both brilliant and inferior teachers. But this diversity of interpretation of the teaching task—rivaled by anthropologists
and psychologists, and for similar reasons—is strongly encouraged by
the multimarginality of the field.[17]

Marginality, then, promotes difficulties. But sociologists, like certain other marginal men, and the subject which they teach also derive
large benefits from this borderline and *parvenu* status. Less restricted
by traditional pressures than others, and prompted by their focus of
interest to seek previously hidden or obscure relationships, sociologists
have opened new paths in the study of man and society.[18] If these paths

[17] Marginality is, of course, only one of several conditions that encourage multiple role-types among teachers of sociology. Ideological orientations, theoretical allegiances, graduate training, kinds of student-client, involvement in research, and other factors influence conceptions of teaching
role. Moreover, like other social roles, the teaching role can be performed
by a wide variety of personalities. It may be the case that the marginality of
sociology is especially attractive to certain personality types—a matter of
no concern here and one about which only speculation is possible at the
present time.

[18] Robert S. Lynd, some years ago, and David Riesman, more recently,
have suggested this function of marginality (as well as other effects). See,
e.g., Lynd, op. cit., Chap. 2; and Riesman's *Thorstein Veblen*, Scribner's,
1953, esp. Chaps. 2, 7; *Constraint and Variety in American Education*, University of Nebraska Press, 1956, esp. pp. 60*ff.*, 101*ff.*; and *Individualism Reconsidered*, Free Press, 1954, Chaps. 9, 10.

at times seem all too familiar and if, as teachers, these sociologists become routineers, they might refresh themselves and their students by re-examining the innovations of such frontiersmen as Durkheim and Marx and Veblen—as a spur to further exploration and a warning against overready acceptance of even the most prestigeful brands of past, or current, social science. Sociology at its best is bold and sometimes disrespectful; not a few of its leaders have been captains of disreputability. We who are teaching privates should not waste this conferred intellectual wealth.

Teachers, however, more and more face the temptations of the psychic security of academic conventions and less and less, it may be argued, appreciate the advantages of marginality. Standardized departmental curricula, textbooks produced according to formula, the frequently deadening experience of prolonged graduate training, ever-stronger pressures to publish regularly, the mounting popularity of sociology in many schools, and booming college enrollments all contribute to the reduction of spontaneity and flexibility in teaching. But in spite of this increasing "bureaucratization"—a trend not peculiar to sociology [19]—the marginal quality of sociology continues to stimulate unorthodoxies of high educational value. Of course, this does not imply that all "off-beat" teachers are educational assets or that all conventional sociological pedagogues are liabilities. The suggestion is, rather, that sociology is a field that can—and often does—prompt intellectual adventure. On this count, at least some sociologists (although only when they themselves are students of more than their own specialization) reign supreme among teachers of the social sciences.

Such teaching superiority requires the curiosity—and the time, alas —to explore sociology's border regions: to study Freud, for example, as well as Weber; to read, say, *Fortune* and *Dissent* as well as the *American Sociological Review;* more, to know some philosophy and fiction and poetry as well as Parsons. Today, this plea for broadly educated sociologists may seem utopian. But surely teachers who are confined by their specializations and limited in their ability to reveal the diverse applicability of sociological analysis—who, in other words, do not exploit the advantages of marginality—restrict the educational possibilities of their discipline.

[19] I have discussed this point at some length in "Bureaucracy and Higher Education," *J. gen. Educ.*, 5 (1951).

These possibilities are more numerous and challenging than ever before. Courses in sociology are multiplying, ranging in subject from religion and child development to nursing and medical practice. A growing number of "area" courses in American society, Soviet Russia, and "underdeveloped" regions employ teaching teams drawn from various fields, providing sociologists with an opportunity to demonstrate the enormous utility of their own discipline, but also, in some measure, testing their command of others as well.

Surpassing these challenges are the "partial incorporation" [20] of sociology and, no less important, its frequent distortion by contributors to popular culture (and by at least a few instructors in the humanities). Thus such widely publicized "sociological" studies as A. C. Spectorsky's *The Exurbanites* and Russell Lynes' *A Surfeit of Honey*, "sociological" novels, and "authoritative" articles in popular magazines help to create an ever-increasing number of sociological "experts." All people, to be sure, are perforce sociologists (and psychologists) in some degree. But the professional sociologist in the classroom faces today an unprecedented pseudo-sophisticated group of students. Here is a situation calling for informed and resourceful teaching at its best.

The Student Audience and Academic Rivals

Teaching problems are as complicated, then, by the wide diffusion of a semisociological rhetoric as by conflicting conceptions of sociology. Both of these conditions permeate the college scene, a complex and changing environment, marked by departmental rivalries and provincialisms, expanding and overlapping curricula, increasing efforts to develop problem-oriented and area-oriented interdisciplinary courses, running battles between specialization and general education, and so on. These are all matters of consequence for teachers and the teaching of sociology. But here I note only a few problematic features of the changing interrelationships among students, sociology, and other academic disciplines.

Most colleges of liberal arts offer a very wide choice of courses

[20] H. D. Lasswell and, following him, David Riesman have used the term "partial incorporation" to refer to the absorption of *some* social science by teachers of law, thereby discouraging its explicit use in legal training; see, *e.g.*, Riesman's "Law and Sociology: Recruitment, Training and Colleagueship," *Stanford Law Rev.*, 9:4 (1957).

from which to elect, fields in which to specialize, and teachers with whom to study. This diversity gives enormous influence to students in establishing the popularity of any subject, its reputation on the campus, and sometimes its level of prestige in the eyes of deans, presidents, and trustees. Whatever its educational merit or liability, this fact of academic life confronts all teachers and affects all fields, not least sociologists and sociology—and in several ways.

The growing significance of student judgment places particularly dangerous temptations before sociologists. For, in the hands of instructors primarily devoted to academic empire-building, sociology, perhaps more than any other subject, lends itself to exploitation for the sake of popularity. At its worst, sociology can be a "gut" course, or a gossip-column of social life providing spicy entertainment and mass appeal, or both, drawing to its classes in large numbers the lazy and the mediocre. At its best, sociology is a demanding study, the intellectual peer of any, and sufficiently challenging to attract superior students. These are extremes, of course, between which most sociologists ply their teaching trade. Many of them no doubt compromise. But if they are to discourage invidious comparison and, more importantly, raise the intellectual standards of their field, they should risk the dangers of limited popularity by offering sociology's richest goods.[21]

Student-customers, to be sure, differ in intellectual taste and capacity, in aspiration and expectation. Although sharing student status, their *role-set,* to use Merton's term, may vary from field to field, possibly from one type of teacher to another.[22] Conversely, the instructor's role-set and teaching performance may be influenced by distinctive characteristics of the student audience—for example, size, class level, sexual composition, Ivy Leaguism, career expectations, and so on. Such variations

[21] In sociology as elsewhere, there are, of course, teachers who at the same time are enormously popular, exacting, and intellectually superior. But this is an exceedingly rare achievement in any field, not least in sociology.

[22] Merton refers to the teacher more than once in explicating the meaning and utility of this concept in "The Role-Set: Problems in Sociological Theory," *Brit. J. Sociol.,* 8:2 (1957). The applicability of "role-set" to variable role performance of students is suggested by differences in student expectations concerning, for example, male and female or, possibly, youthful and mature teachers. In any event, the assumption of a single predominant behavior pattern on the part of students in their relations with teachers obviously is unwarranted.

must be considered in any realistic self-analysis by the teacher. Social analysis of both his manifest and latent roles [23] similarly should include exploration of the effects of different instructional settings and audience traits.

In certain respects, however, student audiences seem to display striking similarities. Their attitudes toward the world around them, their views concerning job and marriage, and, if the Jacobs Report is any indication, their imperviousness to the value implications of social science distinguish them from earlier college generations. The teaching sociologist's client-public is no longer composed of persons many of whom are deeply concerned with social disorganization, the possibilities of social change, the urgency of reform or even revolution. Students to-day—although no less so than many of their instructors—are interested in organization rather than disorganization, adaptation rather than change, and especially those skills that seem to spell conventional success in work, family, and leisure pursuits. Large-scale institutional and cultural changes promote these interests, influencing both teachers and students as well as the nature of sociology itself.[24] And they no doubt account, in some measure, for the plethora of courses in the *tactics* of group life carrying such labels as "group dynamics" and "human relations."

Yet there are also some students who are concerned with social strategy and policy, deeper social analysis, even the pursuit of noninstrumental knowledge about human conduct and the social order. Justifiably or not, these rare birds are the principal targets of some instructors, who

[23] Cf. Gouldner, *op. cit.*

[24] These changes and their consequences are the subject of a large literature today. Varying interpretations are presented—*e.g.*, in David Riesman, *The Lonely Crowd*, Yale University Press, 1950; William H. Whyte, Jr., *The Organization Man*, Simon and Schuster, 1956; Erich Fromm, *The Sane Society*, Rinehart, 1955; C. Wright Mills, *White Collar*, Oxford University Press, 1951, esp. Chaps. 5, 6, 7, 10, 12, and *The Power Elite*, Oxford University Press, 1956, esp. Chaps. 13, 14; and, most recently, Max Lerner, *America as a Civilization*, Simon and Schuster, 1957. Many sociologists regard these works (or some of them) as non- or semi-sociological because of their essayistic character, ideological bias, and limited or overly free use of empirical materials. But many teachers, I suspect, assign them (or some of them) to their students. Few sociologists would deny their importance as symptomatic of significant social and cultural trends.

find in this undergraduate elite the chief rewards for their devotion to the teaching role. I have in mind this minority primarily, though not exclusively, in the following comments on sociology's competitors in the intellectual market of the college.

Both student and faculty appraisers necessarily draw comparisons between sociology and other subjects, especially anthropology, history, political science and economics, and psychology and social psychology. Even a brief glimpse at these neighboring fields—fields that function as important *reference areas* [25] for the assessors of sociology—reveals certain problems, some of which have been touched upon above, facing sociology as a teaching enterprise.

Much of the foregoing discussion applies to social and cultural anthropology. No less than the "science of man," anthropology is subject to imperialistic interpretation, especially as it moves from the study of nonliterate societies to Yankee City, industrial plants, and modern hospitals, and as it makes use of theories and methods of other "behavioral sciences." Anthropology also wears the three faces of science, humanity, and reform and shares with sociology the advantages and disadvantages of marginality. On these counts (and others), anthropologists and sociologists are increasingly interchangeable in research and teaching, often living side by side in single academic departments.

Notwithstanding these similarities, anthropology's distinctiveness persists, partly, of course, because of its unique traditions, contributions, and tasks. But these are matters for the informed.[26] Uninformed stu-

[25] The term *reference area* signifies a field (or, in other contexts, an ideology, value scheme, set of beliefs, etc.) which the actor has in mind when appraising another field—*i.e.* an area on the basis of which evaluation or judgment rests—in part. ("In part," of course, because probably there is never a pure case.) The affinity of this concept with *ethnocentrism* is apparent, but use of the latter term usually accents evaluation whereas *reference area* subsumes "strictly objective" judgment as well. Clearly, this concept should not be confused with *reference group*, which usually signifies the social category ("group") toward which behavior is oriented. Reference groups and reference areas might be considered different "dimensions" of social action which, though interrelated in the concrete case, are analytically distinct.

[26] The relations between sociology and anthropology are ably discussed by G. P. Murdock and Howard Becker in John Gillin (ed.), *For a Science of Social Man*, Macmillan, 1954.

dents, and many of their teachers, picture anthropology as a new and fascinating field which not only reveals exotic and enviable practices of the "primitives" but, seemingly unbridled by dreary disciplinary restraints, ranges freely among such subjects as personality, sex, Plainville's class system, and life in Hollywood. Little wonder, then, that some students—and at least one British philosopher [27]—consider anthropology more "interesting" than sociology.

Impressions of anthropology in college circles contrast sharply with views of history. Hoary with respectability, history is an essential part of liberal education, which undergraduates may find exciting or dull, depending largely upon period and teaching prowess. But for many serious students, history, in comparison with sociology, is apt to be concrete, packed with meaty substance, and relatively untroubled by the abstract theoretical issues of historiography itself. The historian's typical disregard of explicit theory (and of sociological contributions) carries an appeal, for it encourages him to roam in the changing human scene as widely as the philosopher. And history's manifest interest in large-scale change and events of international dimensions, both generally slighted by American sociologists, may seem to some students a sign of vigor and humane concern.[28]

The nagging question "What *is* sociology?" is rarely asked of history—or of political science and economics. The academic legitimacy of these latter fields is seldom challenged and, again like history, they are

[27] Stuart Hampshire, "Can There Be a General Science of Man?" *Commentary*, 24:2 (1957). Hampshire writes: "One of the most elementary facts about sociology is that the literature of this science is very dull. . . . The literature of social anthropology is far from dull." This comment illustrates a fairly common impression found among persons unfamiliar with much of the work in the two fields. Anthropology's appeal as more "interesting" than sociology seems to be particularly widespread among teachers of the humanities.

[28] The wide separation between sociology and history in both research and teaching is regrettable, I believe, but not beyond remedy. Recent efforts to narrow this breach appear in Mirra Komarovsky (ed.), *Common Frontiers of the Social Sciences*, Free Press, 1957, Part I; see esp. the contributions of Leo Lowenthal and Marjorie Fiske, Lee Benson, Paul F. Lazarsfeld, J. R. Strayer, and Henry David. See also Louis Gottschalk, "The Historian's Use of Generalization," in Leonard D. White (ed.), *The State of the Social Sciences*, University of Chicago Press, 1956; and Lipset, *op. cit.*

viewed as offering rich substance to their students. College men especially consider the study of political science or economics (or a combination of the two—a much more likely event than the combination of one or the other with sociology) [29] as an avenue to jobs in government or business. Both male and female students, of varied or no vocational aspirations, are impressed by the fact that these special social sciences, even at the introductory level, confront questions of application and policy. In some schools, political science is "government" or "politics," and economics, although more demanding as a theoretical discipline, carries the repute of practicality. Sociology presents some of these attractions, of course, but images of sociology are less clear-cut and its status in the college community is more problematic.

Psychology also displays similar imperialistic and multifeatured characteristics. In these respects, psychologists may surpass sociologists, for not only are there "psychologies" of almost everything, but scientific, humanistic, and reformistic goals are all pursued with zeal. Students are sometimes discouraged when shuttling between the behavior of rats, the revelations of Freud, and the moral doctrines of Fromm. But this variety has its own appeals, offering on the one hand shrines at which those of different interests may worship and on the other alternative careers to follow (for students so minded) under a single professional banner. Psychology and anthropology are sociology's close allies in current efforts to build an inclusive science of man,[30] but in the competition for students—and therefore for future sociologists—psychology remains a strong and active rival.

Social psychology plays contrary roles in the bid for students—as a loyal partner and as an ambitious competitor. Both sociology and psy-

[29] The limited relations between sociology and political science and economics, as in the case of history, should be extended, I believe. Some of the problems here are discussed by David Riesman in "Some Observations on the 'Older' and the 'Newer' Social Sciences," in White, *op. cit.*; relations between two of these disciplines are treated systematically in Wilbert E. Moore, *Economy and Society*, Random House, 1955, and Talcott Parsons and Neil Smelser, *Economy and Society*, Free Press, 1957.

[30] A growing literature reports these efforts, the most imposing of which theoretically is Talcott Parsons and Edward A. Shils (eds.), *Toward a General Theory of Action*, Harvard University Press, 1951; see also the briefer but lucid discussions by Parsons and Theodore M. Newcomb in Gillin, *op. cit.*

chology staked claims in this border field many years ago. Its subsequent expansion has taken place, academically, in the curricula of both disciplines, encouraging some psychologists to teach sociology of their own making and prompting a number of sociologists to become, so to speak, psychologists. In whichever academic department courses in social psychology are offered, students are apt to confront theoretical and empirical materials, as well as teachers, that they have met elsewhere. Yet social psychology—by definition a marginal discipline; a subject working in the frontier-area of the behavioral sciences (in some of its efforts); one in which *both* the investigation of the always intriguing personality and the study of society and culture take place (where, as Hans Gerth and C. Wright Mills put it,[31] Marx and Freud or G. H. Mead and Max Weber join forces); and a field in which blossom more and more of the new-fangled courses of the "group dynamics" variety, with their emphasis upon the tactics of social life—presents attractive possibilities for students. Thus social psychology is potentially a powerful bidder in the market of higher learning.[32]

Sociology has other rivals, of course, including the arts, literature, and philosophy. Teachers of the humanities are often its severest critics, portraying sociology as a jargon-laden subject, a self-styled science of the obvious and picayune, or even as an instrument of moral anarchy.[33] It is not surprising that sociology elicits these reactions among persons who are trained in the felicitous use of language (which, nevertheless, is frequently missing in their own brands of technical terminology) and,

---

[31] *Character and Social Structure: The Psychology of Social Institutions*, Harcourt, Brace, 1953, p. xiv.

[32] These remarks should not be construed as invidious. I am concerned here with certain characteristics that help to make social psychology a strong rival of sociology in college education, not with the scientific and intellectual significance of the diverse modes of research and teaching in social psychology. This field is marked by impressive accomplishments, as the names of Gordon and Floyd Allport, Hadley Cantril, Richard Crutchfield, Otto Klineberg, David Krech, Kurt Lewin, Gardner Murphy, Theodore Newcomb, Muzafer Sherif, and Edward Tolman, to mention but a few major contemporary contributors to aspects of this multisided field, suggest.

[33] This accusation, made by Joseph Wood Krutch among others, is cogently discussed by Adolph S. Tomars in "Moral Relativism and Moral Anarchy," a paper presented at the annual meeting of the American Sociological Society, 1957.

more significantly, who are professionally committed to the appreciation of artistic insight, moral evaluation, and the sacredness of individualistic "amateur sociology." Comments by exponents of the avowedly humanistic disciplines are needlessly acid at times; and all too often they distort sociology and the efforts of its representatives. Yet teaching sociologists should also be students of its many ramifications: of the humanities as well as science. Or such is my conviction.

Bibliography

To my knowledge, there are no large-scale studies of sociology as a teaching enterprise. The following are a few of the many volumes that might be consulted in undertaking such a study.

Barzun, Jacques, *The Teacher in America*, Little, Brown, 1945. This lively book about college teachers and their milieu illustrates the humanist's rather characteristic bias against sociology. Excellent reading.

General Education in a Free Society, Harvard University Press, 1945. Part V of this well-known report presents a widely held view of the appropriate place of the social sciences, including sociology, in the liberal-arts curriculum.

Gillin, John (ed.), *For a Science of Social Man*, Macmillan, 1954. Seven leading scholars, two representing each of the following disciplines, discuss "convergences in anthropology, psychology, and sociology."

Highet, Gilbert, *The Art of Teaching*, Knopf, 1951. This book contains lessons for teachers of sociology, as well as of other fields, taught by a popular pedagogue.

Komarovsky, Mirra (ed.), *Common Frontiers of the Social Sciences*, Free Press, 1957. A rare, perhaps unique, collection of research studies demonstrating important relations between sociology and history and between sociology and economics.

Lerner, Max, *America as a Civilization*, Simon and Schuster, 1957. See Chap. 10, "Belief and Opinion," and especially pp. 732-49, on "The Higher and the Lower Learning," for a brief but informed treatment of the social context and trends of college education. Chap. 2, "The Idea of American Civilization," is a good illustration of the effective use— and occasional abuse—of sociological concepts by a writer of distinction.

Mercer, Blaine E., and Edwin R. Carr, *Education and the Social Order*, Rinehart, 1957. This collection of readings contains useful contributions in Chap. 9 on "The School as a System of Formal and Informal Organization" and Chap. 10 on "The Teacher."

Mills, C. Wright, *White Collar*, Oxford University Press, 1951. Chaps. 6 and 7 accent the bureaucratization of the professions; see especially the controversial portrayal of "The Professors," pp. 129*ff*.

The President's Committee on Education Beyond the High School, *Second Report to the President*, Washington, D.C., 1957. This appraisal of current problems suggests some of the difficulties faced by teachers of sociology (and, of course, by representatives of other disciplines).

Riesman, David, *Individualism Reconsidered*, Free Press, 1954. Part III of this collection of essays contains suggestive observations concerning marginality and it advantages.

————, *Constraint and Variety in American Education*, University of Nebraska Press, 1956. Part I of this perceptive volume treats variations among colleges and Part II discusses contributions of and interrelations among the social sciences in academic circles.

Ross, Ralph, and Ernest van den Haag, *The Fabric of Society*, Harcourt, Brace, 1957. Written as "an introduction to the social sciences," this volume gives the lie to the notion that textbooks must be dull, routine, and "strictly objective"; science, social science, history, and the humanities are treated in Part II.

The Teaching of the Social Sciences in the United States, Paris: UNESCO, 1954. Surveys of policies and procedures in economics, political science, international relations, sociology, anthropology, social psychology, and law by representatives of these disciplines.

The University Teaching of Social Sciences. Sociology, Social Psychology and Anthropology, Paris: UNESCO, 1952. A fact-studded report, which includes discussions of the interrelations among the three disciplines, their characteristics in various countries, functions of teaching, and proposed reforms.

Waller, Willard, *The Sociology of Teaching*, John Wiley, 1932. Though written many years ago and pertaining primarily to the public school in the United States, this book contains still-unsurpassed discussions of the informal structure of education and the social psychology of teaching.

Warner, W. Lloyd, Robert J. Havighurst, and Martin B. Loeb, *Who Shall Be Educated?* Harper, 1944. Although primarily an examination of the limitations on educational opportunity imposed by social stratification, this study contains suggestive portrayals of the teacher and his different "role-sets" with relation to varied student groups.

White, Leonard D. (ed.), *The State of the Social Sciences*, University of Chicago Press, 1956. See the contributions by James G. Miller, Harold D. Lasswell, David Riesman, Lawrence A. Kimpton, Leo Strauss, James

L. Cate, Louis Gottschalk, and F. A. Hayek for discussions of various questions raised in this paper.

Whitehead, Alfred N., *The Aims of Education and Other Essays*, Macmillan, 1929. Although published almost thirty years ago, these essays contain discussions of educational aims and the interrelations of the sciences and the humanities of current relevance.

Wilson, Logan, *The Academic Man: A Study in the Sociology of a Profession*, Oxford University Press, 1942. This volume, published sixteen years ago, is the only first-rate empirical study of the college teacher; sociologists are not treated as such.

Znaniecki, Florian, *The Social Role of the Man of Knowledge*, Columbia University Press, 1940. This short book is perhaps the most important single work on scholars or schoolmen, their various types of subroles, and distinctions between the scholar-role and that of technologist, "sage," and creator or explorer; an essential theoretical discussion.

Index to Both Volumes

Abel, Theodore, 74, 587
academic freedom, 70-71
Adams, Stuart, 433
Adams, W. A., 396
Adelson, Joseph, 378
Adler, Mortimer, 535
Adoratsky, V., 86
Adorno, Theodore W., 49, 54, 378, 380, 381
adult socialization, 456
  (*see also* socialization)
"affective neutrality," in doctors, 244
age, conservatism and, in college teachers, 72
  eminence and, 62
age structure, demography and, 316
agricultural colleges, recruitment of sociologists in, 366
Albrecht, Milton, 208
Allport, Floyd H., 545, 546, 596
Allport, Gordon, 47, 286, 596
Allport-Vernon test, 286
Almond, Gabriel, 110
Alpert, Harry, 563, 587
Alsop, Joseph, 351
Anderson, Bo, 65
Anderson, C. Arnold, 360-375, 387, 392
Anderson, Odin W., 232, 236, 238
Anderson, W. A., 361, 362
anomie, criminality and, 510, 513-515
  deviant behavior and, 513-515
  forms of, 481-483
  localized conditions of, 480
  mental illness and, 507
  social disorganization and, 480
  social structure and, 464
  suicide and, 183

Anthony, P., 393
anthropology, 584, 593, 594
anti-Semitism, 49-50
  Hitlerian, resistance to, 53-54
  (*see also* intergroup relations)
apathy, consensus and, 88
  political, 94-95
applied research, conversion to policy research, 371-373
  in medical sociology, 240-242
  organizational analysis and, 407-410
  (*see also* research techniques)
Argyris, Chris, 421
Aristotle, 545
art, contemporary American studies in, 203-209
  ideational and sensate types, 204
  intellectual backgrounds in sociology of, 199-203
  Marxian analysis of, 200
  relation of to society, 197-200
  sociology of, 197-213
  Spencer's theory of, 201
artist, contemporary studies of, 206
  need for study of, 209-212
  problems of, 210
  relation to society of, 202
arts, classification of, 197, 212
Asch, S. E., 298, 547
Ashmore, H. S., 392
associations, voluntary, 88
Aubert, Vilhelm, 529, 530
audience research, in mass communications, 541-542
Auerbach, Erich, 199
Austin, G. A., 300
authoritarian personality, F-scale for testing of, 49, 54-55

Revised November, 1964

haRPER 🔥 torchbooks

HUMANITIES AND SOCIAL SCIENCES

American Studies

---

† The New American Nation Series, edited by Henry Steele Commager and Richard B. Morris.
‡ American Perspectives series, edited by Bernard Wishy and William E. Leuchtenburg.
* The Rise of Modern Europe series, edited by William L. Langer.
‖ Researches in the Social, Cultural, and Behavioral Sciences, edited by Benjamin Nelson.
§ The Library of Religion and Culture, edited by Benjamin Nelson.
Σ Harper Modern Science Series, edited by James R. Newman.
° Not for sale in Canada.

DANIEL H. HUNDLEY: Social Relations in our Southern States.‡ Edited by William R. Taylor   TB/3058

HELEN HUNT JACKSON: A Century of Dishonor: The Early Crusade for Indian Reform.‡ Edited by Andrew F. Rolle   TB/3063

ROBERT H. JACKSON: The Supreme Court in the American System of Government   TB/1106

THOMAS JEFFERSON: Notes on the State of Virginia.‡ Edited by Thomas Perkins Abernethy   TB/3052

JOHN F. KENNEDY: A Nation of Immigrants. Revised and Enlarged Edition. Illus.   TB/1118

WILLIAM L. LANGER & S. EVERETT GLEASON: The Challenge to Isolation: The World Crisis of 1937-1940 and American Foreign Policy   Vol. I TB/3054
                                              Vol. II TB/3055

WILLIAM E. LEUCHTENBURG: Franklin D. Roosevelt and the New Deal, 1932-1940.† Illus.   TB/3045

LEONARD W. LEVY: Freedom of Speech and Press in Early American History: Legacy of Suppression
    TB/1109

ARTHUR S. LINK: Woodrow Wilson and the Progressive Era, 1910-1917.† Illus.   TB/3023

ROBERT GREEN McCLOSKEY: American Conservatism in the Age of Enterprise, 1865-1910   TB/1137

BERNARD MAYO: Myths and Men: Patrick Henry, George Washington, Thomas Jefferson   TB/1108

JOHN C. MILLER: Alexander Hamilton and the Growth of the New Nation   TB/3057

JOHN C. MILLER: The Federalist Era, 1789-1801.† Illus.   TB/3027

PERRY MILLER: Errand into the Wilderness   TB/1139

PERRY MILLER & T. H. JOHNSON, Editors: The Puritans: A Sourcebook of Their Writings
    Vol. I TB/1093
    Vol. II TB/1094

GEORGE E. MOWRY: The Era of Theodore Roosevelt and the Birth of Modern America, 1900-1912.† Illus.
    TB/3022

WALLACE NOTESTEIN: The English People on the Eve of Colonization, 1603-1630.† Illus.   TB/3006

RUSSEL BLAINE NYE: The Cultural Life of the New Nation, 1776-1801.† Illus.   TB/3026

RALPH BARTON PERRY: Puritanism and Democracy
    TB/1138

RALPH BARTON PERRY: The Thought and Character of William James: Briefer Version   TB/1156

GEORGE E. PROBST, Ed.: The Happy Republic: A Reader in Tocqueville's America   TB/1060

WALTER RAUSCHENBUSCH: Christianity and the Social Crisis.‡ Edited by Robert D. Cross   TB/3059

HEINRICH STRAUMANN: American Literature in the Twentieth Century. Revised Edition   TB/1168

FRANK THISTLETHWAITE: America and the Atlantic Community: Anglo-American Aspects, 1790-1850
    TB/1107

TWELVE SOUTHERNERS: I'll Take My Stand: The South and the Agrarian Tradition. Introduction by Louis D. Rubin, Jr.; Biographical Essays by Virginia Rock   TB/1072

A. F. TYLER: Freedom's Ferment: Phases of American Social History from the Revolution to the Outbreak of the Civil War. Illus.   TB/1074

GLYNDON G. VAN DEUSEN: The Jacksonian Era, 1828-1848.† Illus.   TB/3028

WALTER E. WEYL: The New Democracy: An Essay on Certain Political and Economic Tendencies in the United States.‡ Edited by Charles Forcey   TB/3042

LOUIS B. WRIGHT: The Cultural Life of the American Colonies, 1607-1763.† Illus.   TB/3005

LOUIS B. WRIGHT: Culture on the Moving Frontier
    TB/1053

Anthropology & Sociology

BERNARD BERELSON, Ed.: The Behavioral Sciences Today   TB/1127

JOSEPH B. CASAGRANDE, Ed.: In the Company of Man: 20 Portraits of Anthropological Informants. Illus.   TB/3047

W. E. LE GROS CLARK: The Antecedents of Man: An Introduction to the Evolution of the Primates.° Illus.
    TB/559

THOMAS C. COCHRAN: The Inner Revolution: Essays on the Social Sciences in History   TB/1140

ALLISON DAVIS & JOHN DOLLARD: Children of Bondage: The Personality Development of Negro Youth in the Urban South || TB/3049

ST. CLAIR DRAKE & HORACE R. CAYTON: Black Metropolis: A Study of Negro Life in a Northern City   Vol. I TB/1086; Vol. II TB/1087

CORA DU BOIS: The People of Alor. New Preface by the author. Illus.   Vol. I TB/1042; Vol. II TB/1043

EMILE DURKHEIM et al.: Essays on Sociology and Philosophy: With Analyses of Durkheim's Life and Work. || Edited by Kurt H. Wolff   TB/1151

LEON FESTINGER, HENRY W. RIECKEN & STANLEY SCHACHTER: When Prophecy Fails: A Social and Psychological Account of a Modern Group that Predicted the Destruction of the World || TB/1132

RAYMOND FIRTH, Ed.: Man and Culture: An Evaluation of the Work of Bronislaw Malinowski || °
    TB/1133

L. S. B. LEAKEY: Adam's Ancestors: The Evolution of Man and his Culture. Illus.   TB/1019

KURT LEWIN: Field Theory in Social Science: Selected Theoretical Papers. || Edited with a Foreword by Dorwin Cartwright   TB/1135

ROBERT H. LOWIE: Primitive Society. Introduction by Fred Eggan   TB/1056

R. M. MacIVER: Social Causation   TB/1153

BENJAMIN NELSON: Religious Traditions and the Spirit of Capitalism: From the Church Fathers to Jeremy Bentham   TB/1130

TALCOTT PARSONS & EDWARD A. SHILS, Editors: Toward a General Theory of Action: Theoretical Foundations for the Social Sciences   TB/1083

JOHN H. ROHRER & MUNRO S. EDMONSON, Eds.: The Eighth Generation Grows Up: Cultures and Personalities of New Orleans Negroes || TB/3050

ARNOLD ROSE: The Negro in America: The Condensed Version of Gunnar Myrdal's An American Dilemma   TB/3048

HENRI DE SAINT-SIMON: Social Organization, The Science of Man, and Other Writings. || Edited and translated by Felix Markham   TB/1152

KURT SAMUELSSON: Religion and Economic Action: A Critique of Max Weber's The Protestant Ethic and the Spirit of Capitalism.|| ° Trans. by E. G. French; Ed. with Intro. by D. C. Coleman   TB/1131

3

History: Renaissance & Reformation

R. R. BOLGAR: The Classical Heritage and Its Beneficiaries: *From the Carolingian Age to the End of the
Renaissance* TB/1125

JACOB BURCKHARDT: The Civilization of the Renaissance in Italy. *Introduction by Benjamin Nelson
and Charles Trinkaus. Illus.* Volume I TB/40
Volume II TB/41

ERNST CASSIRER: The Individual and the Cosmos
in Renaissance Philosophy. *Translated with an Introduction by Mario Domandi* TB/1097

EDWARD P. CHEYNEY: The Dawn of a New Era,
1250-1453.* *Illus.* TB/3002

DESIDERIUS ERASMUS: Christian Humanism and
the Reformation: *Selected Writings. Edited and
translated by John C. Olin* TB/1166

WALLACE K. FERGUSON et al.: Facets of the Renaissance TB/1098

WALLACE K. FERGUSON et al.: The Renaissance: *Six
Essays. Illus.* TB/1084

MYRON P. GILMORE: The World of Humanism, 1453-
1517.* *Illus.* TB/3003

FRANCESCO GUICCIARDINI: Maxims and Reflections of a Renaissance Statesman: *Ricordi. Trans.
by Mario Domandi. Intro. by Nicolai Rubinstein*
TB/1160

JOHAN HUIZINGA: Erasmus and the Age of Reformation. *Illus.* TB/19

ULRICH VON HUTTEN et al.: On the Eve of the
Reformation: *"Letters of Obscure Men." Introduction
by Hajo Holborn* TB/1124

PAUL O. KRISTELLER: Renaissance Thought: *The
Classic, Scholastic, and Humanist Strains* TB/1048

PAUL O. KRISTELLER: Renaissance Thought II:
Papers on Humanism and the Arts TB/1163

NICCOLÒ MACHIAVELLI: History of Florence and of
the Affairs of Italy: *from the earliest times to the
death of Lorenzo the Magnificent. Introduction by
Felix Gilbert* TB/1027

ALFRED VON MARTIN: Sociology of the Renaissance.
Introduction by Wallace K. Ferguson TB/1099

GARRETT MATTINGLY et al.: Renaissance Profiles.
Edited by J. H. Plumb TB/1162

MILLARD MEISS: Painting in Florence and Siena after
the Black Death. *The Arts, Religion and Society in
the Mid-Fourteenth Century. 169 illus.* TB/1148

J. E. NEALE: The Age of Catherine de Medici°
TB/1085

ERWIN PANOFSKY: Studies in Iconology: *Humanistic
Themes in the Art of the Renaissance. 180 illustrations* TB/1077

J. H. PARRY: The Establishment of the European He-
gemony: 1415-1715 TB/1045

HENRI PIRENNE: Early Democracies in the Low
Countries: *Urban Society and Political Conflict in the
Middle Ages and the Renaissance. Introduction by
John Mundy* TB/1110

J. H. PLUMB: The Italian Renaissance: *A Concise
Survey of Its History and Culture* TB/1161

FERDINAND SCHEVILL: The Medici. *Illus.* TB/1010

FERDINAND SCHEVILL: Medieval and Renaissance
Florence. *Illus.* Volume I: *Medieval Florence* TB/1090
Volume II: *The Coming of Human-
ism and the Age of the Medici* TB/1091

G. M. TREVELYAN: England in the Age of Wycliffe,
1368-1520° TB/1112

VESPASIANO: Renaissance Princes, Popes, and Prel-
ates: *The Vespasiano Memoirs: Lives of Illustrious
Men of the XVth Century. Introduction by Myron P.
Gilmore* TB/1111

History: Modern European

FREDERICK B. ARTZ: Reaction and Revolution,
1815-1832.* *Illus.* TB/3034

MAX BELOFF: The Age of Absolutism, 1660-1815
TB/1062

ROBERT C. BINKLEY: Realism and Nationalism, 1852-
1871.* *Illus.* TB/3038

CRANE BRINTON: A Decade of Revolution, 1789-
1799.* *Illus.* TB/3018

J. BRONOWSKI & BRUCE MAZLISH: The Western
Intellectual Tradition: *From Leonardo to Hegel*
TB/3001

GEOFFREY BRUUN: Europe and the French Imperium,
1799-1814.* *Illus.* TB/3033

ALAN BULLOCK: Hitler, A Study in Tyranny.° *Illus.*
TB/1123

E. H. CARR: The Twenty Years' Crisis, 1919-1939: *An
Introduction to the Study of International Relations*°
TB/1122

GORDON A. CRAIG: From Bismarck to Adenauer:
Aspects of German Statecraft. Revised Edition
TB/1171

WALTER L. DORN: Competition for Empire, 1740-
1763.* *Illus.* TB/3032

CARL J. FRIEDRICH: The Age of the Baroque, 1610-
1660.* *Illus.* TB/3004

LEO GERSHOY: From Despotism to Revolution, 1763-
1789.* *Illus.* TB/3017

ALBERT GOODWIN: The French Revolution TB/1064

CARLTON J. H. HAYES: A Generation of Materialism,
1871-1900.* *Illus.* TB/3039

J. H. HEXTER: Reappraisals in History: *New Views on
History and Society in Early Modern Europe*
TB/1100

A. R. HUMPHREYS: The Augustan World: *Society,
Thought, and Letters in Eighteenth Century England*
TB/1105

HANS KOHN, Ed.: The Mind of Modern Russia: *Historical and Political Thought of Russia's Great Age*
TB/1065

SIR LEWIS NAMIER: Vanished Supremacies: *Essays on
European History, 1812-1918*° TB/1088

JOHN U. NEF: Western Civilization Since the Renaissance: *Peace, War, Industry, and the Arts* TB/1113

FREDERICK L. NUSSBAUM: The Triumph of Science
and Reason, 1660-1685.* *Illus.* TB/3009

RAYMOND W. POSTGATE, Ed.: Revolution from
1789 to 1906: *Selected Documents* TB/1063

PENFIELD ROBERTS: The Quest for Security, 1715-
1740.* *Illus.* TB/3016

PRISCILLA ROBERTSON: Revolutions of 1848: *A Social History* TB/1025

ALBERT SOREL: Europe Under the Old Regime. *Translated by Francis H. Herrick* TB/1121

4

6

RELIGION

Ancient & Classical

Biblical Thought & Literature

Judaic Thought & Literature

Christianity: Origins & Early Development

KARL HEIM: Christian Faith and Natural Science TB/16

IMMANUEL KANT: Religion Within the Limits of Reason Alone.§ *Introduction by Theodore M. Greene and John Silber* TB/67

JOHN MACQUARRIE: An Existentialist Theology: *A Comparison of Heidegger and Bultmann.*° *Preface by Rudolf Bultmann* TB/125

PIERRE TEILHARD DE CHARDIN: The Phenomenon of Man° TB/83

Religion, Culture & Society

JOSEPH L. BLAU, Ed.: Cornerstones of Religious Freedom in America: *Selected Basic Documents, Court Decisions and Public Statements. Revised and Enlarged Edition* TB/118

CHRISTOPHER DAWSON: The Historic Reality of Christian Culture TB/305

C. C. GILLISPIE: Genesis and Geology: *The Decades before Darwin*§ TB/51

WALTER KAUFMANN, Ed.: Religion from Tolstoy to Camus: *Basic Writings on Religious Truth and Morals. Enlarged Edition* TB/123

JOHN T. McNEILL: A History of the Cure of Souls TB/126

BENJAMIN NELSON: Religious Traditions and the Spirit of Capitalism: *From the Church Fathers to Jeremy Bentham* TB/1130

H. RICHARD NIEBUHR: Christ and Culture TB/3

H. RICHARD NIEBUHR: The Kingdom of God in America TB/49

RALPH BARTON PERRY: Puritanism and Democracy TB/1138

PAUL PFUETZE: Self, Society, Existence: *Human Nature and Dialogue in the Thought of George Herbert Mead and Martin Buber* TB/1059

WALTER RAUSCHENBUSCH: Christianity and the Social Crisis.‡ *Edited by Robert D. Cross* TB/3059

KURT SAMUELSSON: Religion and Economic Action: *A Critique of Max Weber's The Protestant Ethic and the Spirit of Capitalism.* ‖ ° *Trans. by E. G. French; Ed. with Intro. by D. C. Coleman* TB/1131

ERNST TROELTSCH: The Social Teaching of the Christian Churches ° Vol. I TB/71; Vol. II TB/72

NATURAL SCIENCES
AND MATHEMATICS

Biological Sciences

CHARLOTTE AUERBACH: The Science of Genetics∑ TB/568

A. BELLAIRS: Reptiles: *Life History, Evolution, and Structure. Illus.* TB/520

LUDWIG VON BERTALANFFY: Modern Theories of Development: *An Introduction to Theoretical Biology* TB/554

LUDWIG VON BERTALANFFY: Problems of Life: *An Evaluation of Modern Biological and Scientific Thought* TB/521

JOHN TYLER BONNER: The Ideas of Biology.∑ *Illus.* TB/570

HAROLD F. BLUM: Time's Arrow and Evolution TB/555

A. J. CAIN: Animal Species and their Evolution. *Illus.* TB/519

WALTER B. CANNON: Bodily Changes in Pain, Hunger, Fear and Rage. *Illus.* TB/562

W. E. LE GROS CLARK: The Antecedents of Man: *An Introduction to the Evolution of the Primates.*° *Illus.* TB/559

W. H. DOWDESWELL: Animal Ecology. *Illus.* TB/543

W. H. DOWDESWELL: The Mechanism of Evolution. *Illus.* TB/527

R. W. GERARD: Unresting Cells. *Illus.* TB/541

DAVID LACK: Darwin's Finches. *Illus.* TB/544

J. E. MORTON: Molluscs: *An Introduction to their Form and Functions. Illus.* TB/529

ADOLF PORTMANN: Animals as Social Beings.° *Illus.* TB/572

O. W. RICHARDS: The Social Insects. *Illus.* TB/542

P. M. SHEPPARD: Natural Selection and Heredity. *Illus.* TB/528

EDMUND W. SINNOTT: Cell and Psyche: *The Biology of Purpose* TB/546

C. H. WADDINGTON: How Animals Develop. *Illus.* TB/553

Chemistry

J. R. PARTINGTON: A Short History of Chemistry. *Illus.* TB/522

J. READ: A Direct Entry to Organic Chemistry. *Illus.* TB/523

J. READ: Through Alchemy to Chemistry. *Illus.* TB/561

Communication Theory

J. R. PIERCE: Symbols, Signals and Noise: *The Nature and Process of Communication* TB/574

Geography

R. E. COKER: This Great and Wide Sea: *An Introduction to Oceanography and Marine Biology. Illus.* TB/551

F. K. HARE: The Restless Atmosphere TB/560

History of Science

W. DAMPIER, Ed.: Readings in the Literature of Science. *Illus.* TB/512

A. HUNTER DUPREE: Science in the Federal Government: *A History of Policies and Activities to 1940* TB/573

ALEXANDRE KOYRÉ: From the Closed World to the Infinite Universe: *Copernicus, Kepler, Galileo, Newton, etc.* TB/31

A. G. VAN MELSEN: From Atomos to Atom: *A History of the Concept Atom* TB/517

O. NEUGEBAUER: The Exact Sciences in Antiquity TB/552

H. T. PLEDGE: Science Since 1500: *A Short History of Mathematics, Physics, Chemistry and Biology. Illus.* TB/506

9

GEORGE SARTON: Ancient Science and Modern Civilization TB/501

HANS THIRRING: Energy for Man: *From Windmills to Nuclear Power* TB/556

WILLIAM LAW WHYTE: Essay on Atomism: *From Democritus to 1960* TB/565

A. WOLF: A History of Science, Technology and Philosophy in the 16th and 17th Centuries.º *Illus.*
Vol. I TB/508; Vol. II TB/509

A. WOLF: A History of Science, Technology, and Philosophy in the Eighteenth Century.º *Illus.*
Vol. I TB/539; Vol. II TB/540

Mathematics

H. DAVENPORT: The Higher Arithmetic: *An Introduction to the Theory of Numbers* TB/526

H. G. FORDER: Geometry: *An Introduction* TB/548

GOTTLOB FREGE: The Foundations of Arithmetic: *A Logico-Mathematical Enquiry* TB/534

S. KÖRNER: The Philosophy of Mathematics: *An Introduction* TB/547

D. E. LITTLEWOOD: Skeleton Key of Mathematics: *A Simple Account of Complex Algebraic Problems* TB/525

GEORGE E. OWEN: Fundamentals of Scientific Mathematics TB/569

WILLARD VAN ORMAN QUINE: Mathematical Logic TB/558

O. G. SUTTON: Mathematics in Action.º *Foreword by James R. Newman. Illus.* TB/518

FREDERICK WAISMANN: Introduction to Mathematical Thinking. *Foreword by Karl Menger* TB/511

Philosophy of Science

R. B. BRAITHWAITE: Scientific Explanation TB/515

J. BRONOWSKI: Science and Human Values. *Illus.* TB/505

ALBERT EINSTEIN ET AL.: Albert Einstein: Philosopher-Scientist. *Edited by Paul A. Schilpp*
Volume I TB/502
Volume II TB/503

WERNER HEISENBERG: Physics and Philosophy: *The Revolution in Modern Science* TB/549

JOHN MAYNARD KEYNES: A Treatise on Probability.º *Introduction by N. R. Hanson* TB/557

STEPHEN TOULMIN: Foresight and Understanding: *An Enquiry into the Aims of Science. Foreword by Jacques Barzun* TB/564

STEPHEN TOULMIN: The Philosophy of Science: *An Introduction* TB/513

G. J. WHITROW: The Natural Philosophy of Timeº TB/563

Physics and Cosmology

DAVID BOHM: Causality and Chance in Modern Physics. *Foreword by Louis de Broglie* TB/536

P. W. BRIDGMAN: The Nature of Thermodynamics TB/537

P. W. BRIDGMAN: A Sophisticate's Primer of Relativity TB/575

A. C. CROMBIE, Ed.: Turning Point in Physics TB/535

C. V. DURELL: Readable Relativity. *Foreword by Freeman J. Dyson* TB/530

ARTHUR EDDINGTON: Space, Time and Gravitation: *An outline of the General Relativity Theory* TB/510

GEORGE GAMOW: Biography of Physics∑ TB/567

MAX JAMMER: Concepts of Force: *A Study in the Foundation of Dynamics* TB/550

MAX JAMMER: Concepts of Mass *in Classical and Modern Physics* TB/571

MAX JAMMER: Concepts of Space: *The History of Theories of Space in Physics. Foreword by Albert Einstein* TB/533

EDMUND WHITTAKER: History of the Theories of Aether and Electricity
Volume I: *The Classical Theories* TB/531
Volume II: *The Modern Theories* TB/532

G. J. WHITROW: The Structure and Evolution of the Universe: *An Introduction to Cosmology. Illus.* TB/504

A LETTER TO THE READER

Overseas, there is considerable belief
that we are a country of extreme conservatism and
that we cannot accommodate to social change.

Books about America in the hands of
readers abroad can help change those ideas.

The U. S. Information Agency cannot,
by itself, meet the vast need for books about
the United States.

You can help.

Harper Torchbooks provides three packets
of books on American history, economics,
sociology, literature and politics to
help meet the need.

To send a packet of Torchbooks [*] overseas,
all you need do is send your check for $7 (which
includes cost of shipping) to Harper & Row.
The U. S. Information Agency will distribute the books to libraries, schools, and other
centers all over the world.

I ask every American to support this
program, part of a worldwide BOOKS USA campaign.

I ask you to share in the opportunity to
help tell others about America.

EDWARD R. MURROW
Director,
U. S. Information Agency

[*retailing at $10.85 to $12.00]

PACKET I: Twentieth Century America

Dulles/America's Rise to World Power, 1898-1954
Cochran/The American Business System, 1900-1955
Zabel, Editor/Literary Opinion in America (two volumes)
Drucker/The New Society: *The Anatomy of Industrial Order*
Fortune Editors/America in the Sixties: *The Economy and the Society*

PACKET II: American History

Billington/The Far Western Frontier, 1830-1860
Mowry/The Era of Theodore Roosevelt and the
  Birth of Modern America, 1900-1912
Faulkner/Politics, Reform, and Expansion, 1890-1900
Cochran & Miller/The Age of Enterprise: *A Social History of
  Industrial America*
Tyler/Freedom's Ferment: *American Social History from the
  Revolution to the Civil War*

PACKET III: American History

Hansen/The Atlantic Migration, 1607-1860
Degler/Out of Our Past: *The Forces that Shaped Modern America*
Probst, Editor/The Happy Republic: *A Reader in Tocqueville's America*
Alden/The American Revolution, 1775-1783
Wright/The Cultural Life of the American Colonies, 1607-1763

*Your gift will be acknowledged directly to you by the overseas recipient.
Simply fill out the coupon, detach and mail with your check or money order.*

HARPER & ROW, PUBLISHERS · BOOKS USA DEPT.
49 East 33rd Street, New York 16, N. Y.

Packet I ☐   Packet II ☐   Packet III ☐

Please send the BOOKS USA library packet(s) indicated above, in my
name, to the area checked below. Enclosed is my remittance in the
amount of _____ for _____ packet(s) at $7.00 each.

_____ Africa   _____ Latin America

_____ Far East   _____ Near East

Name_____

Address_____

_____

NOTE: This offer expires December 31, 1966.